Problem-Driven Management

Problem-Driven Management

Achieving Improvement in Operations through Knowledge Management

Beatriz Muñoz-Seca and Josep Riverola
IESE Business School
University of Navarra
Barcelona–Madrid
Spain

This English edition first published in Spanish and translated by G.M. Traductores, Barcelona, Spain, 2003

This English edition first published 2004 by
PALGRAVE MACMILLAN
Houndmills, Basingstoke, Hampshire RG21 6XS and
175 Fifth Avenue, New York, N.Y. 10010
Companies and representatives throughout the world

PALGRAVE MACMILLAN is the global academic imprint of the Palgrave Macmillan division of St. Martin's Press, LLC and of Palgrave Macmillan Ltd. Macmillan® is a registered trademark in the United States, United Kingdom and other countries. Palgrave is a registered trademark in the European Union and other countries.

ISBN 1–4039–4137–8

This book is printed on paper suitable for recycling and made from fully managed and sustained forest sources.

A catalogue record for this book is available from the British Library.

Library of Congress Cataloging-in-Publication Data
Muñoz-Seca, Beatriz, 1953–
    Problem-driven management: achieving improvement in operations through knowledge management / Beatriz Muñoz-Seca and Josep Riverola
        p. cm.
    Includes bibliographical references and index.
    ISBN 1–4039–4137–8 (cloth)
      1. Knowledge management. 2. Organizational learning. 3. Problem solving. 4. Total quality management. I. Riverola, Josep, 1940– II. Title.
HD30.2.M876 2004
658.4′038—dc22   2004046493

10 9 8 7 6 5 4 3 2 1
13 12 11 10 09 08 07 06 05 04

Printed and bound in Great Britain by
Antony Rowe Ltd, Chippenham and Eastbourne

Contents

List of Figures

List of Tables

Prologue

Hello, dear[1] reader! The book you are holding in your hands is the result of more than 12 years of effort to put down in writing some general but extremely attractive ideas and focus them on the task of increasing firms' present and future profits.

Even at the risk of being too general and synthetic,[2] we would start off by saying that there are four central ideas in this book:

- Knowledge is the driving force of permanent improvement.
- It is not difficult to implement a system that produces learning and permanent improvement.
- The system is vital for the firm's productivity and competitiveness.
- The manager must understand that what is important is not to do but to enable others to do.

Background and a little history

Our story starts way back in 1987 when the authors mutually expressed their disappointment in the implementation of quality ideas and methods. At that time, the quality movement had advanced far enough for its limits to be visible. It seemed that the ideas were moving in the right direction to achieve an initial success but, after a short time things came to a halt and it was very difficult to get them moving again. Many companies implemented quality circles during those years. Today, not a trace of them remains. From the vantage point provided by our respective professional activities, one in the university and the other in business and public administration, we saw many companies engage fierce battle for quality, only to emerge from the fray licking their wounds. Even then, with the sweeping tide of the ISO-9000 certifications, we felt sure that that path would not take us straight to our desired goal. We drew some consolation from the discovery that, to quote a Motorola vice-president, 'The ISO-9000 is the worst thing that has ever happened to quality.' But such consolation did little to alleviate the situation. Quality seemed to be like a fire in a hay barn. It started off with a blaze, producing

---

[1] Although we do not know the reader, there is no doubt that the reader is our customer. If he has bought the book, he has exchanged money (which has cost him effort to earn) for an expectation of results. If he has not bought the book and he is reading this: (a) Stop reading and rush out and buy it, (b) in any case, he is investing time, which he probably has in short supply, to understand our ideas. And that too has merit ... In short, it is our obligation to try and satisfy him, giving him a service that matches the investment made. Hence, the use of 'dear'.

[2] A not insignificant risk. If we continue along the path of synthesis, we could say that this book has only one message: 'Do good and avoid evil.' But generality is the enemy of operationality, so we decided not to say it.

immediate results, and then quickly burnt itself out. All of its variants suffered similar fates. For example, for a time, the Kaizen (continued improvement) was in vogue. But, after a few faltering steps, it too fell by the wayside, never to rise again.

One of the basic problems seemed to be that the quality programs ground to a halt when the senior management ceased to devote itself to them directly. If management stopped pushing, the quality drive started to lose definition and eventually became diluted in the company's general dynamic.

It seemed to us that no one had a clear idea about what drove continued improvement.[3] The key questions were focused on identifying the driving forces that pushed the firm's operations forward and on what should be done to put this forces into motion. Another important question was to find out how a self-sustaining permanent improvement process could be obtained – a process that would not stop when management ceased to focus on it.

In 1990, one of the authors attended a series of meetings held in Boston in which the subject of knowledge enterprises and knowledge as the key to companies' growth was discussed. The idea was fascinating. And in a way, it had already been foretold by the classics. Simon himself, to whom many of the ideas contained in this book are owed, had marked the path to follow. Midway between artificial intelligence and management science, Herbert Simon had carried out an in-depth study of the problem-solving process as a source of knowledge and progress. However, there was no clear awareness of how knowledge should be integrated in the firm's operating life. The central issue was, how knowledge could be used to improve the firm's productivity, making its operations more competitive. Some authors, particularly those of the Harvard school, started to approach certain managerial issues from a knowledge viewpoint, although still without making a solid operating link between business and mental processes.

At that time, we started to work in earnest on the subject.[4] We compiled information, observed companies, organized and generated our ideas and, in particular, worked with companies and institutions that wished to go beyond an initial effort in quality. One of the authors has extensive experience in education while the other comes from the depths of operations. These opposing poles have probably provided the inspiration for the work carried out during this time. Gradually, the central idea on which this book is based became clear to us: *the driving force of permanent improvement is knowledge.* Simple and obvious, but it took us a long while to realize this.

---

[3] There is a big difference between continued improvement and permanent improvement. Continued improvement is incremental improvement, little by little, doing new things a little better each time. Permanent improvement encompasses any type of innovation or change, from the most trivial to the most revolutionary. Permanent improvement is the endless quest for progress, the non-acceptance of consecrated procedures and the consolidation of a system that empowers the human ability to overcome obstacles.

[4] The idea was so fascinating that one of the authors gave up his previous career and started a new one in order to concentrate on it. He does not yet know whether his decision was right or wrong. Time will tell …

Improvement is knowledge

As we try to show in this book, the two subjects – improvement and knowledge – are so closely intertwined that it could be said that they are one and the same thing. *Improvement produces learning, learning produces knowledge and knowledge produces improvement.* This leads to a synthesis of both concepts which is considerably removed from the way in which each one has been treated individually up to now. Knowledge management has been viewed in many ways but a lot of the noise is now concentrated on document management. In fact, some authors have already changed the field's name and start to talk about 'document management' instead of 'knowledge management'.[5]

But this conceptual synthesis is not enough. The serious issue is how knowledge management can be used to improve the firm, from a practical and highly operational viewpoint. And this requires providing *practical implementation ideas*, so that the manager can start acting straight away, and, in the process, can see for himself that both immediate and future results are obtained. From this point of view a concept arises as the main practical issue, the concept of a problem and the problem-solving process. This has proved to be the missing link in the above causal chain, the link that allows its fruitful application. So much so, that we believe it opens up a new approach in improving operations. We call this approach *Problem Driven Management* (PDM in short).

And this is another of the book's central issues. In this book, the reader will find an attempt to turn *implementation of a knowledge-based PDM* into something operational, to the point of providing formulas or procedures for action. Although far from being a manual, we believe that that the book contains sufficient practical ideas to enable the interested reader to push the implementation process forward himself.

The manager's responsibility for learning and improvement

We believe that firm's managers are responsible for the development of the people who work under them and with whom they interact. Not only do they play a key role as referents, but their attitude and daily work often are a source of inspiration for the people around them. We are increasingly of the view that everybody that works in a company is actually a manager of it. As we will see, the path to operating progress is to make full use of all the talent that the firm possesses. And this is only possible if each individual has the opportunity and the initiative to contribute. This has a lateral but very clear implication. Firms' human resources and training departments must confine themselves to providing professional support to managers, something akin to the role of the firm's legal department. This

---

[5] Curiously enough, even while still in its infant stages, knowledge management has lost appeal for many people. Perhaps the name has been bandied around too much, without contributing any new operating concepts, and this always disappoints. Concepts wear out quickly in the consulting world.

is because *a firm's real personnel and training managers are all of its managers, each one in its own field.*

Interestingly, in recent years, human resources departments have fervently embraced the idea of knowledge management, understood as the storage and dissemination of the knowledge held by the firm. Some have focused their activity on the creation and operation of information systems based on this function.[6] This is not only wide of the mark but in fact produces exactly the opposite effect, in that it makes people lose sight of the fact that the immediate goal of any management task is the firm's productivity and competitiveness. This is the job of line management. Hence, the people responsible for permanent improvement and, therefore, for knowledge management are, once again, the firm's line managers. In this book, we will see how the commitment to permanent improvement, with the corresponding firm's progress, requires a change of mind-set among the managers, because it is associated with a new paradigm.

To date, all managers have been educated in the idea that they had to diagnose problems, draw up action plans and then implement them. However, this leads to the disastrous attitude of 'me Tarzan, you Jane' or 'I think and you work', which is so deeply rooted in many companies. Sometimes, executives talk in terms of delegation, participation and other similar words but, deep down (almost) all of us think that we are the only ones that see things as they really are. We know what must be done, others must do what we say. This happens at almost all levels of life, but managers have the power to make it happen. Or at least, to try to make it happen. In other social structures, this is not so. In some families, the father is boss (or thinks he is boss) but the real reins of power are somewhere else. The same thing happen in some companies. Someone thinks he is in command and many *pretend* to obey him.

This idea is *necessarily* mistaken. If we want to exploit the knowledge held by the company to attain improvement, *everybody must apply this knowledge* to the performance of actions that improve the firm's productivity or competitiveness. We need them all. Every brain must be involved. And not for humanitarian, ethical or charitable reasons. This is not the old idea that 'the poor worker has such an alienating job". This is very nice, but it is an altruistic approach. And all improvements that are introduced for altruistic reasons fail in crises. When the money stops flowing, the first victims are good intentions.

Everyone must participate because it is the *only way* to achieve *greater present and future benefits for everyone involved.* It is a win–win situation. I must act out of selfishness because what is best for me is best for everyone else. It is the only way to keep the system stable. Someone can argue that this is 'good natured' selfishness. We think that the adjective is redundant. When the situation is the best for everyone, when viewed from each individual's personal selfishness, the situation is

---

[6] With the explosion of technological jargon in recent years, it seems that anyone who doesn't have an advanced system to show must hide away in a cupboard. We know of some managers in areas that traditionally have a low technological content who have installed special information systems, 'not to be any less than those guys …', as one manager said.

stable and the spirit of improvement remains alive. The actions we propose in the book originate from this postulate. There is no altruism in what we propose,[7] everything lunges upon logical, implacable conclusions. And we want the reader to remember this.

The true change of paradigm that drastically affects the manager's life is that he no longer has to *make action plans to do things*. He must *make action plans so that other people make action plans to do things*. There is a double indirection in this statement. The manager does not do. He creates an environment in which the organization's other agents can do things, those that are best for them and for the firm.

One of the authors used to say to his managers that he only wanted them to do three things: 'Develop your people, help them reach where they cannot reach alone, and manage the resources allocated to you. And leave for home at five o'clock!'

Technology and knowledge management

A few words about technology. There are voices in the market who say that special, technologically advanced systems are needed to support knowledge management. We think that, this is completely false. No convoluted computer systems are needed that lay on top of the firm's information system. In our experience, sometimes these systems are implemented by managers who want to leave their mark on the firm, perhaps because the function they perform is becoming empty of content.[8]

We propose that the reader forget about technology during the first 12 chapters of this book. And when he comes to the thirteenth, that he judge for himself the type of technology he requires to do what we recommend. In that chapter, we will propose a structure for the knowledge's information system. It is based on simple things – programs that are within the reach of any company. Ah! And above all keep this book away from your computer specialists, because they may fall into the temptation of applying technology to everything that is said here.

Reader's guide

The book contains a lot of material that may be skipped on a first reading. We recommend that the reader get a general idea of the subject before going into the details of implementation. In order to guide the reader, we have marked with an asterisk beside the section's title those sections that we recommend omitting in a

---

[7] And if there is, we ask the reader to let us know, so that we can eliminate it in future editions. Sometimes, we can't avoid falling into the soap opera culture …

[8] Is it a phenomenon similar to the mobile phones? We have a friend who says that delegation is on the decline in companies, because managers are continually monitoring activity through their mobile phones. And he adds: 'But deep down, what they want to do is make sure that everyone remembers that they are there and they are important for the company.' Is he right?

first reading. The sections marked with an asterisk contain supplementary or applicational material and can be postponed for a second reading.[9]

The book consists of 14 chapters, divided into three parts, and an appendix. The first part, *Basic Principles*, encompasses the first three chapters. It presents the book's common conceptual substrate. Chapter 1 deals with the problem-solving process, a basic prerequisite for the entire book. We explain a model of the process, basically taken from Simon [1989] and we explore the effect that knowledge acquisition has on the whole. It is a fairly conceptual chapter and the reader should scrupulously skip the asterisked sections or he will get a mistaken idea of the weight of the rest of the book.

Chapter 2 explains the operating consequences of the model presented in the previous chapter. Various classifications of knowledge are presented, from different viewpoints, and the idea of collective knowledge is introduced. Knowledge categories and the competence typology are identified. Finally, the idea of knowledge repository is introduced, both for the agent and for the organization, thus differentiating individual learning from collective learning.

In Chapter 3, to soften the content and trend of the previous chapters, we present a first application of the ideas given in these two chapters. It is a simple but important application to project management in projects with a high degree of uncertainty. This type of project, which already forms the majority of the projects undertaken by companies, is difficult to manage because the classic project control techniques fail miserably. This explains why such cherished techniques as PERT in practice are only useful for working on the management of projects that people already know how to manage.

The second part, *On better doing*, is composed of Chapters 4 to 7. This part presents the operations knowledge required to apply the book's ideas to the firm's operations and to achieve *excellence in customer service*. Chapter 4 discusses operations from a general viewpoint. The relationship of operations with service and the company's mission is presented, exploring the contents of the firm's operations 'box' and introducing the Business Activities Sequence, BAS.

Chapter 5 introduces the *six basic variables* for design and control of the operating system. These variables are very important, because they synthesize all of Operations from the top management viewpoint. Top Management has only to establish their values and the operations' people will be able to operate the system in accordance with the denoted mission. Therefore, they are a way of operationalizing the firm's mission, without having to go into detailed decisions that can and must be left to the agents involved. The *six variables technique* itself shows how a context can be created in which the others can act, while at the same time preserving the firm's mission.

Chapters 5 and 6 form a single unit, although they have been split to keep their length within digestible limits. The variables do not only perform the function of control pedals. They are also firm's knowledge repositories – and the way to

---

[9] Although perhaps only those readers who are insomniacs, irrepressibly curious or downright masochists will actually read the book again.

discover, systematize and catalogue a large part of the firm's knowledge. These two chapters provide a detailed discussion of each variable and suggest procedures that use the variables to uncover the knowledge existing in the firm.

The management of *permanent improvement* owes a lot to quality. So it is only fitting to acknowledge this. Chapter 7 addresses quality as the predecessor of good thinking. Quality is analysed as the management of the interactions with customers. The virtuous circle of quality, the forerunner of the *permanent improvement cycle*, is described. In a way, this chapter is an interlude before attacking the implementation of the PDM.

The third part, *On good thinking*, is composed of Chapters 8 to 14. In this we present a complete outline for implementing a permanent improvement and knowledge management system.

Chapter 8 starts the presentation of the improvement system's central ideas. It discusses how to perform a *knowledge inventory* that is, how to identify *what – we know* and its competitive capacity. This is not a simple task, it requires a certain methodology which is presented in the chapter. These techniques enable the firm's competences to be diagnosed with enough detail for its use in devising business development plans.

After presenting the knowledge inventory methodology, we immediately put it into use. Therefore, Chapter 9 returns to the field of more practical action in an attempt to achieve immediate results. A simplified knowledge management methodology is presented. This methodology uses a large part of the model. We deal only with the simple first case of *sporadic improvement action*, to enjoin the firm's agents to perform an improvement plan. It is not yet a permanent improvement system, a system ready for recurrent usage. The methodology has been tested in practical situations with very good results. It starts with the analysis of the 'moments of truth' and continues by detecting problems, listing the knowledge available in the firm and applying it to solve, or destroy, the operating problems affecting service. The chapter provides a set of forms for applying the method.

Chapter 10 focuses on *learning*. It tries to answer the question, 'What should the manager do so that the firm (its people) can learn each and every day and apply this knowledge to do things better?' Conceptually, this question is answered with the description of the *internal cycle*, or knowledge generation cycle. This is a model that describes the operating conditions that must exist in the firm to achieve maximum learning. With these ideas, it is now possible to understand how learning should be addressed in order to achieve productive, competitive results.

Chapter 11 supplements Chapter 10 with a presentation of the conditions that ensure that knowledge is *applied to improving the service* given to the customer. These conditions become a practical general guideline for implementing the permanent improvement system, this time from a general viewpoint that ensures recurrent action by all of the agents.

Chapter 12 presents some horizontal measures required to implement the permanent improvement system and concentrates on two of them, training and organizational structure. Training introduces the subject of the *training system's design*.

We discuss the role of the manager as an educator and propose guidelines for designing training plans along these lines. We also establish organizational criteria and describe organization structures that, in our experience, attain the desired result.

Chapter 13 completes the implementation process by analysing the role played by technology. Specifically, a structure for the *knowledge management system* (KMS) is presented which is superimposed on the usual information system and integrates learning and permanent improvement in the day-to-day work of the firm. Some ideas are given for implementing a KMS using components already available on the market, without requiring large-scale spending on IT resources or new systems separate from the firm's classic ones.

Chapter 14 contains a checklist for the firm's management, listing the main issues to achieve a complete operating implementation. Management can decide the degree of detail to which it is wished to carry out the implementation and the chapter shows the different types of improvement system that are obtained when different features are added to it.

Finally, we give in the appendix, some details on the tools that we have used in the course of the book.

Acknowledgements

As in any book of this type, many people have influenced its preparation and it is only right to acknowledge them. First of all, our colleagues at IESE, particularly our colleagues in the Operations Area. Special mention should be made of Juan Antonio Pérez López, whose ideas were critical in the development of many of the concepts discussed here. Also the members of the Information Systems department have contributed to criticizing the material we present and (possibly) making it easier to understand for the reader.

The many managers who have attended our general and specialized courses have been exposed to this subject and have given us feedback, sometimes positive and sometimes negative, which has contributed to the permanent improvement of what is said here. Particular mention should be made of the EMBA students at Madrid, who have had to endure the practical application of some of these issues.[10] All in all, they make up a group of 3,000 people who had to sit through our divagations at one stage or another of the book's development.

Another special mention must be made of the long-suffering IDE (Institute of Business Development) faculty and students in Ecuador. During the last seven years, they have seen us grapple with these issues and witnessed the evolution of our thinking in the annual courses we give at that institution. Thanks to all of them and particularly to Hugo Pérez (the current professor of Operations), Miguel Rodríguez (the owner of the chalk) and, in particular, his first dean, Wilson Jácome. Wilson: you know that we are going to create an association dedicated to

---

[10] Guys, the book's finished! But the next stage is worse still, because now you'll have to study it in detail ...

you. Neither do we forget the conversations with Antonio Rodríguez and the cheerfulness and good humour of Xavier Vidal and his charming family. Our deepest gratitude to all of you.

During the many years that this book has been in the process of writing, we have been assisted by a number of research and administrative associates. María José Marhuenda and Beatriz Cuadrado are two of the former. Fátima Gonzalez-Aller, Guadalupe Moragues and Marta Silvela belong to the latter. Marta, with her numerous readings, has become a veritable expert in the subject. All of them have helped organize these pages into a more or less coherent whole. IESE's doctorate students have made many suggestions to improve this book's preliminary drafts.

Finally, the authors would like to thank each other for having put up with each other long enough to complete this project.

As in our previous books, each author thinks that all the bad bits in the book have been written by the other author. And he or she may be right ...

Part I
Basic Principles

1
Knowledge and Problem Solving

In this chapter, we outline the basic concepts which underpin the rest of the book. We start by giving a working definition of knowledge which we can use to establish the starting point for our subsequent discussion. After having described the mechanisms for problem solving, we give several different classifications of knowledge. This chapter is necessarily rather abstract, with little relation to business reality. To rectify this, Chapter 3 gives a first business application of the concepts developed here.

Knowledge

What do we mean by the term 'knowledge'? We are sure that the reader is aware that this question has been discussed by the finest minds of Western thought – from Aristotle to the present day. Obviously, in the wake of such illustrious predecessors, one runs the risk of seeming not just trivial but even ridiculous. So we would ask the reader to refrain from engaging in profound philosophical considerations and to remember that our purpose at this point is eminently pragmatic: we want to identify knowledge so that it can be later used to generate a long-term advantage for the firm.

Webster's Dictionary defines knowledge as: 'The product or result of being taught, the body of things that are known, or which are contained in science' and gives as synonyms the words 'information', 'folklore', 'science', 'wisdom'. Although these definitions can be operationalized, they are too general and too limited for our present purposes.

The dictionary accepts that it is very difficult to observe the existence of knowledge and reduces its presence to the detection of its effects. Knowledge is stored within the individual, probably in the neuronal interconnections in the brain. This makes it almost impossible to observe it directly.

This difficulty in observing knowledge lies at the heart of the problems that arise when we attempt to evaluate its existence. Supposedly with the intention of increasing the volume of knowledge held by their students, educators have long debated the correct way of proving its existence. Examinations, tests or continual assessment form part of the body of experiments used to detect the presence of knowledge. All of these tools are based on observation of the results obtained by the individual when he performs certain activities, presumably with the assistance of the knowledge he possesses.

There are many different types of activity that are used in practice to assess the existence of knowledge. All managers carry out an intuitive assessment of the people they interact with, which includes an appraisal of their knowledge (or skills). However, it is rare for the procedure used in these appraisals or their outcome to be formalized in any specific way.

Example 1.1 shows how one firm identifies the existence of knowledge. Basically what it does is ask people questions, jazzing it up with a little high-tech. Of course, such approaches are not particularly satisfactory. Their basic failing is that they contain no clear concept of what knowledge is.

From an operational viewpoint, it is perhaps less important to know 'what knowledge is' than to 'be able to detect the existence of knowledge'. So, in this book, we will follow this indirect approach. Accepting the impossibility of knowing what knowledge is, we identify it by a certain type of result. This is in line with the best twentieth-century scientific tradition. In physics, for example, people have given up finding out what an electron is and define it by its behaviour. We don't know what it is, but we do know how it behaves.

In our analysis, the main observable arising from the existence of knowledge are the results obtained in problem solving. That is why we have placed the concept of 'problem' at the heart of our presentation. The basic underlying hypothesis is that any problem requires a certain type of knowledge to solve it.

Of course, scientific rigour would demand at this point a precise definition of what a problem is. As we do not wish to be excessively rigorous, we will confine ourselves here to giving an operating definition of *problem* (Pérez López, 1991). In this definition, a problem is *a situation that is unpleasant for someone*.

This definition isolates three basic features of any problem:

(a) A problem requires the existence of an agent who is interested in it. In the absence of any interested agent,[1] there is no problem. The agent providing

Example 1.1   Identifying knowledge

Metra, S.A.

The company Metra uses the following procedure to determine the existence of knowledge. The company has software that provides intranet access to a central database which contains its employees' knowledge profiles. Each employee can create his own knowledge profile (using a standard form available on the intranet). The employee can choose from a master list containing several hundred items of knowledge, also available on the intranet, or add his own proposals. Each employee then rates his level of knowledge on each item. This profile is stored in the database and is accessible to all of the company's employees. No objective assessment is performed of these profiles.

---

[1] Like trees that fall down in a wood when there's nobody there ...

the reference need not be the same as the agent who solves the problem. The motivational link between the two is complex and is related to the most profound ideas about human behaviour.

(b) A problem arises from the agent's activity and this activity creates a situation. A situation is a configuration of the world that is obtained at a specific moment in time. The configuration also includes the internal state of the agent concerned. This process introduces a time component into the notion of problem.

(c) Finally, the existence of a criterion of like or dislike is required. This criterion obviously depends upon the agent and it is the source of a high degree of subjectivity in the nature of the problem. A problem is a problem 'for someone'. 'Universal' problems only exist as such because all the parties involved agree to view the situation as unpleasant.

Algebra could be conceived of as knowledge. However, for us, since we are interested in the mechanics of the application, this is too broad. The problems for which algebra provides a solution are too broad. The different subsets of algebra provide a much better understanding of knowledge. For example, 'solving linear equations' is an item of knowledge that allows anyone who possesses it to solve any system of linear equations. Of course, for 'solving a system of linear equations' to be a problem, it must be agreed that looking at a system of equations and not knowing the value of the unknowns can be regarded as an unpleasant situation for someone.[2]

In another area of activity, 'knocking in nails with a hammer' is an item of knowledge that solves a range of problems that share in common the action of inserting nails into a hard surface. In this case, 'knocking in nails with a stone' is not the same type of knowledge because it does not solve the same type of problem. Both types of problem are subproblems of a more general problem: 'knocking in nails'. Although they are similar, they are not exactly alike. For example, the former class contains problems such as 'hammering nails into teak wood'. The second class of knowledge will probably be unable to solve this problem.[3]

Using these ideas, we can establish a rather formal but nevertheless highly useful (on the basis of our experience) definition of knowledge for the type of work in which we are interested. *Knowledge is the ability to solve a certain set of*

Example 1.2 An example of an unpleasant situation

$$2x - 3y = 5$$
$$x + 2y = 20$$

---

[2] One of the authors is of the opinion that there is nothing unpleasant in not knowing the solution to a system of equations. Therefore, for that author, there is no problem! And, in fact, there isn't. See example 1.2.

[3] As the reader's fingers will discover if he tries to apply it ...

problems. Therefore, we identify a knowledge with classes of problems that it can solve, and in the following pages, we will often talk about knowledge associated with a problem.

> *Knowledge is the ability to solve a certain set of problems*

This so important to us, that we have named the whole approach presented in this book 'Problem Driven Management'. Problems are the main objects to be dealt with and the driving force behind knowledge acquisition and applications.

Without going into formalisms, which serve no useful purpose at this level, it is worth stressing that classes of problems have a structure that is inherited from its set-structure. Using this structure – perhaps primitive but a structure nonetheless – we can talk about inclusion between two classes of problems, about the connection and intersection between classes, and, in general, about all of the operations defined between sets. Because of the correspondence between knowledge and classes of problems, we see that knowledge also inherits this structure. Therefore, we can talk about subknowledge and intersections and complements of knowledge. For example, if 'solving linear equations' is a subproblem of 'solving equations', then the knowledge associated with the first problem is a subset of the knowledge associated with the second.

Although this discussion does not make a great contribution to our analysis, it at least demonstrates that operationalizing knowledge in terms of solving problems is something more than just a more or less apt change of name.

When we are dealing with knowledge, we are dealing with classes of problems and their solutions. This is something that can be verified by observation and, in practice, it is the central element in many tests used to identify knowledge. In this type of exercise, identifying the presence of knowledge is reduced to the entertaining intellectual game of ascertaining whether a certain class of problems is solved.

To complete our tour of the consequences of our definition of knowledge, we should briefly address the issue of knowledge deduced from other knowledge by means of logical reasoning. Going beyond the set structure, identifying knowledge with problems introduces the possibility of inferring the existence of knowledge from other knowledge postulated as existing. For example, what is the relationship between 'knowing how to write' and 'knowing how to solve linear equations'? Obviously, one is not a subset of the other – the relationship is more complex than this. We should be able to say that knowing how to solve linear equations entails knowing how to write or, at least, that the knowledge 'knowing how to write' exists very probably as a component.

In this relationship the existence of certain knowledge 'is inferred from' the existence of a body of other knowledge. This relationship enables us to infer the existence by applying an inference mechanism. This relationship can be given formal content by developing a *logic* of knowledge, based on the structure of the knowledge sets,[4] and which ultimately leads to a deductive formalism. Example 1.3 gives a classic example of formal reasoning on 'knowing what' and, therefore, of reasoning on knowledge.

Example 1.3 A nice example of inference between items of knowledge

---

The Three Wise Men

Once upon a time, there was a magnanimous King who had staffed his Court with the best talent in his kingdom to try and ensure the well-being of his subjects.[5] Three talents stood out above the rest, so much so that they were called 'wise men'. One year, on the anniversary of his coronation, the King wished to put his wise men to the test. He ordered five beautiful, jewelled helmets to be made, three made of gold and two made of platinum. Everyone knew this, including the wise men. Of course, the gold helmets were golden and the platinum helmets were platinum-coloured...very different from the gold colour! The King then ordered the wise men to kneel, stood behind them, chose three helmets and placed them on their heads. He then sat them on three chairs so that each one could see the other two.

The rules stipulated that none of them could take off their helmet and there were no mirrors in the room.

The King asked the first wise man, 'Do you know what metal your helmet is made of?' The wise man answered, 'No, Sire, I don't.' He asked the second wise man the same question and received the same reply. He then asked the third wise man the same question. This time, the answer was, 'Yes, Sire. I know what metal my helmet is made of.'

Dear reader, what colour was the third wise man's helmet?[6]

---

[4] Intuitively, it should be possible to do this by copying the construction of the algebra of propositions starting from set theory. However, there is a series of technical problems which complicate matters. The whole problem arises because the relationship 'knowing *x*' is more complex than originally thought because it refers not to objects but to the logic's propositions themselves. This gives rise to a second-order logic with complex formalisms. Consequently, for the moment, there is not much scope for practical application of such a system.

[5] The reader will readily infer from this beginning that the situation is imaginary...

[6] We will use the abbreviations G = Gold, P = Platinum and X = Any. A configuration is a given combination of helmets. For example, GPG is a configuration. As the first wise man did not know which metal the helmet was made of, he cannot be seeing two Platinum helmets. Otherwise, he would have deduced that his was made of Gold, as there are only two Platinum helmets. Therefore, either both are made of Gold or one is made of Gold and the other is made of Platinum. In symbol form, the possible configurations are {XGP, XPG, XGG}. The second wise man has heard the answer and therefore knows that these are the possible configurations. But he is able to see the first wise man's helmet. If the first wise man's helmet was P, the possible configurations are PGP, PPG and PGG. However, PGP is impossible because then the second wise man would know that his helmet was made of

In example 1.3, we use logic to infer consequences that are not present in the situation's premises, in other words, knowledge 'is inferred' from other, previously existing knowledge by exploiting the structure between them.[7]

The problem-solving process

In order to explore the structure of knowledge in greater depth, we must study the process by which problems are solved. Problem-solving processes have a long history of detailed study by philosophers and scientists from different schools. Generally speaking, the formalization of a problem-solving process is presented in terms of a methodology – a sequence of steps which, if they are exactly followed, hopefully give the desired result.

Here, we face a curious situation. The general methodologies for solving problems, although of capital importance in real life, are rarely if ever taught at school. They seem to be transmitted from mother to child, as part of a body of common knowledge which is not formally learnt. In the process of human learning, we acquire methodologies for solving certain *classes* of problems. Learning takes place within the context of specific problems. Initially, these are elementary problems, such as stacking blocks or placing objects in containers. Later on, at school, all kinds of methodologies are conveyed for solving specific problems, for adding, for formulating a mathematical problem, for drawing. On rare occasions, these methods are systematized in a general form, isolating common features that can be applied to a broader range of problems. The educated agent is in a good position to solve problems for which he has obtained a methodology. But, in new situations that he has not encountered previously – and this is an increasingly frequent occurrence in the business world – his methodological preparation is very limited. He must develop a specific methodology for each new case. Implicit hypothesis is that the individual himself can generalize and bring together all the parts,[8] so that he can apply this synthesis to types of problems that he has never encountered before.

As a result, agents develop problem-solving processes within each culture, as an intrinsic part of their approach to life. During most of the history of mankind, the environment has been the main source of problems for people. Therefore, different

---

Gold. Therefore, the only possible configurations are PPG and PGG. If, on the other hand, the first wise man's helmet is made of Gold, the possible configurations are GGP, GPG and GGG. Therefore, in total, {PPG, PGG, GGP, GPG, GGG} are possible. The third wise man knows this, because he has heard the answers. However, he has also said that he knows his helmet's colour. Therefore, the situation cannot be GGX. Because knowing that the other wise men have gold helmets does not identify his, as GGP and GGG are both possible. It must be one of the remaining configurations {PPG, PGG, GPG}. Whatever the case, his helmet is always Gold!

[7] For a very complete discussion of this process, the reader should see Fagin *et al.* (1995).

[8] This category of general methodological concepts is usually governed by rules such as: 'you've gone down a blind alley here, you'll have to undo part of what you've done.' Or 'continue along this path, you seem to be getting somewhere.'

cultures, which have come about in different environments, have developed different methods for solving their problems.

Western culture is deeply marked by the Cartesian method: divide a complex problem into parts, solve the parts and then bring them together again to obtain the solution to the specific problem. The method gives very good results in problems that have a structure that can be broken down. Yet some Eastern cultures feel an intrinsic aversion to separating a whole into its parts. They consider that the unity of the whole should be viewed as such, the whole is not additive, it has a behaviour that goes beyond the sum of the parts. The problem-solving methodology based on this premise will not give the same results as, for example, the Cartesian method. It may be more appropriate for some types of problem and less appropriate for others.

Fortunately, perhaps encouraged by the advent of the computer, more attention is being paid recently to the formalization of problem-solving processes. A few decades ago, Polya (1945), a Hungarian mathematician, wrote a delightful book which should be read by anyone interested in problem solving. In this book, he reviewed everything he had learnt about the subject, after a long, brilliant career as a mathematician. In the 1960s, Herbert Simon, Alan Newell (Simon, 1981) and their colleagues analysed the problem-solving process in some detail and proposed an approach which, to the minds of the authors of this book, continues to be one of the best. Cognitive science has compiled these methods and developed others that are more organized. Strange as it may seem, the people who work in the field of quality seem to be unaware of their existence and have developed their own methods (sometimes oversimplified).

In Simon, the process of solving a problem is basically described through the application of a series of transformations to a situation, which gradually turn it into something that has the desired features and is no longer unpleasant for the agent.

Before going into a detailed discussion of the problem-solving process, it is worth dwelling for a moment on the analysis of two major categories of problems that are particularly interesting from the company's viewpoint. We present this problem typology, also originally proposed in Simon and taken up again by Pérez López, in the next section. It will help us gain an improved understanding of the situation's components.

Problem typology

One possible classification of problems would be by their degree of structuring. Depending upon the need for change that demands their solution, we will distinguish between two categories (Pérez-López):

- *Structured problems*. These are problems in which the decision maker can define with precision and in a verifiable manner what is understood by a 'pleasant situation'. In this case, the problem's solution requires the construction or identification of an object to which the 'solving' criteria can be applied and which responds positively to all of them. This type of problem includes problems that can be solved by applying a sequence of operations, or solution 'procedure'. The decision maker may not know the procedure, but when he knows it, he is able to solve the (family of) problems. Therefore, this knowledge is associated with procedures. Thus, structured problems are associated with process knowledge.

- *Non-structured problems* are those in which it is not possible to define *a priori* what a satisfactory solution is. The decision maker only perceives the situation's 'pleasantness' when he actually experiences it and, even then, it may be impossible (or very difficult) to prove its validity objectively. For this type of problem, it is difficult, probably impossible, to specify a procedure for obtaining acceptable solutions. Creative, tailor-made answers are required whose outcome is often unknown.

Many problems are not structurable, at least given the current state of the art. And when this happens, the decision maker cannot avoid feeling the anxiety associated with lack of structure. This type of situation is commonplace in management tasks. Choosing a company's mission is a non-structured problem. There is a high degree of arbitrariness in the 'solution' to this problem. The experts have designed strategic planning processes that seek to eliminate the anxiety from decisions. But this merely superimposes an artificial structure onto the problem in order to obtain a solution. When this happens, a transformed problem is being solved, which may have only a passing resemblance to the original problem. Many strategic planning processes commit this sin. *Solving non-structured problems requires an active search for the solution by the decision maker, a personal involvement with the problem to be solved.* These features have led some authors to say that these problems (and their associated knowledge) are the most important part of the managerial skills.

*The basic solution process

Having got this far, we can now outline a general problem-solving methodology. This methodology conceptualizes the process of solving a problem as a *search process*. The solver looks among a series of possibilities for a solution that is pleasing to him. During the process, he redefines the problem's structure, broadening or narrowing horizons and defining alternatives and possibilities.

This way of conceiving the problem solution process is the outcome of observing many cases of problem solving by human agents. When faced with a problem he does not know how to solve, it is commonplace for a human to carry out a more or less elaborate search.

According to this paradigm, the functional components of the problem-solving process are always the same, and identical to the components of a search process, namely:

1. Goals and constraints.
2. States of the problem.
3. Measures of distance.
4. Set of transformations.
5. Search mechanism.
6. State of the knowledge.

Let us suppose that our problem is, for example, 'to win a chess game'.[9] This is a well-structured problem which has a well-defined procedure for solving it. As the number of alternatives is finite, all we have to do is to try all the possible alternatives and choose the best. There's just one minor drawback. The number of alternatives is staggering so it is best not to attack the problem using this exhaustive procedure.[10] Let us see what the components of the problem-solving process are in this case.

1. *Goals and constraints.* In this case, the goal is easy to define: 'checkmate the other player's king', and it is easy to test by applying the rules of the game. The problem is well-structured and the overall goal does not alter as the activity progresses. The drawback with such a generic goal is that it is a long way from the decisions. For example, it is difficult to use it in the opening phase, because it does not enable us to readily discriminate between the different moves (different openings). In this case, for example, the immediate goal is usually formulated as 'obtaining maximum mobility for the pieces'. The implicit hypothesis is that obtaining mobility helps win the game, that is, attain the overall goal of 'checkmating the other player's king'.

   The same thing happens in the firm. The general goal of any company is *indefinite survival*. However, at certain times during the 'game', this goal is not very meaningful and must be put aside in favour of other goals that are easier to test.

   Goals can be structured in a hierarchy. Thus, goals can be split into subgoals, which can be further divided almost endlessly. This structure is both an advantage and a disadvantage.

   The advantage is that subgoals are easy to test and transmit. A subgoal may have a very clear meaning in a particular context, in which the general goal is not able to convey the message. Many management by objectives practices try to achieve this advantage by systematically decomposing (top-down) the firm's general goals and formulating them explicitly in each particular context.

   The disadvantage is the difficulty in coordinating the simultaneous impact of interlinked goals. Ideally, achievement of all the individual goals should ensure achievement of the general goal. In practice, this rarely happens. It is

---

[9] Simon himself used chess for his research on problem solving. To a certain extent, he was responsible for the tremendous amount of time that has been invested in the last forty years in developing 'smart' programs for playing chess.

   In defence of all those who took part in this effort, the main outcome sought was not the programs but knowledge about the problem-solving process through chess. However, it must also be said that the knowledge obtained is probably much less than expected, it is doubtful whether it is effective to devote so many hours to such a specific subject, since in recent years, the most successful programs have been focused on 'playing chess well' rather than learning about problem solving. However, speculative science is after all only 'a game before the eyes of the gods ...'.

[10] However, the success of recent programs (such as Deep Blue in its confrontations with Kasparov) depends to a great degree on the capacity of the hardware. Thanks to the hardware's high level of performance, it is possible to examine hundreds of millions of combinations in a relatively short time. The machine's sheer speed enables it to implement to the letter the method proposed in the text. Is it possible to learn anything using this method?

very difficult to devise a hierarchy of goals that meets this condition, although there has been considerable effort among the specialists.

Goal structure is in a state of continual flux and change. At any given time, the decision maker has a definition of the features that the object (abstract or concrete) that materializes the solution of the problem must meet. These features can often be expressed either as conditions or as constraints. In the former case, they are exposed as propositions of degree (sufficient, maximum, a little, etc.). In the latter case, they impose conditions of *belonging* that the result must meet. As a result, the problem can be approached simply as a problem of feasibility. A solution is pleasing to the agent if it meets all the constraints stated by him. When there are criteria of degree, the problem may be presented as one of optimization or relative goodness of the solution. However optimization needs invariance of structure, at last for long enough to achieve the optimum. This is why optimization ideas are normally only applied to structured problems.

Qualitative goals are often hard to assess, particularly if there are several decision makers working together on the solution of a certain general problem. One approach is to describe the goals and constraints in a measurable form. Here one has to define the way in which an object's features can be measured and, therefore, implies the presence of quantitative criteria. This is an important point because quantitative criteria normally do not completely characterize the goals, and as a consequence quantitative criteria end up by being only proxies of the initial concept.

In non-structured problems, the goals of the problem-solving activity are not known *a fortiori*. As the problem evolves, a process takes place whereby the problem is defined. Ideally, this process should lead the decision maker to structure the problem or, at least, some of its components. Goal definition in this type of problem is progressive. A simple way of stating a progressive definition of a goal is to use conditions that are progressively introduced or removed. As we have said, most top management problems are non-structured. Typically the emphasis is on feasibility, on satisfying all of the accumulated constraints.

A problem such as 'developing a business vision for the firm' illustrates this situation. A business vision contains a series of elements and one of them, the mission, normally states a series of conditions that are imposed on the business and its results. See Example 1.4.

Example 1.4   A firm's mission

The Mission of the High-Speed Train

The mission of the High-Speed Business Unit is to provide an integral transport service that satisfies the needs and expectations of its customers and of all the people who work at high speed, to achieve profitability, market leadership and social respect.

The problem is now to find a way (one will be enough!) to meet these conditions. In the process of solving the problem, the high-speed unit will have to define what profitability, leadership and social respect mean, expressing them in terms of concrete goals and conditions. In any case, the problem's general structure will be the same: To find a way of fulfilling the conditions or, to find a feasible solution.

2. *The state of the problem's solution.* In the case of the chess game, the game's state is contained in the position of the two players' chessmen and in knowing whose turn it is to move. This is the only thing that matters for the future. It does not matter how this position has been reached – the future only depends upon the current situation.

The problem's state is the description of all the elements of its history that are relevant for the future. This condition is very difficult to verify in most practical cases. Often, the complete state should be the system's entire previous history, because there may be subtle aspects of this history that influence the future. In chess, the player's mental condition is part of the problem's state and this possibly depends upon hundreds of circumstances that go way beyond the chessboard, such as the results of previous confrontations, whether or not they get on with each other, how much practice they have had, among many others. It therefore becomes necessary to simplify the description of the state, reducing it to its most important components.

The description of the state simplifies if we can *represent* the problem. This technique, *representing* a problem, consists of projecting the problem, which is expressed in a domain that is foreign to us, onto a conceptual universe with which we are familiar.

Although this may sound pretentious, it is something that the reader does continuously. For example, using pen and paper to reflect on a problem is simply transposing its statement to graphic symbols. In another example, identifying defects in a production process may be a difficult problem unless an adequate representation is provided, for example, in the form of a control chart. An excellent example of the power of representation is shown in Example 1.5.

In each case, the different representations of a problem may give rise to different approaches to the problem's solution, with different qualities of the solution obtained.

It is difficult to expect a person to discover by himself the most suitable representation of his problem. This is more an art than a science. However, something can be done. As a representation has many contact points with a *model*, the modelling theories and techniques in specific areas of knowledge provide powerful aids, provided that the problem can be typified as belonging to one or more of these areas. The most widely used representations for well-structured problems are the geometric and algebraic representations. A well-conceived drawing is often the best way of analysing many types of problem.

Part of the system's state is the list of subproblems in which the overall problem has been divided, if it has been done, and a specification of how the

Example 1.5   Representation of problems

The Power of Changing the Representation

Project management. Let us assume that a project must be carried out by completing a series of activities A^1, A^2, ... A^n. Let us assume n = 4. There are precedence relationships between these activities such that an activity cannot start until others have been completed. To set the conditions, let us assume that 2 needs 1, 3 also needs 1, and 4 needs 2 and 3. Let us assume that the activities' durations are given as 2, 3, 4 and 2 days, respectively. How long will the project take to complete? The reader can start to reason using these activities, precedences and so on. He will probably not be able to get very far until he finds the following representation. Each activity is represented by a node or a circle on a sheet of paper. Each circle is numbered. If circle i must precede circle j, an arrow is drawn from node i to node j. The resulting network is a representation of the project. Each arc has a length equal to the activity's duration. In this representation, the project's minimum total duration is the length of the longest path between node 1 and node 4. This is known as the CPM representation. A more complete example will be given in the next chapter. The keen reader will realize that 'we have not represented the problem' in diagram form but in word form. The reader should develop the graphical representation from our word representation for himself.

---

recombination could occur. For example, at a certain stage during a chess game, the player may concentrate on taking an extra pawn, controlling a diagonal or blocking a bishop.

The drawback of an overly complete description of the state is the large quantity of interrelated components that may be necessaries describe it. Marketing specialists say that when the customer has more than seven objects to choose from, he becomes confused, tends to withdraw and not buy. A similar situation arises with states that are too 'rich'.

The state can often be organized as a pyramid, with successive planes representing successive levels of disaggregation in the problem's solution. The aggregate problem is on the first level and is fully solved when the last plane is resolved. This simplifies the solution process, enabling a few elements on the same level of abstraction to be handled at each stage. The art of decomposing or disaggregating – pure Cartesianism – is fraught with difficulties and even the most experienced become caught in the trap of forgetting the whole and giving too much importance to the part. This is particularly liable to happen if the decision maker finds the subproblem pleasing or if the problem's other components contain personal risks that are not in the subproblem. In such cases, the agent redefines the general problem, and solves the wrong problem! Efficiently solving the wrong problem is often more serious than not solving it.

3. *Measures of distance.* Ideally, simply observing the problem's state should be enough to decide whether we are in the presence of a solution. However, it is rarely easy to judge from a given state how far away we are from attaining the solution.

To guide us in the solution process, it is interesting to have measures of distance that seek to determine how far away we are from obtaining the 'solution' to our problem. It is not always possible to define this type of measure. In the case of chess, people have tried to determine the value of the two opponents' situations by giving weights to the pieces. Sometimes it is possible to decide that a certain advantage dominates, in that if both players play well, experience has shown that the player having the advantage achieves checkmate. For example, in many cases having the advantage of a rook seems to be decisive. Chess players know that 'position' is important. Sometimes, pieces are sacrificed to improve a position, enabling a player to move more easily while the other player finds his movements hindered. Assessing a position is more an art practised by the chess player than the application of simple rules of assessment. After more than four decades of experience in programming computers to play chess, modern chess-playing programmes use sophisticated procedures to assess positions.

4. *Set of transformations.* At any given time during the solution of a problem, we can use a collection of transformations. These transformations can be applied to the current state, to make it evolve towards new states. To continue progressing in the solution process, the problem solver selects one from among the series of possible transformations (that he knows). The transformation chosen will be applied to the problem's state to modify it and produce a new state. The ability to efficiently solve problems seems to be associated with the ability to keep the best transformations active on an ongoing basis. The number of active transformations must be sufficient to ensure progress but not so much as to clutter the brain with a large quantity of irrelevant transformations.

Some transformations are sophisticated and are implemented with the help of someone else, an expert, who is told the desired result not just of an application of the rules but of the whole process of solving a subproblem. The expert delivers the solution to the subproblem without the decision maker having to bother finding it for himself. Therefore, a transformation may arise from a subsidiary problem-solving process performed by the same individual or by someone else.

Most people are familiar with the group problem-solving technique in which a 'leader' divides the problems into subproblems which he gives to the different members of the group. This is a top-down technique which depends to a great extent on the 'leader's' skill in producing transformations that it is not necessary to undo later on.

In the case of chess, the set of transformations is very simple. They are all the possible moves that the pieces can make in a given position. Generally speaking, the number of alternatives is small, as many squares on the board are occupied or inaccessible. Here too, a transformation selection process takes place by

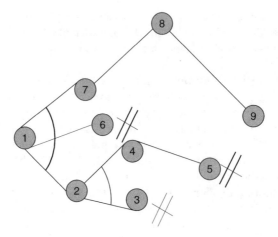

Figure 1.1   Diagram of a search process: exploration

which many of them can be eliminated. This phenomenon, sometimes known as 'solution pruning', eliminates those solutions that are obviously 'bad'. For example, to surrender a queen for a pawn does not seem to be the best of moves and probably should not be considered except in very extraordinary situations.

The application of transformations requires judgements *a priori* on their value *a posteriori*. This in turn requires an evaluation *a priori* of their relevance. This evaluation may come from experience, sensations perceived by the individual on previous occasions, abstract knowledge contained in certain types of theories or models, or information received by the subject from the environment. For example, many books have been written in chess that try to teach the reader how to identify and assess transformations, or piece moves. Most of this literature is concerned with experiences, from which very few conclusions can be drawn that could be used to develop an evaluative theory of chess. Hence the difficulty in applying transformations, which some masters seem to be able to do with great ease, but whose exact mechanism has yet to be clarified.

5. *Search mechanism.* Figure 1.1 shows how a search process can be conceptualized as exploring a certain tree.

The circles represent states of the problem with which the decision maker has been grappling during the process. The lines joining the states represent movements made by the application of transformations. For example, by applying a transformation of the problem, it has gone from state 2 to state 3. Two parallel lines mean that when this state was reached, it was decided to not continue exploring it and the decision maker returned to a previous state. The arcs at each node suggest that many alternatives have to be considered in each node and that only a few have been explored. For example, in node 1, three alternatives have been explored. Node 9 probably rates as the problem's solution.

The manner in which a decision maker builds the search tree is the outcome of his own search methodology. For example, one decision maker could systematically explore all of a state's possibilities before continuing to investigate the partial solutions obtained. This type of search is known as a *breadth search*, or extensive search. It is typically used by decision makers who have little information, or knowledge, about the different alternatives in each node and therefore wish to obtain a full list of the possibilities before continuing. If the breadth exploration is performed by levels, we are talking about an *exhaustive search*, a basic mechanism used in problem solving which consists of applying all of the transformations that are known, hoping that one or other of them gives the desired result. This is not a very intelligent mechanism but, in certain situations, it may be the only possible one. For example, it is necessary when the solution is elusive and could be found, with the same likelihood, at any point, which suggests that the neighbouring solutions are not very informative.

Using the above elements, the decision maker performs a search for the solution. It is a search because the object must be found without it being possible to identify *a priori* its position and how to get there. Generally speaking, the search mechanism has three basic components:

- *The transformation selection mechanism.* The choice of a transformation is usually based on the implicit maintenance by the decision maker of a series of heuristics, or evaluation and selection criteria. These heuristics form part of his knowledge base and, therefore, can be recharged by learning.
- *The backtracking mechanism.* This is used when a state does not seem to be promising and it is necessary to undo part of the road that has been travelled. Again, it is based on interim solution assessment criteria, often related with distance from the solution.
- *The mechanism for selecting the solution to be explored next.* As we have seen, there are systematic rules, for example, breadth search. Experience shows that good problem solvers usually explore *in depth*, choosing at any given time the most promising node and then continuing from it.

6. *Knowledge state, heuristic rules and models.* At last we have arrived at the knowledge base! This aspect deserves a full section to itself, which will be the next section. In a way, the description we have just performed of a problem-solving process is only justifiable from a practical viewpoint because of the light it sheds on how individuals' knowledge bases should evolve to improve the complete solution process. In the course of the previous description, we have discussed the knowledge managed by the solver and which he may hold to varying degrees in his knowledge base. The manager's task is to provide the problem-solving agent the knowledge that will help him improve his performance in each of the different parts of the process.

*Searches and learning: the role of knowledge

Simon's model of the problem-solving process (Simon, 1991) places a particular emphasis upon the search process. In his work on Soar (an artificial problem-solving system), Alan Newell (1982, 1990) explored in depth the relationship between the search process and learning. The idea is represented in Figure 1.2.

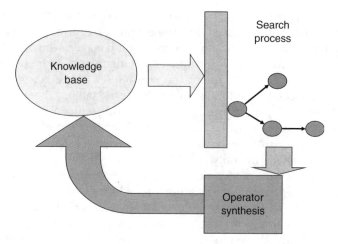

Figure 1.2   Search process and learning

When the decision maker faces a problem that he has never encountered previously, his knowledge base probably contains few elements that are directly applicable to the problem in question. Possibly the only thing he can use is a generic methodology of the type we have discussed above. Therefore, the agent must concentrate on performing a search process among the problem's states, trying to find a 'solution' state. Newell describes the process as an appearance of 'impasses' – points at which the decision maker does not know what to do immediately and where he must try to find in his knowledge base (or deduct from what is contained in it) the appropriate tools for breaking the impasse. Likewise, as he progresses in his search, the agent creates a series of 'chunks' or 'shortcuts'.

As the agent progresses from a state A to a state B (Figure 1.3), he may have to explore an intermediate tree of possibilities. This exploration, if it concludes successfully, shows him that if he applies transformations a, b, c and d, he can progress from A to B without any problems. Now this information can be consolidated in a macrotransformation, in a 'chunk' which groups all four transformations used in a single transformation. By this means, an 'operator' or aggregate procedure (called W, for example) is synthesized which the agent can use to reach B every time he finds himself at A, without having to explore intermediate states. The next time the agent finds himself at A and he is at an impasse, when he looks up his knowledge base, he will find the operator W which will enable him to avoid having to perform the exploration.

The reader will recognize this process from his own practical experience. Let us describe one such experience. In 1991 one of the authors travelled to China. The problem was getting around an unknown city, the country's capital, Beijing. In the absence of additional information,[11] the only way to explore the city was by

---

[11] And the maps of Beijing that were available in 1991, which is when the experience occurred, were all in Chinese, rendering them virtually useless.

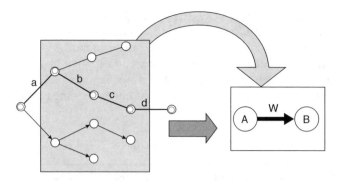

Figure 1.3 Search process between problem states

searching. Starting from the hotel, the home location, and given the existence of a bicycle, the indispensable requisite, the usual procedure is to explore the area, moving progressively further away from the home location. As the exploration progresses, we store the chunks in our memory, for example, procedures that enable us to go from the Friendship Hotel to the Zoo, from the Zoo to the Drum Tower, etc. 'Turn left to the first wide avenue. Turn to the right until you pass a market, ...' is a procedure that can be applied the second time we tour the city so that we do not have to explore the area between the Friendship Hotel and the Zoo.[12]

This learning procedure, adding chunks to the knowledge base, is very powerful for explaining and predicting the time needed to solve a problem. In fact, Newell (1982, 1990) uses it to deduct the famous 'learning curve' which relates the time taken to perform a task with the number of times the task is repeated.[13] Although we will not go into this deduction here, a few simple considerations will help understand the nature of the time needed for a problem-solving tasks.

Any search process is essentially combinatorial. The time required, in the worst-case scenario where the solution is only identified after having explored all the states, is proportional to the number of states. $T = k\,N$, where N is the total number of states and k is the proportionality constant. The time taken to perform the task is proportional to the number of states explored E, where E is a fraction

---

[12] Note by the other author. The only problem with this procedure is, in this case, the limited space in the memory for filing the chunks. I am obviously referring to the other author's central memory.

[13] Until Newell, the learning curve was an empirical rule observed in practice, but never justified. The idea of the experience curve is that the time taken to perform a task always decreases by a constant percentage if the number of times it is repeated is doubled. An 80 per cent curve is a learning curve that predicts that the time taken to perform the task will reduce 20 per cent when the number of times it is performed is doubled, wherever we are along the curve. Thus, the percentage reduction will be the same when we go from 1,000 performances to 2,000 performances as when we go from 100 to 200 performances. It is easy to prove that the learning curve's general expression has the form $T = T_0 x^a$, where x is the number of times the task is performed and T_0 is the task's baseline time.

of the total number of states N. Therefore, the time reduction between an exploratory situation and a known situation, in which we have a perfect shortcut, will be exactly E times, since in the latter case only one state is explored. The time reduction is therefore equal to the number of states explored in a search situation. In many real-life problems, the states' space grows exponentially with the size of the problem. Example 1.6 gives a few cases that illustrate some of the possibilities.

Example 1.6   Number of possible states in some examples

Some Examples of the Number of States

(a) In the case of Beijing, the states are represented by all of the street intersections. To simplify, if the maximum distance we wish to travel is n blocks, there are at least n^2 street intersections. For example, to explore a route that has a length of 10 blocks, we must devote a time that is proportional to 100. As can be seen, the power makes the time increase quickly as the distance is lengthened. When the distance is doubled, the time is quadrupled.

(b) Chess. Let us assume that we wish to examine moves up to a depth of 3, that is, the next 3 moves by both players starting from the current situation. If m is the average number of moves that can be performed at every move, the time required for an exhaustive exploration is of the order of m^6 as this is the number of possible states (squares).

(c) Production scheduling. Let us assume that we have 10 jobs to sequence on a machine. We know each job's duration and the changeover times that will be involved if job i is sequenced after job j. We wish to schedule the operation so that the total time until completion of the last job is as short as possible. The number of states is $10! = 10 \times 9 \times 8 \times \ldots \times 2 \times 1$. In other words, there are 10 ways of choosing the first job, 9 ways of choosing the second job (because only nine jobs are left to assign). 10! is equal to 3,628,800, which is a pretty high value. Now let us suppose that instead of 10 jobs, there are 20 jobs to sequence. There are now 20! possible states. However 20! gives a nice round figure of 2,432,902,008,176,640,000. If $k = 0.001$ seconds, that is, it takes a thousandth of a second to explore a state, the time required for the exhaustive exploration would be a trifling 77 million years!

(d) Production scheduling. Let us assume that we have 10 jobs to schedule. Each job must be processed in two machines. There are no changeover times but each job takes a different time in each machine. Of course, both machines can operate simultaneously. We want a schedule that minimizes the time to completing the last job. The number of possibilities is the square of case c).

(e) Definition of a staff allocation plan. A large spanish department store has the problem of structuring its sales staff's shifts and working hours and adapting them to customer service requirements, which vary depending upon the day of the week and the month. Each person can start his or her work at a different time from the others. Negotiating with the employees, it is possible to organize very variable working hours subject to a few restrictions, such as, for example, the maximum time on duty without a break is 4 hours, the break between two periods on duty on the same day cannot exceed 3 hours, etc. The problem is creating a schedule for all of the store's staff. An exhaustive exploration would lead to a consideration of each person's allocation status at each hour of the day. Of course, the problem accepts different versions of growing complexity. However, the number of possibilities is enormous, more than the previous case.

Of course, the reader will be wondering what would happen if he used a procedure that was more intelligent than the exhaustive search. Couldn't we be a little more sophisticated? Yet even assuming that the search method is very sophisticated,[14] and that the exploration only considers a small percentage of the states' total space – 1 in 1,000 possibilities, for example – the time required in some of the previous cases is still enormous.

The problem is clear. The state space in most practical problems is vast and any search method, no matter how sophisticated it may be, has a performance time that grows exponentially with the size of the problem x. For all of these cases, the solution time is $T = k \exp(x)$. It is possible to reduce this time through the creation of chunks. If, for example, we are working with case d in the previous table, any agent who had in his knowledge base the chunk discovered by Johnson would be able to solve the problem in very little time. Example 1.7 shows Johnson's rule. Two orderings are sufficient and as the ordering time is $x \log(x)$, this is the process's duration.

The time reduction is very significant. From $\exp(x)$ to $x \log(x)$! Stored knowledge has been used to shorten the solution time substantially. In this case, the stored knowledge came from a procedure devised by Johnson. However, in many cases,

Example 1.7 Johnson's rule

Johnson's rule:

(a) Order the jobs in the first machine in order of increasing process time.
(b) Order the jobs in the second machine in order of decreasing process time.

---

[14] And some very sophisticated methods have been developed in the area of artificial intelligence (see, for example, Russell and Norvig, 1995).

it is the problem-solver himself who stores chunks that will simplify his work. Of course, using a chunk when it should not be used can complicate the process and, to prevent this, it is necessary to use heuristics, or logical reasonings that put limits on the application of the rule. For example, we know that Johnson's rule is optimal for the case we have described, but minor changes in the situation may make it not only subopting, but even harmful!

*Knowledge and searching

It can be seen from the previous section that any problem-solving process toggles between two situations: the search (or exploratory phase) and the knowledge application (or knowledge phase). Each of these situations has advantages and disadvantages which are listed in Table 1.1.

A few remarks need to be made about the table:

- *The exploration does not guarantee the result.* The feeling of progress may even disappear and the procedure itself may seem meaningless. This is particularly liable to happen when the distance to the solution does not decrease monotonically during the exploration. Anybody who has tried to solve the famous Rubik's cube knows that at a certain stage of the solution it is necessary to undo the work done, increasing the distance to the solution. On the other hand, the mere application of existing knowledge, by decreasing the challenge, may trivialize the problem and frustrate the agent. For example, the reader could consider the 'difficulty' that he would have in adding two 3-digit numbers.[15] If his daily (problem-solving) work was confined to applying his 'addition' knowledge, his frustration would (probably) be considerable.
- *The imposition of time limits* on an exploration is both a limitation on the solution's quality and a cost reduction. The advertising agency that imposes strict time limits on its creative staff is lowering the solution's quality. Of course, in this case, quality can be maintained with higher levels of knowledge, skill or experience – in short, better creatives and (all other things being equal)

Table 1.1   The two phases of the problem-solving process

Exploratory phase	Knowledge phase (chunks)
• Requires a lot of time (which increases exponentially)	• Requires little time
• May be frustrating	• May be trivial
• Does not guarantee a result in a given time	• Guarantees the result
• Provides learning	• Adds information and experience
• Room for creativity	• Room for erudition
• The way to go where nobody has gone before	• Nothing new is obtained

---

[15] One of the authors: 'Well, for me, that would be quite a challenge ... !'

more expensive staff. The balance between personnel costs and the solution's quality (and time) is a key aspect of the management of creative activities.

- *Exploration leads to discovery and, therefore, to learning.* The outcome of an exploration process can be very rich in knowledge because not only gets the result but also the chunks used. The use of knowledge adds experience on how to use it rather than learning on the problem itself. Further on, we will see the difference between these two types of knowledge, which we can call *domain* and *process knowledge.*

- *Exploration paves the way for creativity.* The very nature of the exploration process makes the agent stop and ask at every turn, 'And now what?' The application of knowledge provides fertile ground for erudition – the consideration of wide types of knowledge that are not obviously related to the problem's target area.

- Finally, and most importantly, the *only real way to explore spaces where no man has gone before* is, by definition, *exploration.* Therefore, in innovation, creativity and, in general, all of those aspects that imply opening up hitherto unknown paths, exploration is not only the only possible problem-solving method but also the most preferable.

The problem-solving theory we have presented here is the most complete we know. The reader may think that it is rather abstract, but this is not really the case. Actually it is one of the few methodologies that has been described in sufficient detail to be programmed in a computer. All of the elements that we have mentioned can be represented symbolically giving rise to computer programmes. The reader will no doubt come across one or more of these in his daily life. Most computer programmes that compete with a human contain at least portions of the methodology we have examined.

2
The Properties of Knowledge Within the Firm

In this chapter, we discuss the main properties of knowledge from the firm's point of view. We start with the more general management properties that make knowledge one of the firm's assets. We will then consider the taxonomies of knowledge that help to organize it. Finally, the chapter includes a series of complementary but highly important issues such as knowledge materializations, knowledge in intellectual processes, collective knowledge, and the firm's core competencies.

Primary management properties

Example 2.1 describes some of the most important properties of knowledge from the management point of view.

*Knowledge extension and intensity

The total 'quantity' of knowledge existing in the firm has two components: one intensive and the other extensive. The extensive component is related to the number of people who hold the knowledge. It provides a preliminary measure of the stock of knowledge held. However, people may hold knowledge with different degrees of intensity. The intensity of knowledge is the level of knowledge existing in each individual. As we shall see later, scales of intensity can be defined which enable this property to be estimated in each individual, at least approximately. The firm's total knowledge is thus the *sum of each individual's knowledge, weighted by its intensity*. Of course, this definition is only indicative, being difficult to apply in practice. However, it at least provides a first notion of the valuation of knowledge assets, a subject that is of great interest to accountants[1] and about which we will have little to say in this book.

Both of these aspects, extension and intensity, should be taken into account in any decision involving knowledge. For example, increasing the number of people in the firm who are proficient in a certain type of knowledge will obviously

---

[1] As our purpose is to earn money and not just to count what (little) we have, we have deliberately ignored the accounting aspect of knowledge in this book.

Example 2.1 Management properties of knowledge

Properties of Knowledge

- *Knowledge is volatile*. Due to the nature of its storage, in people's minds, the evolution of knowledge is subject to the changes that take place in its carriers. For example, one of the firm's specialists may leave and, when this happens, the firm loses knowledge.
- *It develops by learning*. The knowledge development process is basically one of learning. Therefore, the management of learning is a key variable in the efficient management of knowledge. The learning process is a mechanism for personal improvement, an individualized mechanism that depends not only upon each individual's skills, but also on the learning experiences encountered along the way. Chapter 10 in this book contains a more detailed discussion of this process.
- *It is transformed into action driven by motivation*. The use of knowledge in solving a problem is a transitional process from interiorization to interaction with the world. The motivation for using knowledge is crucial for effective use of the knowledge acquired. But, this book is not the place for a detailed analysis of motivation and its implications (see Pérez-López, 1991).
- *It is transferred without losing any of its content*. Knowledge can be bought and sold, transferring to the buyer the same problem-solving ability as is held by the seller. This feature is in the basis of economic theories of knowledge.

---

increase this knowledge's stock. This would be a good decision if the aim is to increase the firm's productivity. The more trained people in a firm, the easier it will be to implement complex processes and resolve complicated situations. However, for the firm's competitiveness, the knowledge's intensity is more important. The creation of competitive advantage depends more upon the intensity of the knowledge held in the firm than on its extension. Therefore, actions that seek to improve competitiveness should concentrate on increasing the level of individual knowledge.

One subject that helps to shed light on these considerations is knowledge transfer between firms. When knowledge is transferred extensively, which is typically the case in most training processes, the immediate effect is to increase the knowledge's extensiveness in the acquiring firm, providing very little immediate competitive advantage. This effect has been widely observed and explains the poor outcome of numerous technology transfer processes between developed and developing countries.

Knowledge can increase the buyer's productivity. However, the seller retains the knowledge as part of his assets, with greater intensity than the buyer. Consequently, he maintains his competitive advantage. In order to increase his competitiveness, the receiver of the knowledge must develop its intensiveness – that is, he must invest money in developing his knowledge's intensity above the level obtained in the transfer. There is no successful process for transferring technology (a type of knowledge) that has not required a considerable investment in its intensive development.

*Knowledge for action

In his work on the basics of management action, Pérez-López provides a classification of knowledge based on its origin and function. This classification is briefly outlined in this section.

Table 2.1 presents this classification of knowledge according to two dimensions:[2] its purpose and its origin.

Regarding the purpose of knowledge, we distinguish between two categories: *operating knowledge* and *reflexive knowledge*.

- *Operating knowledge.* This is the *knowledge* aimed at solving operating problems, problems that deal with the performance of operations, that is, the combination of elementary transformations that change the world's state in well-established ways. Therefore, operating knowledge does not consider problems related with internal learning or with interactions with the other agents in the environment. Some examples of operating knowledge are: knowing how to machine aluminium, knowing how to design K-band antennas, knowing how to make a jacket, knowing how to operate a lathe, among many others.
- *Reflexive knowledge.* This is the *knowledge* concerned with the agent's way of thinking or acting. The agent uses this knowledge to reflect on his own action plans, his knowledge and their respective relationships with the other agents involved in the situation. Reflexive knowledge is a meta-knowledge – that is, a body of knowledge that enables reflection about one's own knowledge. Examples of reflexive knowledge are knowing how to negotiate, knowing how to conduct a meeting, knowing how to lead a group, knowing how to diagnose, and so on.

Table 2.1   Knowledge for action

Origin	Purpose	
	Reflexive knowledge	Operating knowledge
Perceptional knowledge	Cases on general experiences	Cases on specific operating experiences
Abstract knowledge	Rules of thought or action	Rules that are applied to operating categories
Experimental knowledge	Hypotheses on ways of acting	Hypotheses on operating experiences

---

[2] Taken and adapted from (Pérez-López, 1991). The author identifies three categories, which corresponds to the solution of operating, explicit and implicit problems. In her doctoral thesis, Muñoz-Seca [1992] also adds a third category, less clear but nevertheless suggestive. For the purposes of our discussion, the two categories presented here are sufficient.

As regards the origin of knowledge, we use three categories:

- *Perceptional knowledge.* This is the result of the accumulation of experience, or cases, in the agent's historic (or perceptional) memory. The data are poorly organized, accumulating in the memory as a consequence of the agent's personal experiences. This knowledge is sometimes called 'case knowledge' or casuistics. This knowledge can be used to solve problems if a case retrieval mechanism is available which calls up those cases that are 'similar' to the situation that the agent wishes to solve. Often, the 'experience' accumulated by executives in firms is simply perceptional knowledge – an accumulation of experience that is not necessarily structured.[3]
- *Abstract knowledge.* This is composed of rules about the behaviour of the different parts of the problem and the effects of different types of actions on its solution. The rules of logical thought, logic, belong to this category of knowledge. Most well-established scientific and technological knowledge also belongs to this category. Abstract knowledge contains models that can be learned from books or which can be transmitted by means of simple procedures. That bodies are attracted to each other in direct proportion to the product of their masses and inversely to the square of its distance is abstract knowledge, as is also knowing how to calculate digital circuits[4] and the *modus ponens* rule in logic.
- *Experimental knowledge.* This is the result of the induction performed on the data provided by perceptional knowledge. Using data systematization, it is possible to obtain abstract knowledge, models, insofar as the resulting rules can be validated and enable construction of a predictive model. However, in many cases, this is not so, and the experience is summarized in a series of sometimes conflicting and incompletely expressed hypotheses. This book contains in part experimental knowledge. It does not seek to construct a general theory but to infer a series of situations and, guided by well-established principles, provide certain guidelines (albeit incomplete which require the reader's interpretation in each specific case) concerning the effect of the agent's behaviours.

Perceptional knowledge and memories have a poor internal structure, which makes them difficult to use in practice. The collective memories of the people who work in a firm have an instructive value for subsequent experiences, but are not easy to catalogue, share and exploit systematically.

On the other hand, experimental knowledge is very delicate. It must necessarily deal with the way in which human beings think and act, their freedom, their motivations, and so forth. At present, we do not have broadly applicable tools for

---

[3] One sometimes speaks colloquially of 'undigested' experiences and it is common for an executive to need outside help – training courses, for example – in order to have the opportunity to perform the often mammoth task of organizing his own experience.

[4] As against knowing how to design digital circuits, which is not abstract knowledge but contains elements of experimental and perceptional knowledge, which would have to be separated.

managing this type of knowledge. Although very important, it is still poorly understood.[5]

Consequently, this book will be mainly concerned with *abstract operating knowledge*, given its focus on operating action. In spite of this, it will be necessary to make occasional forays into other types of knowledge.

Types of organized operating knowledge

The classifications listed above structure knowledge to help us understand better its role in action. However, business language often intuitively uses concepts such as abilities, skills, etc. which, if they were to be formalized, would give rise to a different taxonomy of operating knowledge which, albeit closely related, is different from the taxonomy defined in the previous section. Perhaps the explanatory power of this new taxonomy is less than that of the taxonomy presented above. However, it is very close to the idea of knowledge as the *ability to solve problems*, since its rationale can be traced to a practical classification of business problems. Because of this, it is commonly used, even though its semantic value is often not analysed in depth.

All of the types of knowledge that are included in this classification share one common aspect. Being operating knowledge, they are *geared towards action* – that is, towards changing the agent's immediate environment. Although simply a consequence of being operating knowledge, it is nevertheless very important.[6]

The following categories are usually considered:

- *Skills.* An agent's *non-formalized statistical* ability to solve a category of *action* problems. This definition may give the idea that all knowledge is a skill. This is not true. There are words in the definition (highlighted in italics) that are highly significant in this distinction.

   First of all, these abilities are not formalized, because the category of problems is not defined explicitly. The more like a 'skill' a certain knowledge is, the vaguer is the specification of the class of problems it solves. Skills may contain subsets of well-defined knowledge (in the form of abstract, experimental or simply perceptional knowledge), but the whole has a very low level of logical, formal structure. This means that it is difficult to apply the tools of reasoning to this type of knowledge to deduce solutions that are not in the original knowledge base of the person (or processor) responsible for solving the problem. For example, 'knowing how to manage' is a skill. But exactly what problem does this skill solve? It is very complicated to specify and any attempt to define the

---

[5] Again we have to say that, in our opinion, one of the best analyses of the subject is to be found in the work of Pérez-López. Unfortunately, it is not easy to read because its philosophical level is high and, like all pioneering works, it is inconsistent and incomplete.

[6] Well, perhaps not so much, but we also say this to wake up the reader, who by now must be on the verge of drifting off to the land of Morpheus. But how can a sleeping reader be woken by a fragment of a text that he is not reading? The reader will realize that in fact this is only a joke in part as it is also a fine example of Bertrand Russell's paradox!

problem precisely comes up against particular difficulties. The simple act of identifying the existence of this knowledge in a person is so complicated that it has led to the creation of an economic sector composed of companies specialized in 'skill-identifying', the head-hunters.

Second, a skill is statistical. This means that it only guarantees a certain probability that the associated class of problems will be solved and, therefore, it may fail to solve a specific problem, even though the right type of knowledge is apparently held.

- *Technologies. Technologies are formalized (action-oriented) knowledge.* Therefore, technology management is a specific instance of knowledge management. By the term formalized, we mean that, in contrast to skills, they have sufficient structure to enable the full use of logic. Technologies lend themselves to the use of logical reasoning. The reader should briefly reflect on the wonderfulness of this property. There is nothing upfront that guarantees that the result of a thinking process, the outcome of a logical reasoning, could lead to a real, 'true' situation in the physical world. The fact that in most cases logical 'truth' and experimental 'truth' coincide is one of the truly marvellous aspects of science. Any reader familiar with logic will undoubtably recognize that our use of the word 'formalized' is rather informal. In fact, our purpose is to continue using it in this informal manner, since formalization here does not mean 'axiomization' but a rather vague feeling that 'what is correct turns out to be true'.

  A technology is operating knowledge. Consequently, the orientation towards action in the definition of technology is redundant. But the redundancy serves to highlight that the mission of technological knowledge is not merely to know but to act. It is a knowledge that must solve action problems – problems in which the decision maker's purpose is to modify a specific attribute of the environment, to modify the state of the 'world'. Consequently, it is a pragmatic knowledge, which one has not only when one 'knows' but when one 'knows how to do'.

- *Pretechnological knowledge.* This category is a residual component that is not contained in any of the other categories and which contains all of the knowledge that comes under neither skills nor technologies.[7] The term is unusual, but we have no better alternative, unless we were to choose 'other', which seems even less adequate to us.

All firms, being institutions geared towards action, hold portfolios of such knowledge, which becomes part of the firm's 'assets'. Therefore, if we wish to determine a firm's ability to use knowledge, we must first identify its skill, technology and pretechnological knowledge portfolios.

---

[7] The reader should take note here that we are cheating. But it is an universally accepted deceit. When an author does not know what the other categories are in a classification, he bundles them together under 'Other' and thinks no more about it. This tactic is often disguised under high-flown names such as 'residual error', residual categories, etc. So many names to identify residual ignorance!

Knowledge materialization within the firm

Given the intangible nature of knowledge, it must be transformed into material structures so that it can be handled physically. Knowledge must be incorporated into a physical structure which can be transformed by well-established physical means and from which it can be extracted by sensorial means. Knowledge in its pure form is not sufficient to satisfy all of the economy's needs. Food for the mind must be supplemented with food for the body. Therefore, knowledge must be transformed – we will also use the term 'materialized' – into entities that can be included in the firm's and society's basic processes.

Knowledge materialization involves its transformation into a form in which it can be handled, stored, transmitted, retrieved and used easily, without having to go back to the person who originated it. A materialization originates in an *originator*, a custodian of the knowledge, and can be used to solve problems for the *recipient.*

Performing an inventory of the firm's knowledge is almost a compulsory prerequisite for knowledge management. As we will see in later chapters, an inventory should be based on tracing the evidence available on the firm's knowledge. This is an observation process – observation both of problems and of items of knowledge. Therefore, the observation of the existence of knowledge must originate from its materializations, from the phenomenon's observable elements. So that they can be used later in the knowledge inventory, these materializations must be typified. This enables the knowledge extraction procedures to be adjusted to the type of materialization being processed. For this purpose we propose the following materialization typology:

1. *Products or black boxes.* Encapsulated knowledge for which normally only the 'input–output' description is used. A product is a black box. The customer is normally given an input–output description and, sometimes, a small quantity of additional information. Any black box contains knowledge, which can sometimes be extracted, depending upon its degree of integration in the box. For example, the technique called 'reverse engineering' enables the knowledge contained in certain products to be liberated.

Industry knows a lot about how to produce things quickly and cheaply. Therefore, to date, this has been the most commonly used type of materialization to put knowledge into the hands of millions of people. Black boxes – are accumulative. Black boxes can be used within black boxes, in an almost infinite chain of knowledge accumulation, limited only by the physical properties of the interface. In fact, the quickest way to develop a new product is to combine existing black boxes. This is a specially quick way of solving problems. Clark and Fujimoto (1991) carried out a study of the car design procedures used in Japan, Europe and the United States. The shorter development times in Japan were attributed to the Japanese manufacturers' method of combining existing black boxes, thereby bypassing the design exploratory phase.[8]

---

[8] In our jargon. The authors of the book in question do not use these terms, probably because at that time nobody was talking about knowledge management and, perhaps, because they had not had the opportunity to talk with the authors...

The products that the firm designs and places on the market enable the use of a knowledge that the user does not possess personally and which the firm provides him in a ready-to-use form, as black boxes. When the user buys a detergent for washing his clothes, he is buying a body of accumulated knowledge ranging from basic surfactant chemistry to efficient manufacturing procedures. This is the result of a long problem-solving process carried out by many people. If this knowledge is lost, the weekly wash would go back to the Middle Ages, probably using caustic ashes and bleaching clothes in the sun. The large number of interrelations between society's knowledges is one of the distinctive features of a modern society. Not everyone needs to know how to solve all the problems of daily life. They can buy encapsulated solutions which do not require explicit knowledge.

As materializations of knowledge, black boxes suffer from the high degree of specificity of the problems they solve. They are highly specialized. You can use an iron to crack nuts, but your fingers will probably find out that the specific type of problems that the iron is designed to solve does not include the problem of cracking nuts.

2. *Processes*. These are sequences of elementary operations which, when they are performed by a suitable processor, lead to the solution of a problem. By definition, a distinctive condition of these materializations is the existence of a processor. They comprise a very broad category, which depends upon the type of primitive operations that the processor knows how to do. A very stupid processor, an automatic manipulator, may only know how to carry out three types of operation: 'close jaw', 'turn arm' and 'open jaw'. But with these three operations, it may 'know' how to transport parts between two locations, if it uses the appropriate process. At the other extreme, a computer is a processor that is able to execute dozens of elementary information processing operations. These operations can be used to specify processes that run spreadsheets, word processors and pseudo-intelligent programs, to give just a few examples. In fact, in a process, knowledge is found not only in the elementary operations performed by the processor, but also in how they are organized. To produce a titanium part, for example, the processor(s) must know how to carry out the elementary metal processing operations: milling, turning, drilling, and others. However, the secret of a good process is to combine these operations in the right sequence within the processor's basic capacities, together with a specification of the conditions in which each of the operations is performed: milling machine feed rate, cutting depth, and so on.

A materialization in the form of a process is a 'recipe book'-type materialization – that is, it provides recipes for solving a problem. Even one of the authors can come up with a reasonable imitation of an apple pie following the procedure described in a famous cookery writer's book. An extreme case of this type of materialization is the 'frozen recipe'. A precooked frozen dish bought in the supermarket is the materialization of the knowledge required to make the dish, made available to any processor whose cooking knowledge basically consists of knowing how to perform the operation 'heat in the microwave oven for 20 minutes'.[9]

---

[9] An operation that both authors are capable of performing, even though one of them might think otherwise...

3. *Symbolic representations in information structures.* This is the representation of knowledge in a certain language and is based on coding knowledge in the language's symbols. The representation has a *syntax*, a series of rules that the symbols must follow in order to form valid sentences, and a *semantics* or meaning of the symbols when they are related in different ways. In order to be transformed, this intermediate coding must be inserted in a standard physical medium, waves, electricity, paper, etc. This enables it to be transmitted using information channels, store it in appropriate devices and finally retrieve it using the appropriate decoding process. Of course, standard English is a language but, more interestingly, mathematics is a language too, as is also symbolic logic. A good feature of languages is that sometimes the solution of a problem can be described in terms of the truthfulness or falseness of certain propositions (or sentences). In fact, as we are writing in a language, one way of presenting a problem is to give a written description of it and then ask questions which must be answered. It may happen that a question only requires a 'yes' or 'no' answer, although other cases may be more complicated, such as counting the number of things, building a certain type of thing, and so on.

This is a 'textbook' type of materialization, which is based upon coding a knowledge structure. This type of materialization immediately shows the deductive properties of knowledge which we have discussed in the previous chapter. For example, a textbook on chemistry not only tells the reader about the relationships between molecules, the nature of chemical forces, the properties of basic compounds, etc., but also tries to show him how to solve new problems, developing the reader's logical and analytical skills.

The categories of materializations have been presented in increasing order of knowledge *freedom. Knowledge freedom* is a concept associated with its use. The easier it is to modify an item of knowledge to adapt it to other problems that are different from the problem specifically targeted by this knowledge, the freer it is. However, the *freer* it is, the less specific it is and the less power it has to solve a specific problem. A black box can only be used when an interface can be created that provides exactly the required inputs and collects the specified outputs. For example, a gyroscopic system (inertial system) in a plane can only be used to control the course of the type of plane for which it has been designed. If we liberate part of this knowledge using reverse engineering, for example, the knowledge contained in the gyroscopes, the knowledge that has been liberated is freer because now it can be used to build other boxes (perhaps gyroscopes for other planes).

Knowledge in the form of a process is much more accessible and takes much less effort to liberate. It is sufficient to redesign or reorder the elementary operations to change the scope of application.

Finally, knowledge in the form of symbolic representations is the freest. The process by which the table is ordered can be readily altered to perform a sort in decreasing order or to use more complicated information structures. (See Example 2.2.)

Knowledge and intellectual processes

In this section, we classify knowledge according to the manner in which it is involved in intellectual processes, or the agents' higher-order mental processes.

Example 2.2 A symbolic representation of knowledge

A Symbolic Representation of Knowledge

Let us assume that the problem we are interested in is 'ordering a sequence of numbers starting with the lowest'. The reader will probably think that this is a trivial problem. And he would be right if we were ordering, for example, 10 numbers. However, if instead of 10, we have to order 100,000 numbers, the situation becomes more interesting. Fortunately, there are people who know how to order numbers (it's amazing what interesting things people can do, isn't it?). These people have a body of knowledge about ordering methods. The only way to communicate this knowledge is by materializing it. Here is a materialization:

1. Start with an empty list, a results list, in which to construct the ordered series.
2. Look for the lowest number among those which are not yet ordered.
3. Place it in the results list, after the current last number.
4. Remove it from the numbers to be ordered.
5. Go back to step 2 for so long as there are still numbers to be ordered. If there are no numbers left, go to 6.
6. You've finished. The ordered sequence is in the results list.

A processor capable of satisfactorily performing this process, materialized in the English language, should know how to perform elementary operations such as: 'Look for the lowest number among those which are not yet ordered'. Of course, described in this language, a computer would not know how to do it. Another materialization in a language closer to machine language (in a variety of Visual Basic (yuk!) is:

```
Dim data (100,000) as real
Dim results (100,000) as real
Dim i as integer
Dim x as real
While i <= 100,000
    x = Min (data)
    results = Append (results, x)
    data = Remove (x, data)
wend
return results
```

Of course, for some readers this language will be much more abstruse than English. But that is because he does not speak this language. If he learnt it (like learning French), the process would become clear to him. Here, the processor needs to know how to execute the basic operations 'Min', 'Append' and 'Remove'. We could continue materializing the procedure and describe in detail how each of these operations is performed with respect to others having a lower level. But this would be very boring and would not add anything to the example.

Intellectual processes are the main channel for using knowledge in personal action. Later in this chapter, we will see that a *logic agent* uses this type of process to reason about his actions. These processes' ultimate goal is to produce actions, but the substrate used consists almost entirely of knowledge.

A complete theory of these processes does not exist. There are not even theories with a reasonable explanatory power.[10] However, some kind of approach, albeit primitive, is needed to understand both the process used for the logical treatment of collective knowledge within an organization and the process used for the identification of core competences.

Methodologies have been developed in knowledge engineering to describe and diagnose knowledge-intensive processes which move along different dimensions. One of these methodologies, the Common Kads methodology (Schreiber *et al.*, 1999), structures its ideas in the desired manner, that is, around the intellectual process. In the next chapter, we will apply it in more detail to the *analysis* of intellectual processes. However, at this point, we must first present the basic nomenclature of Common Kads before we can continue.

Common Kads proposes three categories of knowledge, depending upon their role in the intellectual process: *area*, *task* and *inference* knowledge.

- *Area or domain knowledge* is the appropriate knowledge about *the intellectual process* applicable to a task. It is knowledge about the *concepts* which will be used and the appropriate *vocabulary* for the process.
- *Task knowledge* refers to the *task's goal*, and to the *method used to perform it*, conceived as the integration of the activities that contribute to achievement of the goal. We will refer to this knowledge as either task or process.
- *Inference knowledge* specifies the *basic inferences* that can be made and which represent elementary logical operations for the thinking agent. These inferences contain the rules which are used to combine existing knowledge and draw new conclusions from it.

At first sight, this classification has components that seem similar to those of the classification of knowledge for action. However, a close examination will show that this is not so and that both can even become completely orthogonal. This is because the classification of knowledge in terms of action only distinguishes between the external and internal aspects of knowledge, without considering their purpose within the intellectual process.

*Bounded rationality and collective knowledge

One of the major problems concerning knowledge within the firm is the treatment of collective knowledge, how it is produced and used and how it interacts with the knowledge of individual agents.

---

[10] However, further on we will dare to suggest a very simple and useful general theory based on Common Kads. Read on…

A firm is, in essence, a group of brains that must draw upon each other's resources. They possess a major part of the company's knowledge and are probably the processors capable of interpreting most of the knowledge materialized in symbolic form within it. The conception of the firm as a group of brains and not as a group of hands is characteristic of a society in which people's value is grounded not on what they are but on what they know. The transition to the company of the future will necessarily require a parallel evolution from muscle power to brain power.

We have already seen that knowledge must be materialized before it can be shared. This gives rise, in any firm, to a stock of knowledge materializations which makes this knowledge available to all those who work in it. This common or collective knowledge stock (almost always stored in digital format) has certain unique properties distinguish it from the individual knowledge (very often stored in neuronal format).

In order to understand the role of collective knowledge, we will consider the functioning of a logic agent and its relationships with other organization's inhabitants.

From the knowledge management viewpoint, it is sufficient to define an *organization* as a group of agents who pursue a common purpose. Each agent in the organization cooperates in the common purpose by performing problem-solving actions. The agent has a domain of competence which contains the classes of problems that the organization has entrusted to him to solve and within which he can make decisions, choosing the appropriate actions. As a problem-solving agent, each agent has a structure like that described in Chapter 1.

Idealizing, we can assume that all of the agents have a deductive capacity based on some type of logic. This deductive capacity enables them to add new consequences to the initial knowledge they possess. This type of knowledge is what we have called in the previous section 'inference knowledge', that is, knowledge about the development of his basic intellectual process (in this case, a logical intellectual process, or based on a deductive logic).

On the basis of the above, we can talk about a 'logical agent'. We will call this agent's mental process his 'inference mechanism'. As a result of his interaction with the environment, at any given time the agent has certain beliefs about the world that may be thought as propositions that the agent believes (considers to be true). These premises have been absorbed by the agent either as a result of his own experience or the experience of someone with sufficient authority to accept his propositions as premises, at least tentatively until they are validated personally.

We do not assume that the agent is infallible, that is, all his beliefs are true, nor that he is omniscient, capable of obtaining all the true consequences that derive from his beliefs. The agent may err both in his reasoning and in the things he believes in.

In more precise terms,[11] any *logical agent* has the following components:

1. A long-term memory,[12] in which fragments of behaviour are deposited that solve partial problems, or 'chunks' to use Soar's terminology, obtained during the problem-solving process.

---

[11] And combining it with the jargon used by Forbus and De Kleer (1994) to make it more complicated and less intelligible...

[12] Along the lines of Soar (Newell, 1982, 1990).

2. *A truth maintenance system* (TMS) (Forbus and De Kleer, 1994)) knowledge store, a store of propositions that the agent considers to be true or valid at that time, accompanied by an inference mechanism that is able to perform deductions on them.
3. A mechanism for obtaining 'valid' premises from observation of the world. These observation mechanisms provide perceptional knowledge about the world, which the agent can transform into premises for his deductions.
4. An interaction mechanism, capable of turning action plans into positive action.

The TMS also contains the elementary knowledge that provides the agent with basic reasoning abilities about the 'obvious' or day-to-day part of the world. This includes knowledge about time and its function, space and its function, intuitive (or folk) psychology, etc. Of course, the quantity of propositions contained in a human decision maker's TMS goes beyond the limits of a mechanical system, at least for the moment.[13]

With this approach, learning is simply changing the agent's knowledge bases, contained in his TMS. Therefore, any change in the TMS's contents, whether performed by the agent himself or carried out by external sources, is characterized as learning.

The *inference mechanism* enables the agent to draw believable conclusions from the contents of the TMS or to detect contradictions between the propositions contained in the TMS. This mechanism is therefore responsible for obtaining new propositions implied by the propositions believed by the agent. Nothing prevents the propositions held by the agent in his TMS, the propositions he believes in, from being false in the outside world. If this is so, the agent will be representing the world incorrectly and his actions will be inconsistent with the world structure. Eventually, if the input–output systems are consistent, the agent will detect contradictions which will force him to review his knowledge base. However, until then, his actions will have been based on mistaken premises!

There is a fundamental logical drawback in this type of agent. The drawback lies in the fact that the agent can know the things he believes in, but not those things he does not believe in. From his point of view, if neither a proposition nor its opposite are in his TMS, he can draw no conclusion whatsoever about the degree of truth to be associated with this proposition. The most that can be said is that 'it is not in his knowledge base'. However, this does not imply any statement as to its truth or falsehood and, therefore, it cannot play any active part in an internal reasoning. It is even possible that the knowledge base may be contradictory without the agent realizing this. This may happen because the agent, his logical mechanisms, or his exogenous inputs, have never found a proposition that contradicts another proposition held in the knowledge base. This only means that the agent does not believe in the existence of a contradiction, not that it does not exist. In fact, the truth determination mechanism used in science (Popper, 1992)

---

[13] Putting common sense into a machine has so far taken more than 3 million rules in the CYC project [http://www.cyc.com] and in spite of this, the machine is still pretty stupid …

subjects the propositions believed to be true to a shake-up in the real world, with the aim of identifying cases in which the proposition is not true. The absence of any such cases only determines the proposition's growing plausibility, not its truthfulness.

If the agent has a logical mechanism that does not make mistakes, the root cause of any contradiction will be found in the incompatibility of a subset of the premises. The role of the inference mechanism is, to a great extent, to identify the contradiction's causes and debug the database to eliminate it. If the deduction mechanism is imperfect, false consequences may be obtained from true propositions and vice versa.

The ultimate nature of a mechanism for inferring truths from premises must necessarily be that of a problem solver, with a highly developed exploratory phase. By definition, the mechanism must be able to infer things that the agent has not inferred previously and, therefore, are not knowledge that he may have filed in his TMS. And, being a basically exploratory system, it will have an exponential behaviour over time, as was explained in the previous chapter. Following the arguments proposed in that chapter, in order to obtain a reasonable process time, it is necessary to impose limits, bounds, on the solution's quality, in this case, on the type of truths that the agent can infer.

The most general TMS is, therefore, a problem solver. Consequently, the number of states, the number of propositions that can be inferred from the premises, can grow exponentially. As the memory's capacity is limited, the system must eliminate believed propositions from its TMS so that it can continue operating.

A logical agent such as that described here has a *bounded rationality*, materialized in: (a) an incomplete knowledge of the world; (b) the impossibility of applying the inference mechanism to deduce all the true propositions; (c) the impossibility of accessing at any time all of the propositions that have been deduced beforehand; and (d) the impossibility of deducing certain truths because of the time (or even space) constraints existing in an exploratory deduction.

Our organization is therefore necessarily made up of agents with bounded rationality who use a common knowledge base. It is important to stress at this point that *organizations do not have deductive mechanisms*, only individual agents possess this mechanism. An individual agent, owning an individual TMS, can carry his associated deductive mechanisms with him. Not so the organization, which can only fill its knowledge store by means of agent's actions or by direct input from outside. The organization can modify the contents of the common knowledge store as new experiences or deductions provided by others show certain propositions to be true or false.

This rule modification mechanism may be understood as a degenerated variety of learning – a type of *learning that may be called organizational learning*.

In these conditions, the organization has two ways of influencing agents' beliefs. On one hand, it can issue *rules* that everyone must obey (or abide by). This would mean that the agents must avoid beliefs that are contrary to the organization's rules. The rules are imposed by the organization and may or may not be accepted by its members, depending upon their personal status. As beliefs cannot

Example 2.3 Plane crashes

Plane Crashes

An asymptotic trend in the number of accidents per mile is observed in air travel. The introduction of new rules, both in plane certification and in air traffic itself, do not seem to have any effect on this trend. As a plane crash has serious consequences and is widely reported in the communication media, the air safety community is wondering why the accident rate is not improving, in spite of the fact that each crash is analysed to determine the cause and the regulations are changed to prevent the cause from recurring.

In air travel, the main mechanism for rule creation is the detection of contradictions. A crash is a contradiction between what should happen – that is, what is deduced from the premises – and what has actually happened. *A priori*, on the basis of the system's conditions, the crash is considered impossible or unlikely. *A posteriori*, the event has happened and therefore it is necessary to determine at what point of the logical development did the contradiction that caused it occur.

The usual procedure after a crash is to try to reconstruct the inference process that has led to the contradiction. The process is carefully reconstructed until the event is understood.

The collective rules of behaviour are changed each time an important event shows that one of the statements previously held to be true is in fact false. To avoid the presence of modifications which lead in turn to contradictions, the specific event is analysed with extreme care by specialized agents until apparently 'absolute' conclusions are reached. The agents then apply the rules within their context.

A crash may occur as a consequence of a failure in one of the agent's logical processes. The failure may be conative if the agent held in his database the information needed to deduce the crash's occurrence. In these cases, the crash can be attributed to many factors – incorrect functioning of the inference system, insufficient time to obtain the right solution, or the agent's bounded rationality. In other cases, the information stored does not contain sufficient premises to deduce the possibility of the crash beforehand. In these cases, the organization tries to create new rules that exclude the possibility of such a state recurring.

The causative situations in a crash are very complex because, after many years of work, rules have been implemented that eliminate all of the simple situations. Because of this, the system is on the frontier of rationality and it is natural that its behaviour should be asymptotic. And even though this asymptote is related to the prevailing state of the art at any given time, it has an immanent component related to the limits of any formal rule creation process.

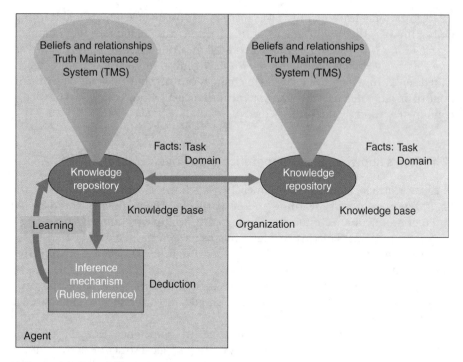

Figure 2.1   Individual and organizational learning

be observed, the organization must focus solely on the agents' acts. Consequently, the organization imposes penalties or incentives to modify the system of personal preferences and motivate agents to abide by the decision rules. In air traffic, for example, the aircraft certification mechanism specifies the rules that aircraft must follow to be acceptable and, therefore, the rules that all those involved in the aircraft's design and construction must accept in their problem-solving process.

The second way in which the organization can influence its agents' deductive mechanisms is by modifying the contents of their individual knowledge bases. Although superficially this procedure is similar to the previous one, there is a substantial difference between abiding by the rules and incorporating them. In the first case, the aim is simply to assure non-contradiction of the results of the problem-solving process with the external formal rules. In the second case, the rules are included as premises in the deductive process itself. They are not verified, they are used. (See Example 2.3.)

Of course, this is one form of individual agent learning. This learning changes the agent's premises and alters his TMS. As a result of the learning, his inference system detects anomalous consequences (contradictions) which must be corrected and produces new consequences which must be incorporated.

This second form gives rise to a higher-order learning in the agents, since each agent can exploit common knowledge directly, through his inference mechanism, to produce new truths which increase his belief database.

Organizational learning only takes place as a consequence of personal learning. Only through the involvement of the agents can deductions be obtained. *Therefore, it is true that,* in this more advanced meaning of learning, *only the agents who possess a deduction mechanism can learn.* Organizations learn in a more degenerated sense, in which there are mere changes of rules, but they are never incorporated in an inference mechanism capable of exploiting common knowledge combined with individual knowledge.

*The firm's knowledge or competence groupings

In a classic article, Prahalad and Hamel (1990) define the core competences as 'the organization's collective learning and, in particular, the manner of coordinating different production techniques and integrating multiple technology currents ... '. Prahalad and Hamel's idea, with a few obvious modifications,[14] can be transposed to our context to illustrate the way in which the firm's knowledge is converted into its competences.

To be consistent, we define a *competence* as the *structured combination of a group of different types of knowledge.* This structure should arise from the use of knowledge to carry out the firm's business processes.

The structured combination of knowledge in competences goes beyond the structure generated by problem subsets or even the logical structure between types of knowledge. A competence can combine different types of knowledge by means of extrinsic relationships which, for example, can involve the use of common resources.

In practice, firms try to identify their core competences with great precision. The goal is to determine both the organization's strengths and those areas that can be eliminated without losing competitive power. One way of approaching the analysis is to base it on the company's knowledge list.

However, it is not easy to identify competences – even when we have the company's knowledge list. A competence is something more than the mere sum of individual aptitudes for solving problems, because of the synergistic effects that are generated by the *relationships* between the types of knowledge of which they are composed.

In order to identify a competence, it is necessary to isolate a group of interrelated items of knowledge that possesses a strong internal structure. This structure cannot be predicted *a priori* from the group but becomes detectable as the group takes shape. In a way, the grouping process itself must contribute to defining the internal structure of the competences which must come into being as a consequence of this process. This feature renders it difficult to use classic grouping methods based upon attributes (see Appendix). With these methods, the grouping

---

[14] With Prahalad's permission and in line with the discussion of the previous section, the phrase 'collective knowledge database' would express the situation more accurately than 'collective learning'.

Example 2.4 Electricity company

> ## Electricity Company
>
> At the end of 1996, a certain electricity company decided to list its competences with a view to identifying business areas that could be spun off from the company's main electricity generation and sale business. The methodology proposed by the company was to identify its core competences and then to use them to group business areas. The project started with a meticulous knowledge inventory, with input from all levels of the company. The inventory listed more than 1,500 items of knowledge. The next step was to group this knowledge and for this purpose, two general techniques were used. One of them was the KJ method, consisting of grouping by mental images and which will be described later in this book. The other technique was a process of eliminating subsidiary knowledge, the MTV method, which uses progressive elimination until only the key items remain. This second technique was necessary because large numbers of items cannot be easily handled by the mental image grouping method. The process uncovered nine core competences, which included: interfacing with public authorities, designing hydroelectric plants, one-off project management, and others. By associating people, resources and knowledge within each competence, the company was split into three business units which later on became separate companies.

is based on attributes defined *a priori* and not on other, possibly more relevant attributes that may be uncovered as the process advances.

Therefore, identifying competences requires a dynamic grouping method which uncovers and makes visible the relationships generating the competence as it is being constructed. Using this method, competence identification becomes a gradual process. These grouping methodologies have been studied in the field of artificial intelligence, within an important form of knowledge representation called 'semantic networks' (see Appendix).

A semantic network organizes objects in the universe in terms of relationships. There can be many different types of relationships. For example, the IS_A relationship, in which an object is stated to be a specific case of another object, and the IS_PART relationship, in which an object is stated to be part of a more complex object, are classic examples. The knowledge typologies discussed in this chapter provide useful definitions of relationships between different types of knowledge.

A detailed presentation of these ideas would be beyond the scope of this book and we refer the interested reader to the specialized literature. A brief introduction is included in the Appendix. Fortunately, our experience has been that an extremely rigorous approach to the subject is not necessary. A grouping procedure such as the KJ (see Appendix) is probably all that is needed in practice – provided that we are aware of the basic features of the competences we wish to produce.

*Competences and process knowledge

Transposing the knowledge categories, according to Common Kads, to the world of competences, we obtain a competence typology that distinguishes between *domain, task and inference competences*. The first are related to the handling of objects and the second to organizational tasks. *Inference competences* are necessary for structuring the knowledge generation process in organizational terms.

- *Domain competences* are those competences, or knowledge groupings whose internal relationships are based on the manner in which the objects in the environment are related to the tasks to be performed. This category groups domain knowledge, specifies the forms, structure and contents (obtained from different ontologies[15]), which make up coherent partial organizations of the body of knowledge forming the competence.
- *Task competences* are those competences whose internal relationships are based on the tasks' goals and the activities that contribute to achieving those goals. In the definition of task, we can include three related aspects: the *task* itself, the *internal result* (for the agent) and the *external result* (for the other agents). This type of competence groups process knowledge.
- *Inference competences* include knowledge of inference, which are interrelated to the nature of the process used to deduce the knowledge that forms the competences.

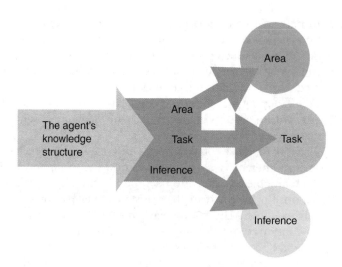

Figure 2.2   An agent's competences

---

[15] Ontology: the objects that exist in the universe (Bunnin and Tsui-James, 1996).

Example 2.5   Telesa

In an electronics firm, we brought together a group of experts in order to solve a technical problem. The group's purpose was focused and its members' expertise was guaranteed, but they did not solve the problem entrusted to them. Observing the lack of results, one of the authors took part in a discussion to diagnose the factors that were blocking the solution. The diagnosis was very clear. The problem was not one of content but one of process. The group did not know how to work as a group to solve problems. They had not realized that groups need to learn how to solve problems and while this may occur naturally, if it does not, a process methodology must be provided that will generate this skill.

Any personal agent can have the three types of competence. Organizations, on the other hand, can have task or domain competences but, as we have stated in the previous section, they cannot have inference competences since they do not possess this mechanism. For each of the competences, in any given situation we can identify the knowledge of which they are composed. This will vary in each case, depending upon the problem area in which the individual operates.

Agents may have a differentiated portfolio of competences. Their area and task competence profile will be specific depending upon the purpose of their work. Their inference competences profile must always be very similar since otherwise their ability to generate ideas will be reduced. Inference competences include (as we will argue in Chapter 10) *problem-solving, creativity* and *innovation absorption* competencies. (See Example 2.5.)

Companies spend time and money on instilling in their workers the knowledge included in the inference competences, using a wide range of approaches to achieve this. For example, one British company is giving free time to its employees to teach them to learn. The employees choose to develop an area of knowledge (task competences, in our vocabulary) which had no bearing on their work in the company. This was adequate, since the company's goal was to familiarize their employees with the *learning process* so that they will be able to learn the inference competences that they will need to perform their work in the future.

3
First Practical Implications: Project Management

In this chapter, we make the first application of the ideas on knowledge structure that were introduced in the previous chapters. Our purpose is to reduce the level of abstraction, passing immediately to the sphere of action without having to wait for the full presentation of the model underlying PDM. Specifically, we would like to show the reader how even the small number of concepts that have been presented already shed considerable light on the functioning of certain operations systems.

In this chapter, we will concentrate on project management, the simplest operations system that exists, but one which contains many of the features of complex systems. Initially, we can work with the system's intuitive structure, without discussing the underlying variables. This issue will be the subject of a more general discussion in Chapters 5 and 6.

What is a project?: The classic idea

According to the classic definition, a project is an operation system geared towards obtaining a single product or service. It may be building a bridge, installing an enterprise resource planning (ERP) system, designing an advertising campaign or writing a book. The project has a limited lifespan and its purpose comes to an end when the product has been obtained or the service has been rendered. Therefore, a project has certain very specific goals, it is performed only once and it has a clearly defined beginning and end.

In the literature on projects, a project breaks down into a series of activities. These activities (or tasks) are well-defined working elements, with clear inputs and outputs, which are not described because it is assumed that there is a processor that merely needs their statement to perform them satisfactorily. It is therefore not necessary to provide the activities' internal process or the method by which they are put forward.

It is assumed that adequate performance of these activities constitutes satisfactory performance of the project. The activities are stated *a priori* and, in a way, are the materialization of the project itself. It is common for the project to be confused with the activities of which it is composed.

As limitations on their performance, a series of stable (almost unchangeable) relationships between the activities are defined and accepted as being valid throughout the project's execution. The immutability arises from the logical nature of the relationships. The most typical relationship is that of precedence. A precedence relationship between two activities specifies that one of them cannot be begun until a certain fraction of the other has been completed. The most normal form of a precedence relationship states that an activity cannot begun until another activity, which precedes the former activity in its entirety, has been *completed*. When all the relationships are of this type, a project's activities can be represented as a network of activities. Although there are several possible formats, in the simplest an activity is represented by a circle (a node) and the precedence relationship between two activities is represented by an arrow. Figure 3.1 shows a network of activities for an 'ERP implementation' project. This project is taken, in summarized form, from the project actually carried out by a certain company. To simplify the discussion, we have taken as basic activities a series of very high-level activities, such as 'creating the database'.

In Figure 3.1, the activity 'creating the structure' cannot be performed until the activity 'implementation plan' has been completed. A similar situation arises with the activity 'test data', which cannot be begun until 'install software' and 'new account plan' have both been completed.

Activities have durations that are specified *a priori*. Generally speaking, these durations may be given by a probability distribution which is assumed to be unchanging for a long enough period of time for it to be used as a basis for the planning process. These durations take into account the manner in which the processor must perform the activity. The duration depends upon the resources allocated to each task. It is assumed that an activity lasts what its 'duration' indicates.

Classically, people distinguish between a project's *planning* phase – the determination of the manner in which the project will be carried out – and the project's

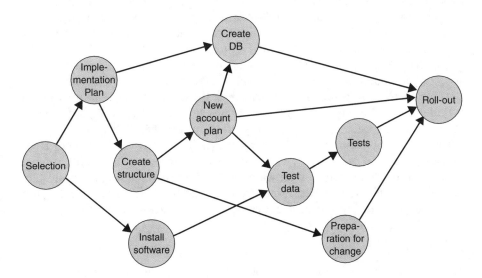

Figure 3.1   Reference relationship between activities

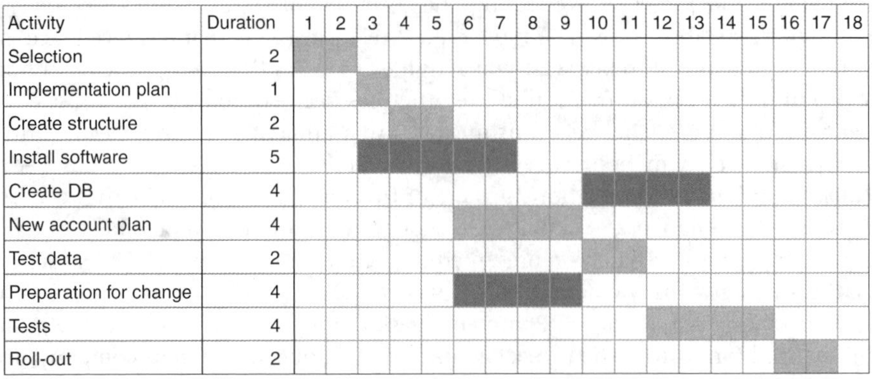

Activity	Duration	1	2	3	4	5	6	7	8	9	10	11	12	13	14	15	16	17	18
Selection	2	▓	▓																
Implementation plan	1			▓															
Create structure	2				▓	▓													
Install software	5				▓	▓	▓	▓	▓										
Create DB	4										▓	▓	▓	▓					
New account plan	4								▓	▓	▓	▓							
Test data	2											▓	▓						
Preparation for change	4								▓	▓	▓	▓							
Tests	4														▓	▓	▓	▓	
Roll-out	2																	▓	▓

Figure 3.2   Gantt chart of the ERP (Enterprise Resource Planning) project

execution phase. During the first phase, most of the project's features are taken as data. In the execution phase, the possibility is considered of probabilistic events occurring that alter the project's activities structure or data. As the project progresses, it is replanned to take into account the new events. In almost all cases, the replanning process is wide-ranging, possibly changing the activities' level of aggregation as the project advances.

In classic project management, the emphasis is focused on managing the interaction of three key aspects: the project's *cost*, its *duration* and the *specifications* of the resulting product (service). Typically, a project's duration is inversely proportional to its cost; the shorter the duration, the higher the cost, as the basic laws of economics suggest. The same thing happens with the specifications and either of the other two parameters. The more complicated the specifications are, the greater the cost or the longer the duration. Project management, viewed from this classic perspective, consists of devising a schedule that situates the project's activities in time. The most commonly used method for representing the action plan is a Gantt or bar chart. Figure 3.2 shows a possible action plan for the project in Figure 3.1, accepting the durations (deterministic and in weeks) shown in Figure 3.2.

As can be seen, a classic operating plan establishes an action commitment for a period of time. The commitment is the promise to carry out each activity in a certain time, in accordance with its position in the Gantt chart.

Thus, from the classic viewpoint, project management is a management technique for a special operating system, characterized by its simplicity and uniqueness. The process incorporates the learning that takes place during the project by means of replanning exercises. Each replanning adds to the system's description the result of all the knowledge acquired about the project's components.

A new approach

In actual fact, the conception of a project along the lines of the previous section is typical of a time in which large-scale social structures were developed. These project management techniques were developed to handle the complexity of the massive projects of the twentieth century. For example, the PERT technique was conceived and applied around the construction of the Polaris submarine. The need to meet deadlines with a certain amount of efficiency in the large public works and space projects made this type of tool necessary.

However, most projects managed in this fashion are fairly well-known and although they are essentially unique, they are grouped in classes having similar components. For example, although each road is unique, road-building projects are composed of very similar activities. Levelling, compacting and tarmacking are activities that are very familiar to construction companies. These projects admit strict planning, with relatively few changes in the nature of the activities to be performed.

This situation changed dramatically at the end of the twentieth century. Most projects undertaken by innovative companies – and to be competitive, you've got to be innovative – share a high degree of uncertainty. This uncertainty appears both in the definition of the result to be obtained and in the process for obtaining that result, the impact on the various agents involved and the nature and quantity of the resources used. Example 3.1 provides a brief overview of the story of IDOM, a renowned engineering firm, with the Guggenheim Museum in Bilbao. In this project, there was no clear idea of what had to be done – or, more importantly, how it had to be done. The project was completely impossible to schedule, at least in its early stages, and yet an estimate had to be given that could tell the museum's owner how much money would be needed to achieve the general goal of giving Bilbao a landmark building.

Example 3.1 The Guggenheim Museum

The Guggenheim Museum in Bilbao

In the early 1990s, Bilbao was a city undergoing a rapid process of deindustrialization. It lacked exceptional landmarks that could make it competitive worldwide. The Olympic Games and the Expo had fuelled remarkable development in Barcelona and Seville, and now Bilbao was lagging a long way behind. The Basque government sought to give the city an activity that would be exceptional, unique. After a period of analysis, it was concluded that this goal could be achieved by providing a facility to house part of the Guggenheim collections. This would require building a unique building whose intrinsic architectural worth would complement the attractiveness of the museum's exhibitions.

The project was entrusted to Frank Gehry, a world-renowned architect. However, like all geniuses, neither he nor his team seemed to be particularly interested in the practical details of the construction or budget. Therefore, the Basque government looked for an engineering firm to lead the project's operating aspects. The company chosen was IDOM. While a respected engineering firm, it had never been involved in projects such as this one. The company decided to take part for several reasons. First of all, it would give a considerable boost to the company's turnover and earnings. However, more important than that, it provided an opportunity to make a name in this type of project and gain appreciation among the architect's team for the company's work. Of course, Gehry's team had never heard of IDOM, nor did they see why a Basque company had to take part in the project. They had their contacts with global engineering consultants who, until now, had always done a good job.

IDOM's involvement was fraught with problems at the beginning. One of the first meetings required the presentation and critical examination of the project's budget. The architect's studio had only given IDOM a few outlines drawn in pencil which, according to Gehry, sketched the future building. In actual fact, the sketch was nothing more than a few lines drawn freehand which could just as easily have been an abstract picture as an outline of the museum. In fact, Gehry still did not know what he was going to do. His ideas would become clearer as the design progressed.

In such conditions, drawing up anything like a reasonable budget was out of the question. However, it had to be done because the final customer wanted to know how much money the venture was going to cost him. So IDOM put together a few figures which included certain buffer mechanisms. Of course, when Gehry's engineers saw IDOM's (a Spanish (?) company) figures, they immediately accused the company of inflating the figures to earn more money or to give itself a large safety margin. After a large number of adjustments, an initial consensus was reached. With time, the architects gave form to the general look of the building. But it was still not clear how it was going to be built. Many of the ideas proposed were impossible or would cost the earth. IDOM had to intervene, providing engineering input for carrying out the construction project. Thus, the project continued to progress until its completion. When the building was completed, IDOM felt that it had played a vital part in the project. But had it met its goals?

This uncertainty is part and parcel of new projects. Their most outstanding feature is that *one finds out what one is doing while it is being done.*

In knowledge terms, domain and process knowledge is initially very small, almost non-existent. Of course, related knowledge is held, but the specific development of the knowledge needed cannot be carried out without prior research.

If we confine ourselves to the scope of the project itself, we see that this type of project is basically a temporary company. It has all the features of an innovative firm. However, it is a firm that has a foreseeable demise. When the project is completed, the company formed by this project ceases to exist.

In the classic approach, the fact that this minicompany is immersed in a 'mother' firm is ignored. The 'mother' firm develops the project and takes on a large part of its results. In the case of Table 3.1, the 'mother' firm is the IDOM engineering company. Once the project is completed, and the customer is satisfied with what has been obtained, it will be dismantled. But the assets that have been created, or obtained, will now form part of the 'mother' firm. And the most important of these will be those assets that take the form of the knowledge, skills or prestige (reputation for knowing) obtained during the project's development.

When planning a project of this type, many difficulties arise. The first of these is that its activities list is unknown and difficult to specify *a priori*. It will only be fully known when the project is completed. Second, there are many different – and often unpredictable – types of relationship between activities. We are no longer talking just about *precedences*. There are all manner of complicated relationships between activities. The relationships of simultaneity take on extravagant forms in which some activities become intertwined with others in complex manners (for an example, see Example 3.2).

Unlike the classic case, the activities' duration is difficult to calculate *a priori*, because the uncertainty in the task knowledge makes it very difficult to adopt a top-down or decomposition approach. In such conditions, it is very difficult to ensure operating control using detailed action plans, particularly in the medium

Example 3.2 The Palau Sant Jordi

The Palau Sant Jordi

As part of the Olympic Ring, built for the 1992 Olympic Games in Barcelona, a covered sports arena was constructed with a capacity of 15,000 spectators and all the necessary facilities for the different sports disciplines. After the Games, it would be used as a venue for all types of large-scale events held in Barcelona. The project was entrusted to a Japanese architect, who designed an undulating roof whose shape was reminiscent of that of a sleeping dragon. The arena was going to be called the Palau Sant Jordi, after Saint George, patron saint of Catalonia and well-known for his skill in rescuing fair damsels from the clutches of evil dragons. Of course, what a sleeping dragon looks like is a matter open to discussion, since the information available on the appearance of dragons does not specify how these creatures rest from their labours. And Saint George was not at hand to fill in the details. The outcome of this mythological feat was a roof that was very complicated to build – especially if you wanted to build it in the traditional manner, starting with the walls and then putting the roof on top. The technique used was to start with the roof first, which was built on the ground and then raised to the appropriate height using powerful hydraulic jacks, in a very bold operation. The construction process was designed in parallel to the design of the roof, with a high level of interaction between the designers and the engineering firm responsible for the project. The reader will probably be pleased to know that the Palau was finished, was used satisfactorily in the Olympic Games and continues to render an excellent service to the city it was built for.

term. The detailed forecast of resource requirements must be replaced by the preparation of flexible allocations enabling resources to be used as and when required in accordance with the present state of progress.

Very often, as in the case of IDOM, the project's goals are stated in terms of the acquisition of knowledge or skills. The agent executing the project must attend to multiple priorities and learning must be combined with efficiency. Seen in this light, a project is basically an opportunity, an innovation, an experience and a style of organization.

The four project management processes

Any firm, and therefore any project, is bound by a twofold purpose. On one hand, if it wants to earn money and survive indefinitely, the firm must be efficient and productive. However, at the same time, the firm must be competitive that is, it must build today its capacity to earn money tomorrow. This capacity is obtained by building and accumulating assets that give it the possibility of being productive in the future. Most of these assets are simply knowledge assets. Indeed, it is possible to say that in most firms, the only asset that provides competitive advantage – the future capacity to earn profits – is what the people who work in the firm know.

As we have said, a project is an individual, perishable operating system. On the basis of this property, it would seem that the only thing that matters in a project is the productivity that is attained with it. However, this is clearly untrue. A project never exists in isolation from a competitive context. Taking things to their worst extreme, even if the project team is disbanded upon completion of the project, it will have generated knowledge in the agents who took part in it and that knowledge can provide those agents with future competitiveness. This knowledge will accrue to the firms that employ the agents in the future. Only if the disbandment is accompanied by the total disappearance of the agents from the active economy[1] will we really be able to talk in terms of disappearance of knowledge, or, to put it another way, a reduction of society's knowledge assets with an associated loss of society's competitiveness.

The same thing happens if the knowledge used in the project cannot be used to generate other products and services. The knowledge generated will become obsolete and eventually will be lost. This often happens when the project completed is very innovative, advanced or one of a kind (see the Expo 92 project in Example 3.3 below).

For these knowledge-generating projects, particularly those with a high degree of uncertainty, the management of competitiveness, that is, the management of the acquisition and future consolidation of potentially usable knowledge, becomes just as important as the correct (productive) performance of the project.

---

[1] For example, because they retire to enjoy the financial fruits earned during the project.

Example 3.3 The Expo 92 Project

The Expo 92 Project

In 1992 a Universal Exhibition was organized in Seville to commemorate the 500th anniversary of the discovery of America. This glittering event was prepared as an example of the innovative capacity of Spain in general and Andalusia in particular. Many companies took part in the organization of the event, which brought around it, during the five-year preparation period, some of the world's finest brains in the leisure and entertainment industry. The Spanish government wished the Expo to be a future landmark and whole-heartedly devoted its efforts towards achieving this goal. Vaguely aware that after the project was finished, on 12 October 1992, the show would end and each of the participants would return to their winter quarters, the event's managers contracted a team of sociologists and economists to perform a study about what use could be made of the knowledge that was generated during the process. Unfortunately, the team performing the analysis confined itself to considering the physical assets generated at the Expo, without studying in depth the accumulation of knowledge this entailed. As a result, a very ambitious plan was drawn up which sought to turn the Expo site into a technology park, using the existing communications infrastructure. Experience showed that it was impossible to execute this plan because no knowledge assets had been generated that were capable of driving the creation of new, competitive services. Subsequently, another study showed the knowledge assets that had been generated (by inventorying them) and proposed a series of actions that sought to exploit them for the region's development. In the end, as a result of political vicissitudes, including the massive amount of money spent on the Expo, which exhausted possible sources of finance, the knowledge was allowed to disperse and much of it was not used since no products had been developed that could be sold immediately on the markets.

This gives rise to the need to manage not only the project as such but also the secondary knowledge generation and improvement processes. The goal of this management process is to ensure that once the project is completed, the firm or group that has carried out the project has acquired the knowledge assets in the best possible manner to ensure its future competitiveness.

Therefore, in this type of project, 'project management' has more than one meaning. In fact, as we will discuss later, there are four different meanings that can be applied to this expression. The firm must address all four aspects simultaneously if it wishes to obtain competitive, productive results from the project.

The four aspects are obtained from the combination of two basic dimensions, each of which can be broken down into two levels[2] (see Figure 3.3).

The first dimension is related to the *formulation of the project's goals*, or what it wishes to achieve with the particular project. Any project has both competitiveness or *strategic* goals and productivity or *operating goals*. These goals are not static. By definition, as we have already explained, the project's shape becomes progressively clearer as its execution progresses. It follows from this that the task of stating goals is not a 'once-and-for-all' thing, but an activity that must be periodically repeated throughout the project. Therefore, it is necessary to manage the continual redefinition of both strategic and operating goals. In this dimension, the problem to be solved consists of identifying what can and cannot be achieved and what can be done to achieve that which is achievable at any given time during the project. Basically, the project is subject to a continual redesign process in which the project's manager regularly updates an explicit idea of what is hoped to be achieved by the project in both strategic and operating terms.

The second dimension addresses how the project *achieves results*. From this viewpoint, it is possible to consider short-term or *operating* approaches and long-term or *strategic* approaches, both for the customer and for the firm. Consequently,

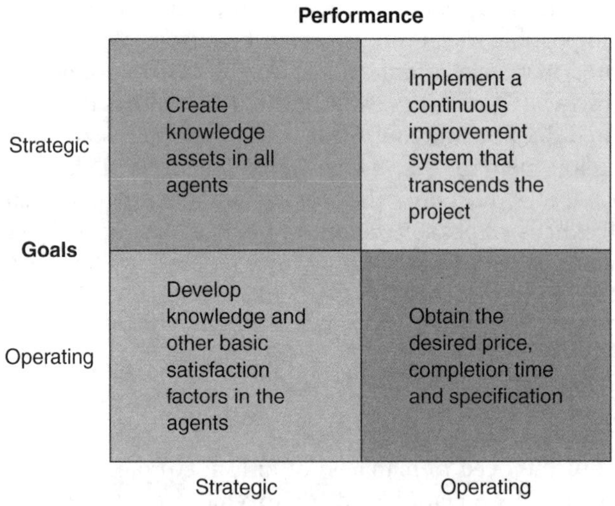

Performance

Goals	Strategic	Create knowledge assets in all agents	Implement a continuous improvement system that transcends the project
	Operating	Develop knowledge and other basic satisfaction factors in the agents	Obtain the desired price, completion time and specification
		Strategic	Operating

Figure 3.3   The four aspects of project management and the four management processes

---

[2] Any professor and/or consultant worth his salt must have a 2 × 2 matrix to show and a three-letter acronym (preferably in English). No more than 2 × 2, because popular belief has it that larger matrixes are incomprehensible, or at least incomprehensible for managers (!). And no more than three letters for the same reason. As the reader will see as the book progresses, we abide strictly by this condition, presenting several 2 × 2 matrixes, of which this one is the first, and many three-letter anagrams.

there are two different types of performance: the *strategic performance*, which conceives and carries out actions from a long-term viewpoint, and the *operating performance*, which does the same from a short-term viewpoint.

We must now combine the two ways of achieving results, or carrying out the project, with the two ways of formulating the project's goals to give four different management processes. Figure 3.4 shows the four management processes.

1. *Strategic management of strategic goals.* This is where the infrastructure required to guarantee the agents' learning and the resulting increase in the knowledge base of the firm managing the project is considered. It includes aspects such as ensuring the inclusion of external knowledge by absorbing the suppliers' knowledge, the exploitation of alliances to obtain knowledge, and the implementation of measures to absorb knowledge from this project. This management process rarely generates income because it is concentrated on investments that are not directly related to the project's cash flows.
2. *Strategic management of operating goals.* In this case, the infrastructure created must reflect the project's operating goals. These are concentrated on the customer's satisfaction and, although outside the project as such, are related to it. Here the firm must manage both the factors involved in the customer's immediate satisfaction and the measures required to assure the customer's learning (courses, technology transfer, training, etc.).
3. *Operating management of strategic goals.* The aim here is to use the project to ensure, day by day, the obtainment of cumulative improvements that provide future competitiveness for the firm. Note that in this case, as the project progresses, the goal is to capitalize on the improvement obtained from its execution or from the problem-solving processes that arise in the project. Specific actions in this area are usually concentrated on establishing analysis methodologies such as that proposed in Chapter 4.
4. *Operating management of operating goals.* This assures attainment, in the course of day-to-day activities, of the completion time, price and specification fulfilment goals that make up the project's operating purpose. This management process is virtually identical to the classic project management process described previously.

Of these four management processes, knowledge acquisition goals appear in at least three. In two cases, they are direct: the customer and the firm must both learn from the project. In other cases, the management process is concentrated on the two faces of learning: on the use of knowledge. This can be achieved by implementing a PDM system whose principles will be discussed extensively in the following pages.

This brief analysis shows the ubiquity of a new equilibrium which does not appear in the classic conception of projects: the equilibrium between efficiency and learning. The most efficient way of proceeding at any given time is not necessarily the way that provides the most valuable learning experience for the agents involved in the project. Therefore, the manager has the responsibility of balancing these two sources of results into a coherent whole that encompasses all four aspects defined in this section.

*Intellectual projects

It often happens in innovative projects that the project has a high degree of intellectual content. Writing a book could be considered to be a project of this type,[3] but so also could many of our previous examples – such as implementing an ERP, writing a complex software program or executing a strategic plan.

In these cases, it seems that the limits between some of the management aspects from the previous table become extremly fuzzy. Where does the performance of mental activities to attain operating completion of the project begin and where do the activities that produce learning end? It becomes very hard to define this with any precision and even harder to separate the two aspects.

Difficulties often arise in describing in operating terms the activities or tasks involved in performance of the project. For example, if we are writing a novel, 'imagining the plot' could be one activity. But its breakdown into subactivities is not clear – even when the activity has been completed. Although methodologies or processes are explained and taught for carrying out this type of activity, it often contains magical elements, such as references to 'inspiration' accompanied by appeals to the muses and other extracorporeal aids.

In intellectual projects, it usually happens that the phases that are richest in knowledge are summarized in a few high-level activities for lack of a methodology for itemizing them and acting on them. Diagnosing, planning, discovering and creating are some examples of verbs that describe situations that it is difficult to systematize.

And yet the literature, particularly the technical literature on software development, offers some useful suggestions. Software development is a type of project that has a high commercial value and significant operating difficulties. On one hand, it has a strong intellectual, even creative component. On the other hand, there is the need to produce software to carry out tasks having a high degree of complexity and which involve a large number of people. As a result, strict methodologies are needed for sharing knowledge and exploiting the synergies that can be achieved in the project. These problems are addressed in the literature on software engineering, where attempts are made to give some answers, in the form of procedures that guarantee the projects' success. Unfortunately, their high complexity and short history have prevented researchers from dispelling the mist and bringing in the light in this

---

[3] Although the reader may be sceptical about this, to write a book you do need at least a couple of ideas as well as the ability to spin them out to 300 pages without losing the reader on the way. If he has any doubts on this, let the reader try to find more than two ideas in some of the popular management books, probably including this one …

field of activity.[4] However, even at this stage, there are a number of ideas that can be extrapolated to other intellectual projects.

As an example of what is being achieved – and as an illustration of certain aspects of intellectual projects – we will briefly comment on the Common Kads methodology.[5] This methodology has been developed to analyse knowledge-intensive projects with the aim of improving and supporting them along all four dimensions of project management given in this chapter. As we have seen in the previous chapter, Common Kads contributes an important classification of process knowledge. In the analysis of intellectual projects, Common Kads makes full use of these knowledge and competence categories.

The methodology's rationale is very simple. The goal is to analyse existing processes in an intellectual project and break them down into their component parts in a manner that is similar to the analysis of business processes (Chapter 5). However, in contrast to the latter, the methodology seeks to identify:

(a) The *logical objects* being processed, contained in domain knowledge. This normally consists of building a thesaurus in which both the objects and their attributes are defined in detail. This standardizes their use by all the agents involved, establishes a common vocabulary and makes them available for systematic study.

(b) The *logical processes* (or *task knowledge*) which are used at each stage of the project to perform each task of the business process. For each logical process, a reasoning method is specified to implement it. This association can be obtained empirically – that is, by identifying the agents who implement the method and extracting it by means of observations and interviews. The methodology itself has developed a standard zoo of methods that have been listed and typified and whose structure is documented in detail. The standard methods are associated with standard tasks, which have been taken from observation of a large number of business processes. Figure 3.4 shows some standard types of task. Experience shows that more than 80 per cent of the processes can be described with these types alone. Once a standard task has been identified, it is associated with a method. Figure 3.5 shows a method for the task *diagnose*. There may be many methods for the same standard task. For example, the task diagnose is not always performed using the same method. The analyst is responsible for documenting the method, but a variety of pre-established methods are available that help him in this task. For example, the

---

[4] Some people propose, rather cynically, that it is precisely because nobody can make head or tail of it that there are so many methodologies. We are not so pessimistic but it is true that large-scale software projects lead to systems that have very low quality levels. For an example, one has only to look at a certain family of operating systems that have all sorts of quirks. One of the authors once saw (on one of these systems) the following error message: 'Press any key to continue and any other key to cancel ...' After pressing a key, the system displayed a blue screen with the message 'The system is trying to show the close dialog ... ' and then disappeared into hyperspace. To get the computer to work again, it had to be unplugged and rebooted ...

[5] Common Kads (Schreiber *et al.*, 1999).

method shown in Figure 3.5 is based on hypothesis generation and testing. From among the hypotheses generated, one is selected and tested, associating it with observables derived from the interaction with the world. The hypotheses are validated by observation and, if necessary, they are discarded, formulating new ones in their place. We could easily imagine another method based, for example, on the progressive refinement of a hypothesis. Many of these standard methods are described in the literature on artificial intelligence (Russell and Norvig, 1995).

(c) *Use of inference knowledge* Once the method has been stated, methodology tries to break it down into individual components that should not be broken down any further, thereby giving rise to elementary logical operations. These basic operations are inference knowledge. In Figure 3.5, the inference knowledge is shaded in a dark colour. In the same way as for activities, the methodology's authors identify about twenty types of standard inference knowledge, ranging from 'abstracting' to 'selecting'. The four types of inference knowledge shown in Figure 3.5 are included in these twenty typical types of inference knowledge. The types of inference knowledge, reduced to a readily manageable number, can now be supported by computer processes that help perform the entire project.

A more detailed discussion of the Common Kads methodology is beyond the scope of this book. Such a discussion would require an entire book in itself. However, this brief outline should convince the reader that:

1. Using this type of analysis, an intellectual process can characterized quite reasonably, maintaining inference knowledge as the primitive operation.
2. The processes can be reordered so that efficiency losses are minimized by interaction between the operations and, once this is done, the methodology can be used to determine how to support the individual components through the use of technology.

Elementary tasks

ANALYTIC
Classification
Assessment
Diagnosis
Monitoring

SYNTHETIC
Design
Configuration
Allocation
Planning
Programming

Figure 3.4   Common Kads methodology: Basic tasks

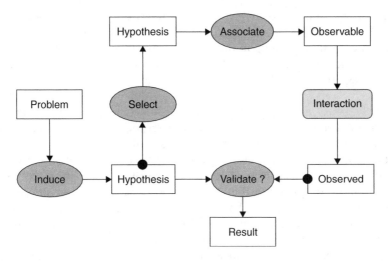

Figure 3.5   Standard method for the task diagnose

In intellectual projects, knowledge is the common axis on which the whole must turn. Basically, the four management processes manage and process knowledge.

Executing projects with a high level of uncertainty

Given the initial definition of the project's strategic and operating goals, a working method must be defined that can make them a reality. However, if the project itself only becomes clearer as it progresses, the way in which this clarity must be obtained is nebulous at the very least and we need some kind of anchor, in the form of a methodological approach, that helps us in this task. In this section, we will address the subject of how to create a project development program, when the program emerges over time as a result of the project itself. The reader will no doubt perceive the recursive nature of the difficulty. A project program is needed in order to execute the project. But we won't know how to do this until we have the project ...

The way to break out from this recursiveness is to generalize, using the concepts given in previous chapters. One simple central idea is sufficient: *executing a project is basically solving a problem,* and, therefore, benefits from the structure described in Chapter 1. The problem is formulated by stating the project's goals at any given time.

Rather an elegant definition, isn't it? The first implication is that the lack of adequate knowledge will mean that there will be exploratory phases during the project. Any exploratory phase compromises the project's result because of the time and quality constraints mentioned previously. From the action viewpoint, we are interested in identifying the measures that minimize this risk. One way of minimizing the risk *is to create a context in which knowledge is identified, absorbed and used as quickly as possible,* preferably at the very instant that it is generated by the action of any of the agents involved in the project and as a result of any of the four basic management processes. All of this in the service of the project's goals.

The context will depend upon the type of competence involved. Therefore, we will adapt to the project situation the three types of competence described in the previous chapter.

(a) *Domain competences*. The lack of domain competences is basically manifested by the *inability to list the objects to be handled*. In the case of a project, the main objects are the activities of which the project is made up, the resources that these activities must use and the relationships between activities. Of course, the degree of ignorance is never total. At least, it is always possible to list the objects that represent the project's goals and they provide the starting point for further exploration. The main tool for handling these competences is a top-down decomposition method (see Appendix). This method is well-known and comes from the design world, where it has achieved considerable maturity in the field of software development. In these areas, the method is used to progressively define the structure of an artefact. However, it can be generalized perfectly well to address any situation of the type we are describing. The idea is that, at any given time, a description of the project is only held to a certain level of detail. As this is the only information available, maximum use must be made of it in all the project's management tasks. There's no choice, as anything else would be simply sighing for better knowledge of the project. And sighing without action is nothing more than poetry. When this method is applied, for example, to managing the project's activities list (or structure), the starting point is a single high-level activity: 'do the project'. This activity is used in the best possible way for all planning (trivial, because of the briefness of the description) and execution (horrible, for the same reason) functions. As soon as a more refined description can be obtained for any part of an activity, it is immediately added to the project's activity base. Thus, while the project is being performed, the activities list is progressively decomposed and enriched, exploiting at any given time the available base in the best possible way. All of the process can be structured around a dynamic database, to which the agents contribute as they work. This is not the place for a detailed discussion of such a management system, but the reader can probably guess what to do to implement it.

(b) *Task competences*. The possession of task competences seeks to avoid the exploratory phase, which occurs when one does not have the necessary knowledge to perform an *individual activity*. Task competences must focus on the method for performing the task. Once one has an activities list, each activity must be associated with a method. In a traditional project, the different activities have as their basis the task knowledge which we know is necessary to perform them. Very often, task knowledge is expressed at a high level by simply adding the verb 'know how to' to the activity's name. If the project is to build a power station, the activities' task knowledge could be 'know how to choose the site', 'know how to negotiate fuel contracts', and hundreds or thousands of other pieces of knowledge, each one associated with a particular activity. In these cases, the method associated with the task is probably well-known and does not need additional refinement. When this is not the case, the method's description can be iterative, obtained using a top-down process. The advantage here is that pre-defined methods can be used, if it has been possible to decompose the activity into typified subactivities.

For many activities, the method for performing a task can be delegated to the agents performing them. However, even if this is so, the project's management system must maintain a subsystem that documents the status of the method associated with each task, probably described in an unified language that materializes it and makes it readily accessible to any agent. The task competences appear as a result of the direct learning performed on the project itself. Upon completing the project, the method used for the project's activities and its results become part of what is known.[6]

(c) *Inference competences* These competences are focused on the ability to keep all the other competences up to date and, therefore, on the manner in which the participating agents successfully conclude their projects. This is reflexive knowledge, knowledge about the manner in which the knowledge process is performed (Arcos, 1998). It typically refers to the high-level procedures which are used in the development of the other two competences. For example, the top-down decomposition procedure mentioned earlier is basically knowledge within an inference competence, the competence concerned with 'concretion in the project's description'. A project without this type of competence would be chaotic, because the entire project would be basically exploratory, both in its execution and in its planning and learning. In many projects, if the group of agents performing the project has experience in other projects, these competences will probably already exist, to differing degrees, within the project. In any case, it is not possible to expect the people involved in operating management processes to have the appropriate perspective to systematize inference competences. To develop such projects, it is advisable to have agents working specifically on the subject, who accumulate expertence and systematize it in the desired competences by means of a 'reasoning about reasoning' process. These competences are usually disseminated – not necessarily formalized – by training. In many cases, the project's organizational structure itself is most effective in providing training, with the managers taking on the role of trainers.

*Estimating duration

For each competence, it is at least possible to conceptualize, and sometimes to estimate, the source and magnitude of the need for exploration. Applying the ideas presented in the first chapter, this may help estimate the time required to attain a certain quality.

Let us assume that the project contains certain levels of inference competences that enable the process we are going to describe to be performed. Let us also

---

[6] In practice, when a project is completed, the learning obtained about the methods is acknowledged by the suggestive phrase 'If I had to start again, I wouldn't do it like that.' A futile lamentation as the project will probably never be repeated in the same form.

assume that at a given stage of the project we know the knowledge required for a certain competence. For example, if we are building a road, we must know how to roll and flatten the earth, lay the roadbed, lay the tarmac, etc.

Let us imagine that we create a knowledge requirement profile such as that shown in Figure 3.6.

In Figure 3.6, we plot the knowledge on the abscissa and, on the ordinate, some measure of the intensity with which we need to 'know', for example, a lot, some, a little … Now we put on top the knowledge profile that is available in the company's competence. Let us assume that the result of the overlay is Figure 3.7.

The reader will clearly see that, in some areas, the competence has 'too much content'; in other words, 'we know too much', while in other areas, we have a knowledge deficit, 'we know too little'. There is a knowledge gap generated by the difference between the knowledge requirement profile and the current profile.

The gap between the two curves will necessitate the presence of an exploratory phase in which the basic methodology will be the search (or exploration).

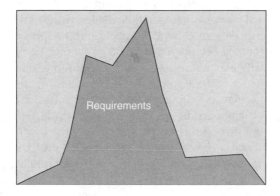

Figure 3.6   Knowledge requirements of a project

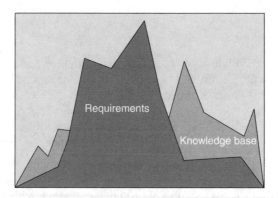

Figure 3.7   Knowledge requirements and the current knowledge base

Knowledge	Exists	Necessary
File ordering	Yes	No
Access to relational databases	Yes	Yes
User interface	Yes	Yes
Natural language interface	No	No
3D graphics processing	Yes	Yes
Client-server technology	No	Yes

Figure 3.8 Knowledge possession

In the first chapter, we saw how an activity's expected duration depends upon the proportion of exploration with respect to application. If the activity is partly defined, if task knowledge is lacking, the activities' expected duration will have exponential components.

One way of estimating the possible duration of one of these activities[7] from the size of the gap is to consider that the part corresponding to the application phase has a linear relationship with respect to the size of the problem. Let us say that the problem's size is x. For example, in software development, x may be the number of program lines to be written. Let us suppose that the necessary knowledge is that contained in Figure 3.8, which we have simplified by rating possession of an item of knowledge as 'all' or 'nothing'.

For each item of knowledge held to a sufficient degree, we can now calculate the time required to apply it, possibly knowing the number of times it is applied in the program and how. This estimate will give a time of Kx, where K is a proportionality constant.

As 'client-server technology' knowledge is necessary, we could choose between hiring an expert (in which case the problem would be solved linearly) or doing the implementation ourselves, using manuals and books that are available on the market. In this case, we will spend an exponential time exp(cx), where c is another constant, in an exploratory phase. The final result is that the time will take the form Kx + exp(cx). The exponential explosion will depend on the constants' relative values but, in the end, the explosion will happen anyway.

A similar phenomenon is to be found in the systems that do not scale up well. These systems contain an exploratory component, because nobody knows how to solve the problem by simply applying knowledge.

*Intrinsic complexity

To close this chapter, we will state that there are problem-solving tasks which can never be typified by the direct application of knowledge and which will always

---

[7] A way that is 'simple to understand, but difficult to apply, like many of the recipes given in this book', according to the opinion of one of the authors, and 'difficult to understand and easy to apply, like many of the recipes given in this book', according to the other author's opinion.

Example 3.4   HighTechSA

HighTechSA

HighTechSA took part in the Spain–United States compensation programme after the Spanish Air Force bought 60 F-18 planes. The compensations were projects or assignments which the companies that were supplying the plane's components sent to Spain with the aim of creating jobs and generating technological development. One of these compensations was the manufacture of the cockpit's main display, the so-called Head-up Display. The American manufacturer agreed with HighTech to carry out assembly of the display in Spain. The parts arrived from the United States and were assembled in HighTech's plants. When the programme was started, HighTech realized that the assembly instructions were given fully specified, with no room for improvising or learning. Everything was planned – to the smallest detail. To assemble the unit, it was enough to know how to move one's hands and operate certain tools (complicated but used routinely). Obviously, the American company had no interest in facilitating learning (technology transfer) between it and HighTech. HighTech decided that it was worth spending money on learning, even if it took longer. It negotiated a more relaxed delivery schedule and, with the additional time obtained, prepared a learning programme. It sent the engineering department the specifications of the product to be obtained and asked it to develop a process. The original process, that of the American company, was kept out of its reach, being held by a monitor who could only give suggestions in extreme cases and validate the proposals with the original. The validation consisted of comparing the processes and scrutinizing the differences. In addition, each assembly worker would be accompanied by an engineer who would 'look over his shoulder' to see what was happening and document it for subsequent analysis. The result was a lot of learning but a substantial decrease in the output. The cost was much greater than that originally budgeted but the difference could be viewed as the cost of the learning, the cost of the course followed by the company's engineers.

---

require an exploratory phase. In recent years, there has been recognition of the existence of problems which can be stated simply but which do not seem to be reducible to the mere application of knowledge. These really are well-structured problems! Therefore, we could formulate a general law which states: *In any project-related problem, one must expect an exploratory phase of exponential duration, which will limit the attainable quality of the result.* Although nothing more than an application of the ideas expressed in the previous chapter, this statement is able to account for mysterious situations which arise in any project, such as the need to specify results suboptimally.

Table 3.1 An actions table

	Domain	Task	Inference
Strategic management of strategic goals	Create a system for maintaining the project's composition	Create a standard methods library	Provide training in integrated competence management
Strategic management of operating goals	Decrease the uncertainty, and challenge, by means of working parties to progress in identifying the project's structure	Advise on the development of task methods. Distribute standard methods	Provide training activities on the work itself, adapting the challenge to the demand
Operating management of strategic goals	Create a system by which the agents take part in defining activities and resources	Assist in applying the methods. Support the solution of specific problems that arise in applying a method to a task	Provide training on improvement. Implement support systems for solving general coordination problems
Operating management of operating goals	Immediate use of the knowledge database in CPM planning modules adapted to learning	Implement procedures for monitoring performance and quality of the results. Assess the methods used	Systems for resolving emergencies. Create working parties to share all types of experience acquired during the project

Conclusions for action

One way of summarizing the ideas contained in this chapter is to construct a table which relates the four types of management to the three types of competence, so that each type of management is associated with actions on competence that lead to an improved level of achievement of the project's goals.

Note that the actions table (Table 3.1) is far superior to the typical actions proposed in the treatises on project management and this is to be attributed to the additional richness contributed by the consideration of knowledge.

In the present environment of structural uncertainty, project management needs a much broader approach than has hitherto been the case since the classic methods are no longer sufficient. There is a need to add another dimension: knowledge requirements and the learning this entails. In this chapter, we have confined ourselves to applying some of the ideas put forward in previous chapters to the world of project management. Albeit a fragmentary view for the moment, it does illustrate the need for action not only on the operations system, but also on the creation of a metastructure superimposed upon the system which assures the desired strategic results. This is a key feature of knowledge management and a consequence of the results–learning dichotomy.

Part II
On Better Doing

4
The Beginning of Good Doing: The World of Operations

Sometimes after analysing the literature, one may think that it is possible to describe improvement phenomena separately from the target of the improvement. This is essentially the viewpoint taken by the quality approach, which considers that the same procedures can be used, for example, both to improve sales and to improve the efficiency of the financial process.

It is certainly true that there are common elements in any improvement process. In fact, Chapter 2 is an elaboration on the main general aspect of improvement: problem solving. However, more general means less powerful. The generic tools – those which are applied to any problem – do not have the same power as tools that are more specifically adapted to a certain domain. To use the jargon of Chapter 2, inference knowledge by itself is too generic a tool. To give it greater power, both domain and process knowledge are needed. In this chapter, we will begin the presentation of domain knowledge in operations.

Domain knowledge in operations

Two basic approaches can be taken to build the subject matter of operations. The first is that of professional advice. This consists of taking the viewpoint of the people who are responsible for carrying out operations at different levels: worker, technician, foreman, operations manager or general manager. Each level needs 'clues', ideas to enable it to improve. Therefore, for each level, we could review actions that are currently working well in the world and considers those factors that seem to be necessary for success. There is no attempt to develop a logic of the domain; the aim is simply to offer alternatives for action. This is the approach taken by most business books.

The second approach consists of creating a knowledge structure that helps the professional to understand the relationships between the variables of which operations are composed. With the help of his truth maintenance system (TMS) he will then be able to propose alternative actions that lead him towards the desired objective. This is the typical framework used at university level.

Both of these approaches have drawbacks.[1] The emphasis on the recipe, on describing actions that have worked for others, may be reduced to a series of guidelines that are useful so long as the environment is similar to that of the prototype situation and remains unchanged. In rapidly changing or highly competitive situations, however, imitating successful actions is a slow, unreliable way of progressing. Domain elements are required to develop solutions specifically geared towards the problem in hand.

Unfortunately, we do not have a general theory, a comprehensive model of operations which, in the manner of physics, would enable a totally deductive approach to be adopted. In operations, it is not possible to deduce by logical reasoning from a set of axioms, all of the consequences of a particular action. We must therefore adopt a mixed approach, an intermediate stance. To help us in this task, we will try to establish a general reference framework strongly focused on action.

Strategy and operations

Any assessment of the effectiveness of operations should be based upon a general concept of the *firm's purpose*. A lot has been written about this subject and the interested reader may find numerous references in the literature (Buffa, 1983; Skinner, 1985; Hayes *et al.*, 1988).

Classic economic theory normally assumes that the firm's purpose is to maximize profits. Yet this criterion is too restrictive and has perverse connotations. It should be banished once and for all from the business world.[2] It poses all manner of problems: the definition of profit itself, the time period over which it is applied, the difficulty in introducing risk considerations in the earnings generating process, and so on.

In recent years, this classic goal has again reared its evil head disguised as a neoclassic goal. People have started talking about maximizing 'value for the shareholder'. This criterion is every bit as perverse as that of profits. The shareholder is only one of the firm's many stakeholders, and possibly not the most important one at that. Behind this criterion there lurks an underlying goal that is much more

---

[1] The type of literature targeting each group is substantially different. For the first group, which is assumed to be very busy and not very keen on reading but with plenty of money to spend, the goal is to produce literature that contains easy-to-follow maxims and instructions. The result is the typical 'airport' book – sparing in text, generous in illustrations and amusing stories. Rather than help the reader, the author seeks to sell books and, at a later date, consulting services. The second type of literature would be the off-the-peg textbook, many replicas 'with variations' on a few basic texts. They are often more concerned with techniques than with problems and the knowledge they contain is rarely geared towards improving action.

[2] Curiously enough, there are still some people in the business world who say that their goal is to maximize profits. Even the classic economists themselves acknowledged that the only good thing about this criterion is that you could do math with it. Perhaps for this reason it still forms the basis of the microeconomic theory taught in many universities. Even though it is ridiculous, the theory that can be generated with it is mathematically much simpler than with other alternatives, so perhaps the reason why it is kept alive is so that people can write papers.

cynical than the previous ones and, therefore, is rarely stated explicitly. Observation of companies shows that everything seems to happen as if the firm's implicit goal was to maximize the (economic and political) power of its (senior) executives. This is an hypothesis that can explain the activities observed during some of the major bank mergers or the stock market manoeuvrings of certain companies.[3] It also accounts for the cynicism of certain firms who proclaim their concern for the customer and then stab him in the back when they can exercise their power.

Faced with this situation, certain authors (Cyert and March, 1965; Nelson and Winter, 1982; Simon, 1969; Rubinstein, 1997) put forward approaches that question the optimizing goal while suggesting the need to consider all of the firm's stakeholders. In real life it is normally necessary to set priorities and bargain and, in these cases, the stakeholder holding most power within the firm will dictate to the others. In the event of conflicting interests, the bargaining will be limited by the firm's survival capability, which is a goal which all the groups typically accept as being above their personal interests. In this sense, the firm's survival is usually placed as the ultimate goal to which all other goals should be subordinated. Therefore, we will adopt this criterion as the firm's purpose. For us, *the ultimate goal of any firm is indefinite survival.*

Of course, indefinite survival cannot be achieved without a level of profits that guarantees adequate compensation for the various agents that contribute to the firm. However, the survival criterion is very powerful because it also includes risk and opportunity considerations. For example, survival implies the adequate remuneration of equity so that new shares can be sold in the future and, consequently, introduces the concept of risk. Likewise, it includes the long-term satisfaction of the various stakeholders. The criterion implies that the firm's components should learn to cooperate, because failure to do so will limit their lifespan.

By accepting the firm's indefinite survival as its purpose, we are attributing to the firm a capacity that is only found in the more highly developed organisms, those that are able to survive by deploying forms of behaviour that prevent their disappearance. Without the positive involvement of its components, the firm will tend towards increased disorder,[4] thereby endangering its continued existence. To counteract this trend, positive action is needed.

---

[3] A friend of ours said that, once again, the dark hand of power was behind the criterion of maximizing value for the shareholder. Because many executives receive part of their compensation in stock options, the way to become rich is to concentrate effort on increasing the shares' value. And many times this is much easier to do than concentrate on improving the quality of the company's service.

[4] A firm is a living organism. One way of understanding nature is to view living organisms as highly organized forms that increase the existing amount of order: ordered structures arising from a much less organized environment. Viewed in this light, the second law of thermodynamics works against life. This law, in its most sophisticated form, states that the universe's disorder increases continuously and that any transformation increases the total degree of disorder of its entropy. Therefore, just as with any living organism, the firm is bound by the inexorable laws of decline and disorder.

This generic survival criterion is difficult to apply in practice. To assess an action in terms of this criterion, it is initially necessary to determine how it contributes to a firm's long-term survival. This is not easy when considering an extensive and, in principle, indefinite time framework.

Viewed from the strategic analysis viewpoint, the *search for sustainable competitive advantages* is a means that enables the firm to survive in the long term and to counteract situations that endanger its existence. Therefore, in order to survive indefinitely, the firm must be able to compete – that is, to obtain and retain certain advantages over its competitors. Consequently, when the survival criterion is replaced by that of increasing sustainable competitive advantage, the criterion's operationality is increased. It is also brought closer to the area of operations: on one hand, by providing a method for assessing actions and, on the other hand, by locating the survival criterion in time and space. In order to assess an action, it is enough to consider whether it allows the firm to increase its capacity to compete efficiently, here and now.

There are two aspects of the *competitiveness* concept that are particularly important. First, *competitiveness is a relative notion*. This means that a firm's competitive advantage depends upon how much better its service is compared to those of its rivals on the long range, always referred to the way it has chosen to be 'the best'.

Firms often address their competitiveness myopically 'to do things better than my competitors'. This idea, although correct, holds a number of great perils. One of them is that it may seem that it is sufficient to work as well, or perhaps a little better, but not much better than our competitors. The idea is that if the competitors do not do it, it is probably because 'the customer does not appreciate it'. There are many examples of cases in which this ill-founded interpretation has led to disastrous results. Example 4.1 gives two case studies.

Example 4.1   If the customer does not appreciate it, is it worth doing?

Zapatos Castilla

Zapatos Castilla had developed a dyeing process that achieved a very strong colour fastness. Its competitors did not have this technology. A value analysis revealed that customers did not value the high additional colour fastness provided by the process. The process was changed and the feature was eliminated. Everything went well until one of the company's biggest competitors also found the way to give additional colour fastness. This rival started to promote this feature to its customers, creating an awareness of its advantages. Colour fastness soon became a standard requirement. Zapatos Castilla realized what was happening as soon as the competitor started its campaigns. They quickly tried to make up for lost time but they had already lost their advantage. In addition, Castilla incurred a double process change cost, eliminating the colour fastness and then restoring it. When the dust finally settled, the company had lost an advantage that it had initially held over its other competitors.

The Spanish Motorcycle Industry

In the 1950s and 1960s, there were five major motorcycle brands in Spain. Bultaco, Montesa, Sanglas, Ossa and Derbi provided a variety of models that were 'suitable' for the market at that time. The Japanese manufacturers were unable to offer quality and owning a Japanese motorcycle was considered 'a poor choice' among the initiated. The Spanish machines were reasonably reliable and the features they offered were sufficient to keep the customer happy. The Japanese did not believe this to be true and implemented large-scale programmes to improve their machines' quality much beyond what the customer valued at that time. The result can be readily seen by the reader in any street of the world.

Example 4.2 Ford's strategy

Ford's Buying Strategy

In the automobile market, the pressure to reduce costs is reaching extreme limits. The large OEMs are caught in a pincer with the three major technology suppliers (brakes, fuel supply and transmissions) on one side and the customer on the other. Production has already squeezed off much of the fat by all sorts of efficiency-boosting programmes, from JIT to Lean Production. One way that is still open to reduce prices and maintain margins is to save every possible penny on purchases. Thus, one tactic may be to encourage global competition between suppliers, leveraging the advantages of geographic areas with lower labour costs, better resources, and so on.

Along these lines, Ford like many other large companies has developed a buying system using Internet tendering. The company posts its purchasing requirements on its website and waits to receive offers from companies interested in supplying by the same medium. Ford then chooses the company that offers it the best conditions. And all this on a global scale. Single suppliers and stable customer–supplier relationships have become a thing of the past.[5]

The second peril appears because the notion of competitiveness is *dynamic* in nature. Competitiveness is a struggle for survival and, in this sense, it is a Darwinian, evolutionary force. It is not sufficient that the firm should be the best at a *particular moment in time*. It must continue to be the best over all time. In the

---

[5] Such practices can't help but send a shiver up the authors' spines. On one hand, it seems to be a manoeuvre by someone who finds himself in a desperate situation. On the other hand, it seems a way of exploiting those countries that are trying to use their lower labour costs to boost their own growth. Global competition reduces all companies' margins, including those in these geographical areas. Sometimes, one catches oneself wishing that the shark was not white but yellow…

struggle to be the best, firms undergo a process of natural selection, producing competitors that are increasingly-better adapted to the aggressive environment. And the more competitive (aggressive) the industry is, the easier it is to develop 'sharks' or 'killing machines'.

The world of operations

Operations focus essentially on *activities that transform certain inputs into outputs essentially products or services*. It corresponds to what could be called the firm's 'know-how', the ability to built entities that did not exist *a priori* by means of the transformation of certain inputs.

In industrial companies it was usually called 'Production'. But the distinction between products companies and services companies is a fairly artificial one. In fact, *all companies are service companies*. An industrial company does not just deliver an object to its customer. It delivers much more; in fact, it delivers a complete package of potential sensations to be 'experienced' throughout the product's useful lifecycle. Buying an object implies starting a relationship between the two parties involved in the contract – a relationship which will take on an increasingly concrete form as the interaction progresses.[6]

Accordingly, all types of companies have *operations*. By contrast, only manufacturing companies have a *production* process. Therefore, in this book, we will refer interchangeably both to the two classical types: pseudo-industrial companies (steelworks, textile mills, electronic firms, etc.) and services companies (hospitals, restaurants, hotels, etc).

*The actors[7] in operations

The success of companies is not easy to explain.[8] However the literature and our own experience show that the best firms, the most competitive, achieve a high degree of the internal consistency, which is transmitted to their environment.[9] In this respect, two types of consistency seem to be necessary: an *external*

---

[6] When someone buys a luxury car, he is not buying just a car,– in the sense of purchasing a product consisting of an engine, four wheels, the steering wheel, the seats, and the rest. He is also buying the look of envy from his next-door neighbour when he sees the new car and the ashen face he will have when he receives the bills from the bodyshop...

[7] One of the authors' says that the operations world is like a play where the actors change their costume but the plot remains the same: 'being the best' is timeless – it's the wrapping in which it is presented that changes!

[8] For us, success is equal to competitiveness.

[9] After being adequately processed. In recent years, with the growing fashion of putting computer technology into all sorts of activity, the customer resource or relationship management (CRM) has been identified as an information system that is able to exploit the information contained in these experiences. How these ideas should be given concrete form is open to debate. The experts often identify the empty box and give it a name. How it should be filled is the manager's problem.

consistency between customers and strategy, and an *internal* consistency between strategy and the operations structure that supports its implementation.

A company's competitiveness is the outcome of the interaction between three actors: the customer (the decision-making component of the market), the strategists (those responsible formulating company's way to compile), and the operators (those responsible for the operating decisions). The later two operate within the company, both, each one in his own field of activity. The company manages its service from the joint work of these two agents' (strategists and operators) decisions.

A happy customer enters into a *stable business relationship* with the company. This enables the company to continue learning about its customer's preferences and, by this means, to continue to satisfy his expectations. A stable relationship helps the company achieve its long-term goal: the survival. If the priority is to achieve the greatest possible satisfaction in the continuing interaction with the customer, all three agents must have an interest in maintaining a high degree of consistency. First of all, the company's two internal agents must cooperate in order to attain the desired way of competing and, second, the satisfaction obtained from the exchange by the company and the customer must be sufficient to maintain confidence in the prospect of future satisfactions.

This interaction between the agents takes place around three basic objects: the mission, the customer and the operations box. (See Figure 4.1.)

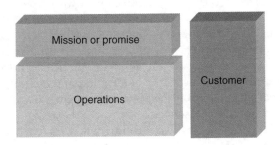

Figure 4.1   The three players

Example 4.3   Fading

Fading's Promise in BTS

- We have extensive experience in the provision of global solutions to improve our customers' performance.
- We have detailed knowledge of the operators' operating requirements.
- We deliver an integrated product designed for our customer, executed and implemented by us.

The *mission* generates the 'promise' that the company makes to its customer. The promise reaches the customer before the act of consumption. Therefore, the promise is conveyed through classic communication channels – basically marketing actions such as advertising. Example 4.3 gives one of Fading's promises. Fading is a small Spanish company specializing in the development and supply of Portable Cellular Telephony Stations (BTS).

The *customer* is the party who receives the service and is attracted to the company by the promise it makes. For example, a customer may approach Fading hoping to obtain a custom-designed, reliable, quality product that satisfies his desires, with turnkey supply and which reduces his operating costs.

The company's promise creates expectations. *The customer's satisfaction results from the interaction of his expectations with the service actually obtained.* Indeed, greater satisfaction is achieved when reality surpasses prior expectations.

In order for the customer to be satisfied, a real service must be delivered that at least matches the expectations raised by the promise. This has to be built and delivered to the customer through some process. This is the role of operations. *Operations is everything in the company that transforms the promise into a tangible reality for the customer.*

The moments of truth

The customer comes into contact with the mission through service. In order to obtain the service, the customer comes into contact with the reality of operations and it is these that deliver the service or product. Ian Carlzon (1988), SAS's CEO during the 1980s, coined the phrase moments of truth (MOT) to help describe the customer's interaction with the reality of operations. The *moments of truth* are the events that have most impact on the result of the interaction. It is in these moments that the customer assesses his interaction and identifies the value that the company gives him to fulfil his expectations. By identifying the moments of truth, we can better design our service.

Some managers find it rather overwhelming when their service's moments of truth are listed. When they are shown this list, they become aware of the enormous number of apparently trivial details that are vital in securing a satisfactory perception of their company. When the product is not a differential element of the total service offered, the MOT component takes on great importance. The idea provides a way of decomposing, identifying and measuring the abstract concept of 'service quality', behind which lie supposedly intangible elements of the customer's assessment.

In all MOTs, it is necessary to isolate the contents supplied by each of the interacting parties. In turn, these contents are the result of design decisions concerning the context in which the interaction takes place. Heskett *et al.* (1990), authors of acknowledged repute and fathers of the service assessment movement, identify some of these decisions, such as job design, employee empowerment, employee selection, reward and recognition, and matching tools to the service's purpose. These characteristics make up what they have termed the '*service's internal quality*'.

They also identify the *service's external value*, which includes the customer's expectations and his measurement of what he receives. It is in this function that the pure personal interaction takes place and the ability to solve problems, offer alternatives and implement them operationally takes on particular significance.

The customer's perception is obtained through these interactions. And, sometimes, these interactions contain within them inconsistencies that produce a dissatisfied customer.

Example 4.4   The MOTs in the Strait Crossing operation

The Moments of Truth in the Strait Crossing Operation (SCO)

Each year, during the months of July and August, more than half a million Moroccans load up their cars somewhere in Europe and travel to their home towns or villages to spend their holidays with their families. Most of them drive down to the port of Algeciras, on the southern tip of the Iberian Peninsula and try to cross to Africa using the network of ferries operating from this port. The movement of vehicles becomes a veritable avalanche at the time of peak demand in early August and long queues form to board the ferry. For the travellers, the port is the 'destination' because it is the most important differential milestone of their journey. As part of the process to improve the SCO service, the moments of truth in the customer's waiting period at the port of Algeciras were identified. The most important were the following:

1. Arrival at the port through the main entrance. Associated with the bewilderment produced by arrival in an unfamiliar environment after many hours of motorway driving (often more than 30 hours). Need for guidance and welcome to have the sensation of having reached their destination.
2. Buying the ticket. Associated with the marketing process to which the shipping companies subject the customer. Need to clarify special offers, terms and prices. Security in the choice.
3. Arrival at the waiting area. Assurance of FIFO discipline. Perception of an ordered, safe, comfortable area to wait the required number of hours until embarkation.
4. Leaving the waiting area and arrival at embarkation. Respect for queuing discipline. Clarity in the instructions given and in the interactions with the harbour employees.
5. Embarkation. Organization of embarkation, quick, problem-free. Provision of the necessary information to assure physical and mental safety on board.

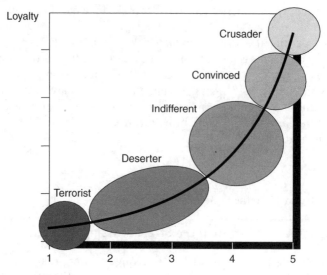

Figure 4.2   Customer types

The customer[10]

An effect of competitive advantage is the capacity to *obtain and maintain the customer's satisfaction*. The customer's satisfaction is a time-extended experience. Therefore, from the operating viewpoint, it is important to measure the customer's real degree of satisfaction with the service received. This kind of information is hard to obtain, as it is not enough to simply ask him.[11] The only immediate way of ascertaining this satisfaction is to observe his interaction with the company.

Figure 4.2[12] gives a customer typology in terms of customer satisfaction with the company over time. At one end, there are the *crusaders* customers, who recommend the company to all of the people they come into contact with. Less visible but normally more numerous is the group of *convinced* customers. A satisfied customer is normally a convinced customer. This type of customer maintains his interaction, repeating purchases and showing an attitude that is beneficial for the company. A company is truly competitive when it gains and keeps a 'stock' of satisfied customers (convinced and crusaders) who will remain loyal in their

---

[10] We always say that customers are 'frivolous, capricious, spiteful and resentful', but they are the ones who are doing the buying!

[11] This is a point that crops up time and time again in the book. The obvious way of obtaining information, asking those who hold it, is not appropriate as the observer interacts with the observee. Since the observee is not a machine, his answers often depend on what he perceives as important in the interaction. It's the case of the respondent who tells the interviewer what he thinks he wants to hear...

[12] Graciously lent by our colleague and friend Jaume Ribera.

interaction with the company. This continuity in the relationship is, the basic feature that defines customer satisfaction.

Seen from the viewpoint of results for the company, the convinced customer is far superior to the crusader customer. The latter gives the company more than the company delivers to him. Out of altruism, or kindness, he decides to do a favour to his fellow men by proclaiming the results of his interaction. However, this generous action runs contrary to one of the basic maxims of any interaction that we have adopted as a basic postulate in Chapter 1. The customer's relationship with the company is, and must be, an absolutely selfish situation – both company and customer must gain in the exchange of services. This rationality principle leads to the possibility of obtaining a stable equilibrium.[13] The customer does not change because the company is his best choice, and the company serves him because serving him is, in turn, the company's best choice.

At the other end of Figure 4.2 are the terrorist and deserter customers. The terrorist customer broadcasts negative publicity about the company, points out its failings and often protests and complains about them. The deserter customer is the one who silently goes to another company if he considers that his expectations have not been met.

For the company, the worst customer is the deserter. On the other hand, *the terrorist customer is one of the greatest sources of improvement* that the company has. He offers free of charge a diagnosis of our weaknesses which, duly captured and processed, enables us to diagnose and solve service problems. Of course, this is always provided that the company takes notice of him.

The case of Example 4.5 shows a situation in which terrorist customers, tired of playing their role, become deserter customers. When a customer deserts us, we always find excuses to think that the fault is his and not ours. However, the truth of the matter is quite the contrary. A customer always leaves us because *we have not satisfied him.*

The customer's loyalty is an indicator of the efficiency and consistency of our operations. This only ceases to apply in situations of power, when a monopolistic company keeps unsatisfied customers – customers who are waiting anxiously for a rival company to appear on the scene to run away with him. From the neighbourhood garage to airlines, monopolies, real or tacit,[14] exist in our world. Typically, the customer keeps a tally of all the dissatisfactions and, when the opportunity presents itself, he will bring the company to account for all them. For example, the reader could reflect on what will happen in the Flynow case if a high-speed train starts to run, connecting Timbuktu and Pernambuco in just two hours.

According to the previously stated rationality principle, a long-term relationship between a company and its customer is only achieved if the company is *the best*

---

[13] A concept which concurs with that of Von Neumann and Morgenstern (1944) addressed in their classic treatise on games theory.

[14] The reader will agree that often we are subject to implicit agreements between companies to maintain prices and not unleash a price war.

Example 4.5   VueleYa's customer

Flynow Airlines

Flynow Airlines offers an air shuttle service between Pernambuco and Timbuktu. Between these two cities, there is a high volume of passengers who wish to sell things to the inhabitants of the other city. The company has defined its service as 'Arrive and fly'. Regardless of the time he arrives at the airport, the customer will be able to fly to the other city within an hour. However, the service has a large number of inconveniences for the passenger.

Let us look at one of them. The plane always travels full. As it is not possible to book a seat, the best seats are always taken by those who arrive first at the plane's boarding gate. The one who arrives last may have to sit between a chicken vendor, with his chickens, and a goat dealer, of course accompanied by his goats. As the airport is not a sequential system, there is no check on the order of arrival at the plane's boarding gate and the FIFO rule (first come, first served) of queue ethics is not applied. So the first customer to arrive at the airport may be the last one to get on the plane. The queue discipline system applied is more like NIFO.[15] For example, there are lengthy neurasthenic queues that are not beneficial to anyone. The mechanism is the following. As the passengers enter the waiting room, they sit on the benches provided. However, as boarding time approaches, the nervousness rises in crescendo because the first person at the check-in desk will be the first one to board the plane. The tension mounts until a chance movement triggers a catastrophic reaction. As one man, almost all the passengers rise and rush for the queue. In just a millisecond, a hundred-person queue has been generated.[16]

Curiously enough, the company has already been informed by its terrorist customers of this and other similar effects that passengers find very inconvenient (such as the lack of space in the overhead lockers because of the massive presence of regulation-sized suitcases, complete with wheels, which are not checked in to save time). The company refuses to listen to these complaints because it thinks that its service is 'arrive and fly', that it is giving a good service and that this is enough to keep the customer happy. The complainers are an 'insignificant minority' in the opinion of Flynow's sales department.

---

in some area of activity and continues to be the best over a period of time. In any other situation, there is no stable equilibrium.

Therefore, *competing is being the best*[17] *in an area that generates satisfaction for our customer.* Only by being the best, and continuing to be the best, will the company

---

[15] The most nervous (or sometimes the most neurasthenic) first.

[16] Of course, to the detriment of the elderly, expecting mothers and non-officer military personnel.

[17] Here, being the best should be interpreted in a broad sense. It does not mean being the best in a limited aspect, such as being the best at answering the telephone, or in some internal, more economic-oriented aspect. It should be possible to convey this status of 'being the best' to the customer's perception.

be able to retain the customer's loyalty. *Being the best is our competitiveness criterion* that operationalizes the generic purpose of survival.

Defining the mission or promise

Strategy plays a mediating role between customers and the firm's operations structure. The operations structure links internal strengths and weaknesses to external opportunities and threats. Operations[18] closes the gap between the general appeal of the industry in which the firm operates and the firm's specific advantages in that market.

This is not the place to analyse the ways of defining the firm's strategy. Suffice to say that there are different methodological approaches that can put suitable tools in the reader's hands. Of course, defining a firm's strategy is an exercise that encompasses all of the firm's areas and, therefore, requires defining a comprehensive framework that covers the entire firm. This specification is the basis for establishing the framework for the firm's operating decisions. In this book, we will not consider the soundness of the firm's strategy, the manner in which it has been decided, nor even whether it has been formally defined. We will assume that somebody is capable of converting the firm's mission into a small number of criteria. This is sufficient, from a logical viewpoint, to establish an adequate operating structure.

We propose five families of criteria or *dimensions* for assessing the firm's service. Three of them are averages of certain basic dimensions of the service: *cost, time and breadth*.[19] These basic dimensions do not remain stable over time. It is also necessary to include criteria related with the rate of change. We will group them in another dimension which we will call the service's *innovation* dimension. Finally, the basic dimensions show a *variability* over time which has to be taken into account. All criteria related to the dimensions' variability over time will be grouped in another dimension, which we will call the service's *consistency* dimension. Therefore, the five dimensions are (see Figure 4.3):

1. *Cost.* Measures of efficiency associated with profits.
2. *Time.* Time taken to react to the environment.
3. *Breadth.* Planned variety, potential and real services portfolio.
4. *Innovation.* Ability to make changes in the service.
5. *Consistency.* Degree of variability between what is forecast and what actually happens.

*Details of the five dimensions

Cost. This dimension is intended to contain all the criteria related to the efficient use of resources. For the customer, the service's monetary value may be based on

---

[18] For a more precise formulation of these concepts, see Hax and Majluff [1991].

[19] The choice of dimensions is the outcome of a synthesis of the many measures found in practice and trying to reduce them to a small number of categories, seeking the most concise description possible.

price, which normally means the cost of obtaining the service. However, this simplification is misleading. If there exists a long-term interaction between the customer and the company, the assessment of the service should include other monetary elements, which are often much more important than the price. A certain car model may have a lower purchase cost but much higher maintenance costs, which erode the advantage gained by the lower purchase price in the medium term.

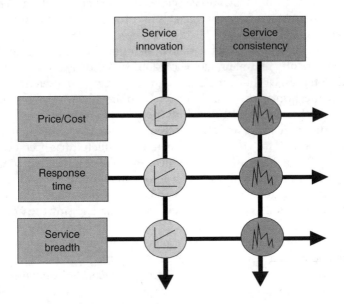

Figure 4.3   The five dimensions

Example 4.6   The dimensions in Danobat

By way of example, let us see how Danobat, a Spanish company belonging to the Mondragón group and specializing in the production of machine tools mainly for the automobile industry, defines its strategy using the five dimensions we have just listed. This company's general mission is to provide a specialized approach to product innovation and development in the field of advanced technology machine tools and capital goods.

- *Cost*, reduce the product's price.
- *Time*, decrease the time between the approval of the order and when the machine is delivered to the customer.
- *Breadth*, adapt our product offerings to our customers' individual requirements.
- *Innovation*, offer the market's latest solutions.
- *Consistency*, the specifications stated in the quotes should be clearly identifiable in the individual machines.

Time. This dimension consists of all the criteria that contain purely time parameters. One of the most important is the lead time, defined as the time between the customer request for a service and the time when the company starts to render this service. In the case of a consumer product, it is the time between when the order is received and when the customer receives his product.

Breadth or range. These are criteria related to the planned variety existing in the company's services, and in the way customers should perceive this variety. One important feature of this dimension is that it does not assess a single service (one interaction) but a portfolio of services. The company interacts with many customers to whom it may be rendering different services.

A highly specialized company has a low breadth; a highly diversified company has a high breadth. There are at least two aspects to be considered in the breadth of services. The potential breadth of services – *potential* portfolio or adaptability of the service – and the *real* breadth or the structure of the portfolio of services offered. The operations system's structure must be assessed on the basis of the potential variety – the services that *can* potentially be obtained from the existing structure. The real variety, the services that are actually being rendered, is less than the potential variety and may perhaps only amount to a minute fraction of it. We know the case of a company with a flexible, automated production line that is capable of assembling many different types of telephones but which, for various reasons, only manufactures one type. In this instance, practice has reduced the potential variety to the real variety.

Innovation. This dimension is related to the dynamics of the company's service over time. Basically, it tries to measure the company's capacity for implementing changes that improve its service. Therefore, change and improvement are two key concepts in the innovation dimension.

This dimension can include all of the rates of change of the system's other dimensions. The innovation criterion should reflect changes in service's price, response time, performance, and so on. The common denominator is *change*.

This dimension plays a very important role in the dynamic assessment of the service by the customer. It can be argued that the customer perceives the improvement in the service and expects it to be maintained. Consequently, the degree of innovation influences the rate at which the customer's expectations can change. It is a virtuous (or vicious) circle in which expectations increase proportionately to the magnitude of the change and the appreciation of the same degree of change becomes proportionately less. To maintain expectations, the company may find itself committed to a process of rapid and, sometimes, destructive change.

Consistency. This dimension introduces the scatter, in space and time, of the parameters defining the service. Any criterion has random characteristics that are produced by the interaction of hundreds of factors. These factors lead to difficulties in obtaining consistently the same result in the presence of the same actions. Consequently, most criteria are random variables in both space and time. For example, the delivery date is random. Although its mean value may be fully

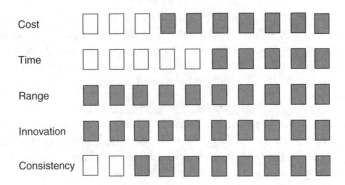

Figure 4.4   The dimensions assessed

controlled and specified, some lead times may be shorter than the average and others are longer than the average. This scatter may have marked effects on the service's goodness. Although most customers may be satisfied with the company's lead time, some – those that have suffered the extreme values of randomness – may remain unsatisfied and eventually be lost. In this case a high fluctuation will mean a continual drain of customers and a deterioration of their expectations.

In the traditional literature, it is common to see quality-related criteria under this dimension. Reliability, reproducibility, maintainability, etc., represent the need to control random phenomena and, consequently, the need to reduce uncertainty by means of procedures, methodologies or experiments that contribute to understanding and controlling the phenomenon's 'uncontrollable' aspects.

Dimensions as a management tool

The dimensions are an important management tool. Synthesizing a strategy by enumerating a few criteria and announcing priorities helps to solve concrete operating problems. Knowing that time has a higher priority than cost helps operating personnel to order the actions to be carried out.

There are many ways in which priorities can be defined. However, in our experience, it is not necessary to use complex procedures.[20] A simple procedure is shown in Figure 4.4 and explained in Example 4.7.

*The complete operating margin (COM)

The COM is *the difference between what the customer receives and what operations could give him.* It is the company's competitive cushion. Even if the customer does not receive it, the company is physically able to produce it. If competitors or

---

[20] There are plenty for those who want them, as the reader can see for himself if he takes a look at the voluminous literature on multicriteria decision making ...

Example 4.7   Quantifying the mission

> To make the task easier to perform, we usually suggest that management distribute 100 points among the 5 dimensions. This gives approximate weights for each dimension. In our previous example, if time is the most critical dimension, management can give it 50 points (50 per cent of the total assessment). The remaining 50 points are then divided between cost and consistency, giving a higher weighting to cost. The dimensions range and innovation have been omitted, not because they are unimportant but because they are not priorities for the company. Figure 4.4 shows this assessment in diagram form.

customer expectations change but remain within the COM, the same operations system can be used to deliver the new service.

The basic idea is that both the service given to the customer and the firm's purpose can be measured in terms of the same five dimensions introduced in the previous section. Both the promise and the customer's perception can also be translated into these five dimensions. Then we can compare them.

For example, let us imagine that a company promises to deliver its service within 24 hours. The customer agrees to this, receives it at the stipulated time, at the promised cost and in accordance with his expectations. However, it is possible that the company's operations system could deliver the service in just 12 hours. The company has a safety margin, a buffer, in the lead time. It does not use this time 'buffer' because it does not need it, as its customer is happy with the 24-hour lead time.

If a competitor should suddenly appear offering delivery in 18 hours, the company can react quickly, equalling or surpassing the offer and delivering in 12 hours. It has not been necessary to modify the operations structure. The company was already prepared for this and only changed its promise.

The buffers or safety margins that the company has in each of the five basic dimensions form the *complete operating margin*. Changes in operations are usually slow but a company that has no COM will have difficulty in responding to aggressive actions by competitors.

In the monetary dimension, the cost at which the customer gets the service (the cost at which he is happy) is by definition the selling price. As the minimum cost at which the company can offer the service is its direct cost, the complete operating margin is equal, in this dimension, to the company's *contribution margin*.

Operations' internal structure

So far, we have been discussing operations as a homogenous whole. In actual fact, this is not so, and it is advisable to break down the operations' contents into slightly smaller parts.

We represent the operations' contents in a sequential structure which we call the *business activities sequence (BAS)*. The BAS is an expansion of the part related with operations in Porter's (1995) *value chain*. The BAS encompasses all those activities that take place in operations from an idea to a satisfied customer. In total, there are ten activities: research, design and development, quality assurance, process design, input and output logistics, production, customised integration, keeping the promise, and continuity of the interaction. Figure 4.5 shows the BAS divided into three subchains: the design chain, the value addition chain, and the service chain.

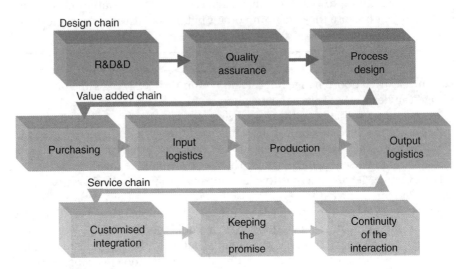

Figure 4.5   The BAS

Example 4.8   Coordinating the BAS

Coordinating the BAS

A typical case of coordination of different companies' BAS is that of the Italian furniture companies. Located in the north of Italy, these companies, most of them small, initiated a procedure that has now been imitated in many parts of the world.[21] In some circles, this system has been known as the cluster system. Each company specialized in specific activities of the BAS and all of them entered into cooperation agreements with one another to associate and reach out to the end customer together. Thus, some companies specialized in R&D, others in production, others in delivery, others in maintenance. Between them, they formed a composite BAS that was capable of delivering a very competitive service to the customer.

---

[21] The Danish government instituted a programme with official financial support in which the cooperation style was copied. The US government also did a similar thing to support small companies in the southern states.

In any company, it is possible to define the *critical* activities of its BAS. These are those activities that have the greatest influence upon the company's competitive capacity. The critical activities determine the competitive capacity of the whole. A greater competitive capacity in a non-critical activity would have little effect upon the company.

The BAS is a chain, because its weakest link limits the efficiency of the whole. All of the BAS's activities must be carried out at the right level, although the *critical* activities are those that have the greatest influence on the result. In order to *improve operations*, we must improve the BAS's critical activities.

Not all companies have all of the BAS's components. Most companies have some of these activities, but look to secure the others in agreements with other companies or in outsourcing.[22]

Although it is presented as a chain of activities, the BAS does not have a linear structure. All of the BAS's activities are closely interrelated. Design for manufacturing (DFM) is a clear example of this interrelation. DFM was invented to solve the problems that arose when a new product was designed for a robotic line. From

Example 4.9   Design for the BAS

DFB: Design for the BAS

When the Banco de Santander tried to introduce home banking about 10 years ago, it did not take into account the serious problems that this would cause in the rest of the BAS. It seems that the underlying hypothesis was that the rest of the BAS was going to remain invariant and that only the production aspects, the transformation box, would change. Things actually turned out very differently. Many of the BAS' activities changed radically. It was quickly seen that the right type of production was to be different, affecting this function. Input and output logistics were dramatically affected. Finally, and perhaps most importantly, the classic processes suffered significant distortions when they operated with the new product. The technological medium changed the way these processes were carried out. Neither the telephone system of the time[23] nor the technology proposed (Minitel) were adequate to support an idea that was original and innovative. The bank's customers spurned the service, even though the idea was very attractive.

---

[22] The authors wish this book to become a classic and to run to at least thirty editions. Consequently, they have debated heatedly whether we should mention trendy issues such as the much publicised e-business. As we foresaw when we first wrote this chapter, the e-business fad did not take long to burn out. Therefore, now is the time to talk about e-business. Two years ago, one of the authors argued that for a book to be a hit, he would have to add an 'e' in front of all the words. E-that e-is, e-talk e-about e-BAS, e-operations, e-book, e-company ...

[23] When we were 'subscribers' and not customers (of course, perhaps now we are customers but treated like subscribers).

then on, the idea has been expanded, turning it into a generic conception that seeks to simplify and accelerate the process from generating an idea to when it comes off the production line. When Cadillac applied DFM to the design of the Seville model, a 50 per cent reduction in the number of components decreased assembly time by 19 per cent, which brought benefits in purchasing (less suppliers and less transactions), production (less operations, simpler materials management, etc.), aftermarket service (less components to repair) and logistics (warehouse management and easier transportation). The DFM concept can be generalized to the entire BAS (DFB or 'Design for the BAS'). The aim is to design right so that the other activities in the design chain can be performed easily and efficiently.

*BAS: the design chain

The BAS's design chain consists of three activities: RD&D, Quality Assurance, and Process Design.

(a) RD&D

Research, development and design encompasses all of the activities that go from generation of an idea to its materialization in a product or service. It includes all aspects – functional, organic, aesthetic, and economic – ranging from the purest research work to its transformation into a product, process or procedure.

Design must not only address the BAS itself, but also the BAS of the suppliers and customers who work with the firm. To use currently prevailing jargon, it must address all of the firm's supply chain. Any modification which includes internal changes may also include changes in the service rendered by suppliers and employees.

Introduction time of a product or service

Clark (1991, 1993) proposes that a product's development should be analysed like an innovation process. Therefore, the charts which we will develop in Chapter 8 may shed light on this activity's behaviour. We will confine ourselves here to introducing a few criteria that are specific to the response time:

- *Time to product.* This is the time required for the physical creation of the product – from when someone has an idea about a service to when it is physically materialized in an efficiently reproducible manner. Here 'efficiently' may express many things, including perhaps the large-scale, economic production of the service, something which may not be achieved until long after its birth.
- *Time to acceptance.* This is the time required for the service to be assimilated by customers. Remote banking was developed as a service to streamline paperwork and reduce the number of trips to the bank. The service was conceived, designed and materialized in a software package. However, it should have been understood that in the two communication media involved, conventional

telephony and Internet connection,[24] the reaction was going to be very different. The customer was not 'educated' enough to understand what the Internet path meant and this innovation would require a long assimilation time.

To use the language of Chapter 1, the *time to product* is the result of a *problem-solving process inside* the firm. Everything that has been said there is applicable here. Therefore, there will be an exploratory component and a knowledge-based component. The degree to which each one is present determines the response time. On the contrary, the *time to acceptance* is associated with changes that take place in the *problem-solving process outside* the firm. Here, it takes more time and effort to endow the environment with the necessary knowledge to shorten the exploratory phase.

Designing a service

An important aspect in designing a service is the determination of the value of the service's different features. Classically this aspect is addressed by the value analysis techniques used in product design. In the case of services, value analysis must be generalized slightly and in this section we suggest a possible procedure.[25]

A service's features may come under different categories and can be found in varying degrees of intensity. It is typical to consider two grades of presence of a certain feature: *present* or *absent.*

The types of service features that we consider are the following:

- *Service appeal features*: those that contribute an intrinsic value if they are present, but which do no harm if they are absent. For example, personalized attention to each customer is an appeal feature.

Example 4.10 Response time

> According to a recent survey, 80 per cent of domestic video users cannot remember the function of more than six keys on the player's remote control. The other keys are divided between those that are never used but are there and look nice and those that are used after reading the manual. Even in an appliance that has been on the market for many years, the degree of exploratory problem solving may still be high, leading to frustration in the use of the device. A crucial feature of domestic video players is the degree of additional knowledge required to use them (which must be minimized).

---

[24] We wonder whether the reader has tried to communicate by Internet in Spain outside of the large cities. It is a heroic exploit, almost on a par with the crusades. One of the authors gets in such a foul mood that it is impossible to continue working with him after his frustrated attempts to be virtually present in the world.

[25] There are other very interesting approaches. For us, the most interesting is that of Shoji Shiba (Shiba *et al.*, 1993) based on Kano diagrams, of which the one presented here is a simplification. The general procedure is based upon the use of sophisticated aggregation and analysis methods, which we will describe further on.

- *Harmful features*: those that contribute a negative value to the service if they are present, but whose behaviour is neutral if they are absent. Dirt in a restaurant is a clear example of a harmful feature.
- *Proportional features*: those that contribute value if they are present and impair the service if they are absent. Speed of delivery is usually a proportional feature.
- *Inversely proportional features*: the opposite case of the above. They are negative when they are present, but the more absent they are, the more positive their contribution is. Queues are a clear example of this type of feature. The more queues there are, the worse is the service delivered. The less they are found in a service, the higher the positive rating given to that service.
- *Necessary features*: those that do not contribute value if they are present, but which have a negative influence on the service if they are absent. The inclusion of toilets in the design of any large-scale public service is a typical necessary feature.
- *Indifferent features*: their existence does not contribute any value nor do any harm to the service.

These properties are summarized in Table 4.1.

Analysing a service's value by identifying its features and classifying them in the above categories provides a comprehensive vision of the service's properties.

(b) Quality assurance

Quality assurance is composed of a group of activities intended to attain and guarantee the service's quality, maintainability, repairability and reliability. Although Chapter 7 will be specifically devoted to the quality concept, we should clearly differentiate at this stage between the concepts of quality 'control' and quality 'assurance'. By *quality control*, we mean those activities that assure that the specifications of a product or service are met. *Quality control* is confined to the detection, verification and control of the parameters defined in the specifications.

Consequently, quality control aims to ensure that *no defects reach the customer*, even though the operations system may produce them.

This concept of control does not introduce the idea of improvement in action. In Example 4.12, the control is limited to rejecting the substrates whose holes are out of tolerance. No analysis is carried out of the causes of the variability (or variation) to determine how the appearance of further defects could be prevented.

Table 4.1   An analysis for a service's properties

Types of feature	Present	Absent
Appeal	+	0
Harmful	−	0
Proportional	+	−
Inversely proportional	−	+
Necessary	0	−
Indifferent	0	0

Example 4.11 The underground service to Madrid Barajas Airport

---

Designing a Service: The Underground to Madrid Barajas Airport

The managers of the Madrid Underground and Barajas Airport contacted the authors to analyse the design of the service in the stations that connect Barajas to the centre of Madrid. This situation arose as a result of the need to improve *all* of the aspects related to air traffic from and to the capital – particularly considering the competition that air travel would have to face from the high-speed train.

The assignment's basic methodology focused upon a features analysis exercise, as described here. The systematic reflection process uses this methodology as inference knowledge and also has recourse to domain knowledge obtained from the BAS. The whole was structured as an exploratory problem-solving process. The outcome of the analysis was a variety of additional features which added considerable value to the service at very low cost. The proposals concerned the Barajas and Nuevos Ministerios stations, the transportation process itself, on-board services and pre- and post-transportation.

The exercise was completed with an estimate of the two times mentioned in the text, completion time and acceptance time. The estimate revealed the possible need for an exploratory process by some of the agents involved, leading to the identification of the knowledge which had to be added to the environment to simplify the problem-solving process. Finally, ways of providing this knowledge to the agents were proposed, special ways being required in this case because it was not possible to implement a classic training plan for the outside agents.

Example 4.12 Quality control

A Spanish company must drill holes with a diameter of 100 microns in a ceramic substrate. These holes will house the pins of integrated electronic circuits. If the hole is too large, the circuit will not be positioned correctly and if the hole is too small, the pin will not enter fully and may produce a faulty contact after soldering. We want the circuit to be correctly assembled, to make a good electrical contact and to not come loose when the substrate vibrates. Translated into specifications given by the engineering department, the hole must have a diameter of 100 microns with a tolerance of ± 5 microns. This means that if the hole has a diameter of more than 105 microns or less than 95 microns, it will not meet the required expectations. After adjusting the tools, the company starts production and regularly takes samples of the circuit boards produced, measuring the holes to check that they are being made to specification. If the statistical process gives alarm signals, all the boards are inspected one by one, discarding the faulty ones. If the statistical process indicates that everything is OK, the entire batch is accepted.

However, we can expand inspection by trying to diagnose or understand the defects' causes. When a problem appears, we look for the root of the problem in order to try to eliminate the causes.

Quality assurance encompasses all of those activities that ensure that the operations system does not *produce* defects or, to put it another way, that we do exactly what we want to do.

(c) Process design

The last activity in the design chain is process design. For efficiency reasons, the systematic obtainment of a service should never contain exploratory components. Furthermore, for consistency reasons, the variability between different performances of the same service must be as low as possible. Therefore, according to Chapter 2, knowledge must be inserted in the process.

There are many ways of inserting knowledge in operations, but the usual procedure is to *materialize* the knowledge required to solve all of the transformation's problems in the form of procedures, rules and skills that enable the processes to systematically carry out the transformations with a high level of consistency. This is the nature of the process design function.

Process design is an operation whereby process knowledge is encapsulated. Again, the obtainment of a good or service can be formulated as the solution of a series of problems. The problem is to materialize the product from the design and it must be solved using the knowledge resources available to the firm. The transformations will applied by processors[26] specialized in a range of transformations or, to put it another way, who are specialized in the solution of certain families of problems.

Although each processor has a certain stock of knowledge, normally it is not enough to solve the overall problem. Although a machine workshop may have specialized machining centres – for example, lathes, mills, shears, etc. – that can perform a very wide range of operations, the union of this knowledge is not enough to solve the overall problem of processors.

Designing a process requires a global vision of the process; it is not enough to define and design each of the subprocesses or operations of which it is composed. Designing the interfaces between operations is just as important as the operations themselves. If the resulting process is to fit smoothly into the company's strategic goal, this must be taken into account in the process's conception.

*The value addition chain

This chain consists of the following activities: purchasing, logistics (both materials input and output), and transformation (or production). It could be identified with the operating part of the supply chain, although a supply chain includes other aspects that are not considered in the BAS.

---

[26] Think about machines, shopkeepers, butchers, clerks, and so on.

(a) Purchasing or procurement

The purchasing activity includes all of those operations whose purpose is to obtain products or services meeting the required specifications as regards price, lead time, quantity and quality. Price is important because purchases very often, represents more than 50 per cent of the finished products cost. Lead time is particularly important for coordinating with production and with the end customer, and the purchases' quality and specifications have a direct effect upon the firm's service.

The main subareas in this activity are: assuring the flow of materials and services required for the firm's continued functioning; keeping stocks and waste to a minimum; finding and nurturing competitive suppliers; standardizing the items bought; and obtaining the goods and services at the right price.

Supplier relations are another critical part of the purchasing activity. Supplier policies cover a very broad range. At one extreme, there are companies who choose suppliers basically on the basis of price. When considering the purchase of a component, they ask a large number of the possible suppliers to give an estimate and finally give the order to the supplier that makes the best offer. A company who operates this way could continually change its sources of supply. These companies usually only provide information about their short-term requirements, have more than one source of supply for each component, have higher raw material stock levels, and usually do not have reporting systems integrated with their suppliers.

At the other extreme are those companies who build a long-term relationship with their suppliers, ignoring occasional short-term opportunities often they have a single-source policy which guarantees future business for their suppliers, keep their suppliers informed about future requirements, they put in place joint contingency plans and they work actively with their suppliers to improve their reliability and lead times.

A close relationship with suppliers has effects on the whole BAS. The quality assurance functions will be much simpler; the customer firm is guaranteed a flow of materials and components that meet the requirements for the production process, information interchange between the two companies is improved increasing productivity, and end customers are offered shorter lead times, increasing competitiveness.

Many companies have realized that one of the most important sources of *knowledge input* into the company takes place through suppliers. These not only offer products and services but also training in their use, that is, knowledge related with the use of products and services.

A useful approach to analyzing the purchase activity is structure it in terms of two dimensions. One considers the knowledge contents of the products or services bought. Here, people usually distinguish between two types of product: strategic and operating. *Strategic* products are accompanied by a significant knowledge content. This knowledge is provided by the supplier and is related to the way in which the product is used. To use *operating* products, low levels of knowledge are required. On the second dimension, products can be classified in two categories: direct and indirect. *Direct* products are included in the firm's service. *Indirect* products are not included in the service. *Direct products influence the firm's competitiveness.* In fact,

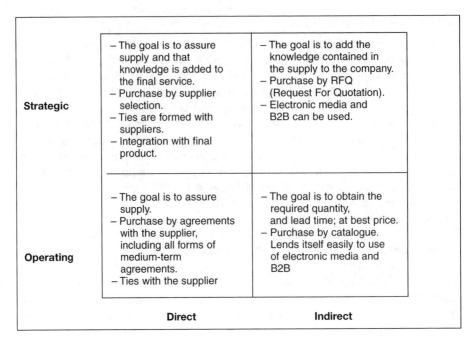

	Direct	Indirect
Strategic	– The goal is to assure supply and that knowledge is added to the final service. – Purchase by supplier selection. – Ties are formed with suppliers. – Integration with final product.	– The goal is to add the knowledge contained in the supply to the company. – Purchase by RFQ (Request For Quotation). – Electronic media and B2B can be used.
Operating	– The goal is to assure supply. – Purchase by agreements with the supplier, including all forms of medium-term agreements. – Ties with the supplier	– The goal is to obtain the required quantity, and lead time; at best price. – Purchase by catalogue. Lends itself easily to use of electronic media and B2B

Figure 4.6   Properties of purchasing

they add to the way of competing by contributing features to the service that increase its value in terms of functionality, price and lead time. Indirect products usually only add marginal value to the final service but contribute to the firm's productivity.

Figure 4.6 shows in synthesized form the properties of purchasing for each of the resulting four product categories. Of particular interest is the suitability of using, B2B-type electronic media.

(b) Logistics

The term logistics suggests the movement of things from one place to another, with storage along the way. A firm's logistics system is the body of capabilities, equipment, people and policies that enable the flow of goods – from purchase of the raw materials to distribution of the final product. The task of logistics is to design and operate the system implementing policies that enable control, coordination and efficient flow of goods. Logistics is also concerned with transportation, storage systems and stocks.

There are two types of logistics: input and output. Input logistics deals with the system that assures that the necessary resources are available for performing the operations. Output logistics deals with the same operations, but from the perspective of the need to put the product in the place chosen by the customer to use it.

Example 4.13 Logistics in action

Logistics in Action

Through logistics, firms can face challenges, create value and increase their market share and earnings. An example are selling procedures where logistics is totally integrated in the sale action. This is the case of presale or direct sale, extensively used in drink distribution to pubs, or in domestic heating fuel. In these situations, a well-designed distribution network as regards number of vehicles and route, depending upon their customers' demand, will have a significant influence on the firm's sales.

Firms that sell through the Internet usually have their Achilles heel in logistics. The most successful firms are those that can use the Internet for the moving of their services. Companies like Amazon.com lose money above all because of the need to maintain complicated (warehouses, transportation, and so on) and often poorly managed logistics systems.

The possibility of using economies of scale in transportation and the pressure to reduce the cost of moving goods, which adds little value to the final product, give rise to complicated handling processes, increasing service lead times. This is the case with many companies producing in the Far East.

Typical logistics operations are: picking (retrieving products from the warehouse to make up shipments for complete orders), packing, palleting (loading on pallets to facilitate product handling), loading and unloading, distribution (splitting large shipments into components in distribution centres), and so on.

Logistics technology is sophisticated – from the simplification of transport operations to product storage and picking in the warehouse, and requires sophisticated software and hardware.

This leads some to propose logistics as being a separate area from operations. The same people recommend outsourcing logistics to specialists. In our opinion, this is often true but one should not lose control of the logistics system. It is an important part of the BAS and may easily become the weakest link.

There are two basic alternatives in designing a logistics system: push or pull. A *pull* system concentrates on reducing the time to perform the activities once the customer's order is received. With a fast turnround in order deliveries, it is not necessary to hold large stocks; the quantities required can be produced and sent quickly within the lead time required by the customer. Each level in the supply chain may hold small inventories which are monitored by stock control policies triggered by the demand from the levels below. This is the system typically used by companies that have implemented just-in-time procedures.

The *push* system forecasts requirements, prepares plans and send the items to the distribution system's intermediate nodes in advance and on the basis of demand forecasts. The forecast is usually carried out in a coordinated manner in order to unify criteria and provide estimates of future demands and their time sequence. Those systems rely heavily on the intensive use of computer applications (MRP or DRP[27]).

(c) Transformation or production

The last activity in the value chain is transformation. Transformation is the process by inputs are turned into finished products. In other words, the process of using resources to change the state and condition of certain 'materials' and obtain final products or services. Having defined the transformation process and secured each activity's input and output elements, the mission of production is to guarantee the efficient performance of this transformation activity.

*The service chain

The service chain has undergone dramatic changes in recent years. From being a kind of Cinderella topic, it has now become the star of the BAS. All firms have a service chain and they can use it to gain significant differential advantages.

Automobiles are bought for their effectiveness and functionality, but also for their service chain. The reader could similarly consider his washing machine, his fridge and many other items that are in daily use. When the purchasing decision is made, one thinks about general features but the existence of maintenance and repair services is an important consideration. There are companies who use their service chain to stand out from their competitors. The El Corte Inglés department stores position their service chain as one of the key differential features in their relationship with the customer. In this department store chain, customers buy for the added value perceived in the 'No questions asked' refund policy, free installation and service warranty.

The service chain includes activities associated with commissioning, customer satisfaction with the product or service-including user training-physical installation and advice during use. It is also concerned with all the aftermarket activities which guarantee that the product/service performs as defined as advertised, both when new and during the estimated (by the customer) service life. It includes warranty fulfilment activities, repairs, upkeep, and other related activities. Finally, the service chain includes upgrading activities, adapting to new uses and, in general, all of those aspects that supplement and complement the product/service.

Many firms are using this type of activity in order to win new customers. Thus, for example, there are warranty contracts that remain in force even if the product is resold, with the original supplier continuing to provide the necessary support to the new owner. Further, some department store chains have expanded their maintenance department so that they can repair not only the products they sell but also those of other manufacturers.

The service chain is formalized in three main activities: customized integration, keeping the promise, and continuity of the interaction.

---

[27] Distribution resource planning, a kind of MRP but reaching further down the logistics chain. More of the same ...

Example 4.14 CRM

CRM

It has become fashionable to talk about customer relationship or resource management (CRM). Although firms all over the world have been doing this for many years, the phrase stresses individualized attention to customers through the use of information technologies.

A clear example of how this is achieved with the help of technology is the Ritz Carlton hotels' information system. In these hotels, all customers are individualized according to their customs and preferences so as to be able to give them a more individualized treatment. To achieve this goal, all the hotel employees who come into contact with the customer try to identify his preferences and enter them in an information system that is available throughout the hotel network when that customer returns to the same hotel – or to any other hotel in the chain.

(a) Customized integration

The core element of customized integration is the individualization of the service. A specific aspect of this function is installing the product in the customer's home. A good installation avoids problems, produces a knowledge transfer towards the customer and, in general, helps the customer to arrive at a truer determination of the value of his purchase. However, this function goes much further, including matching the product to each customer (mass customization) and all of the operating aspects which lead to individualized attention. Customers do not want to be a number – they want to be identified and attended to individually. And this is a very complicated thing to do when the number of customers is very large, with a high turnover. Consequently, the core elements of this activity are all of the operations that are associated with the service delivery process and the measurement of this process.

(b) Keeping the promise

The activity of keeping the promise includes all of those activities that ensure that the product or service remains functional throughout the entire period it is planned to enjoy it. In the case of products, the product must be kept operating in the same condition as on the day it was bought, over the course of the product's expected lifetime.

These activities are normally associated with the physical maintenance of the product or service and with the identification of the image held of the company by the customer. This activity enables firms to differentiate themselves by, for example, their 'greenness' or environment-friendliness. There are many hotels who ask customers not to leave their towels for laundering every day in order to help maintain the ecological balance.[28]

---

[28] And, of course, reduce their costs.

This activity must contain a decision-making capacity with the customer, the existence of suitable tools to perform this, and a server profile matched to these requirements.

(c) Continuity of the interaction

Finally, the service chain must consider those activities that update and upgrade the product's features, that is, it must enable the customer to fully exploit all the service that the product can give. The idea is that the customer buys company, not a specific product or service. Therefore, this activity must include 'lock-in' actions which ensure that the customer is provided a suitable services portfolio by the firm.

People talk a lot about customer loyalty programmes. The authors think that this is a rather funny concept, which suggests that obstacles will be placed in the customer's way to prevent him escaping from the company's clutches. In our opinion, the best loyalty programme is a good service. The customer does not need locking mechanisms, nor should they exist from an ethical viewpoint. So long as the company gives him the best service, the customer will remain loyal. If it doesn't, there is no loyalty mechanism that can possibly keep him happily chained to the company. Many travel companies give points and loyalty cards and then treat their customers like dirt. The best loyalty mechanism is obtained through the satisfactory continuity of the customer–company interaction and not in the awarding of points.

5
The Basic Variables of Action in Operations (I)

An operations system is a highly complex element, probably the most complex to be found in any firm. Although the BAS provides an initial simplification, each activity in the BAS is also complex in itself. Most of the distinctive knowledge held by the firm will be found and used in operations. Firms have relatively similar financial, accounting, personnel and even sales systems, using almost identical knowledge. However, the operations system, and its BAS, is unique to each company. Its activities use product, process and management knowledge which are often unique.

Therefore, it may seem very complicated to synthesize and diagnose many activities of the BAS. And this may indeed be the case if the correct level of aggregation is not chosen. The pitfalls are either concentrating too much on the details or, on the contrary, being excessively general. Through the detail, we can venture into the description of the nitty-gritty of operations. Since there can be several hundred or several thousand operations in an operations system at any one time, an exhaustive description is usually out of place. Excessive aggregation leads to schematism and an inability to distinguish the essential features that make the system work.

Experience shows that it is possible to develop an intermediate-level description that is sufficient for most purposes but which, at the same time, can be refined to enable the entire operating improvement process to be structured around it. It is possible to identify just six decision variables which are sufficient to define the structure of any activity in the BAS. This description is based upon conceptualizing each activity in the BAS as a continuous stream of transformation activities, which consume inputs and produce services. To use an everyday example, we conceive each activity as a tube that transforms input – which enters the tube at one end – into the desired output obtained from the other end. This analogy may be rather unscientific,[1] but it is extremely useful. Conceived in this way, structuring an activity in the BAS is like building the tube that transports it. The six properties that are typical of any tube are shown in Figure 5.1.

---

[1] And it almost embarrasses us to include it in a serious book like this.

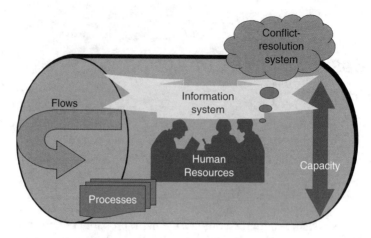

Figure 5.1   The tube and the variables

1. The structure of the processes.
2. The structure and sizing of the capacity.
3. The structure and composition of the flows.
4. The structure of the human resources.
5. The information system.
6. The conflict-resolution system.

Each activity in the BAS can be described using only these six variables. Therefore, the six variables provide a high level taxonomy of the operating problems. A systematic analysis of these variables ensures that most of the problems associated with each specific activity in the BAS are questioned. However, it is also possible to associate a specific questioning methodology with each variable – a methodology that can be translated into procedures, questionnaires and rules of action by means of which it is possible to carry out a thorough diagnosis of the situation without having to be an expert in each one of the individual parts of the activity.

Specifying the variables

In this section, we will describe in some detail the nature of the variables, leaving the detailed analysis of their functioning and effect to a later point. Although we present them sequentially, in ideal conditions the variables' values should be determined simultaneously as all of them are interrelated.

- *Processes.* These are the *transformations* within the tube. The reader will remember that the idea of processes as materializations of knowledge has already been discussed in Chapter 2. The emphasis there was on the knowledge contained in processes. Here we are basically interested in the elementary transformations' effectiveness and the effect that their combination in different configurations may have on productivity and competitiveness. To obtain a service, a series of manoeuvres or transformations must be performed on the system's inputs. We will call these manoeuvres *operations*. This is a primitive concept, difficult to describe precisely, because what an operation is may depend on the degree of aggregation with which the problem is viewed. For national accounting, steel production is an operation which takes coal, ore, flux, etc., as inputs and produces different types of steel as an output. For the production scheduler in a steel plant, the operations are much more detailed, perhaps including the blast furnace, the converters and other items of equipment. For the maintenance foreman, the operations are even more detailed, involving discrete activities: open valve, close gate, etc. In each case, what an operation is depends upon the elementary capacities, the knowledge, held by the *processor* performing it. It must be possible to perform an operation with the knowledge held by the processor. For example, if the processor is a computer, an operation may be an instruction. The computer understands the operation and is able to perform it without any further decomposition. We order our computer to 'add 3 and 2' (in its language 3 + 2). And the computer will add. If we ask it to build a bridge, an intelligent computer should answer 'how?'. It needs the process – the programme that tells it how to combine its elementary capacities to achieve the goal that has been proposed. What an operation is and what a process is therefore depends on the knowledge held by the processor who must perform them. At a high level of abstraction, for a processor who possesses considerable knowledge, a complex process may be an operation. However, when the processor is not perfect, and must improve and learn, it is advisable to apply the old Cartesian method of breaking the process down into component parts. And this decomposition leads us to operations.

- *Capacity*. The tube's *width*. Technically speaking, this is the maximum output rate that the system can attain – or, to use more business-like terms, the maximum product or service that we can produce per unit of time. As we will see, capacity is a multidimensional concept and a thorough analysis will reveal a considerable degree of complexity. Superficially, this appears to be a simple concept, which is easy to measure and quantify. However, this is not the case at all. Many operations decisions concern capacity. From employing another worker to subcontracting work to third parties or working overtime, these are all capacity decisions. It could be argued that all operations decisions are about acquisition or use of capacity.[2] It is not easy to design capacities, as can be seen in the many badly designed situations that one finds in real life – airports where horribly long queues form to catch a taxi, hospitals that collapse at the beginning of holiday periods, etc. Problems involving lack of capacity usually manifest though the appearance of waiting lines. Many of the hold-ups observed in operations can be traced to capacity forecasting and management problems. And many services are affected by waiting lines![3]

---

[2] The reader would do well to think about this statement because it will help him to understand the nature of the phenomenon. However, once he has thought about it, he should forget it quickly before he slides into futile generalization.

[3] If the reader should see either author at any public place, we can provide objective proof that we spend a significant percentage of our lives waiting because of lack of capacity!

- *Flows.* The manner in which the items (materials, customers, and so on) *flow* within the tube. Think about how water flows in a river. The river can be described in many ways but a very precise image is obtained by describing the structure of its current, its still pools, its rapids, the rate at each point and the different parts where water accumulates in the river. Describing the river is to describe the structure of the water transit times and the stocks created by this structure. Just like in our tube. All flowing items generate stocks. All items show a specific structure of waiting times. The only difference with respect to the river is that, in our system, several types of fluid (several types of item) flow simultaneously. Some authors identify five different flows in any system (Forrester, 1961). These are (different types of) materials, customers, orders, information and money. Therefore, it is not sufficient to describe each item's flow structure (in terms of stocks and times). It is also necessary to define the manner in which the different items share the system. The reader can therefore deduce that flows are a dynamic reflection of capacities. When capacities vary over time, and process rates too, flow analysis is basically the study of the capacity's dynamics.
- *Human resources.* The most important feature of most processors is their capacity. However, there is a particular type of processor with special dynamic features which requires an individualized analysis. This processor is the operations' people or human resources. This book is not the right place[4] to discuss the behavioural features of human resources. That job is more properly left to the experts in industrial psychology. What we are interested in here are the individual's three operational features – features that interact and determine the individual's effectiveness within the operations system. The three distinctive capabilities of these 'free processors are': their *freedom*, their ability to *generate knowledge* and learn, and, finally, their ability to *use the knowledge* that they possess (their intelligence[5]). Analysing the three distinctive features of human resources sheds light on the manner in which the processor will behave in the operation and, consequently, on the operations' dynamic behaviour.
- *Information system.* We now come to the variables that control the system's behaviour. Human resources are processors that are able to make decisions. In any firm, the number of operating decisions is very high. Considered in isolation, most of them are probably fairly insignificant but together, operating decisions are very important for competitiveness. Any delay in starting a certain operation for an order may mean that the order is not delivered on time. Well, anyone can have a bad day. But if wrong decisions are made systematically or full use is not made of the existing capacity, any number of orders may be delayed, which is very damaging for the firm's competitiveness. When there are many interrelated decisions, the problem arises of how to coordinate them. *One of the necessary conditions for coordination is that each of the agents has the necessary information to make decisions.* This information should reflect the effect of

---

[4] And neither author feels he or she has the moral authority to address this task…
[5] We use here Aristotle's definition of teleological intelligence as 'the ability to use knowledge for a purpose'.

all of the other decisions. This is why the information system is so important. Of course, one could philosophize endlessly about information systems for operations. A lot has been written on the subject and a lot more has yet to be written. However, to improve the operations system, it is not necessary to go into any detail about these aspects. The main point to be considered at this time is how operating decisions can be distributed and coordinated.

- *Conflict-resolution system.* The information system coordinates the movement of information between the operations' decision makers. However, each decision maker faces an individual need to decide in the way that is best for the firm's competitiveness, given the information available. We have already seen in Chapter 2 that each agent has, at least conceptually, a truth maintenance system (TMS) that enables him to infer results from his knowledge base and, in particular, from the firm's rules base. These rules are materializations of knowledge, ready for immediate use by the agent; they encapsulate knowledge not held by the decision maker but which can be used to support (or constrain) him. Sometimes, they form part of the firm's 'culture'[6] – unwritten rules, criteria we 'believe' in, procedures which are sanctioned as 'exemplary' or 'correct'. And sometimes they crystallize, they become obsolete and, rather than providing support for those who must decide, they act as a constraint on operations. It is very important to identify the rules that already exist and create those that are required for the optimal functioning of operations. This is the scope of the variable we are considering here: the analysis of 'why we make this decision like this and how should we make it in order to do it better ...'.

This concludes our brief description of each of the variables. If the reader wishes to explore them in greater depth, he should read the detailed description given below. In each case, we briefly present the conceptual rationale of their analysis. In addition, we include management checklists that seek to give a broader view of the type of issue that general management should consider in each case.

*Analysing processes

The content of the first action variable revolves around processes and their redefinition. The subject of process analysis has become very popular since the massive publicity given to process re-engineering.[7] However, few people realize that these ideas date back to the pioneering work carried out in industry at the beginning of the twentieth century. The pioneering works by Taylor (1911) and Gilbreth (1972) were ahead of their time. As so often, re-reading the classics helps deepen our knowledge and understanding of a problem.

The world of processes has been extensively studied in industry. However, it is only now that people are starting to carefully analyse the service firm's processes.

---

[6] Although we are not very sure what this means.

[7] In a process re-engineering study, the processes are analysed taking into account:

(a) Whether several tasks can be combined into one.

(b) Whether the workers have any decision-making capacity.

In the services world, the elementary (or unit) operations often have a much lower technical content than is the case in industry. Filling in a form is an operation that almost everyone feels capable of doing. The same can be said about making a sandwich. It does not seem necessary to pay attention to something that is so 'known' or trivial.[8]

However, this perception is unfounded. An intuitive approach to operations leads to a high degree of variability in both the results and the resulting service. Two omelettes made using the same intuitive approach may differ considerably in their presentation and taste. The intuitive approach relies to a large extent on the operators' know-how. If the processors do not carry out the operation to perfection, because they lack the necessary knowledge, then knowledge must be inserted in the system by means of a decomposition and redefinition of the processes performed. The process's components must be examined in order to assure the outcome of the operations. Companies like McDonald's or Burger King have departments that specialize in process design, and this function is highly formalized. These departments calculate how often the cooked French fries or hamburgers must be replaced so that the customer does not receive them cold, how long the meat takes to grill, etc.

In small companies which start developing a service activity that is more or less new for employees – for example, pizza deliveries – the business's basic service is initially implemented by means of intuitive operations. Then, as the firm progresses, the process is gradually refined, putting into practice what they have learned.

The process design function has also undergone considerable development in clerical tasks, essentially because the introduction of computers or automation has made it necessary to review the methods or processes used. Re-engineering has played a significant part in furthering these ideas – in some cases achieving spectacular results through the systematic analysis of a process and its structure.

However in recent years, the indiscriminate use of classic process redesign 'à la Hammer' (Hammer, 1992) has led, for example, to the excessive outsourcing of activities. The company loses so many things in its enthusiasm to concentrate on

---

(c) Whether the process's steps are performed 'naturally' or whether they can be performed simultaneously.

(d) Whether there are flexible processes that take into account the problem's degree of difficulty.

(e) Whether the task is performed at the most efficient time in order to achieve a higher level of rationalization.

(f) Whether controls are reduced.

(g) Whether the number of external contacts with the customer is reduced: a single contact point for greater efficiency.

(h) The process's custodian; contact point with the customer, he must have the information to solve the problem.

(i) Search for technological efficiency: The value of technology not as a replacement but as a means for opening up new horizons – enabling technologies.

[8] Compared with a typical chemical operation, such as 'flocculation'.

what is essential that becomes too thin,[9] losing the capacity for interdisciplinary enrichment. It becomes a load of people specialized in just one thing or a 'hollow company'.

Two ideas dominate the process diagnosis methodology that we introduce below. The first is that everybody within the firm must be able to perform process analysis – not just a select few who decide *how* things must be done. To ensure the full exploitation of the knowledge base existing in the firm, everyone who has knowledge must contribute to the result. This introduces the *need* to perform process design in a distributed manner, in which the process designer basically plays the role of a facilitator rather than a decision maker.

The second key idea is the emphasis on the *competitiveness* of the outcome of the redesigning exercise, rather than on its efficiency. Process redesigning should be focused on today's customer, but always keeping one eye on tomorrow's customer. It must create learning within the firm, by generating knowledge that can be transformed into future competitive advantage.

In the following pages, we will present a methodology for process analysis. The methodology identifies four stages:

1. Description of the current situation.
2. Questioning the process: the WWWWH technique.
3. Proposing modifications.
4. Using technology to facilitate the process.

Description of the current situation

We propose the decomposition of a process into its elementary units (operations) and then an examination of the manner in which these operations are performed. Therefore, our initial goal is to identify the process's operations and the way in which they are combined in the baseline situation. This will enable us to generate new ways of carrying out operations, which we will finally assemble into a new, coherent process. As the process is also an activity when viewed at the right level of aggregation, the techniques that question individual activities can also be used to question the entire process.

There are many ways of breaking a process down into its individual components. However, most of them eventually lead to some kind of chart. Although graphic representation is not strictly necessary in all cases, its use requires a certain decomposition methodology and, above all, facilitates subsequent questioning both by the analyst himself and by other people. In recent years, highly sophisticated computerized decomposition techniques have been developed. Some of these enable the simultaneous creation of a computerized model of the process, which can be subsequently used to simulate and validate the process.[10]

---

[9] Anorexic, some would say.
[10] Some of these methods are GRAI and SEM (Wallace *et al.*, 1987; see also Larios, 1995). There has been considerable interest in these more complex techniques but, so far, the results have been rather disappointing.

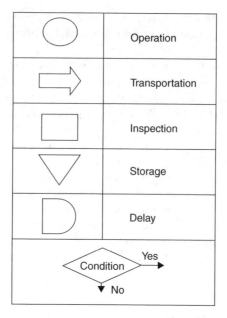

Figure 5.2   Process symbols

However, most of these techniques are too complex to be of any practical worth to the unskilled user. We recommend[11] a simple charting technique that is used routinely in industry but more rarely in services. Its main advantage lies in its simplicity, which enables it to be used by anyone and, in our experience, successfully.

The technique is a condensed visual representation of a process's sequence of stages in which five categories are used to classify all of its activities. The five categories employed are intended to draw the analyst's attention to the types of activity which can be eliminated or modified with the least disruption. The activities categories are represented graphically using standard symbols (see Figure 5.2).

The classes of activities associated with these symbols are defined as follows:

1. *Operations*. Activities that imply the transformation or handling of products or services that are used to obtain the final service.
2. *Transportation*. Activities that imply the physical movement of elements used or produced by the process from an origin location to a destination location.
3. *Inspection*. An activity involving verification of any of the features of the element being processed. Normally, this does not imply the element's modification.
4. *Storage*. A planned delay in the flow of the elements treated by the process. The delay is planned when its existence forms part of a technical or economic goal pursued by the process.

---

[11] This technique was originated by F.W. Taylor. Using his studies, Lilian and John Gilbreth refined the method, adding new categories of elementary operations and introducing certain symbols called 'Therblig' to represent them.

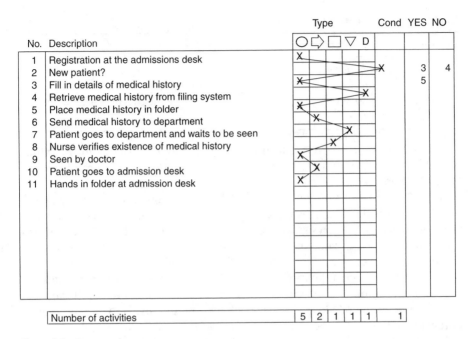

Figure 5.3 Process chart

5. *Delay.* Any incidental delay in the process which is not planned but happens because of some circumstance.
6. *Decision.* A simple two-path decision based on a single (perhaps composite) condition.

The decomposition and charting technique consists of identifying the different operations contained in the process, listing them on a purpose-made form and recording in the case of each one the type of activity involved. The result is a complete list of activities, classified by order of performance, together with their type. As we have said, the list provides an initial basis for subsequent criticism. The example given in Figure 5.3 gives a simplified breakdown of the process of treating visits to a clinic.

Questioning the process: the WWWWH technique

The process must now undergo detailed scrutiny in order to determine whether everything that is done contributes in one way or other to the firm's mission. There are many ways in which one can question the process. Many people prefer to use their intuition and view the process from different viewpoints, seeking to understand their unity. These approaches may be very useful if the analyst is familiar with them. However, in many circumstances, the person who must question the process needs a simple technique that ensures that he does not leave out any of the important things that must be considered and which works well, irrespective of the user's training. One of these techniques – and the authors' favourite – is

Table 5.1   Questionnaire for an activity

Question	Answer
Why is registration performed?	Because it is necessary to know each patient's details
Why is it necessary to know the details?	To retrieve the patient's medical history.
Why…?	So that the doctor can read it.

the five question or WWWWH technique, whose name derives from the initials of each of the five questions that the 'questioner' must ask continuously: 'Why? Where? When? Who? How?'

The WWWWH technique consists of interrogating each of the process's operations with the five questions. In practice, there are a number of different ways in which this analysis can be performed. For example, one school proposes starting by applying the 'why' test to each activity, iterating it on each answer up to a total of four times. Thus, the analyst asks 'why' four times consecutively for each activity. Of course, the exercise does not consist of answering the question more or less satisfactorily, but of questioning each of the answers. For example, in the previous case, we could choose the first activity 'Registration at the admissions desk' and perform the test on it, as in Table 5.1.

As can be seen, the questioning has led to the root of the need for the operation. The purpose of the registration operation is to obtain information for the doctor. The questioning continues, asking ourselves whether there are better ways of obtaining this information. Where is it done? Must it be done there? How is it done? Are there better ways of doing it? And so on. By this means, the method scrutinizes the operation until its structure is changed or the present structure is accepted (if there is no better way of doing it).

According to some authors (Van Gundy, 1984), this is the most useful technique for redefining a process, because it provides a systematic way of compiling and analysing the process's most relevant data. According to the same author, the disadvantage of the technique is that it is time-consuming and may seem somewhat tedious.

However, this criticism is only valid when the same analyst must scrutinize all the operations, as in the top-down approach. This situation does not arise when the process of questioning is allocated among different people in the organization. Consequently, with our approach, it becomes a very attractive tool to use. Normally, each question is accompanied by a checklist of subsidiary questions that have relevance for the overall question under consideration.

Forms

One systematic way of applying the technique is to use a form (sometimes written on a blackboard, especially when the exercise is being performed by a group), as in Table 5.2. On this form, the activities are listed one by one and the answers to each question are recorded. As the activity is questioned, a record is made both of the diagnosis and of the creative alternatives that appear.

Table 5.2 Form

	Question	Diagnosis	Alternatives
Why	1. What is done? 2. Why is it done? 3. Is it necessary? 4. Could it be eliminated? 5. Could it be replaced by a simpler process? 6. Could it be combined with another? 7. Could it be outsourced? 8. What should be done?		
Where	1. Where is it done? 2. Why is it done there? 3. Could it be located later on? 4. Could it be done without the customer knowing that it was being done? 5. Where should it be done?		
When	1. When is it done? 2. Why is it done then? 3. Is it always necessary? 4. Does it interfere with another process's flow? 5. Could it be done less often? 6. Does it add value to the service? 7. Where else could it be done?		
Who	1. Who does it? 2. Why does that person do it? 3. What qualifications are needed? 4. Could this person be replaced by someone less qualified? 5. Could a subcontractor do it? 6. Could a machine do it?		
How	1. How is it done? 2. Why is it done that way? 3. How else could it be done? 4. How should it be done?		

*The use of knowledge

Knowledge makes a process much more efficient and effective. Therefore, when analysing processes, it is important to determine how the firm's knowledge can be applied to improving its operations. This subject has already been discussed in Chapter 1 and there is little we can add at this point. Suffice to say that the approach of considering technologies as 'enablers', a core approach in the work of some authors (Hammer, 1992), is subsumed in the more general approach we have presented. Consequently, the aim should be to apply any *knowledge* to improving an operation.

Table 5.3 Management checklist of processes

1. The problem: synonyms	—Where do I place the emphasis, on machines or men? Should I automate? —What type of machines, production centres or production lines should I have? —What type of operations must my processors perform?
2. Alternatives	Mainly manual operation. —Specialized, low-output machines —Polyvalent, high-volume, high-efficiency machines —Flexible machines —Combined machine centres —Integrated, computer-controlled systems —Structure of the production operations —Repetitive? —Different each time, with a high degree of creativity? —Can they be grouped in categories, types?

3. Form of assessment	1. Operating properties
	   —Level of investment and their financial valuation.
	   —What are the machine set-up times?
	   —Difficulty in the operations and their effects on the quality and number of people.
	   —Costs and times involved in maintenance, repairs, replacements, etc.
	   —Set-up times, unit costs and learning curves.
	2. Relationship with criteria
	   —Effect on the type of orders I can have.
	   —What do my processes contribute to the assessment of the criteria?
	   —How do they affect the capacity to introduce new products?
	3. Relationship to the firm's knowledge
	   —Must my staff be able to learn many skills that are continually changing?
	   —What permanent problem-solving capacity does my staff have?
	   —Is my differential my staff's skills?

4. General policies	1. My differential are my people and their knowledge.
	2. Maintain a classic, mixed man-machine type of process.
	3. The firm wants flexible automation and little highly skilled labour.
	4. I am going to invest in large-scale automation (high efficiency).
	5. The process rate is set by the machine or the transportation system.
	6. The process rate is set by the personnel:
	   —totally
	   —with restrictions

*Analysing capacity

In this section, we present a capacity analysis technique which can be used to diagnose the problems associated with the capacity of the BAS's functions. The basic idea is that each individual processor has a capacity that can be easily calculated when it processes a certain item. However, the capacity of the system, of all the processors taken together depends upon their individual capacities and the relationships between each one. Even if a processor is very fast, it is possible that the system's total output may be limited by a slower processor that interrelates with the former. The total production capacity is therefore the result of the different processors' interaction with the items they must process and the demands made by the latter on the former. We need to take the processors' individual features and combine them in an adequate manner to diagnose the entire system. To simplify, in this section we will consider that all operations are performed at a constant rate and in a consistent manner over time. Although this virtually never happens, the high degree of comprehension of the phenomenon that is obtained with this hypothesis justifies its use.

From the technical viewpoint, we will be performing an *analysis of average capacities on the long term*. This is because, in this analysis, the processor's instantaneous rates are not important. Only their average, long-term rates are. If a machine operates for four hours producing 1,000 units an hour and stops for another hour for maintenance, the machine's average (long-term) rate is $4,000/5,000 = 800$ units an hour. Even though in actual fact it has never made 800 units in an hour!

Basics: processors, operations and capacity

The main objects in capacity analysis are:

- *Items.* These are the elements that are produced in the system under consideration. For instance, in the purchasing function, the different items may be different product lines to be bought. In an airport, it may be different types of traveller, who exhibit different habits in the use of the various processors that constitute the airport. Each item requires a certain process or sequence of operations that are to be performed by the system's processors.
- *Processors.* As we have already said, these are unit elements capable of performing transformation operations. Each processor can carry out a certain number of operations – a concept which we have already analysed. These operations consume processor capacity. Generally speaking, we assume that the process time for a certain operation performed on a certain item is known. Often, particularly in the case of service operations, this process time is random (irregular and variable) over the different units of an item. This does not mean that it cannot be measured. It is simply measurable in distribution, so that only the probability law that represents the phenomenon can be known.
- *Capacity.* Each processor has an average capacity. This capacity is the maximum average output that the processor can perform in an unit of time – boxes per month, for example, in the case of a machine that packages coffee. This average

capacity can be expressed in many different ways. A typical one is in units of a certain item. For example, a cashier can attend to 50 people an hour. Of course, there is one minor problem with stating the capacity in this manner. If the item to be processed changes – if the type of customer changes in the example – it is no longer so easy to estimate the new items' production capacity. For this reason, we prefer to adopt a simpler approach. A processor's capacity will be measured *by the number of standard[12] hours available for carrying out production during a certain period of time*. For example, our worker may have a production capacity of 8 hours a day. Or 40 hours a week. Or one hour in an hour... Why not? One advantage of this system is that two identical processors have a joint capacity of 2 hours per hour, three processors have a capacity of 3 hours per hour, etc. These capacities are very easy to calculate. On the other hand, there are efficient people who have a capacity of 1.2 hours per hour (they are capable of working at a rate of 120 per cent of the standard). The cost of this simplicity is that the capacity consumptions must be estimated in the same units in which the capacity was measured. We will look at this in the next paragraph.

- *Capacity consumptions*. In each operation, a processor working on a particular item consumes a certain amount of its capacity. This consumption can be estimated by the processor time required to carry out the operation. In the case of our friend the cashier, the processor time consumed by a customer is $60/50$[13] = 1.2 minutes per customer. For each operation, each item's process time must be estimated for each type of processor. There are many ways in which this estimate can be performed – from manual timing systems to synthetic time methods based on computer simulations.

We can now turn to the analysis of capacities. The basic idea is expressed by the 'formula':

> For all processors:
>
> Capacity used by the items <= Processor's available capacity

However, the capacity used by the items depends on each one's output, so we can say:

> | Capacity of one processor used by the items | = | Sum over all the items of (Item's capacity consumption in the processor × Number of units to be produced) |
> |---|---|---|

The way in which the number of units produced is given will lead to two types of analysis. If the desired production of the different items is given, we can determine

---

[12] A standard hour is the amount of work that a standard worker can produce 12 per hour. And what is a standard worker? As always, all agreement and a definition. In analogy with other standards, we could say that a standard worker is a worker preserved in the Louvre Museum of Weights and Measures...

[13] Remember that we have said that the cashier could attend to 50 people per hour.

what capacity is required to obtain it. In this case, we are dealing with a load or feasibility analysis for a production plan.

By contrast, if the units to be produced are not initially stated – only giving, for example, the percentages of each item that must be produced – the system's maximum output can be calculated on the basis of the existing capacities. In this case, we are dealing with a bottleneck (or scarce resources) analysis, we concentrate on this case below.

An example of bottleneck analysis

The Eco travel agency organizes trips to Ecuador. This country has a rich natural and historic heritage, and any trip that would cover everything that the country has to offer would be excessively long. Therefore, to adjust the supply to the expected type of customer, the agency has designed a series of packages offering different experiences.

There are three types of package:

- Fauna package (FP), which stresses the observation of animals in their natural habitat.
- Nature package (NP), which concentrates on exceptional scenery (such as the Amazon jungle).
- Culture package (CP), which shows visitors the country's history and culture.

To simplify, we will assume that the company operates the following resources:

- A log cabin complex in the Amazon jungle (AJ).
- A hotel in Quito (HQ).
- A ship at the Galapagos Islands (GS).

We will dispense with the distinction between single and double rooms, assuming that there are only double rooms and that these always contain two people.[14] The log cabins in the jungle offer a total of 40 rooms, the hotel has 120 rooms and the ship has 40 cabins. Each package is composed of consumptions of no more than the three resources listed.

> The system's items are the three packages FP, NP and CP. The processors are the resources AJ, HQ and GS.

Each item's composition and its capacity consumptions are given by the following 'Route Sheet'.[15] Observe that in practice there could be successive visits to the same group of processors (a possibility which is not considered in Table 5.4).

---

[14] Only stable couples are allowed. In that way, we avoid any promiscuity...

[15] This is the name given in industrial practice to the sheets that specify an item's route, the operations performed on it and in which processors. Normally, they contain information on each operation's capacity consumptions. Of course, the text version is highly simplified. The graphic format we use is very easy to see, but it quickly becomes tedious when they are many possible routes. In such cases, the tabular format must be used.

Table 5.4 Route sheet

	FP	NP	CP
AJ	2 nights at the log cabin complex.	4 nights at the log cabin complex.	
HQ	2 nights in Quito	1 night in Quito	5 nights in Quito
GS	5 nights in Galápagos	3 nights in Galápagos	2 nights in Galápagos

Table 5.5 Capacity analysis 1

	FP	NP	CP
AJ	2	4	
HQ	2	1	5
GS	5	3	2

Table 5.6 Capacity analysis 2

	FP	NP	CP	Capacity
AJ	2	4		40
HQ	2	1	5	120
GS	5	3	2	40
Mix	0.4	0.4	0.2	

To analyse the capacities, we will construct a table based on the diagram above (Table 5.5), in which each row represents a processor and each column an item. Where a row and a column intersect, the item's consumption capacity in the processor is indicated,[16] that is, the (standard) duration of the stay.

We complete the data, by adding to the right edge of the previous table (Table 5.6) the processors' capacity, in this case, the total number of rooms available for AJ, HQ and GS.

A room is a single processor with a capacity of one night per day. Therefore, on the basis of the remarks in the previous section, the total capacities are numerically equal to the number of rooms.

Finally, we add a final row in which we place the percentage share that we want each product to have in the company's product mix. In this case, we would like to have 40 per cent of fauna package (FP), 40 per cent of nature package (NP) and 20 per cent of culture package (CP) (see Table 5.7).

We can now readily calculate the capacity consumption per unit of mix and the production of mix units if each processor was on its own. The consumption and production columns in the next table (Table 5.7) show these quantities.

---

[16] If the item makes several visits to the processor, the overall consumption is the sum of the capacity consumptions for all the visits.

Table 5.7 Capacity analysis 3

	FP	NP	CP	Capacity	Consumption	Production
AJ	2	4		40	2.4	16.67
HQ	2	1	5	120	2.2	54.55
GS	5	3	2	40	3.6	11.11
Mix	0.4	0.4	0.2		BN production	11.11

- The consumption column is the result of averaging the stay duration by percentage of the mix and it is therefore the average consumption per mix unit.
- The production is obtained by dividing the processor's capacity by the consumption in the processor of one mix unit.

We show in the last row of the column Production the lowest of all the production values. It is the maximum output that the system can give. Here, it is 11.1 couples from the mix per day. By Rounding up, we can say that of these 4.4 have the FP package, 4.4 have the NP package and 2.2 have the CP package. Of course, all the time we are talking about average and long term production.
Some remarks:

1. The bottleneck, the processor(s) that limit the system's output, is the Galapagos ship. Of course, this is with the desired mix. If the mix is changed, the bottleneck will change.
2. The system's output is the same as the bottleneck's output. The other processors are underused. It is easy to calculate the *occupation* of any processors by dividing the system's output by its maximum production. For example, for AJ, 11.11/16.66 = 66.6 per cent; for HQ, 11.11/54.5 = 20.3 per cent. Obviously for GS the occupation is 100 per cent.
3. 11.11 mix units go through the processors HQ and GS – that is, 11.11 customers from one or other of the types. However, this is not the case of the processor AJ. Only two types go through this processor. As the presence of both types in the mix is 80 per cent, only 11.11 × 0.8 = 8.88 customers pass through the processor AJ. If the reader has any doubts, he should verify that with this number of customers, the usage is precisely 66.6 per cent, as stated in point 2.
4. The capacity of the different groups of processors is clearly imbalanced. As the occupation shows, there is idle capacity, capacity that cannot be used, both in AJ and HQ. In order to use this capacity, one could change the mix or increase the capacity of the bottleneck GS.[17]

---

[17] The optimal mix, which achieves the best return from the system, can be readily calculated using linear programming techniques, which are within the reach of all mortals now that they are included in spreadsheets. The goal would be to maximize the margin with the constraint that the capacity cannot be exceeded. Having reached this point, a Solver's Manual works miracles.

5. If GS's capacity is increased, GS would eventually cease to be a bottleneck and now AJ would be the bottleneck. In fact, GS's capacity can be increased until the output is 16.66, at which point there will be two bottlenecks. This gives a capacity of 60 cabins. After this point, only AJ will be a bottleneck.

6. A *perfectly balanced* system is one in which all of the processors are bottlenecks. It attains maximum capacity usage, but has management problems. Any incident suffered by any processor affects production. This does not happen when there is only one bottleneck. In this case, only the incidents suffered by that particular bottleneck will affect total output.

7. It may be impossible to obtain a perfectly balanced system because the capacity may only be available in indivisible blocks. For example, it is possible that we cannot add 20 cabins to the system because efficient ships must have 40 cabins and capacity must be increased in entire ships.[18]

8. Capacity may be *hard* or *soft*. 'Hard' capacity is that which cannot be exceeded. For example, the fact that a day has 24 hours is a hard capacity. Obviously these capacities give rise to hard constraints, logical constraints, that must necessarily be fulfilled. In other cases, the constraints may be soft. For example, in our case, we could transfer customers to other (competing) ships at the times of peak demand. This would enable us to exceed the ship's capacity and make better use of the rest of the system. We could also arrange for some customers to sleep on the deck, offering a special discount for the inconvenience. This situation, in which it is possible to eliminate a strict capacity constraint, paying a price for it, may be addressed using special methods, or simply using the method presented here and performing a series of trial and error exercises (recommended!).

9. The consumption data may be inaccurate or random. Because of this, it is advisable to examine the result's sensitivity to errors in the consumption data. This is easy to do, again by the trial and error method, using a spreadsheet.[19]

10. The analysis does not provide any information on delays or stocks in the different parts of the system. For example, we do not know whether there will be any type of delay between HQ and GS. As we have said, the analysis corresponds to an average, long-term situation and, therefore, assumes that the flows take place at a constant rate and without any variations over time. In such conditions, it is not possible to calculate the stocks that accumulate due to momentary rate imbalances. The average input and output rates in each processor must be equal for all processors and its value must match the bottleneck's output. Of course, this does not mean that this equality must always exist. In practice, rates are never stable. In practice the equality between averages

---

[18] The problem with determining optimal capacity in the presence of indivisibilities can be solved using more advanced methods. We do not include them here because one of the authors does not believe in them. But if the reader would like to contact the other author, we will be pleased to tell him about them.

[19] Although it can be made very complicated. One of the most interesting approaches when it is made complicated is that of Wagner (1975).

Table 5.8 Capacity analysis 4

Groups of processors	Items				Capacity	Consumption	Production
	Item1	Item2	...	Itemn			
Proc1 Proc2 . . . Procm	Capacity consumptions				Capacity	Calculation	Calculation
	Mix					Maximum *P*	Calculation

is obtained by absorbing the rate fluctuations in the stocks. On average and over the long term, due to the equality of average rates, it is not possible to see the phenomena that give rise to stock.

Structuring the analysis

After having considered the previous example, the reader can now understand the general analysis methodology, which is outlined below:

1. Description of the current capacity. This requires:
   - Determination of the items to be considered. We must start with a few product families having clearly differentiated features.
   - Identification of the groups of processors. For each group of processors, specify their individual capacity.
   - Compilation of route sheets, indicating the operations performed on each item and each item's capacity consumption in each processor.
2. Now fill in the table above (Table 5.8). The data are written in the boxes indicated. Make sure that the units are consistent.
3. Study the bottlenecks, usages and other parameters, and adjust capacity optimally to the demand.

Analysing flows

As we have said, this variable considers the capacity's dynamics – that is, *the way in which the items accelerate or slow down in the system, and the times during which they remain in each part of the system.* The system's response time to an order depends critically upon this variable. In order to analyse this variable, we must examine what the process rates are like, and what flows result from these rates, at each moment in time. Only rate imbalances in time give rise to delays and stocks.

Let us consider any processor in the system. For example, in the previously discussed case, let us consider the processor GS. We have seen that the average input in GS is 8.8 couples per day. However this average rate can be obtained in many

Table 5.9   Management checklist for capacity

1. The problem: synonyms	—How many shifts? —How many workers? —How many operations centres, what type and where?
2. Alternatives	—Overtime —Second or third shift —Recruit more workers —Buy more machines or equipment —Subcontract —Buy capacity hours —Another production unit —Networking —Polyvalence

3. Form of assessment	1. Operating properties
	  —What are the costs (fixed and variable) in each of the possible forms?
	  —What properties: barriers, constraints (knowledge, resources, etc.), rigidities, limitations, etc. are there in each of the possible cases?
	  —How much time is needed to increase or decrease the capacity?
	  —Availability of each type of capacity: abundant, scarce, etc.
	2. Relationship with criteria
	  —How do the different types of capacity relate with the criteria for competing?
	  —What type of criterion comes out best with each alternative?
	3. Relationship with the firm's knowledge
	  —Is the way of providing capacity possible within the knowledge currently existing in the company?
	  —Does it provide something unique to the company's knowledge base?

4. General policies	1. Maintain stable capacity or adapt. 2. Obtain it as required or plan it. 3. Decentralize or centralize. 4. Hold in-house or subcontract. 5. Long-term agreements or market contracting.

ways. One way is that exactly 8.8 couples arrive at the ship each day.[20] Of course, 8.8 couples a day must also leave the ship. Another way is to load batches of 40 couples and to operate with a full ship. However, this production rate is unsustainable as the ship's maximum occupancy is 66.6 per cent. This means that loads

---

[20] Rather difficult, because 0.8 couples is not a couple. It also means that each day they must be taken to the ship from wherever they may be. Perhaps by helicopter? Consider it simply as an illustration.

must be spaced further apart. There are times when the ship is at full load and others when the ship is empty. Specifically, the ship must be empty 33.3 per cent of the time. Furthermore, as the stay duration is different for each item, loading must be done differently for each item. Quite a mess!

The basic tool for putting some order into the analysis of instant rates are the input–output curves. We will introduce the basic ideas below and then apply them to clarify the Galapagos ship operation.

Input–output curves

Let us consider any processor in isolation. Generally speaking, any repository or place where there are inward and outward flows of items can be analysed using this procedure. From this viewpoint, a processor acts like a storage tank. Therefore, let it be a tank like the one shown in Figure 5.4.[21]

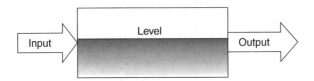

Figure 5.4   The processor as a tank

At any given time, the tank's contents are at a certain level. The level decreases if output is greater than input and rises in the opposite situation. Let us assume that the items' input rate is 50 units a day for one day, followed by three days in which no material enters. Likewise, let us assume that the output rate is 25 units a day for one day and zero the next day and this structure is maintained indefinitely. In both cases, the rates are constant throughout the time in which they take place. Observe that the average, long-term input and output rates are equal. Specifically, they amount to $50/4 = 25/2 = 12.5$ units/day. What level will the items have in the tank at any given time? One way of finding this out is to plot a graph of the rates, proceed step by step identifying at each moment in time the net rate at which the level rises or falls. Then the rates are accumulated, giving the stock. This is what we have done in Figure 5.5.

Observe that there is accumulation on the first day, because the net input rate is $50 - 25 = 25$ units a day. The level is maintained on the second day, because both rates are zero. Finally, the level falls on the third day because the input rate is 0 and the output rate is 25, which gives a net rate of $0 - 25 = -25$ units. The result is the curve with a truncated pyramid shape at the bottom of Figure 5.5.

A simpler procedure than pursuing rates is to use *accumulated input* and *accumulated output* curves, which we will call respectively the *input curve* and the

---

[21] The reader can think in terms of a water tank which is filled from one tap and emptied through another. But, please, keep it quiet; these 'unscientific' analogies are bad for our image...

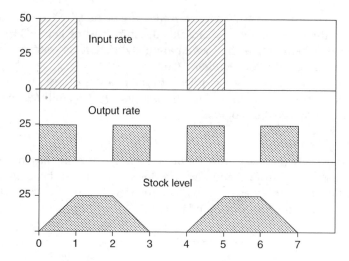

Figure 5.5   Levels in the tank

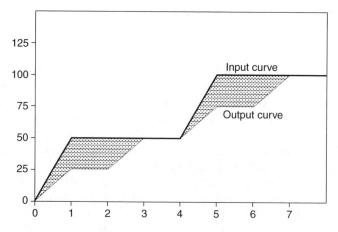

Figure 5.6   Input–output curves (Example 1)

output curve. The input curve is the graph of the total inputs accumulated up until each moment of time. Likewise, the output curve is the graph of the total accumulated outputs. These curves are plotted for the case described above in Figure 5.6, input–output curve Example 1.

Both of the curves have a rising slope. The reader should see that the vertical difference between the two curves represents the stock and corresponds exactly to the stock calculated in Figure 5.5. Therefore, the stock can be read directly from the input–output curves, without requiring any further constructs. However, that's not all. It is also possible to read directly from the curves the time that a certain item remains within the tank, provided that the inputs and outputs have a FIFO

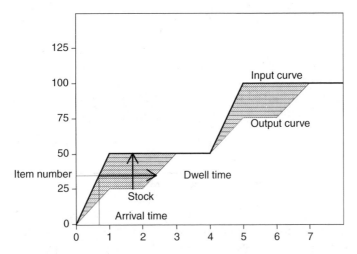

Figure 5.7 Properties of the input–output process

(first in, first out) behaviour. In this case, a given item's dwell time, in the jargon called *waiting time*, is the horizontal distance between the two curves – input and output – measured at the time of arrival of the item in question. To understand better why this is so, the reader can imagine that we stamp a number on each item as it arrives. The output will take place when it is that number's turn to leave, that is when the y-axis of the output curve matches that of the input curve, at the arrival time. Figure 5.7 summarizes these important properties.

The average stock can be calculated easily by dividing the shaded area by the total time, the average time can be calculated using the same procedure. Observe that, by definition, if the stock must remain finite (and it must!), both curves can separate, only for a certain time, and then they must join again. In fact, both curves' slope must be equal, on average and over the long term. Since the average slope is simply the average output rate this follows from our previous remarks.

Figure 5.7 also shows the close relationship that exists between times and stocks. If there are stocks somewhere, it is because the items spend some time there. Conversely if something spends time in a given place, stock will form there. Therefore, stocks and times are two sides of the same coin, dual visions of the world of flows. This duality is expressed in a simple equation relating average stock and average waiting time. On average and over the long term, it must be met that:

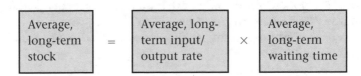

Average, long-term stock	=	Average, long-term input/ output rate	×	Average, long-term waiting time

Or in symbols, calling λ the value of the average, long-term input rate (which must be equal to the output rate), N the average stock and W the average waiting time:

$$N = \lambda \times W$$

This simple formula, which the reader may be familiar with even has a name. It is known as Little's law.[22]

A nice application of the input–output curve analysis is the examination of the 'tragedy of the commons' (Example 5.1).

Example 5.1

The Costa Brava Motorway

The coastal motorway connects the beaches of the Costa Brava with the city of Barcelona. On Sundays during the summer months, it is common for the motorway to become jammed since most of the people who live in Barcelona choose to return to their city between 8.00 p.m. and 12 midnight. However, traffic during most of the afternoon is quite light and the motorway has plenty of spare capacity. A few years ago, the Motorway Operator decided to promote travelling on off-peak times on Sundays. It distributed leaflets among drivers leaving Barcelona listing the advantages of returning to Barcelona at 7.00 p.m. and the ills that would befall those who waited until later. The result that Sunday was the worst traffic jam ever seen on a Spanish motorway. The average delays were extremely high, way above the hour required on average to make the trip. It is easy to understand why by looking at the two situations' input–output curves (see Figure 5.8).

The graph on the left shows the case of a typical Sunday. To simplify, the operation time – the normal, jam-free travelling time – is assumed to be negligible. If this were not so, one would simply have to shift the output curve to the right by a time equal to the travelling time.

The input curve – the total number of vehicles entering the motorway – is drawn with a thicker line. The output curve follows the input curve (all those who enter leave) while there is spare capacity, until about 8.30 p.m. After that time, a queue is formed which peaks at 9.30 p.m., as shown by the vertical arrow. The vehicle entering the motorway at that point will experience a delay given by the horizontal arrow, roughly one hour (in addition to the normal travelling time).

The graph on the right shows the case of the terrible Sunday. All arrivals take place at 7 o'clock. Consequently, at that time the input curve jumps suddenly upwards. All the cars are on the motorway (vertical arrow) at that time. Therefore, the last car to arrive will have to wait the distance indicated by the

---

[22] Nothing to do with being small. It is given this name after John Little, a MIT professor who formulated it rigorously for general applications more than 40 years ago.

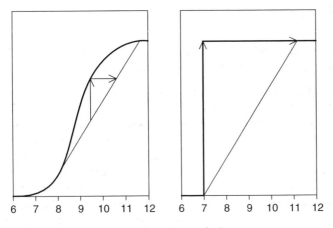

6 7 8 9 10 11 12   6 7 8 9 10 11 12

Figure 5.8   Analysis of input–output curves (Example 2)

horizontal arrow, equal to the time required for all the vehicles to pass (except his). And, what is more, the poor chap who was the last to arrive, just after 7 o'clock, waited 4 hours, more than all the rest... We will come back to this subject at a later point but it gives a first glimpse of the evil effects of batch creation.

*Times

Because of the duality between times and stocks, it is possible to create a standard typology of waiting times in the operations system. This typology, composed of seven types of times, includes most of the reasons why hold-ups occur in the system. Of course, the accumulations are always caused by differences between instant input and output rates, but the differences do not always have the same causes. And these causes must be understood if we are to act on them. Therefore, the times typology also provides a typology of causes of delay. And each cause of delay must be solved applying specific measures – measures tailored to the cause in question. Only by understanding the causes is it possible to devise measures that reduce stocks. This is an obvious truth that has led to the failure of many stock reduction policies that have confined themselves to treating the symptom without treating the disease causing it.

The basic operations times are:

- operation,
- set-up,
- batch,
- interference or queue times,
- buffer or safety times,

- planned,
- disruption.

In the following, we will briefly describe each type of time, as their identification and treatment are fundamental for actions on the flows variable.

1. *Operation times.* The times used in the performance of transformation operations required to attain the appropriate service. Performed by the processors, they are basically the times that have been determined in the capacities variable. *The typical way of reducing operation times is to simplify the process by eliminating unnecessary operations.* To achieve this, it is necessary to go back to the process variable and apply the ideas prosecuted there. Another common way of decreasing these times is to increase the processors' speed. This has two consequences that must be considered carefully. On one hand, a processor's maximum speed (especially that of a mechanical processor) is determined by the operation's quality, profitability, safety and reliability requirements. If a processor is not operating at its 'maximum' speed (compatible with the above conditions), it is being wasted. However, if it is being operated efficiently, any attempt to make it work faster will have a negative effect on one or other of the above qualities. Second, in many processes, the operation time is very small compared with the total process time. In most situations, particularly services, it accounts for less than 20 per cent of the total time. Therefore, an action on the operation time will have little effect on the total time. And the effort required to achieve the reduction may be considerable. The reader could consider the case of manual (human) processors. Any attempt to increase in their capacity (or speed) may lead to a significant deterioration in the company's relations with the person.

2. *Set-up time.* Time required to change the activity performed by a processor. It generates delays because the items that the processor must process have to wait until preparation is completed. The existence of time set-up generates economies of scale that give rise to other waiting times. *The way to reduce preparation times is identical to that for reducing operation times.* A rigorous study of the process (or method) may bring to light ways to reduce or eliminate it. However, unaware of its direct importance, there are still many companies that do not look at this type of time. In fact, until the advent of JIT (Just In Time) almost no one paid attention to the changeover times, tending to consider them a necessary or inevitable evil. However, with the introduction of JIT methodologies were developed to reduce these times.[23] Most methodologies are structured around a few basic ideas. For example, do not carry out any adjustment with the processor stopped that can be done with the processor operating, standardize changes and create procedures for them, etc. Each case normally needs *ad hoc* procedures. Hence the importance of applying process analysis to these times. Creativity and experience can achieve spectacular results. One company known by the authors, specializing in plastics injection,

---

[23] Such as the RDE (Rapid Die Exchange) methodology for changing dies in presses.

achieved reductions of 500 per cent by applying a few rules of common sense. Moral: give some attention to these times and make the effort to reduce them because they are responsible for the existence of the next (bad!) time.

3. *Batch time.* One of the main causes of waiting times. This is the waiting time that happens when several items have to 'travel together'. Here 'travel together' means undergoing a process as a batch. The travel metaphor helps to make the phenomenon easier to understand. When several people must travel together, each one must wait until the others have finished the current operation before they can start the next stage of the journey. This gives rise to a delay which we call batch time. Batch times are extraordinarily frequent. They appear whenever, to achieve some type of economy, items are not processed one by one but are grouped together to create batches. For example, a bank's loan committee may meet once a week to discuss the loans that are pending approval. Why not meet once a day? Typically it is much more efficient to allocate a particular day for this task. So, lets have weekly meetings! This is a reasoning based on process economies. Its effect is clear. If the meeting is held on a Tuesday, for example, the loan applications that arrive on Wednesday must wait six days to be examined. A waiting time of five days is created for the sole purpose of minimizing the inconvenience for the committee's members. Example 5.2 gives another example with air traffic.

If the reader examines his company's processes, he will probably be surprised by the ubiquity of batch times. All types of transportation, meetings, formalities, etc., are accumulated in batches for greater efficiency, on the basis of decisions that are made after only a superficial consideration. In the process, inactive waiting times accumulate. On average, if the time between consecutive processes of a batch is T and items arrive constantly at the service, the delay produced by the batch is $T/2$. This is because the first has to wait a full time

Example 5.2 Batch time on planes

To travel to America, high-capacity planes are used. Let us assume that the plane's capacity is 300 seats. Of course, the reason for using this type of plane is the economies obtained. It is much cheaper to transport 300 passengers in a single plane than in 300 single-seater planes, even if it is only because each plane needs a pilot. But now the batch time delays start. The plane cannot close its doors until the last passenger has boarded. The first one on board must wait one hour until the plane fills. A batch time. Upon arrival, when our patient passenger goes to collect his suitcase, he must wait until it comes off the conveyor belt, among the more than 500 suitcases that this sort of plane usually carries. Another batch time.[24]

---

[24] As the reader will be fully aware, Murphy's law is invariably met for suitcases: our suitcase will always be the last one to come out (if it hasn't been lost ...), no matter when we boarded.

T while the last does not wait. Therefore, the average value is $T/2$. One immediate consequence of a delay is that there is stock. Obviously, the resulting stock is called batch stock. And, by Little's law, its average value is $\lambda T/2$, where λ is the service demand. Of course, the batch size is $Q = \lambda T$, the total demand between services. Looking at it another way, the delay (and the stock) is proportional to the batch size! A nice way to waste time … ! *The batch time is reduced by examining the causes of the economies and eliminating those which play against having a small batch.*

4. *Interference (queuing) time.* This is the second major cause of waiting times. And also the most mysterious. Delays caused by interference (also called congestion or queue phenomena) occur whenever the items' arrival or departure rates are random, even if the processor has sufficient capacity. Let us assume that the rate at which customers arrive at a service is 10 customers per hour and the (maximum) service rate is 100 customers an hour, both being average rates the actual rates being random quantities. The reader will observe that the average usage (occupancy[25]) of a system with an average arrival rate of λ and a maximum departure rate of μ is precisely $\rho = \lambda/\mu$. In our case, $\lambda = 10$ and $\mu = 100$, therefore $\rho = 0.1$. But, even though the occupancy is only 10 percent, there will be interference delays! This is because the rates are random. Management often experiences considerable difficulties in understanding the nature of this type of time. Delays *always* happen because the instant arrival rate is greater than the departure rate. However, and this is the crux of the matter, this condition can arise when the arrival and departure rates are random – even though the average maximum departure rate (or average capacity) is much greater than the average arrival rate. Intuitively, queuing phenomena are the result of random microvariations in the input and output rates. The big surprise is that the delays that occur are much greater than what they may seem to be at first sight. There is a negative feedback phenomenon, delays give rise to more delays, so that the system amplifies the consequences of variability, which may reach explosive proportions. It is worthwhile pausing a moment to take a look at this phenomenon. This we will do by means of the case described in Example 5.3.

Figure 5.9 shows the input–output curves of a sample taken from the case. The times are in minutes. It is only a sample, a possible case, because, being a random phenomenon, other observations, of the same phenomenon will be different. During the six minutes plotted, there are 16 arrivals and 16 services (why?). The time periods during which the output curve matches the input curve correspond to the idle times in the system. In total, they should add up to 50 per cent of the total time. However, the reader will note the significant presence of interference delays. There is a large gap between the two curves

---

[25] It is interesting to note that in the literature ρ is used to denote occupancy. This has been so since time immemorial (beginning of the 20th century). Was the original author afflicted by a speech defect, in addition to being a bad speller, writing 'roccupancy' instead of 'occupancy'?

Example 5.3 The taxi service at Kulatuka airport

The taxis at Kulatuka airport are caught at the exit of the national terminal. Travellers leaving the terminal must go to a pre-established pick-up point where they queue for a taxi. Let us assume that at an off-peak time the average number of travellers arriving at the pick-up point is 60 travellers per hour and that loading the taxis takes 30 seconds on average. The system's occupancy will be 60/120 = 0.5, that is, 50 per cent. Let us assume, for the purpose of simplicity, that only one taxi is loaded at a time and that the phenomenon can be considered to be in the steady-state, the input and output rates are on the average constant over a given period of time. Let us consider what happens with the first traveller. Let us say that he arrives at the pickup point at 10 a.m. and the queue is empty. He will immediately get into a taxi and let us say that the taxi leaves the pickup point at 10 h 0 m 45 s. It has taken 45 seconds to load. As arrivals take place every minute, on average, probably no-one will have yet arrived. 'Probably' refers to the probability of the time between customer arrivals being greater than 45 seconds. To economize in writing, let us abbreviate as A the (random) time between arrivals, which on average is one minute. We will also abbreviate 'probability' to 'P'. Therefore, the P that a queue will form is P(A > 45'), in words, the probability that the time between arrivals is greater than 45 seconds. Now, let us assume for a moment that the next A is 25 seconds. Let us say that, by chance, the loading time for this customer is also 45 seconds. This second customer will first wait 45 −25 = 20 seconds (the remaining time required by the first customer to finish service) and will then use 45 seconds to go through service himself. Therefore, he will leave the airport 65 seconds after arrival. Now, the third customer to arrive will experience a delay with a probability equal to P(A > 65). This is the queue on a queue phenomenon! The second customer's probability of having to wait was P(A > 45) but a third, identical customer has a probability of having to wait of P(A > 65). The fact that one customer has to wait gives rise to waits by the customers following him, because the customer arriving cannot be attended to until the queue of previous customers has been depleted.

for 50 per cent of the time. Therefore, the interference waiting time will not be insignificant. And we insist, all this with an average occupancy of 50 per cent!

How are interference times reduced? One obvious answer is 'by reducing occupancy'. There are two ways of reducing occupancy. Reducing the demand, the arrivals, which will probably not be the most satisfactory solution in most cases, or by increasing the capacity, increasing the service speed. For example, we could increase the number of processors or obtain additional capacity from outside or use any one of the many ways of increasing capacity which we

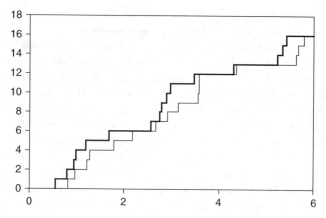

Figure 5.9   Input–output curves (Example 3)

know[26] from way back. However, increasing capacity increases competitiveness (decreases transit times) but reduces productivity. More inactive investment. Therefore, we pay good money to increase the service. As always, this is a sign that we should start the old thinking machine going. How can we reduce interference times without it costing us money? First, we could try to *reduce the direct service time*. In many services, the customer can perform part of the service himself. This is what was discovered by the self-service restaurants, supermarkets, and many other businesses. As service time is operation time, all the considerations about operation time are also applicable here.

Second, we can try to take some of the activities from the server and *allocate them to a less expensive processor*, for which it will be cheaper to obtain additional capacity. For example, in many hospitals, nurses and technicians nowadays absorb part of the work that used to be done by the doctor. The stupidest, but also the cheapest aid is usually the computer, so we should try to see what we can offload onto the computer.

Third, we can accept the idle time in the processors and *allocate them additional jobs* that do not create interference. This last condition is very important because if the server is unable to perform the main service while it is carrying out these secondary tasks, it will create occupancy and therefore interference. The only types of task that can be allocated are those which can be preempted as soon as a customer arrives. For example, a few years ago switchboard operators in many companies used their idle time to open and sort the mail.

Lastly, the best way to reduce interference times is to go back to the universal recipe: *act on the causes*. Act on the factors that generate the interference time. *Specifically, reduce the randomness in the arrivals or performance of the service*. As this is the cause of interferences, by destroying the cause we eliminate the interferences permanently. Here, you have to use your imagination.

---

[26] And hate.

For example, to reduce uncertainty in arrivals, we can use *booking* systems. The booking not only guarantees a service to its holder but also makes the load of the centre known *a priori* and with almost total certainty. To reduce the variability in the service, we can *standardize* the items, taking similar items to the same work station. This can play against the economy of scale generated by having polyvalent servers, so the two effects have to be weighted together. We could also standardize the processor's *operations*, for example, simplifying the process and using mechanical means. Whatever the option chosen, the reader must make sure that the variability eliminated does not come back in through the back door. If variability is eliminated, the servers' occupancy may be increased without interference times appearing. Let us say that occupancy is increased to 90 per cent without this causing any problems. However, if variability is reintroduced at this point, we will find ourselves with a system that generates interference and with a 90 per cent occupancy! The result will be disastrous.

5. *Safety times.* Another time that appears because the world is random. The 'just in case' time. Just in case something happens, you arrive earlier and then have to wait. We sometimes call it the 'important person time'. Because when we are given an appointment by an important person, for example, a minister[27] who we are going to ask for money from and he tells us that he will see us at 12 midday, at what time will we arrive? Depending on the amount we are going to ask for, we may try to arrive 20 minutes early, 'just in case'. Although 100 per cent of the times, he will see us at 1 o'clock! But we never go 'just in time'. We always go 'just in case'.[28] This time is equivalent to a safety stock. Having a safety stock is making certain items wait, just in case we need them. This type of time occurs very often, not just in stock problems but whenever there is an event with risk, as in the case of the minister.

How can the buffer time be reduced? One obvious alternative is to *reduce the cushion*, but then we increase the risk of error unless something else is done as well. Can the reader guess it? Let's go back to the causes! The cause is the variability of the various elements of which the phenomenon is composed. So we

---

[27] Are ministers important? One of the authors had always thought they were. This author had never seen them very close up. The other author said that they weren't. This author had known them very well. The second author (and reading the newspaper) did not take long to convince the first author.

[28] One of the authors uses a double form of buffer stock. He lives for part of the year in a house away from the town. He often has to go to the town to catch a train which takes him to Madrid. This requires driving 40 km along a fairly crowded motorway. Let us say that his train leaves the station at 3.00 p.m. To determine at what time he should leave his house, the author estimates the driving time, adding a generous margin for heavy traffic (one hour in case there's traffic, he says) and then adds another half-hour, just in case. He decides to leave one and half hours before the train leaves, at 1.30 p.m. But as the travelling time already has quite a large margin, the result is double precaution. As is shown by the fact that the time he has to kill at the station, as determined historically by an impartial observer, is about 45 minutes.

should act on the causes that generate variability. One of these causes could be the lack of information. If we have imprecise information about a quantity's possible values, the variability perceived by us will be large. In fact, we can think that the total variability of any parameter is the sum of its intrinsic variability (inherent to the physical phenomenon generating it) and the subjective variability (created by our poor knowledge about the law generating it). As a result, we will think that we need longer buffer times, which will create delays in the items. Therefore, *we must make better forecasts* of all the problem's random variables. These forecasts must be as accurate as possible in order to eliminate the subjective variability to the point that, in the ideal case, the total variability is only composed of the intrinsic variability. And then we should modify the phenomenon's structure to eliminate this variability too. Destroy the problem, not solve it.

6. *Planned times.* These are waiting times that are introduced surreptitiously in the course of planning operations and as a consequence of the specification of the order in which things will be done. They are created indirectly when we try to exploit the different potential economies existing in a situation. They are the result of 'optimized' designs that focus on the cost without clearly considering the side effects on the firm's competitiveness. In fact, all of the times we have studied so far could be considered as examples of planned times if we were to adopt the viewpoint which associates costs with perturbations.[29]

Whenever the production of a certain item is shifted deliberately from its instant demand, stocks will accumulate with the associated waiting times. The most typical case of this type of time occurs in operations planning, when trying to balance the use of different types of capacity over time. Let us consider a specific case Example 5.4.

In this case is the delay (Figure 5.10) above a planned time. The optimization of working schedule has resulted in waiting times. And this has happened because the working schedule exploits the economies inherent in the situation, without taking into account the resulting waiting times.

The only way to reduce planned times is to act, once again, *on their causes*. As the causes of planned times are not always of the same type (as they are in batch times), the first thing that must be done is to identify them. This requires identifying the problem's key elements and reducing their effects as much as possible. One must always be on the watch for the 'balancing pitfall'. There is always the temptation to obtain the 'optimal solution' by assigning a cost to the waiting time, thus obtaining a balance between the operating cost and the waiting cost. Using this approach, one will never get to the heart of the phenomenon and the problem will never be solved. The reader must avoid this

---

[29] For example, in theory, one could think in terms of a stockout cost, which includes all the effects that arise as a consequence of this situation. In this case, the buffer stock appears as a side effect of optimizing total costs, which are the sum of the holding costs and the stockout costs.

Example 5.4 The Hancock Island ferries

Hancock Island, on the east coast of the United States, is connected to the mainland by ferries. The ferries operate 13 hours a day, starting at 8 o'clock in the morning and ending at 9 o'clock at night. Each ferry has capacity for 30 vehicles. During the summer, the number of vehicles that wish to cross to the island is given by the following table, for different times of the day.

Time	8–9	9–10	10–11	11–12	12–13	13–14	14–15	15–16	16–17	17–18	18–19	19–20	20–21
Outgoing	10	40	80	95	120	50	50	60	40	30	10	20	10
Return	5	15	20	30	40	30	40	40	100	120	125	30	20

The table also indicates the number of vehicles wishing to travel from the island to the mainland, also for different times of the day. The full trip there and back – including loading and unloading – takes one hour. The company rents all the ferries from specialized firms. The rental can be either for a full day, or only for certain times. At most, two ferries may be rented for a full day. It is not possible to schedule departures less than 12 minutes apart due to docking constraints. The cost of renting a ferry is $5,000 an hour when it is rented for a full day or $6,000 an hour if it is rented for specific times during the day. The planners wonder what timetable the ferries should have and the number of ferries needed to provide reasonable coverage for the demand.

Let us consider only the trip between the mainland and the island. The analysis of the return trip is similar and the total capacity must be the larger of the two. The cars' input curve is easy to plot from the data given in the table. The cars' output curve depends upon the number of trips performed per hour and this in turn depends on the number of ferries available in each time block. If, for example, there are three ferries operating, three departures an hour can be scheduled. As a general rule, if there are n ferries operating, n departures an hour can be scheduled. As each departure carries a maximum of 30 cars, the hourly transportation capacity is 30n vehicles, where n is the number of ferries. Now, a good planning department would calculate the ferries required to satisfy the demand while at the same time seeking to save taxpayers' money – that is, minimizing the rental cost. This is relatively easy to do with the help of a specialized programme. In this case the best option is to rent one ferry for the entire day and rent extra ferries by the hour in accordance with the following daily schedule [0,0,1,2,3,1,1,0,0,1,0,0,0] where each value corresponds to a one-hour slot.

Having calculated the capacity profile, we can now plot the output curve. We must simply note that in each hourly slot, the departures will be the minimum of the number of cars waiting to board and the ferry's capacity, as it is not possible to carry more cars than are waiting or which fit on the ferry.

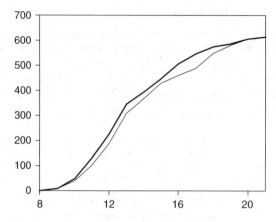

Figure 5.10   Input–output curves (Example 4)

temptation and devote himself to the fruitful exercise of modifying the system's basic functioning so as not to have to 'optimize' it.

7. *Disruption times.* These are the easiest to describe and often the most difficult to eliminate. This is the 'What's this doing here?' or 'Look what I've just found!' time. They are delays that occur for no reason. Delays caused by memory lapses or misplaced information, which give rise to 'black holes' within the firm – bundles of paper piled up in the wrong place, and other consequences of human nature. Their causes are very varied. Lurking in the background there is always the possibility that employees wish to delay certain items for reasons that are unknown. Because of this many managers try to implement controls that constraint people's behaviour. In this way we may fall back into old errors. For many years, magical formulae have been devised to assure the success of certain methods within the firm, which advocated 'involving management' or 'applying pressure'. This type of generic action is typical of situations when one does not know what to do.[30] As we will see later, if by 'applying pressure', one means the art of proposing attainable challenges to people, then 'applying pressure' may work in our particular case. But if this is not the case applying pressure could just suffocate the recipient.

In any case, the most common cause (or excuse) for these waiting times are defects in the information system which lead the firm to lose track of certain transactions. By acting on the information system, it is possible to eliminate these causes (or excuses).

---

[30] In order to promote the application of mathematical models in firms, many years ago a particular professional journal gave the recipe of 'involving the general management'. We have always wondered why general management should allow itself to be involved in these situations. In our experience as managers and one of us being an expert in models, we would never become 'champions of a mathematic modelling action'. There are other, more important and more difficult matters that require the attention of general management for it to allow itself to be drawn into uncharted quicksand…

Table 5.10 Checklist of flows

1. The problem: synonyms	—What should my layout be like? —How do I take my items from one end to the other of the company? —How do I reduce my in-process stocks? —Long delivery time.
2. Alternatives	—It doesn't matter what path the item follows. —Functional distribution, equal processors are grouped. —Processors grouped for similar operations. The items go to the centres. —The processors are lined up one after the other, depending on the item. —Batch size in each case and production stage. —Where should I have stocks? —Buffer stock types and sizes.

3. Form of assessment	1. Operating properties
	  —Where are my delays?
	  —What are the costs of having a mix of items: changes, interferences, etc.?
	  —What type of orders do I have?
	  —How much stock accumulates and how much does it cost me to have intermediate and final stocks?
	  —What are the dominant flows that are created and the alternative paths?
	2. Relationship with criteria
	  —What is the total production time?
	  —What are the trade-offs between time, cost, breadth, etc.?
	  —What criterion comes out as best with each alternative?
	3. Relationship with the firm's knowledge
	  —Is the manner of providing flow within my employees' skills?
	  —Does the way I organize my flow contribute something to my employees' improvement?

4. General policies	1. I am going to organize myself to forecast customer demand and produce against stock. 2. I am going to process individualized customer orders. 3. There are functional centres and the items go to them. 4. I have many different items, I am going to look for similarities in them and organize myself on the basis of these similarities. 5. I have several items that are very different and without any similarities and I am going to organize myself on the basis of each item. 6. Type of production flow: synthesis, analysis or hourglass. 7. Standardization or diversification policies.

6

The Basic Variables of Action in Operations (II)

In this chapter, we complete the description of the basic variables of operations which we began in the previous chapter. The remaining variables to be considered are: human resources, the information system and the conflict-resolution system. The latter two are vitally important as repositories (and sources) of the knowledge held by the firm – principally in the form of symbolic materializations.

*Human resources

In this book, human resources are considered more from the 'resources' aspect than the 'human' one. We are interested here in how operations can use the distinctive features of the human processor and, in particular, of the knowledge he possesses. In fact, this is the central theme of this chapter and, therefore, will not be extensively discussed in this section. We find ourselves before an elegant example of recursiveness. Everything that is said in the other chapters is applicable to this variable. That would be one way of ending the analysis of this variable. But let the reader not be alarmed, there's still more for us to say!

Polyvalence versus speciality

We propose to analyse in some detail one of the most important aspects of this variable from the operating viewpoint. We are talking about the *polyvalence–speciality* dilemma or, in less highflown language, the question: how polyvalent must my staff be? We will investigate the economic effects of polyvalence in a very simple context, but the implications can be applied more generally. Consider the situation of Example 6.1.

Obviously, productivity is increased with specialization. But does this lower the operator's response time as a result of interference times? The exact analysis is rather complicated so we will offer here an approximate reasoning based on simple simulations performed by one of the authors.[1] The observed-queuing times are summarized in Table 6.1.

---

[1] This is an approximation that gives a value for the queuing time that is reasonably close to the actual time.

Example 6.1   Multiusos

Multiusos is a company specializing in household repairs. The main service it provides is to connect the individual customer to the professional repair person. When a person needs a repair in his home, he calls the Multiusos assistance centre. He is attended by an operator who immediately contacts a professional who can solve the problem. Multiusos guarantees the repair and requires professionals to give a cost estimate before carrying out any repair. It also guarantees a maximum response time – from the time the first call is received to when the customer has the professional at his home. There are currently five employees receiving calls. There are 20 calls an hour at peak times and the time required to attend a call is about 10 minutes, including locating the professional and calling the customer to inform him of the current status of his call. The employee normally does not attend to other calls until the current case is resolved. Recently, the possibility has been suggested of specializing the employees' work. An automatic system would screen calls and a particular person would take the plumbing repairs while the other four would deal with other situations: 30 per cent of the calls are for plumbing and the remaining 70 per cent relate to other repairs. The average time required to attend a plumbing call is 4 minutes. For other repairs, the average time is 12 minutes. If the weighted average of these times is calculated, an overall average of 9.6 minutes is obtained, giving an increase in productivity of 4 per cent that can be attributed to specialization. To what extent is this change desirable?

Table 6.1   Example of queuing time

Group	Calls per hour	Number of servers	Service time	Percentage occupancy	Queuing time (mins)
All	20	5	10	0.67	1.87
Plumbing	6	1	4	0.40	2.67
Rest	14	4	12	0.70	4.28

In the case of specialization, if the average of the two queuing times is calculated a value of 3.8 minutes is obtained,[2] which is much longer than the 1.87 minutes wait in the case of polyvalence (see Table 6.1).

The situation is prototypical. Generally speaking, the effects of polyvalence can be summarized in the following statements:

1. Assume equal loads, in a service system if the servers are divided into several subsystems and specialized, the average level of service deteriorates. This is

---

[2] This value is obtained by averaging the values of the table, that is $(2.67 \times 6 + 4.28 \times 14) \div 20$.

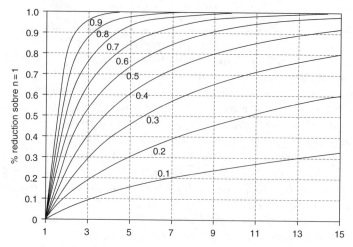

Figure 6.1   Graphic representation of the queuing times

because there may now be free time in one of the subsystems but queuing in the other subsystem. This circumstance cannot occur in the polyvalent case.

2. When the number of servers is increased, maintaining the load at a constant level, the level of service increases. This is a consequence of the law of large numbers. Therefore, a large company has a competitive advantage over a small company if both have a similar load per employee. Figure 6.1 shows the effect on the queuing time of increasing the number of servers, assuming that the load is kept at a constant level. The percentage reduction is given, for different numbers of servers, for the extreme case of specialization in which each server has its own queue. Each curve in the figure corresponds to a certain level of occupancy in each server, from 0.1 to 0.9, in increments of 0.1.

For example, when the average occupancy is 60 per cent – a typical figure in service operations – working in polyvalent groups of five instead of five specialized centres (with a single server) leads to a reduction of 85 per cent (the dot marked on the graph) in the queuing time.

*Analysing the information system[3]

This variable considers the structure of the information system. The information system is the body of mechanisms that move, store and provide information to the firm's different agents so that the agents can *use it in decision making*. The

---

[3] It is a common occurrence in our presentations for someone to ask what the difference is between information and knowledge. As the alert reader will have noticed, we have defined knowledge with some precision, deliberately leaving the meaning of the word

information system may be on a computerized, manual or verbal medium, but it always exists in some form or other.

Of course, the information system handles also information that cannot be associated directly with a decision. The typical example is financial accounting. Some of the firm's stakeholders – the shareholders or the State – demand that the firm maintains an information repository which shows its assets and the sources resources invested in them. However, even in this case, no matter how unlikely this may seem, the information is associated with decision making: by the shareholder, to decide whether his money is in the right place; and by the State, to decide whether the firm must be watched more closely in case anomalous situations arise. Indeed, one school of thought asserts that there is no information in the absence of decision making. And that the information's value is positive only if its presence changes the decision that would have been made if the information had not been available.

Operating decisions

The operations information system does not address all of the decisions made within the firm. It concentrates on operating decisions, intended to solve operating as opposed to strategic problems. The properties of both types of decisions are shown in Figure 6.2 (Anthony and Govindarajan, 2001).

The most important features of operating decisions are their low individual importance and their recurrence over time, which provides the possibility of *solving these decision problems by iterative methods*. Because the problem occurs recurrently – if we don't succeed in destroying it – each occurrence is an opportunity to refine the process. In fact, an exploratory process takes place on the consecutive occurrences of the problem. As long as the problem does not change, eventually the best solution is obtained.

By contrast, since strategic decisions are non-recurrent, the possibility of progressive refinement does not exist. An error made in a strategic decision is much more difficult to correct than an error made in an operating decision.

It is easy to find examples of operating decisions. Most decisions in an operations system are of this nature. Problems involving allocating employees to tasks (for

---

'information' wreathed in ambiguity. Perhaps it is worthwhile briefly clarifying the matter. In fact, there is a hierarchy – an artificial one, to some extent – that starts with symbols and ends with knowledge. The hierarchy can even be extended to include transmission systems, protocols and other niceties. Symbols are the primitive content that conveys on horseback some kind of content. It is also necessary to distinguish between data and information. Data are normally associated with the messages' gross content. We could say that data are the first human interpretation – intelligible to the agent – of the symbols content. A datum has very little structure. Information is data given to some sort of structure. *Information* contributes a structure that goes beyond the data themselves. We can also use Russell and Norvig's definition (Russell and Norvig, 1995), information = data and structure; knowledge = information + reasoning. We do not know if this will help or confuse the reader. Perhaps a little of both. But at least we avoid being overwhelmed by e-mails demanding to know the distinction between these concepts.

Operating	Strategic
■ Low individual importance	■ High individual importance
■ Collectively important	■ Individually important
■ Short-term	■ Long-term
■ Recurrent	■ Non-recurrent
■ Limited scope	■ Broad scope
■ Impact on service	■ Impact on competitiveness
■ Delegated	■ Performed by agent

Figure 6.2   Types of decision

example, in a department store), daily decisions concerning cash management in a bank, network operation decisions in a telecommunications company, or opening and closing counters in a supermarket are just some examples of operating decisions.

Strategic decisions are normally associated with the operations system's design. For example, purchasing land to open a new shop, hiring a new employee, closing a large contract with a major supermarket chain are examples of this type of decisions. Operating and strategic are relative concepts. For a firm that controls a chain of 1,000 shops, opening a new shop may be an operating decision. However, for a firm that only manages two shops, it would be a strategic decision.

Operating decisions comprise a continuous flow of decisions that produce a sustained load on the people responsible for them. Thus, the level of dedication required by operating decisions renders it necessary to distribute them among several people.

This phenomenon is seen more clearly in the growth of one-man firms. In the early stages of a small company's life, most operating decisions are made by a single person – its owner or entrepreneur. This person has a mental model of the firm in which the different operating decisions are related. To use the language of Chapter 2, the owner's TMS is the only one that exists. This means that the presence of inconsistencies is minimized, because they are detected and eliminated. Furthermore, much better use is made of knowledge because it is concentrated and associated with the same agent who solves the problems.

For example, this decision maker can relate the amount of cash to be held to the purchases that must be made in forthcoming days, and with the payment and collection dates. He/she can take into account the mutual constraints – conditions imposed by the context and which must be met in order to guarantee the system's feasibility.[4]

---

[4] In Simon's terminology (Simon, 1981), which replaces economic optimality with a long-term acceptability. In our terminology, we would say that optimality is not important. What's important is to earn enough money today so that we can survive until tomorrow and that assets are created within the firm that ensure that tomorrow we will survive to the day after…and so on. All of this is consistent with the generic mission of any firm which is indefinite survival.

As the firm grows, the volume of operating decisions increases, which eventually renders it necessary to distribute the decisions among several decision makers. At this point, a coordination problem appears which in turn leads to the necessity for an information system.

When there are several decision makers, each of them has to make sure that their TMS's remain consistent with the firm's mission, and, specifically, with the other decision makers' decisions. Purchasing managers must make their decisions so that the firm's operations have the materials needed to carry out the production plans. In turn, these plans must be coordinated with the sales department so that production is matched to what the sales department needs to give a satisfactory service to its customers. Therefore, coordination must be achieved by sharing common information. Each decision maker must be able to see the status of those parts of the system that affect his area of responsibility. The information system propagates, in a logical and consistent manner, the conditions that are not directly observable to the decision makers that need them for their activity.

The need to make operating decisions in a coordinated manner also leads to the creation of policy systems that establish conditions (rules, restrictions and priorities). This will be discussed in the sixth variable. But, the information system must also propagate, in a consistent manner, the logical consequences of the reasoning carried out by the agents with the input from common knowledge and, specifically, from the policy system.

*Types of information

In any activity of the BAS, information is produced that is associated with the performance of all of the operations' events. Each one generates information, at least, on the *type of event* and the instant in *time in which it occurs*. Furthermore, information is generated on *changes of state* in the system components affected by the event, resulting in *criteria values* and changes in the *list of events that have yet to occur*.

The information system consists of four parts: *collection, preparation, adaptation* and *distribution* of the information. This covers a broad range of issues, from coding of information in a form suitable for the transportation medium, to reduction of the information by means of data synthesis and extraction algorithms. Unprocessed information is normally unmanageable and must be systematized by grouping it in categories in databases. Once systematized, it becomes accessible in trough standard procedures. The information on operations is usually systematized in broad categories which refer to the system's different entities and their attributes. Thus, it is common to systematize in terms of information on: *entities, processors, the system's structure variables* (the six *variables*), *criteria values, events* and *knowledge*.

*Components of the information system

The managerial design of an information system is not confined to determining how the information will be managed. The design also includes identifying the operating decisions, assigning them to specific people and designing the mechanisms which provide these people with the information they need to ensure that their decisions are consistent with the organization's objective. To coin a phrase, the information system must make sure that 'everybody is playing in the same ball game'.

Therefore, a high level of logical consistency is required from the information system. The information system must not consider propositions to be true that are untrue in the real system, and vice versa. Consequently, it must accurately transmit all of the real system's propositions. This is an intuitive condition but, at the same time, devilishly demanding. On one hand, it demands that the information system not generate 'errors'. It cannot make mistakes, for example, when adding the entries on the assets side, or make logical errors in the bookkeeping.[5] This condition is equivalent to saying that the system must be able to infer only the results that follow logically from the information held. Considering that no TMS is capable of deducing all the valid consequences of the information held, the closer it is to meeting this condition, the more powerful the system will be. Since, as we have seen, not all truths can be deduced within a TMS, the system must be open to the entry of truths that it is not capable of deducing by itself. In particular, it must be open to the entry of decisions which must be made by a human or by an element that is extraneous to the system.

One of the typical errors that IT specialists have made during their short history has been their insistence on creating powerful information systems that integrate most of the relevant information. Although this defect seems to have been largely overcome, the emphasis on company-wide ERP systems (Enterprise Resource Planning, of which the SAP is the most well-known) also tends towards this direction. These systems have two main features:

1. *They tend to be closed.* It may be difficult or even impossible to introduce unforeseen true (and important) propositions. For example, it may be important for a construction company to know when a particularly severe rainy season is near (the Niño phenomenon in Ecuador, for instance). However, this information is not incorporated easily in an ERP. Consequently, the company's dependence upon such a system may give rise to pathologies insofar as it prevents the propagation of the effects of these additional conditions. On the other hand, a powerful system creates the sensation of completeness. The fact that a fragment of the world is very well modelled leads to the idea that the system is the world. And deductions made in a fragment of the world may not be valid in the real world.[6]

---

[5] To make sure that this didn't happen, in the Renaissance an Italian friar called Lucca Pacciolo invented double-entry bookkeeping. This system introduced what in modern language would be known as redundancy for error detection. In accounting, the figures must tally exactly, that is, the sums obtained by different processes must be equal. One of the authors argues that this humanly impossible no matter how hard the arithmetic may try. And probably anyone who has tried to add more than three numbers at a time would agree with this.

[6] In the United States, there have already been a number of lawsuits against ERP vendors because the system has led to incorrect conclusions that resulted in company losing money. The first sentences to be handed down have not yet enabled any trend to be determined for or against the ERP vendors.

2. *Their internal consistency is very high.* The greater a logical system's internal consistency, the more quickly and widely the consequences of an erroneous statement, an error, introduced by chance in the system, will be propagated. In a simple system, the error may be propagated within a limited area around its starting point. If there is a mistake in the sales accounting, neither the customer's account nor the cash account will tally. In a powerful, integrated system, this error may propagate to forecasts, from there to the production plan, to purchasing, and so on. The entire system will feel the effects of this error. This property, combined with the existence of mistrustful people, has been the cause of quite a few failures of theoretically powerful, integrated systems. When a powerful system gives an invalid result, for example, when it says that we have a stock of chairs but I am not seeing a single chair in the warehouse, the users may lose confidence in the system. And if the need is pressing, parallel information processing mechanisms tend to be developed. 'The computer is wrong', people say 'Don't trust it.' This gives rise to a generalized sensation that entering data, or propositions, into the system is a waste of time because it won't serve any useful purpose. And important things cease to be entered, with the result that the system's world and the real world are increasingly further apart. The consequence is schizophrenia and lack of consistency in the decisions universe.

A management analysis of the IS needs to use a methodology that avoids both of these pitfalls. The methodology is based upon differentiating the parts of the system that may be logically complete – that is, they essentially contain all of the valid propositions for a fragment of the world, of the parts of the system that cannot become logically complete since they are lacking in omniscient processing agents. A specific case will help us to explain these ideas.

Let us consider an information system that helps us operate a customer relationship management (CRM). A CRM is simply an information repository that contains data on the specific features of each customer. The repository is used to prepare personalized offers that have the maximum appeal for a certain type of customer while also bringing benefits for the company. A possible structure for the information system is shown in Figure 6.3.

The system essentially consists of a series of information capturing operations that appear each time the customer interacts with the company. These operations change the system's master database. Each time the database is used, a customer selection operation (shaded in dark) extracts customers having the desired features and creates a personalized offer for them.

In this diagram, the information collection chain is a *process sequence* – a complete collection of transformation operations that can be performed almost automatically and which do not require any involvement on the part of a decision maker. A process sequence must be implemented efficiently and consistently. A process sequence has a well-defined scope and a finite model, in the sense that all the demands that the system makes on its services can be considered beforehand. In a process sequence, the information system can do all of the work.

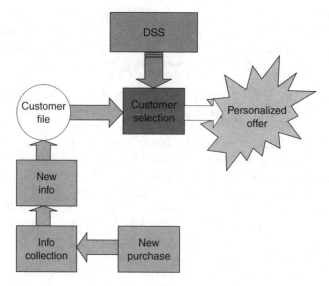

Figure 6.3   Diagram of a possible structure for the information system

However, the dark box is a very different element. There, a *decision* takes place, which someone makes using the system's information. This is an interval in the system, a break which enables the entry of propositions from outside. For this reason, we call it a *decision interval*. It is a break in the flow, that the system must anticipate in order to enable the entry of propositions from an outside agent.

An outside agent who makes decisions often needs support to use the information available. To make easier its problem-solving process, particularly during its exploratory phases, it needs to view the problem's context from different angles that help it obtain new states, evaluate the current state and develop solution heuristics. This task is open-ended. It is impossible to predict *a priori* what will be the demands of our decision maker. Consequently, we now need a system that can accommodate the potentially infinite number of requests in the decision maker's problem-solving process. This type of system, represented in Figure 6.3 by the top box, is called a decision support system (DSS).

Thus, the three functional components of an IS are the *process sequences*, the *decision intervals* and the *DSS*. From the management viewpoint, the crucial issue is the detection and positioning of the decision intervals. Once this has been done, it is relatively simple to specify the other elements. Figure 6.4 summarizes the properties of all IS's components.

It is important to highlight the features of a DSS from the viewpoint of the problem-solving process described in Chapter 1. The mission of a DSS is to expand its user's scope, helping him to construct and explore alternatives. From this viewpoint, its mission is to expand and facilitate the decision maker's exploration capacity. Generally speaking, a DSS will not shorten a decision maker's decision time. On the contrary, it will probably lengthen it by increasing the number of

Process sequences	Decision intervals	DSS
• Not discretional, defined by procedures. • Require little initiative and knowledge. • The human's role is basically one of input • The only integration required is through the data. • Each sequence may be separate from the others. • Automatable, transactionally or *ad hoc.* • They can and should be fully automated.	• Require initiative and knowledge. • Its information requirements vary depending on the system. • The human's role is to make decisions and incorporate them in the system. • Must be integrated with the firm's mission. • Cannot and should not be automated. • But must be supported.	• To support decision making. • Open-ended, dominated by the decision maker. • Exploratory by nature. • Flexible retrieval technologies. • Simple, problem-oriented interfaces.

Figure 6.4   The properties of an information system's components

alternatives that need to be explored. Thus, the main effect is not the quickest decision (this would be obtained using the appropriate conflict-resolution system), but the possibility of obtaining, over the same timespan, a higher quality solution. This enrichment is the outcome of:

(a) The ability to examine more solutions by reducing each solution's evaluation time.
(b) The ability to generate more states through improved knowledge and analysis of the problem.
(c) The possibility of performing better assessments of the state and, therefore, applying better heuristics and knowledge to obtaining the appropriate solution.
(d) The learning obtained by solving a greater number of partial problems.

A DSS is justified because the quality of the solutions obtained outweighs the fall in productivity, at least in the short term, that its use may entail.

The integration of an information system may take the extreme pathological form in which the decision intervals are *closed.* In these cases, which are fortunately quite rare in their acute phase nowadays,[7] it becomes impossible to use the system in making decisions that are outside of its bounds. Two options are then open. Either the company surrenders to the system and accepts what it proposes or it develops an informal information system that is run in parallel to the formal system. Both of these cases represent pathologies, but we have

---

[7] Although it is returning again with virulence because of the ERP. In fact, the modern disease – a mutation of the old disease – is worse, because now they close … in the design phase!

Table 6.2   Design methodology for an IS

- Document the present system.
- Identify the decisions and their decision intervals.
- Assign decisions to people.
- Identify the required information.
- Identify process sequences.
- Identify DSS requirements.

---

observed them often, particularly in those systems that are guarded by a powerful technical team.

*Designing an IS: methodology

To design an IS from the management viewpoint, we propose the methodology summarized in Table 6.2. This methodology has been designed for the use of the firm's management.

Document the present system

The present system can and must be the starting point for any redesign. When the present system is questioned, it helps us to understand the components that the future system must have. Since it is operating in the firm, it probably represents a significant part of the required system. The present system must be questioned in order to identify its problems in fulfilling the mission. This questioning, for which the WWWWH methodology can be used, starts with a description of the process intelligible to all the people involved. There are many methodologies that can be used to describe an IS but we recommend a very simple one which we present in the following section.

Identify the decisions and their intervals

Having obtained the description of the current system and questioned it, all the decisions that have been identified and which must be coordinated must be listed. The list should be complete enough to assure a proper design. Nothing more is required.[8]

Allocate decisions to people

Each decision must have a person – static or dynamic – who is responsible for its making it. This person must insert in the system additional information describing his decision, appropriately parameterized. For example, in the case of a purchase decision, the decision maker must indicate what product has been bought, in what quantity, the delivery date, and so on – all of these being parameters that enable

---

[8] One must not be tempted into exhaustive detail because then everything becomes decisions. At this level, in order to enter a quantity on a keyboard one must decide to sit down, one must decide to put one's fingers on the keyboard, one must decide to press a key… This will lead to inaction through analysis, a process that one of the authors performs with true mastery…

the decision's effect to be propagated. Assigning people to decisions is a complex process. It is in fact the organization's design, one of the key tasks in business management. We will consider these issues in more detail in Chapters 9 and 12.

Identifying the necessary information

Each decision requires – or at least it is recommendable that it use – certain information. For example, in order to calculate next month's sales figures in a typical company, information is needed about customer status, stocks, previous orders, capacity, and so on. It is not easy to identify the information that is needed. Decision makers tend to exaggerate their information requirements – including information which they may only need sporadically.[9] Determining the necessary information is a problem of identifying domain and process knowledge. For well-structured problems in which there are systematic solution procedures, the information is well characterized by the process knowledge. For more unstructured problems, many types of information could be required, depending on the case.

Identifying sequences

Now we must analyse the source of each type of required information and the process that leads to it being obtained. If this process can be described as an algorithm, not involving decision makers, it is a process sequence which can be implemented as a whole. Once identified sequences are listed. This list is essentially a summary of the system's functional analysis.

Identify DSS requirements

Finally, each decision interval must be examined in detail to detect the needs of decision-support information. This cannot be exhaustive, because (a) by the very definition of a DSS, and (b) the dynamics of the situation will require different DSS's at any different times during the system's life. Simply identifying the interval – and preserving its nature – are already two major contributions. The list of decision intervals is another valuable input to the formal software design.

*Graphic techniques

All of the above operations are performed more easily when some sort of graphic representation is used. To focus ideas, we will work with a small case which will help us review the graphic techniques (Example 6.2).

An Information and Decision (ID) flowchart describes the path that the information follows among the firm's various organizational groups,[10] and the

---

[9] The just in case attitude is very prevalent in IS. 'Let's ask for lots of information; you never know when it might come in handy. But the other way round is much more difficult.' The reader will understand if he thinks how many dictionaries (or encyclopaedias) he has bought so that his children could use them, but which have only collected dust on the shelves. But, just in case…

[10] In the classic organization, these groups are usually functional departments. However, in modern organizations, these groups are project groups or something similar. More details in later chapters.

Example 6.2   Petesa

Documents PS-05 to PS-07 are received from the offices. These documents list, respectively, personnel who have joined the firm, personnel who have left the firm, and personnel who are being transferred. These documents are sent to the personnel department, which reviews them and compares them with what has been authorized. If the movement is authorized, it is sent to the IT department, where it is prepared manually and entered on the personnel file. A listing by offices and job categories is obtained each month from the personnel file by the IT department, which sends it to the personnel department. Likewise, listings by cost centres are regularly obtained, which are sent to the personnel and accounting departments. If the incoming movement is not authorized, a telephone query is made after which the same process is followed. Finally, there is documentation generated within the personnel department itself, in the form of additions, deletions and changes added to the personnel file.

relationships with other groups that receive or send information. The description starts from the information to be received by the group. The next step is to specify, using graphical symbols the operations performed on this information, the decisions made and the documents that are generated.

The symbols which we will use, basically for uniformity reasons, are given in Table 6.3.

Structuring a diagram

It is advisable to draw the charts in a format (possibly electronic) such as that shown in Figure 6.5.[11] The chart's top row must indicate the different departments or subdepartments involved in the process to be charted.

Each column represents a group. But several other columns should be added. One column must correspond to the environment of the system being analysed. An additional column should be used for the files – common information repositories that are, (potentially) accessible to all of the decision makers. The vertical axis along the page represents time. When a process takes time, its progress is charted by a vertical line, joining those operations involved. On each line, the document (or information) travelling along it must be indicated. An examination of Figure 6.5 will help clarify the situation better than a verbal explanation.[12]

---

[11] This example is provided courtesy of Professor Rafael Andreu, from IESE's Information Systems department, to whom we owe (together with one of the authors) most of the interesting (?) concepts contained in this section.

[12] We would only point out here that we have broken the convention that time flows downwards in order to simplify the layout of the figure; this is not to be recommended!

Table 6.3 Signs for an information chart

⬭	Indicates a written document. For example, it indicates the document which contains the list of personnel entering and leaving the firm, the listing by personnel centres, and so on.
▭	Indicates an operation that is performed on the information. It is not worth while considering very elementary operations but only those that alter substantially the information or prepare it for subsequent treatment (by computer or manually). In the example, these may be file review operations.
◯	Indicates the existence of a file, normally computerized. It indicates that the information in question is stored in some manner or other. In the example, this sign indicates the existence of a master personnel file.
▢	Indicates a decision that someone makes. The most important decisions, which entail a commitment to continue in a certain manner, must be indicated.
◇	Used to indicate the existence of alternatives, depending on the outcome of the question written inside the symbol. In the example, it is used to represent a manager's authorization.
△	Indicates the obtainment of information generally outside of the company through use of a communication medium.
⬡	It is used to indicate the existence of a complex process which is not described in detail but that is charted separately. It must be used with caution because it tends to over-simplify diagrams. However, not using it makes charts cluttered and incomprehensible ...

*Analysing the conflict-resolution system (CRS)

As we have said, if the environment were stable, or foreseeable, practice, habit and experience would probably be sufficient to establish a system of operating 'rules' – a repository of rules of the organization (axioms of the TMS) whose consistent application would obtain the desired results. If, in addition, the decisions were relatively few or were all made by the same person, it would be possible to carry out all the operations without any need for a more elaborate system.

In operations, most decision making has to do with resource allocation problems. The firm possesses resources (whose levels are determined under the capacity variable) and, for this reason, must provide for situations in which the resources available will be insufficient to obtain the desired service. Resource allocation problems span a broad spectrum of difficulty – from trivial to impossible. The important point to remember is that there is a variety of intermediate situations which require specific domain, task and inference knowledge.[13]

The operators themselves may not be able to foresee situations of conflict until they occur, due to the random nature of the events that influence their occurrence. For instance, if a customer changes his desired delivery date, and it is an

---

[13] The reader will remember that we spoke about these three types of knowledge in Chapter 2.

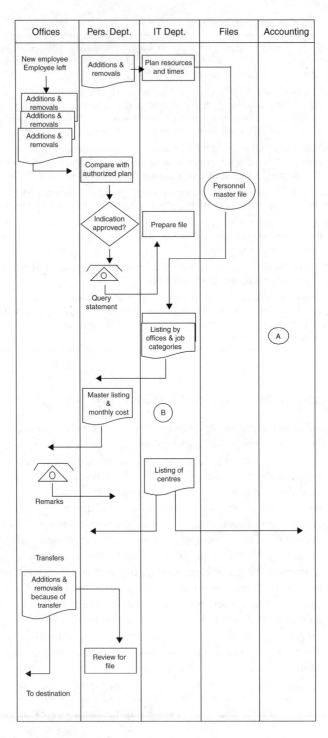

Figure 6.5 Information process chart

Table 6.4   Checklist of the information system

1. The problem: synonyms	— Who should receive the information from whom? — Why is an operation started without having received the order to proceed? — Why can't I find the items I need to operate? — Why aren't the databases up to date and why is the information obsolete? — Where is order xxxx?
2. Alternatives	— There is no need to create an information system. — Informal information: meetings, committees, etc. — Documentation included with the order to proceed. — Real-time information input on progress. — Integrated, computer-based system, ERP, etc.

3. Form of assessment	1. Operating properties
	  — What are the costs of setting up an integrated system?
	  — What type of human resources are needed to operate the system, maintain it, etc.?
	  — What is the cost of not having an information system?
	  — What barriers are there against having the right information?
	  — Operativeness of the database and cost of keeping it up to date.
	  — Degree of motivation of the personnel concerned in complying with the system.
	2. Relationship with criteria
	  — How does my information system related with my criteria, particularly consistency?
	  — What does my information system contribute to my way of competing?
	3. Relationship with the firm's knowledge
	  — Does the personnel have the necessary knowledge to determine priorities?
	  — Does my information system block my personnel's capacity for initiative?

4. General policies	1. The personnel concerned are given access to all the operations information. 2. Only the information required to perform the task is provided. 3. Exception information focused on solving problems. 4. Real-time (how real) or delayed-time system?

important customer, the result may spread to all the operations, forcing changes in resource allocation priorities throughout the system.

The conflict-resolution system lies at the heart of the problem-solving mechanism. *Its intrinsic goal is to form a common knowledge base, materialize it and distribute it so that all of the firm's agents can share it.*

The most commonly used technique for materializing knowledge in the CRS is the use of decision rules, often called *policies*. Strictly speaking, a decision rule is

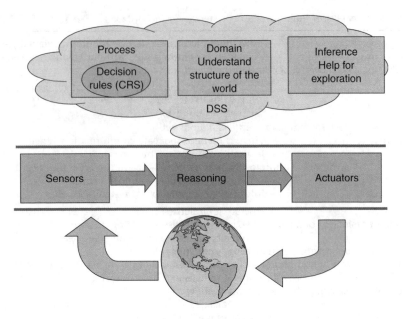

Figure 6.6   Representation of a decision support system

an inference rule whose purpose is not only to deduce a proposition but also to recommend an action. Any decision interval contains a TMS (see Chapter 2). The TMS's inference driver, the system that the agent uses to reason, is composed of the domain, process and inference knowledge available for decision making. This structure provides a functional decomposition of a decision interval. These ideas are summarized in Figure 6.6.

*Components of CRS operations

The operations conflict-resolution system is usually divided into strata or levels of aggregation. Classically, four levels have been considered:

1. The forecasting system.
2. The general resource allocation, or planning system.
3. The detailed allocation, or scheduling system.
4. The follow-up system, subdivided into a further two systems: the launch system and the control system.

Each of these subsystems is formalized by specific rules, examples of which follow:

1. The *forecasting* system tries to use the information available in order to forecast the types of conflict that may arise and when they will happen. The forecast is necessarily probabilistic because the future is random. The degree of certainty in the forecast increases as the forecast horizon shortens.

The forecasting system can be based solely upon the players' expectations, an informal system, or on the quantitative processing of the information available. This is done to obtain maximum leverage from the relationships between the available data. The ultimate basis for forecast is the hypothesis that the future shares invariants with the past – that is, that the analysis of the past enables us to determine those things that will remain on which the forecast can be based. In the absence of any invariants, it is not possible to forecast, the future is totally random and the best forecast may be the current state.

A forecasting system is a *decision-making system*. To forecast is to make a decision and, therefore, should be the responsibility of someone within the organization. Forecasts will be used to build complex reasonings that lead to presumably consistent problem-solving logics. A forecast with nobody responsible for it is a false basis for all that follows, creates mistrust within the organization and is difficult to fit in a permanent improvement system.

2. The *general allocation or planning system* is the first level of aggregation and seeks to determine an acceptable allocation of the firm's aggregate resources to the different aspects of operations. The allocation is usually made in the medium term – over a time period that is long enough to provide for obtaining resources that have a long lead time. For example, if the lead time for material deliveries is two months, the planning horizon must extend beyond this time. Otherwise, there will never be sufficient time to anticipate the correct decisions. Additionally, the resource obtainment plans must take into account the company's basic competitiveness criteria and, therefore, are the result of balancing resource availability with the cost of obtaining resources.

   Among the typical resources that must be addressed by the planning system are: people, materials, money and capital goods (or assets). Therefore, the CRS must contain rules that coordinate these decisions with the firm's strategy. For example, in a hotel a planning rule may be implemented for the recruitment of seasonal workers, specifying that they will be recruited in May and held until October. Another rule may be 'we have very few permanent employees, a chef, a maître, a receptionist and a staff manager. All the others are hired on temporary contracts.'

   It must be remembered that at this stage, the firm has already designed its capacity, the first action variable. Therefore, conceptually, the processor's capacity is one of the problem's data. Here, the general allocation system must resolve the conflict in the allocation of *scarce* resources, taking into account the possibility of its increase or decrease in the medium range.

3. The *detailed allocation or scheduling system* seeks to achieve a feasible short-term allocation of the existing resources assigned in the previous stage. The time period considered must be short enough for the allocation to be stable – that is, so that the events that take place as a result of existing uncertainties do not destroy the allocation's validity. For example, if the firm's customers call every day changing their priorities, it may be useless to try to allocate resources over a time period of one week as, after two days, the situation will change dramatically, invalidating any decisions made previously. Schedules are made trying

to anticipate the effect of external events, knowing too well that uncertainty causes many actions never to yield the expected result. In practice, one knows that schedules (and plans) are almost always not met, but one should try!

4. Finally, the *follow-up system* specifies the manner in which decisions are made after conflict develops, that is, when the allocation conflict has already occurred or is in the process of occurring. As conflicts are unavoidable in uncertain environments, their presence requires the arbitration of emergency procedures which quickly, and at lower levels of the organization, lead to a situation that is consistent with the mission's criteria. Priority rules and immediate action (both automated and manual) rules are two of the ways of specifying this part of the system.

Methodology for designing a CRS

The CRS design methodology is the result of its location within the DSS and inherits from and partially overlaps the information system design methodology. The following methodology is drawn in part from the ideas on intellectual process redesign proposed in Chapter 2. The method's phases are:

- *Identification of the problems* to be solved during each decision interval. For each decision, the typical problems that the decision maker must address in the decision process must be listed.
- *Hierarchical classification* of the problems identified with respect to the context in which they are solved. One useful way is to group them in contexts that are dependent upon the time horizon in which they take place and in accordance with the categories described above (that is, forecasting, planning, scheduling, launch, control).
- *Knowledge identification.* The knowledge available in the DSS must be catalogued using one of the existing methodologies. A simple adaptation of the inventory methodology[14] would be sufficient to catalogue the knowledge required. The three types of knowledge (domain, process and inference) form the basic taxonomy for the catalogue. Observe that in this phase we can exploit the work done in building the knowledge inventory (see Chapter 8), as the general knowledge list can be used to identify the detailed knowledge structure needed here.
- *Proposal of methodologies.* Analysis of the inference knowledge. Creation and presentation of general methodologies to help in the exploration. Although, strictly speaking, this is not part of the CRS, at this design stage we have enough structure to take a preliminary look at this important issue.
- *Proposal of rules.* This is the central point. For each problem, the 'inference rules' that best meet the firm's strategic goals must be estimated, determining their field of validity and generating specific recommendations for their use. This is a complex phase in which formal tools may shed some light. Simulation tools can be used to test alternative policies while optimization tools can contribute

---

[14] See Chapters 8 and 9 for a more detailed discussion.

by providing bench-marks and logical structures that help in the problem-solving process.

- *Forms of knowledge acquisition.* Determination of the way in which specialized knowledge must be acquired (or developed) in each problem context. Here, the ideas of the internal and external cycles, with other methodologies which will be described further on, play a central role.
- *Scope of use.* Finally, a synthesis is required of all of the elements that make up the DSS. This synthesis encompasses all three types of knowledge and should determine the appropriate technologies for using them. This phase also requires the consideration of the motivations and attitudes of the decision makers that populate the system.

The reader will note that the definition of this variable includes a significant part of the operations organizational design process. Indeed, the phases listed encompass most of this process. The main omission is the design of the motivation and objectives system, which is too far removed from the purpose of this book. Indeed, it is only possible to isolate the operations system from the rest of the firm's systems for the purpose of scientific study. But the dividing line has got to be drawn somewhere.

In practice, it is impossible to obtain a clear cut separation and, in fact, compensation design issues have been one of the classic aspects of industrial engineering. With time, they have become specialized subjects that are addressed in specialized books. But all aspects in the firm interact and are closely interrelated.

The conflict-resolution system, more than any other variable, appears spontaneously when it is not properly designed. Conflict[15] is permanent in operations. Within conflict, problems are generated and, therefore conflict becomes a source of permanent improvement. However, the existence of conflict leads to confrontations between decision makers and to organizational aggressiveness. Consequently, all decision makers are highly motivated to ensure that the (continuous) conflict does not lead to (continuous) situations that are traumatic for everybody. This motivation results itself in the birth of *local conflict-resolution systems*, which produce local stability, havens of tranquillity, isolated from the surrounding turmoil. This generates complacency among the agents.

In order that this does not occur, any globally designed system must meet the requirements for security, efficiency and stability needed in the local decision environments. Otherwise, the local decision makers will continuously modify the general system resulting into an informal system but very well adapted to their needs.

---

[15] Some authors (pedantic...?) use the term 'chaos' for perpetual conflict, taking the suggestion from the mathematical theory of singularities (or stability). If the reader prefers, he can use this expression. However, one of the authors feels that chaos is 'too abrupt'. For example, the relationship between the authors (while this book was being written) could be described as being one of continuous conflict, but not necessarily of 'chaos'.

To achieve all this, it is vital to view the problem *from the viewpoint of each of the local subagents*; otherwise, the system's useful life will be very short and evolution will take the real system further and further away from the system designed.

*Some specific rules in the provision of services

To provide a concrete example of priorities in the provision of services, we will briefly study some of the priority rules that the CRS can contain and we will illustrate its possible effects on the quality of the service rendered.

In our analysis of interference times, we have always assumed FIFO (First In First Out) as the wait discipline. In actual fact, this rule is arbitrary, but its use in service systems when the customer is present and, therefore, is physically experiencing the wait, is almost universal. In many cases, particularly in small services, it is the ethical standard *par excellence*. Changing the FIFO rule, particularly when this is done by the customer, is rated very poorly by other waiting customers offending customer is accused of 'jumping the queue'. The arbitrariness of the FIFO ethics becomes obvious when we observe that in some cultures – in China, for example – 'jumping the queue' is not perceived as a breach of queuing ethics. On the contrary, it is viewed as a palpable demonstration of the 'queue-jumper's' superior status. Only the rabble queues. In such societies, queues operate with all sorts of odd *queuing disciplines*.

The processing discipline is also selectable. The manner in which the next processor to be occupied is chosen is irrelevant if the processors are identical and are incapable of feeling put out. However, in manual jobs, certain disciplines which favour task allocation to a certain processor can, once again, constitute a breach of process ethics. Some processors could be described by the others as 'shirkers' because they do not perform their fair share. For example, a process discipline which numbers processors in an arbitrary but constant order and always allocates the job to the lowest-order free processor will bias work allocation towards the low numbered processors, who will be occupied more often than the high numbered ones. This discipline can generate a high degree of social injustice among the processors.

Table 6.5 gives a small survey of service disciplines (combination of queuing and processing disciplines) which are used in practice. Since the number of proposals considered in the literature is enormous, this sample should be viewed merely as

Table 6.5 Some service disciplines

FIFO:	First In First Out. Jobs are processed in their order of arrival, without exceptions.
LIFO:	Last In First Out. Jobs are processed in the reverse order of their arrival. Therefore, when the operator takes a new job, he always chooses the one which has arrived most recently.
SPT:	Shortest Processing Time. When choosing a job for processing, the processor chooses that which has the shortest processing time from among those waiting in the queue. Note that this requires *a priori* knowledge of the job's processing time.
DD:	Due Date. The job that has the closest delivery date is the next one chosen from those waiting in the queue.

an example. The reader will also note one important property that all these procedures share in common: *Almost all of the rules imply discrimination in favour of a certain type of customer and against another*. When one group of customers obtains an advantage, another group loses it. Therefore, the rules are generally a tool for ensuring fair distribution, and for administering scarcity, but they are not a practical way of increasing production or improving the service on a general level.

All of the decision rules imply a value judgement on the attention to be given to each type of customer. In some cases, these judgements are universally accepted as 'ethical'. Sometimes, in services that serve a social interest – for example, hospitals – the ethical standard may not be FIFO but another different rule. Nobody complains because a seriously ill patient jumps the queue ahead of someone with a sprained ankle. In paper queues, which await attention by a human processor (the IN–OUT trays), the queuing discipline is often LIFO, since this is the discipline that is obtained if the papers are stacked as they arrive and the paper that is at the top of the pile (the one that can be seen) is the one that is always processed first. In other circumstances, in the attention that a computer gives to its users when there are several using it simultaneously, the accepted rule is usually a variation of SPT (shortest processing time). The idea is, that at least in theory, the users whose jobs consume least resources may obtain a faster response from the machine. The assumption is that those who have longer jobs don't mind waiting (presumably, they have something important to calculate ... !).

Finally, when the customer is not physically present waiting for the operations' result, it is possible to dispense to a greater degree with the ethical component, using any type of decision rule that obtains the desired service and which is favourable to the interests of the person responsible for operations. For example, a job may be delayed when another one appears with a shorter delivery date (the DD rule) or priority may be given to the orders of an important customer.[16]

What is the effect of giving priority to one class of jobs over others, both as regards the system's output and as regards the service received by customers? This is an important issue and its analysis will determine whether a given rule is suitable for allocating processors to customers. One way of finding out is by trying it out. Simulating is the technical term. A simulation model is built of the operations system and is used to experiment with different rules. This simulation may generate recommendations concerning the use of rules for the various agents involved in the phenomenon.

In order to recommend a rule in a particular case, first the situation in which it will be used must be carefully analysed. If the situation is slightly special – and many business situations are unique in this respect – this analysis may require time and resources and, therefore, cost a lot of money. Or worse still, it may be so specialized that only a few people are able to perform it – people who perhaps do not exist in the company or who cannot communicate with the decision maker in a language which he can understand.

---

[16] Or the WSMB (what suits me best) rule may be used.

There are alternatives. For example, in the case of the decision rules, we have domain knowledge on the effects of applying certain categories of rules in different situations. This helps the designer to make an informed choice without having to perform costly exercises.

The priority rules can be classified by its structure. This structure is partially outlined in the table below. (Table 6.6)

Table 6.6   Types of rules

LP: Load preserving. The rule does not change the load
PR: Preemptive Resume rules. The interrupted jobs are resumed from where they were interrupted.
PI: Preemptive interrupt rules. The same as above, but they start from the beginning again.

It is known that, in general, the LP rules do not alter the total average dwell time. Therefore, although they may change the distribution of waiting times, the average service time remains the same. With the PR rules, in which the interrupted job is resumed from where it was interrupted, the higher priority customer classes do not see the lower priority classes, in other words, there are no interferences between classes and each class only uses the capacity not used by the other, higher priority classes. The PR classes tend to increase production slightly but also enormously increases the variance in the total time in the system.

Table 6.7   Checklist for conflict resolution

1. The problem: synonyms	— Who is in charge of what?
	— Who issues work orders?
	— What purpose does the operations database serve?
	— Who orders who?
	— Who sets priorities?
	— Who controls the quality of what?
2. Alternatives	— The customer's orders arrive at random and are attended to as they arrive.
	— Stocks pull production which is carried out to the warehouse.
	— Sales sends firm orders to operations.
	— There is a sales and production plan which is followed.
	— There is a detailed schedule which is kept up to date.
	— Random orders are mixed with a sales plan.
	— Scheduling includes all items or only the finished products
3. Form of assessment	1. Operating properties
	— Implementation difficulties: resources required (computers, special knowledge, and so on)

— Types of randomness, possibility of complying with schedules, possible scheduling period.
— What type of decision making is required and what are the responsibilities of the various levels
— Effect of priority and scheduling rules on operation times
— Difficulty of drawing up a detailed schedule for all levels.
— Maximum and minimum stock levels and operation batches for stock.
— Degree to which each operator must be responsible for his quality.

2. Relationship with criteria
— How the ways of solving conflicts relate with the criteria.
— Effect on service time and occupancy of operating resources.
— Performance of expected service, particularly consistency with lead times.

3. Relationship with the firm's knowledge
— Do my employees have sufficient knowledge to control their own quality?
— What initiative-taking capacity is being developed within the company?
— What effect does each way of acting have on the company's culture?

4. General policies

1. Organization structure with centralized orders.
2. Clear policies but exceptions handled at the highest level.
3. Creation of supplier–customer relationships between the different departments involved.
4. Production only for downstream demand (JIT)
5. Nothing is made until it is needed.
6. Produce for stock to occupy idle or low-demand periods.
7. Relationships policy between players: sales, production, planning, etc.
8. Items produced as soon as possible or delayed as much as possible, until they become critical.

7
Quality and Service

Introduction

A precedent of some of the ideas discussed in this book is to be found in the concepts of quality. Therefore, it is only fair that we establish this dependence in this chapter.

Over the course of the last decade, quality has been extensively addressed in both the technical and popular literature. It has become part of the conceptual baggage of politicians and engineers, often incorporating a strong emotional component. The idea of quality has left a deep imprint on the corporate world and, now that the initial blaze is starting to subside, it is becoming time to assess its true contributions.

*The history of quality and its meaning

The history of quality is a short but intense one. It started quietly in Europe, and burst into bloom in Japan in the 1980s. In many respects, confusion is still rife about the influence of the cultural context on the approach's success. The recent history of quality is basically bipolar: United States–Japan. However, Japanese corporate culture is a unique phenomenon, so importing quality ideas from there to other cultures (for example, European cultures), after having passed them through the American screen first, gives rise to new vicissitudes and problems.

Example 7.1 The history of quality

> With the replacement of craftwork by the techniques of mass production, the 1920s saw the emergence of a technical approach to quality whose purpose was to prevent faulty products from reaching customers. Its most representative concept is the inspection-based quality control which was developed during the Second World War. The English statisticians Shewart, Fisher, Snedecor and others devised sophisticated procedures which remained a military secret until

after the war. After this time, quality control techniques progressively gained acceptance, particularly in companies' more technical areas. The goods inwards and in-process controls, based on statistical techniques, became widespread in some companies.

In the 1950s and 1960s, quality – now associated with control rather than assurance – continued to be an area that received little attention from companies' general management. The quality theorists tried to endow it with a content that could appeal to senior managers. Deming, Juran and others tried to attract the attention of management professionals, developing a more qualitative, sometimes even missionary approach. In the West, this message mostly fell on dry ground. But their methods' future success was starting to germinate in the resurgence of Japan.

After the Second World War, as part of Japan's reindustrialization plan, the Americans brought many experts to the country to train a new generation of Japanese businessmen. Among the concepts taught at courses and lectures were the statistical quality control techniques and some of the ideas that the pioneers had developed to popularize these techniques. The Japanese found them to be tremendously attractive and very much in line with their culture. They adapted them to their industrial operations, leading to the birth of a quality movement in Japan.

United States realized the significance of this movement when it started to yield spectacular results, culminating in the dramatic moment when United States saw that Japan had overtaken it in terms of competitiveness.

The concern for competitiveness forced American companies to take a close look at their major competitor. In the process, they rediscovered those techniques that they had exported to Japan, albeit now adapted to Japanese culture and values. A renewed interest in quality was kindled in American companies, which reappeared under a different guise. During these years, many companies sent missions to Japan to learn from the Japanese and they started to become initiated in quality concepts through the approach's three chief exponents: Deming, Juran and Cosby who, paradoxically, up to this point had found their most receptive audiences in Japan.

With the Japanese dominating the American market, particularly in the area of automobiles, under growing pressure to compete and desperately looking for new ideas, companies considered making a quantum jump in quality management, moving from a tactical situation to a strategic situation. This led to the concept of total quality – the notion that a company does not sell just its products or services but the entire organization and its success is determined by the level of performance of all its functions.

Interestingly, during the 1990s, western business became a strong evangelist for quality. The concern for quality led to the creation of numerous quality awards all over the world, which are granted to companies that excel in this function.

Example 7.2   Some meanings of the word quality

- **Performance**: In this meaning, an object (or service) has more quality than another when the performance of the former is superior to those of the latter, when measured by a series of commonly accepted parameters. In this sense of the word quality, a Rolls-Royce has more quality than a Citröen 'deux chevaux', the performance of the former is superior to those of the latter as regards measures such as safety, speed, comfort when driving on the open road or in towns, and so on.
- **Compliance with specifications**: From this viewpoint, quality is defined as fulfilment of the expectations regarding a product or service. Discovery of this meaning some years ago led to considerable confusion. Under this meaning, a Rolls-Royce and a 'deux chevaux' have the same quality so long as they satisfy the customer's expectations, which will be different in each case.
- **No defects**: This is a particular instance of the previous definition. A non-fulfilment of a specification becomes a defect when the customer can clearly perceive this non-fulfilment. Like all of the other meanings, a defect is something relative. For example, something that would not be perceived as a defect in a firearm in the eighteenth century would be unacceptable in a modern weapon.
- **Reliability**: According to this meaning, quality indicates the absence of properties that shorten the time between failures that lead to a deterioration in the service's (or object's) performance in normal use.
- **Attention to details**: According to this meaning, the quality of a service or object is associated with the sensation given when great care has been taken in all the details that have a bearing on the user.

As a consequence of its turbulent history, the term quality has been used in a number of contexts and with many different implications. The reader should be aware of the coexistence of, at least, the meanings listed in Example 7.2.

The stages of quality

For a long time, companies have been looking for a system for implementing actions to achieve the ultimate goal: to do things as has been promised to the customer and with assured service. This does not simply mean delivering the promised product or service to the customer, but also taking on the responsibility for future interactions and giving a satisfactory answer in all cases.[1] The quality movement has sought to give the answer, but with mixed results to date.

---

[1] We refer the reader to what was said in Chapter 4.

Example 7.3 The quality culture

Many authors have discussed the reasons for the success of the quality approach in Japan. Now that the mist has cleared, it can be concluded that the following conditions have been necessary, although not necessarily sufficient, for this success:

- The employees' total *involvement* and management commitment. Awareness of a common goal and commitment. Acceptance that innovations lead to the appearance of problems which must be solved.
- The firm's long-term outlook. Total *priority* for quality, encompassing all of the firm's activities; from product planning to sales and aftersales service.
- Involvement of all workers in identifying and *solving problems*. Recognition that problems don't have people to blame for them, but solutions. Development of participation tools – for example, promotion of quality circles by senior management. These expanded outside of Japan though implementation in subsidiaries and branches. Many companies included quality circles in their education and training activities.
- Great emphasis on *training*, using case studies, problem-solving activities, and group discussions.
- *Trust in the problem's scientific aspects.* Development and application of statistical techniques, multivariant analysis, experiment design (*Taguchi*), and so on.
- *Promotion of total quality activities* at national level, with a significant motivation and appeal. Acceptance of attitudes which, in other cultures, seem rather ridiculous or embarrassing, but which have a great communication power. Events such as October, standardization month, and November, quality month, Deming prizes and JIT prizes.

We think that the one great contribution made by quality is to have formulated the three basic goals to be achieved: *to provide a service that is consistent with what has been promised, to fulfil specifications, and to guarantee performance.*

The message is simple but making it a reality requires an enormous effort on the part of every member of the organization. Quality seeks to chart the path to do this, providing operating tools to assist in the task.

As we saw when we described the BAS (see Chapter 4), there are at least two implementation levels for the quality idea which, in some way, form a logical sequence in the idea's evolution. The first is quality control – to avoid defects from reaching downstream stages of the process, or reaching the customer. The second is quality assurance. Quality assurance implies modifying processes so that no defects are produced. Thus, quality assurance goes beyond eliminating defects, focusing instead on eliminating their causes.

However, when these two ideas proved to be insufficient to achieve the goals proposed, the quality movement introduced a third idea total quality. Total quality is not a natural evolution from the quality assurance idea; rather, it constitutes

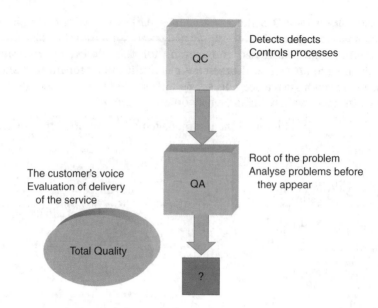

Figure 7.1   Evolution of the quality concept

a side link in the evolution's logic. A much more abstract phenomenon, it focuses its message on a continual desire on the part of the firm to 'do things well' to satisfy its customer.

Different tools are used to implement the quality ideas at each level. Quality control has technical tools – knowledge materialized in the form of procedures – which can be used immediately for solving problems, most of which are structured. The knowledge required in this phase is domain and task knowledge. In quality assurance, since the problems are less structured, the tools draw to a greater extent on inference and task knowledge. These are tools which contain knowledge for 'solving knowledge-related problems'. (See Figure 7.1.)

By contrast, in total quality, there is no precise implementation tool structure. Rather than dealing with formalized knowledge, total quality is concerned with skills that are difficult to transfer and apply outside of their original context. Given this situation, it is not surprising that some companies confine themselves to mimicking the movements of certain leading firms that have implemented this type of system and (because of this or any other reason) have succeeded and become leaders in their sector. The followers copy the procedures, and imitate the leader, but they do not have a complete understanding of the system.

In other cases, faced by a lack of implementation procedures, total quality is replaced by a model with a more restricted scope, but one which is easier to implement. This restriction is a tacit recognition of the impossibility of giving a deep content to the idea. The quality prizes have utilized this approach. In the model used for the European Quality Prize, or the Baldridge Prize, the total quality idea is broken down into a series of attributes, which are then weighted. There are

Example 7.4   What do some understand by total quality?

On a trip to a certain Latin American country, one of the authors passed an army barracks. At that moment, typical military exercises were being carried out on the parade ground. A squadron of soldiers, with camouflage uniform and highly polished boots (whose shine would perhaps defeat the purpose of the camouflage), were marching at a rapid pace. At the same time, they were singing marching songs which sounded more like rap than patriotic songs. When he passed by the barracks entrance, the author read the motto on top, written in letters one yard high. The author has seen many barracks with patriotic messages written above the gates, such as 'Everything for my country' or 'At the service of the people', or some similar cabalistic phrase. At this barracks, the message written above the gates was: 'Our motto is: Total Quality'...

Example 7.5   The European Quality Prize

Created in the likeness of its predecessor, the Malcolm Baldridge prize in the United States, the European Prize is open to all companies who think that they meet the criteria specified by the founding committee. Candidates must submit their structures for scrutiny by a group of experts who evaluate different aspects of these structures. The criteria and their relative weight are shown in the figure. As can be seen, the idea of achieving 'quality' is replaced by that of 'getting a good score in the criteria'. The highest score is given to customer satisfaction, but business performance and process structure account for 29 per cent of the total weight. Thus, under this outlook, having 'quality' consists 14 per cent of having good processes and 15 per cent of performing well financially.

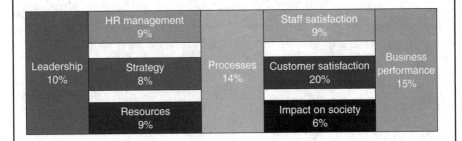

In Spain, the Renfe's high-speed train (AVE) won the European Quality Prize in 1998. Anyone who has travelled on the AVE knows that it is an excellent means of transport with a good service. However, it is also common knowledge that there are a large number of problems with the service. These problems range from difficulties in obtaining the points associated with a ticket, the technical quality of the films shown, or the appearance or behaviour of some of the staff. As a result of the substitution of concepts, these minor problems, which affect customer service, are masked in the prize's nine criteria. However, the AVE unit is aware that a good score does not necessarily guarantee the absence of operating problems.

many different types of attributes and the weighting is an explicit statement of the importance and priority of the actions referred to each attribute. The definition of 'Total Quality' in the 'European Quality model' in terms of attributes indeed simplifies the concept, but it also makes it much easier to apply.

Quality as the management of customer interactions

In this book, we subsume all of the above ideas into just one single, overarching concept. For us, *quality is the management of the interactions that take place in the interface between the customer and the firm*. More specifically, it is the management of the mechanism by which the customer's expectations and the firm's service become satisfactory to both agents.

When *this notion of quality* is applied, it becomes an integral part of knowledge management. However, we do not see quality as synonymous with knowledge management, because knowledge management is much more than quality. Quality must not take on full responsibility for improvement because it is not up to the task. This is because it does not actively use knowledge which, as we will see, is an essential part of the process. However, it does play a key role in managing part of the system – the part that puts the firm in contact with the customer.

Let us consider the main implications of this notion of quality focused on customer satisfaction. Every customer has a hierarchy of needs (Maslow, 1943). This hierarchy extends from those basic factors which cover his fundamental needs to the desire to be recognized as an individual by his fellow men. Now lets apply an idea that has already been introduced in Chapter 4, namely, to *examine the customer's expectations one by one* and to determine what the firm can do to satisfy them. To do this, we will consider the *different attributes of the expectations*. Each attribute implies categories of actions that the firm must carry out to satisfy expectations and which, in many cases, correspond to different visions of quality, such as those described in Example 7.3.

An approach like this is exhaustive and justified in some cases (see Example 7.6). However, a full description of this approach would be very lengthy (Muñoz-Seca, Riverola, Sprague) and is beyond the scope of this book. Therefore, we will confine ourselves to analysing only those attributes that clearly show how the previous definitions of quality are fully contained in the present definition.

Example 7.6   An exhaustive analysis of a customer's needs

A few years ago, the authors worked with a group of local experts on an analysis of the quality of Bulgarian hotels. Following the demise of the previous regime, the resort complexes on the shores of the Black Sea previously used by high-ranking State officials ceased to perform their original function. Most of them were converted into tourist resorts with luxury hotels often having several hundred rooms. However, the pervading spirit among all the parties involved continued to be that of a bureaucracy, with significant quality problems in the service given, which was often spoiled by seemingly trivial situations. Furthermore, the hotel's surroundings, in enclaves such as Varna, lacked the services that other resorts offered to their visitors. Thus, the first tourists who visited the country found that many of their expectations went unfulfilled. The managers of the new hotels felt the need to do something to remedy the situation but all their attempts, based on ideas taken from quality manuals, remained as minor efforts that did not alter the overall situation. In order to effectively address the problem, a comprehensive approach was needed, starting from an integrated concept of a tourist's expectations.

The basic idea is that an inhabitant of a community is accustomed to obtaining the services he needs from a network of personal and institutional contacts, whose structure and configuration are familiar to him. Therefore, any need is solved by using the network available. However, when a tourist goes to another place, particularly if he goes to a foreign country like Bulgaria, his network of contacts breaks down. His links with the environment are changed, problems and new situations arise, and in the absence of a suitable structure, the tourist may find himself bewildered and frustrated. A minor arm injury may become a very distressing experience if there is no access to the local health network.

The hotels are the key point of contact between the tourist and the network of local services. Therefore, when analysing a hotel's services, it is necessary to consider the full hierarchy of human needs, since all of them are addressed in the rendering of those services.

As a result of this work, a series of tools was created to determine customer requirements, and then mechanisms were designed to 'restore the missing links'. The results were presented to a group of hoteliers in Varna. These results were good enough to convince the Varna hotels to cooperate with the group of local experts, to whom all the necessary knowledge was transferred to enable them to continue with the project unaided.

*Service around an object

Let us start by considering the attributes of a service that is performed around a product – that is, as a result of the exchange of a good.

When the exchange takes place around a good, the following expectation attributes must be considered:

- *The customer is more satisfied if he does not find any defects.* One clear and immediate goal of the interface must be to prevent any defects from reaching the customer. But what is a defect? In the absence of any direct feedback from the customer, firms usually consider the matter solely from their viewpoint, defining a series of specifications that must be met by the product to be delivered. They then produce an operating definition of a defect as a non-fulfilment of these specifications. *Specifications* are different from *expectations*. Expectations refer to the possibility of someone 'expecting' a certain functionality. Specifications are an operational, measurable and verifiable definition of expectations given by an agent. The implicit assumption of this approach is that the customer is satisfied if the specifications are met – that is, if the customer's expectations match its operationalization in terms of specifications.

  Focusing on the elimination of defects leads firms to two types of action:

  (a) *A barrier is raised between the firm and the customer that the service must overcome if it is to reach the customer.* This leads directly to quality control. If this aspect is the only one considered, the next consideration would be what is the optimal number of defects to be produced. The idea behind this optimization is very simple. There are two basic costs associated with defects. First, there is the *cost of detecting a defect.* This grows as the percentage occurrence of defects decreases and it grows at an increasing rate due to the diseconomies of scale that arise when one tries to wring the last drops of quality from a process. On the other hand, there is a *cost of having defects* which arises from their presence in places where they can have harmful consequences for one or other of the agents involved. These include repairs, customer complaints, addition of value to products which must then be scrapped (or reprocessed) because of the defect, and other similar costs. The sum of both costs gives the value of the total cost, which, when suitably minimized, gives the optimal number of defects. This argument is summarized in graph form in Figure 7.2.

  Of course, this approach is totally incorrect because it is incomplete. It places too much emphasis on the short term and it omits any consideration of the firm's competitiveness. It can be argued that the cost of a defect is almost infinite, since its existence causes serious damage to the firm's future competitiveness and also opens the door to competitors, enabling them to form a competitive strategy based on the non-presence of defects.[2] If a competitor reduces the number of defects beyond what is reasonable (measured from the cost viewpoint), it will probably incur a higher cost. Furthermore, it may not even improve its competitiveness in the short term because the customer does not expect a product with such good quality. The customer

---

[2] Sometimes, people have tried to convey these ideas by saying that 'quality is free'. As a catchphrase, it's not bad but, obviously, the idea is totally and absolutely false. Quality is never free. Doing things badly is almost always cheaper than doing them well...

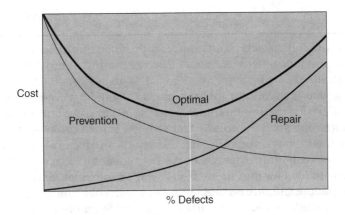

Figure 7.2 Optimal number of defects

'does not appreciate' what the firm is offering to him. However, albeit scorned by some, this tactic has the property of accruing *operative margin* (COM) to those who follow it – a potential energy that can be released at the right time.

(b) *Prevent defects generated by the firm from reaching the point of interaction.* This idea is equivalent to the quality assurance approach. It's in order.[3] This change must affect the firm's processes, which are those that produce the service and which, therefore, may give rise to anomalies that lead to customer dissatisfaction. All of the firm's members must devote themselves obsessively to the task of preventing the processes from producing defects.

- *The customer's satisfaction increases as a result of improvements in the product's or service's performance.* In this case, the concept of 'performance', meaning improved functionality, is added to the customer's expectations. According to this implication, quality must start with the product's design and continue throughout the BAS. In this instance, the creation of specifications, and not just their fulfilment, becomes the critical step in achieving quality. Here, it is accepted that specifications are one of the service's design variables, a variable that must be stipulated after having observed the reality of the customer's wishes. Measuring these expectations is a basic prerequisite for being able to satisfy them later.

- *The customer is more satisfied if the firm corrects the anomalies that occur with respect to his expectations in the use of the product.* This introduces the explicit idea that expectations are a dynamic process that occurs throughout the interaction between customer and firm. Many products, such as education, are deferred consumer goods. The customer's true satisfaction may take years to appear. And, during this period, events happen that endanger satisfaction and which must be settled as satisfactorily as possible. The difficulties raised by this

---

[3] The typical slogan of this approach is 'quality is not controlled, it is produced'.

Example 7.7   Fersa

In a joint committee with a certain country's armed forces, Fersa, a company specializing in military electronics, studied the specifications for a fire control system for use with anti-aircraft batteries. The mission of an anti-aircraft fire control system is to collect data from the radar and, in general, from a group of sensors, about the position and speed of an attacking aircraft. With this information, the system forecasts the aircraft's future position and aims the guns towards that position. After more than three years' work, during which prototypes were built that passed all the specifications, there was a change in the command. Following this change, it was decided that it was not worthwhile upgrading the existing anti-aircraft guns because the air defence tasks could be carried out more efficiently by missiles. The project was abandoned, producing heavy losses for both parties and also a highly demoralized engineering team.

concept are obvious. The customer's expectations do not remain unchanged from the time they are measured and, therefore, sufficient provision must be made for such changes. The longer the time frame – the 'time on the market' – is, the easier it is for discrepancies to appear.

*Service quality: expectations in service activities

The attributes of the previous section must now be extended to a consideration of service operations. Traditionally, in product companies, the scope of the interaction was circumscribed to the environment of the object being exchanged. The satisfaction of expectations was limited to the interaction with the goods in question. When he bought a pencil, for example, the customer's satisfaction was assumed to be based solely on how smoothly it wrote, the strength of the lead and other similar properties of the object.[4]

However, in modern firms, this changes dramatically. It is simply the result of the structure of the service activities, which all companies have within the BAS's service chain.

In services, the agent's higher needs come into play. In most restaurants, for example, the aim is not simply to satiate the agent's hunger.[5] The service's primary feature is the satisfaction of certain higher-order needs: aesthetics, comfort, individual respect or mutual recognition.

---

[4] Although it may seem strange, elementary economic theory continues to postulate this hypothesis by assigning satisfaction (or utility) to the pure act of the exchange. As a result, many students embark upon their career in business with precisely the wrong idea, which they then have to change.

[5] If this were to be so, any transport café would do the job…

A significant change takes place in the interaction whereby the intensity of the interaction – the degree to which the customer interacts with all the private and public aspects of the firm – is increased considerably. A service's quality is assessed during the entire period of the customer's interaction with the firm, but particularly during the moments of truth. Therefore, an adequate discussion of quality should be based on the integral consideration of expectations in the entire firm–customer interface.

The intensity of the interaction between customer and company results from a series of causes:

1. *The customer comes into contact with the inner reality of operations.* In a service activity, the customer moves inside our operations and becomes an integral part of it. For example, in a travel agency, the customer has a direct perception of how the employee interacts with the airline, how he handles the information, how complete it is, and so on. Often, the customer is the passive object of the process. In a hairdressing salon, the customer undergoes the operations of hair-cutting, manicure and styling, sometimes with frustrating or even hazardous results. The conclusion is that the minute details of the manner in which the firm's processes are performed have a great influence on the satisfaction of the customer's needs. A mechanical, impersonal process may achieve the same purpose as a personalized, human service, but the latter has the necessary elements to achieve a better match with the customer's higher-order needs.

2. *Each customer needs a specific, individualized treatment that is appropriately matched to his problem.* Each customer requires an individual service because each customer is both physically and mentally unique.[6] This uniqueness gives rise to a high level of variety in the demand, which must be offset against the variety in the service supply. As a consequence of this 'law of required variety',[7] the people who deal with the customer must have developed problem-solving skills.

3. *The customer comes into contact with the employees who work on the firm's operating levels.* As a result, the customer must interact with people having different levels of training, power or decision-making capacity.[8] In an airline, when a customer complains about a delay, an employee may reply that 'the planes' punctuality is not my problem'. Strictly speaking, this statement may well be true. However, the customer will perceive a lack of interest on the part of the employee to solve his problem. In short, the company will be letting the customer down through its employee.

---

[6] Which implies nothing regarding the customer's quality in either aspect. As Lucy said to Charlie Brown: '*Charlie Brown, you are a unique human being. For whatever it's worth, Charlie Brown, you are you!*'.

[7] A term which we owe to Ashby, who proposed it as a cybernetic principle ...

[8] It is well-known that when one has a friend in a firm's senior management, one is treated much better. In many cases, 'friendocracy' is still the best way to get a good service. However, this has a perverse effect. When the authors perceive that they are being attended to well because they are friends of somebody who has a lot of clout in the company, this gives them a terrible impression of the company's average service, since it means that the customer will not be treated properly unless he is someone important (like one of the authors).

4. *The initiative in asking for the service is held by the customer*. The customer asks for the service when he wants to and is often annoyed if he has to wait to receive it. This circumstance is not found so often in firms that exchange goods. The firm offers a lead time and, within this time, it has a certain degree of freedom in scheduling the operations that give rise to the good, to suit its own convenience or economy.

5. *The perception of the service is very subjective*. It is impossible to objectify a service's quality. A product can be examined objectively, perhaps by performing tests and diagnoses in a laboratory. An engine's horsepower, a car's acceleration, can be measured with precision, leaving no doubt as to its quality. The same cannot be said in the case of services. Some people may like a film (the service is perceived positively) while others may not like it (the service is perceived negatively). In either case, this opinion may be due to subjective, non-objectifiable reasons.[9]

6. *Errors are very difficult to remedy because the customer sees them as personal affronts*. Mixed with his expectations, the customer has ethical judgements. Lack of solicitude by an employee may be interpreted as a lack of ethics, or lack of consideration, and provoke a state of exasperation within the customer.[10] The typical case is that of the queuing disciplines, which we have discussed in Chapter 6. In the West, FIFO is the ethical discipline and any breach of this discipline is seen as an offence.

These are some of the most crucial aspects of the customer–firm interaction in which quality improvement must be carried out. As we can see, this concept of quality enriches the original concept and links it with the other ideas which are addressed in this book.

*Some proposed actions

In this section, we will briefly examine some of the actions proposed by quality with a view to improving the interface between customer and firm.

The range of actions traditionally proposed is summarized in Figure 7.3. In many cases, the literature does not offer detailed description of how the basic recommendations should be implemented. People talk, for instance, of implementing a 'quality culture', but since nobody is very clear as to how this should be carried out, they end up recommending some type of 'group' activity.

---

[9] During the darker periods of Spain's recent history, one of the authors had the opportunity to take part in Cine Forum sessions. These sessions were a means of seeing films that were semi-prohibited (or completely prohibited) out of the sight and hearing of the authorities. However, as well as tasting forbidden fruits, we also had the opportunity to savour some indigestible products of hermetic cinema, which at that time were considered to be masterpieces. *O tempora, o mores*...

[10] Of course, another typical fallacy is that 'the customer is always right'. Sometimes he is, but there are also unbearable customers who not only are not right but should be punished for their behaviour. It is another of those 'famous sayings' that have no basis in reality.

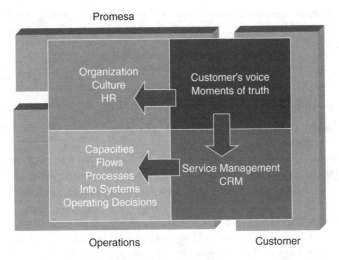

Figure 7.3 Actions for positive interactions

Many classic actions are based on the idea that, for some mysterious reason, sharing experiences will reveal how to 'do things well'. This is why, traditionally, group activities are recommended. Of course, these techniques may be either suitable or unsuitable and their use may either lead to the desired goal or they may be very harmful. *Often, group work is a very efficient way of wasting time.*

Behind this universe of measures, there is a germ that is worth considering it in a little more detail.

Let us consider what happens to a firm that confines itself to performing quality control – that is, it places a barrier so that faulty products cannot reach the customer. In the absence of a continual drive to improve, the firm will embark upon a downward spiral. This is called the 'vicious circle of quality'. Its main feature: trying to solve the problem without carrying out an in-depth diagnosis of its cause.

In such a situation, the worker does not have sufficient knowledge and tools to understand and diagnose the situation. His perception is that there is some outside element that is forcing him to reject part of his work. Even if he is working under self-inspection, where he performs control his own work, there is a foreign agent that hampers its output by setting certain conditions that must be fulfilled, without giving any further explanation.

This leads to the vicious circle shown in Figure 7.4. Pure reprocessing, without any improvement, leads to new defects, with an increasingly negative impact on the agents, who never see their work improve. In short, nobody learns from the mistakes and the problem may re-occur at the most inappropriate time.[11]

As the opposite of the vicious circle, a *virtuous circle* of quality has also been described. In this circle, the worker controls his own process and has the necessary

---

[11] By effect of Murphy's law.

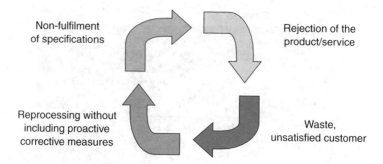

Figure 7.4   The vicious circle of quality

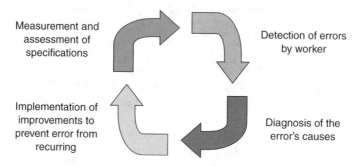

Figure 7.5   The virtuous circle of quality

tools and *knowledge* to diagnose the error's causes and act to correct them. In this situation, the worker has a proactive approach to improvement and, since he understands the reality that surrounds him, he is able to take steps towards it. The firm's actions are not only based on objective data on what has happened, but also on the reasons that lie behind those facts (Figure 7.5). (See Example 7.8.)

The missing link

Everything that has been said in this chapter can be summarized in one simple idea: *Because things never turn out right the first time, because operating problems are recurrent and give us the opportunity to improve, because everyone wants to do their job well, **things must go better each day** and, to achieve this, each worker must be given a framework of action that makes this possible.*

This idea in fact proposes the missing link in the development of quality – a link which we have identified with question marks in Figure 7.1, and which is unveiled in all its glory in Figure 7.6.

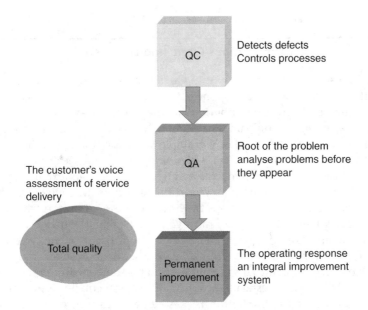

Figure 7.6   Permanent improvement

Although the idea is well known and people talk about it a lot,[12] the notion of permanent improvement has never achieved a dominant status, and has relinquished the place that corresponds to it to total quality. The reason is very simple and has already been suggested in earlier sections. Until now, there was no paradigm that subsumed the causality associated with improvement. For this reason, most of the measures proposed yielded mediocre results in practice and eventually disheartened the agents involved. Only by identifying the drivers of permanent improvement is it possible to lay the foundations for the implementation of this system. This is role achieved by the process of *knowledge management*.

This book's fundamental thesis is that *the driving force for improvement is the knowledge held by the company* (and by the agents who comprise it). Therefore, knowledge management is essentially the implementation of the PDM system and vice versa.

---

[12] Kaizen has been the flagship of this approach. However, in spite of its popularity, Kaizen has been a limited approach that has lacked a dynamic mechanism. How many companies does the reader know that have implemented Kaizen? As the reader will have observed, each time a new concept becomes fashionable, the same old companies say that they are already doing it. Are they really that dynamic? Or are they simply putting a new name to what they were already doing or, simply, generating publicity for themselves? I am sure that the truth is the first statement ...

Example 7.8   Implementation of the virtuous circle

The Virtuous Circle Implemented

We will illustrate this process by using a classic example of a virtuous circle. Now that the Japanese are no longer in vogue, this is the perfect time to acknowledge their great contributions to the world of continuous improvement. In Japan, many companies have implemented mechanisms for applying the virtuous circle. And the classic example is the Kawasaki plant in Kobe. In this plant, each work station has a series of lights that are clearly visible from all parts of the factory. The lights have different colours – for example, yellow, blue and red. The procedure followed in the factory is the following: when a worker discovers a defect, he stops the line and presses a button which turns on the yellow light. The foreman must go immediately to where the problem is (with the line stopped!) to try to find out why it has happened and how it must be corrected. If he is unsuccessful, he presses the button again, this time turning on the blue light. This is an indication for someone from process engineering to come and investigate the causes of the problem. If this investigation fails to find the cause, the button is pressed again to turn on the red light, which will bring on the scene someone who is responsible for the product's design to solve the problem. This is a clear example of the importance given to finding the cause of the problem in this plant.

---

*Quality certifications

We cannot end this chapter without making a few comments about ISO-9000 and its derivatives.

History shows that since statistical control was developed, quality has focused on: *processes*. Processes are also the core of quality's current big star: *certifications*.

The ISO-9000 standards are an international quality standard and must be met by all companies who wish to submit tenders to certain government agencies and be suppliers for certain other companies. Their goal is to keep under control the technical and administrative factors that affect the quality of products or services. We could say that ISO-9000 requires the presence of detection, observation and comparison tools in order to identify the manner in which the BAS's functions affect the customer–company operating interface.

The idea of the certifications is that it is impossible to attain an acceptable quality level[13] unless all of the people within a company follow *procedures* (processes) that are suitable for achieving this goal. And in order for this to happen, the

---

[13] Whatever that may mean, as the ISO standards do not define what is understood by quality. Well, that wouldn't be a bad place to start ...

following requirements must be met:

- A procedure must exist for each relevant operation.
- The appropriate processes for each operation must be documented.
- The processes must be strictly adhered to.

Therefore, the certifications stress the provision of proof of the *existence of the procedures, their documentation and the controls required to ensure their use.*

The certifications have generated impassioned debate both for and against within companies. In itself, the only thing that the certification provides is the empirical observation that the process's specification exists and that it is met.

So why has there been so much discussion about its use? In our opinion, the cause is to be found in the frustration that many companies feel when they see the enormous effort they have made to achieve certification and the comparatively small benefits it has brought them. The certification *does not seek to question processes* in order to examine their match with the firm's purpose, but simply confines itself to documenting and certifying the *existence of processes.*

Only when the certification effort is coupled with a systematic effort to *question* the process (as we have seen in Chapter 5) does the firm obtain tangible results.

On one hand, the way in which the activities are performed must be documented. However, at the same time, it is necessary to question the way in which these activities are being performed – and to change them when the firm's internal or external circumstances so advise. Otherwise, the certification will ossify procedures and turn the firm into something inflexible and static.

This is the proactive approach to certifications. They must be a challenge for the firm. Become certified to help you compete (most of your major customers are asking for it), but look to the added value of systematic questioning to improve.

Part III
On Good Thinking

8
The Knowledge Inventory

In *the process of managing* a firm's knowledge, the first steps must be to identify the knowledge it has and to perform a preliminary evaluation of its competitive features. In this chapter, we address the problem of how to identify a firm's knowledge. What we know and how much we know are the two basic issues that we seek to answer and are usually among the first questions that the authors consider when they want to know more about a company. And the range of answers we find is very broad. Most firms are unable to come up with a quick answer. In fact answering these questions is by no means a trivial undertaking and requires a fairly elaborate process.

Identifying knowledge

Most of the knowledge held by a firm is organized operating knowledge – either in abstract or experiential form. Normally the company wants to draw up an inventory in order to identify deficiencies or new possibilities in what the firm knows.

The implication of this is that knowledge must be inventoried with a high degree of disaggregation, which, in any case, must be similar to that required when inventorying other types of assets. A highly aggregated determination may give the idea that it is possible to solve an overly large category of problems. It is best to carry out a detailed determination, subsequently integrating knowledge in suitable categories.

In this section, we present a knowledge inventory methodology that has been tested in a number of business situations and which enables the systematic handling of the complexity existing in a real-life situation.

Knowledge must be identified with its subsequent use in mind. Depending upon this use, it may be necessary to inventory knowledge belonging to several of the categories of Chapter 2, some of them fraught with conceptual and practical difficulties. In order to avoid complications while covering the widest possible range of practical cases, our definition of purpose is chosen with some care.

Specifically, we conceive two uses for a knowledge inventory:

- *Choosing the firm's key knowledge portfolio (or its core competences).* This decision consists of determining what knowledge (competences) the firm will use to offer a competitive service in the future. This decision will determine what priorities the firm must set in terms of investment, research, knowledge acquisition and training in order to become a leader in the chosen field. Having formed its knowledge portfolio, it must then choose those activities which it must develop, maintain or eliminate. Any decision on activities that does not take into account the development of key knowledge runs the risk of being efficient in the short term but dysfunctional over the longer term.

This knowledge (possibly grouped by competences) comprises a true knowledge *portfolio*. First, the whole has properties that are different from the sum of the parts, because the interaction between types of knowledge adds properties that are very important for their practical use. Second, there are a number of risks that are inherent in the process. The key knowledges for the firm's future – the knowledges which will make it competitive – may not necessarily be the knowledges that were expected. It may be other knowledges determined by circumstances beyond our control. This creates an intrinsic risk similar to that which exists within financial portfolios. Example 8.1 illustrates a situation in which the existence of a knowledge portfolio was very important for the company's survival.

- *Using the knowledge portfolio to create new assets.* As competitiveness is manifested in service to the customer, knowledge must be turned into assets so that it can be used in operations that provide the service. A knowledge inventory provides the raw material for a systematic analysis of the generation of new products, services or processes. A new product requires the presence of a body of knowledge. This knowledge encompasses both the product's design and the process used to make it. In general, it extends to the whole BAS that must support the service. A knowledge inventory provides a means for systematic visualization of the possibilities and shortcomings of a particular development. Specifically, there are three subtypes of questions that can be asked:

  - Given a service, does the knowledge needed to provide it exist? What knowledge is missing and where can it be found?
  - Given a body of knowledge, what services can be generated from this knowledge?
  - Given a body of products and knowledge, how should they evolve so that the firm can remain competitive?

These definitions of purpose are quite clever because they achieve an equilibrium between utility and feasibility. Thus, for the furtherance of utility, we concentrate on developing and building services – an area that holds great importance for designing the future. With regard to feasibility, and referring again to the classification given in Chapter 2, the approach enables us to concentrate on operating knowledge, leaving to one side the difficulties associated with reflexive knowledge.

For the purpose stated, perceptional knowledge is less important. From the feasibility viewpoint, the lack of overall structure of the experiences would force us to list them one by one. This is a slow, time-consuming task since the lack of an underlying structure does not allow an implicit enumeration.

Example 8.1 Identifying key knowledge

Software Castilla, SL (I)

Software Castilla is a small company, which specializes in software develop-ment. It was formed in 1992, after the Barcelona Olympic Games, by a group of people who had played an active part in creating the IT system used during the Games. The company initially undertook a series of turnkey projects in which it designed the software and subcontracted its development to third parties. A knowledge analysis performed in 1993 showed that the company had competitive knowledge, among other things, in the following areas: data-base design, user interface design, information system design and IT project management. The company decided to focus its business on this knowledge. As a result of the Olympic project, there were two Internet experts among the company's founder members. In 1993, this knowledge seemed to be a very specialized area outside of the company's basic lines of business. What is more, the company had no projects in this area.

At this time the company decided to eliminate this knowledge, moving the two experts to another more productive field. Shortly afterwards, Software Castilla's CEO met a consultant who warned him about the risks of concen-trating on a narrow market. Narrow markets are imperfect, in the sense that they may not provide business opportunities for certain knowledge, even though it may be competitive.

During the period 1993–96, in spite of the unflagging efforts made by the company to sell services based on what it considered was its key knowledge, it was unable to build up a substantial order book in these fields. In order to increase its turnover, almost without realizing it, it started to accept projects in areas such as intranet and local networks, which the market was demanding in abundance. By 1997, the company had reassigned virtually all of its staff to projects involving telecommunications, internet, intranet, etc., and was com-petitive in these fields. This had required a substantial investment, particularly in higher project costs, because of the learning involved.

Therefore we will concentrate on identifying organized operating knowledge. Further on, we will come back to the issue of perceptional knowledge in order to comment on a number of developments that enable an effective consideration of this knowledge.

To illustrate our methodology, we will use the case of Example 8.2, which describes the context of a knowledge inventory performed by the authors. We have selected this case to illustrate how the methodology proposed is capable of handling just such a complex situation. Using this methodology, it is possible to involve the entire company in the inventory process, which can be performed at a low cost.

Example 8.2   Knowledge diagnosis at INTA

National Institute of Aerospace Technology (INTA)[1]

INTA, the National Institute of Aerospace Technology, is located on the outskirts of Madrid. Working for the Ministry of Defence, it specializes in the research and development of advanced technologies, particularly in the areas of aeronautics and avionics, air navigation, aerospace technology, telecommunications, and other related areas. INTA has a solid track record of scientific and technological quality, with more than 2,000 employees, most of whom are university graduates and many of them with doctorates. INTA is divided into departments specialized either by technologies or by products, as it also manufactures a certain number of products in cooperation with industry. In addition, INTA renders services such as calibration, metrology, consulting, etc., which it offers to a large number of companies who wish to have access to the institute's technological expertise.

At the beginning of 1993, INTA was embarking upon an ambitious growth stage, initiating new activities, which included the development of minisatellites, the development of a low-cost launching rocket, etc., and which would mean significant changes in how the institution operated. To assess the feasibility of the plans that had been drawn up and to have first-hand evidence that would enable it to identify areas of concentration, INTA's management decided to perform an inventory of the knowledge it already had. It was expected that the number of knowledge items would be very high and it was not considered feasible to delegate performance of the inventory to a small group. A structured methodology was needed that would enable most of the organization to take part in it and which would generate reliable results capable of providing the basis for future action.

A working group was formed whose membership included all of INTA's top-level managers. In addition, this group would be assisted by outside experts when it was considered necessary. The working group was given the task of devising a methodology, communicating it to the organization, organizing the collection and validation of results, and preparing the database which would be the project's end product.

---

*Presenting knowledge

Knowledge should not be inventoried directly – it is much easier to describe problems than knowledge. This may seem to be an exercise in mere semantics

---

[1] We thank INTA's 1993 management team for permission to publish this case and the enthusiasm with which they took up the idea. Although the methodology had been used previously in a number of companies (one of them being a large corporation), the great work done by the project's coordinating group enabled a much better grasp of the way to perform this kind of work.

Table 8.1 Description of knowledge

Knowledge Number

- Operation
- Object
- Conditions
- Goodness

since, at the end of the day, we have equalled both. However, for many companies, problems are an elementary object that is easier to locate than knowledge, even though we know that both things are identical.

During the inventory process, we must systematically record all of the problems that are solved, associating the appropriate knowledge with each problem. To do this, it is recommendable to use a common format which has sufficient representative power to formulate most of the elements involved in the situation. If such a format is not used, each item of knowledge ends up being recorded as a more or less lengthy verbal description of a domain of the problem. Handling large quantities of knowledge items using unstructured verbal descriptions is both time-consuming and difficult. Hence the need for a simple representation, such as the one described below.

In our experience, in the case of operating knowledge, it is sufficient to create, for each knowledge item, a description with the structure (fields) shown in Table 8.1.[2]

This structure can be represented by a data card, by a record in a database, or by an information structure, but always using the fields given above.

Data cards are only useful for small-scale inventories. If it is suspected that the inventory may generate several hundred knowledge items, it is always best to choose one of the other representations. The second is very simple and can be implemented in any commercial database – even in a plain file. The third is more refined and is recommended for more delicate computer applications.

- The 'operation' field must contain a single word, a *verb* that identifies the type of transformation corresponding to the operating problem. They are usually transitive verbs, which indicate an action carried out on an object. The fact that this field must be a verb is not simply a grammatical issue. The use of this format ensures that the knowledge inventoried is primarily task and inference knowledge, about operations which produce objects from inputs. In each practical case, verb dictionaries (ontologies) should be prepared in advance.

---

[2] This format is the outcome of repeated experiments using different representations until one was obtained that combined ease of use with expressive power. There are other, more complicated forms but the representation used offers considerable expressive power and, since it was created, we have used it in all our assignments, with no need for further modification. We could say that it is perfect, but we find this hard to believe and we continue to wait for a case that could dash to pieces our confidence (or lack of it) in this representation. Can the reader find such a case for us? Well, if you can, please keep it to yourself! We would never get over the disappointment…

Table 8.2   Verbs used at INTA

Generation	Logical transformation	Logical-physical transformation	Physical transformation	Physical-logical conversion	Glue
• Design • Specify	• Calculate • Simulate • Optimize	• Integrate • Build prototype	• Manufacture • Operate • Install • Maintain • Calibrate	• Evaluate • Test • Measure	• Manage • Use • Control • Direct

Table 8.3   INTA's dictionary

Material objects		Immaterial objects	
Fixed	Mobile	Signals	Information
• Instruments • Networks • Stations • Power supplies • Motors	• Satellites • Launchers • Aircraft • Transmitters	• Sound • Electromagnetic • Electrical currents	• Frequencies • Programs • Shapes • Dimensions

Particularly when several people are involved in the inventory process, this practice ensures better structured results and, at the same time, highlights the domain knowledge, which is not inventoried directly by this method.

Table 8.2 shows the verb dictionary initially used to describe all of INTA's organized operating knowledge. Of course, the participants could introduce new verbs if the existing verbs are insufficient, but such additions must be carried out cautiously in order to avoid, insofar as this is possible, the existence (and non-identification) of synonyms.

• The 'object' field indicates the object of the transformation or action determined by the verb. Again, object dictionaries are used to unify criteria, although in this instance it is more difficult to produce a dictionary that covers all the possibilities. This is because normally new objects are created as the inventory advances due to the refinement of the existing ones. However, a dictionary may still be useful for the initial stages of the inventory. Table 8.3 shows the initial dictionary used at INTA.

• The *conditions* qualify the object, framing and completing it. They normally help to define the range of objects to which the action is applied. For example, for the verb 'evaluate' and the object 'vibration tests', the condition may be 'frequency = 0–150 Hz, D < 130 mm, acceleration < 5 g, speed < 0.5 m/s, power < 120 kW', which describes precisely the range of tests that can be performed.

• Finally, the knowledge's *goodness* describes the tolerances, precision or quality with which the operation can be performed. For example, in the above case, the value 'with an error less than 0.1 per cent' could be inserted in the 'goodness' slot. The 'goodness' field is complementary to the 'conditions' field and often does not need to be filled in.

Having established a procedure for recording elementary knowledge, we will now consider a systematic way of identifying existing knowledge.

*The inventory process

In order to perform an inventory of the knowledge portfolio, we must first overcome the basic difficulty we mentioned earlier (Chapter 2): as knowledge is stored in people, it cannot be observed directly and its composition can only be inferred by induction – either through the observation of real events or through the performance of experiments.

In order for knowledge to be observable, it must be materialized in some form. Therefore, in practice, we must concentrate on inventorying what is observable, on the *materializations* of knowledge: products, processes and symbols.

The general lines of the inventory methodology are the following:

- Identify the materializations existing in the company.
- Identify the problems that are solved (have been solved) to produce these materializations. Part of this process includes the description of the problem using the format of the previous section.
- Associate problems with knowledge.

Let us now see in more detail what steps are included in each of the above stages.

1. *Materialization in products or services already existing in the firm.* Here we will only give the case of products.[3] It is a recursive, top-down process consisting of the following parts:
   - Cataloguing of the products offered by the firm, or the activities it carries out for its customers. For a garment manufacturer, men's suits, sports clothing, women's suits, etc., are examples of products. At INTA, more than 70 services rendered by the institute were identified, including: software quality services, CAD (computer-assisted design) services, metrology and calibration, aircraft tests, environmental tests, and so on.
   - Each product identified must be broken down into its components, thereby revealing the presence of occult knowledge. The idea is that the product has been obtained as a synthesis of a certain number of problem-solving processes and that if each of the process's output is described, this will give a recursive description of the knowledge involved. There are several possibilities for breaking down the product and, in principle, we should choose that which makes it easiest to identify subproblems. The two possibilities that are most commonly used are functional decomposition and structural decomposition. *Functional decomposition* lists the different functions that are present in the product. *Structural decomposition* lists the product's parts. These

---

[3] See the addendum to this chapter for a description of a procedure specialized in services.

Example 8.3   Example of knowledge decomposition

The Case of a Carpenter Making an Office Desk

The process would start by examining the components of the end product. The office desk is composed of the following elements: drawers, flat boards and legs. This is the structural decomposition. The process of assembling the components into the finished product gives it the functional features of a 'desk', functions that the parts do not have: be able to bear weight, allow a person to work comfortably, adorn the office, etc. This is the functional decomposition. During the 'assembly' process, used operations (that are readily identified from a description of the process) contain the operating knowledge. Some examples of this knowledge are: make plain joints, make dovetail joints, align parts, glue parts and varnish wood.

Decomposition of the product into its components has shown the presence of five knowledge items and has decomposed the product into a further three. Now the knowledge can be recorded in the format presented in Table 8.1. In the case of components, any description that identifies them adequately is enough.

We can now repeat the above process for all of the components. This is the recursive process that we have already discussed. The same procedure gives decompositions at ever deeper levels in the product's/service's tree.

---

decompositions may be immediately accessible if the task is started by listing objects in the form of a thesaurus. The basic idea is that a structural decomposition (the product's components) become a product by solving the 'assembly' problems. In addition to transforming the parts into a whole, these problems also imbue the product with functional features. The assembly problems are solved by the application of certain knowledge to the parts (which are in turn products) to obtain the desired end product. The relationship between the two decompositions is expressed in the following equation:

$$Components + Knowledge = Functionality$$

The equation suggests that knowledge should be obtained from the functional and structural decomposition. Example 8.3 shows one such application.

The recursive process continues until either components are obtained which are black boxes for the firm or the decomposition reaches levels that give rise to excessively disaggregated knowledge for the purpose pursued. Although this criterion is subjective, in practice it is easy to see when a decomposition should not be continued. Example 8.4 shows a partial example taken from INTA referring to the implementation of local area networks.

2. *Processes.* It is simpler to carry out a knowledge inventory using processes, since the elementary operations that implement the process contain within them the

Example 8.4   Knowledge tree for a service

INTA: Implementation of Local Area Networks

- Analyse attenuation problems.
- Measure network tasks.
- Detect anomalies.
- Design and calculate the network.
- Manage the project.
- Components:
—Cables.
  ✓ Select cables (bought)
  ✓ Lay cables (subcontracted)
  ✓ Connect cables
    ✓ Check current continuity
    ✓ Check signal continuity
—Computers
  ✓ Select computers (bought)
  ✓ Create interfaces
    ✓ Select standard cards (bought)
    ✓ Adapt cards (subcontracted)
—Communication devices
—Support devices

---

desired knowledge. If we have a detailed description of the method, the description itself is often expressed in a manner that enables immediate identification of the knowledge. If necessary, when activities are excessively aggregated, a method similar to the one indicated in the previous section can be used to refine them. The authors have carried out knowledge inventories in companies which have few products/services and where processes dominate the system. For example, in an inventory performed for one of Spain's largest electricity companies, 90 per cent of the knowledge was generated from elementary activities contained in the company's processes. These processes ranged from electricity generation in hydroelectric power stations to the maintenance of nuclear power stations and the design of low-voltage switchgear. Although the working group did not have the explicit methods – and their compilation would have been extremely time-consuming – it was possible to delegate the analysis to the lower levels that knew it. The result was very satisfactory.

3. *Symbolic representations.* This type of materialization can be treated in the same manner as products, provided that the concept 'items' is identified with 'symbolic representation'. Specifically, items such as the following must be considered: books and publications, annual reports, technical reports and miscellaneous technical documents, computer programs, laboratory logbooks, etc. Theoretically, each item must undergo a process of scrutiny such as that

described in section 1. As always, in practice, it is wise to exercise judgement and to limit the analysis to those items that are most relevant.

4. *Information system and conflict-resolution system.* Although strictly speaking, these materializations do not differ from the previous ones, these two variables of the operations system contain important information about the knowledge held by the firm. Both are important repositories of collective knowledge, particularly the CRS. In order to obtain knowledge from these two variables, we proceed as follows.

   —*Information system.* The information system is charted in accordance with the ideas stated in Chapter 6. When it is charted, the decision intervals are identified in the manner described. Each decision interval contains knowledge in its formal or informal DSS. Often, the interval's process is purely intellectual and, therefore, can be described using the techniques in Chapter 3. As an added value, analysing the information system helps establish the firm's processes. If it is carried out at the beginning of the inventory process, it may help us to not omit processes which, at first sight, may seem to have little bearing.

   —*Conflict-resolution system.* In this case, it is necessary to interview the company's people, discussing with them what are the basic rules that make it operate and which the company believes in. From the system of rules, knowledge is deduced. Both the rules' antecedent and consequent often reveal problems that are solved and which affect the whole. For example, a rule such as 'IF the customer is a mass merchandiser, THEN its order is scheduled immediately' contains at least one clear indication that the company knows how to schedule production of urgent orders.

   This variable must be analysed after having completed the other phases, as often it adds nothing new and simply confirms the existence of knowledge. This is important in validating the knowledge that has been inventoried.

5. *Refinement.* The result of the process described in the previous points is a list of unrefined knowledge items which may come from different sources and authors. Therefore, it is advisable to subject the list to a refinement and organization process. Two activities are important here:

   —*Validation of the list.* The knowledge lists' internal consistency must be verified, particularly when many people have taken part in drawing it up. It is not uncommon for the firm's personnel – quite deliberately in some cases – to include in the knowledge both knowledge they themselves would like to have and knowledge which their boss would like them to have. This effect, observed in practice, seriously detracts from the list's objectiveness. Fortunately, a simple check that the knowledge that it is believed to hold is supported by the existence of materializations is sufficient to eliminate many inaccuracies.

   —*Refinement of individual knowledge items.* As it is very difficult to propose a complete dictionary of objects, it is common for the objects of some knowledge items to be ambiguous – either because they are too general or because they are too specific. The same thing happens with the other fields. The inventory's ultimate purpose is to be used by a decision maker. Therefore, the description of knowledge must be chosen so that all of the decision makers involved understand its meaning. In our experience, this can be achieved by critically reviewing, one by one, all of the knowledge items obtained. This review should be performed by a group of people on a organizational level similar to that of the people who will use the results. For example, at INTA, the review group was the working party itself, formed by the institute's top-level managers. The party considered all of the knowledge items, one by one, asking themselves whether 'all the members of the party understood the knowledge item's meaning and understood it in the same way'. If this was so, the knowledge item was accepted. If it was not, a review request was generated. This method, which may seem rather imprecise, works surprisingly well in practice and needs no further elaboration. In our experience, the use of more sophisticated methods does not achieve better results and complicates the process.

6. *Organization of the knowledge list.* Once the knowledge list has been refined, we can reorganize it to suit our purpose. The initial list is typically organized by originating location of the knowledge and this organization is often unsuitable for the desired use. There are many ways of reorganizing the list to suit a particular purpose.

For this phase, we usually create a digital information structure from the complete list which is very flexible to use. To do this, we work with a software system that enables a list to be easily reorganized and explored.[4]

The first step in the reorganization process is to differentiate skills from technologies. This can be done using the following process:

—*Technologies* can be detected by inspection or by using a grouping process. In our research we have developed a long technology 'master list' organized hierarchically. Each knowledge item identified is classified in one of the categories of the master list using a sequential procedure. Each branch of the technology master list is reviewed, deciding whether to file the knowledge in it or not. If it can be filed its a technology although the converse is not true. This enables the identification of technologies in the knowledge database.

—*Skills* are detected in the residual knowledge that has not been grouped with the above procedure. Skills have the property that it is difficult to list the features of the processor who can successfully carry them out. Furthermore,

---

[4] We have used a number of software systems for this purpose. One of the first analyses, that of EXPO'92, was carried out on a system based on Smalltalk, a high-level, object-oriented language. Subsequently, we developed applications in Lisp, a commonly used language in artificial intelligence, and more recently, we have worked with representations in Noos (Arcos, 1997), an interesting system for handling knowledge structures, developed at the CSIC's IIIA in Bellaterra by Josep Lluis Arcos and Enric Plaza. In recent years, we have dispensed with most of these elaborations in favour of relational database structures, typically Access, used from Excel. As the reader will see, we have followed a process of progressively lower levels of procedural sophistication. Unfortunately, sophisticated has not proved synonymous to useful.

even having a suitable processor, it is not easy to guarantee that he will be successful. For example, 'painting pictures' is a skill. What defines a good painter? How can one assure that a painter will always paint good pictures?

Therefore, among residual knowledge, the existence of skills can be deduced from the uncertainty in the quality of the solution for each range of problems and from the ambiguity in the processor definition.

7. Finally, it is often necessary to summarize a knowledge list as a series of *core competences*, particularly for dissemination and communication purposes. This process can be achieved by systematically grouping the knowledge list, at several levels, using commonality of purpose as the grouping criterion. The process of creating core competences from knowledge has already been discussed in Chapter 2.

*Perceptional knowledge

In the previous section, we left perceptional knowledge on one side because of the difficulties in inventorying and using it. However, this type of knowledge is very important. It can be likened to the firm's collective memory since it catalogues the firm's interactions with its problems and, therefore, contains elements that enable the problems to be structured and new knowledge to be developed.

The analysis of perceptional knowledge and the techniques for using it have been developed within a branch of cognitive science called case-based research.[5] This research has led to the creation of tools[6] for handling perceptional knowledge within a structure similar to the following:

• All the situations that it is wished to file in the firm's perceptional memory are compiled as 'cases'. Here, a case is a simplified representation of a situation which, in contrast to the case studies used for teaching, includes a record of the actions taken and the results obtained. The main difficulty in this procedure lies in systematically capturing the information when it is generated but, if suitable mechanisms are available, it is no more complicated than capturing structured information, which is a familiar process in any information system.

---

[5] In this section we will confine ourselves to giving a brief introduction to the subject. The reader should go to Chapter 13 for more details.

[6] In our previous book, we took for granted that these tools were going to be widely available in the following years. Seven years have passed since then and there have been no major developments in this field. It appears that the technique's promises have never got beyond the promise stage. Even one of the leading gurus on the subject, Roger Shank, has dropped his ILS at Chicago and is concentrating on other types of project which, although they include previous ideas, differ in the methodology used. As Shank puts it: 'The way to do things well is with case-based techniques but, due to all sorts of constraints (particularly budget restraints), it is not possible to use them and quick fixes have to be developed.' Following Shank, we wish to give the reader an idea of how to do things well, hoping that one day the subject will cease to be weighed down by budget restraints.

- The cases are filed in case-based files. A case-based file is able to retrieve a case using similarity criteria. The operating definition of 'similarity' is not obvious and lies outside the scope of this book. However, we would stress that it is a 'logical' similarity, not one of formal identity. For example, with a system of this type, we could ask the computer to retrieve all the cases that 'deal with a staff problem that took some time to solve and which had harmful consequences for the company'. Such a description is very qualitative and imprecise but a good case-based system should eventually be able to identify and extract cases 'similar' to those requested.
- A user interface is provided in a language that is similar to natural language (like English) and is able to interpret interpellations such as that given in the example above. This way, the user can freely express his thoughts and it is the computer's job to formalize the description and retrieve the information.
- Finally, a case adaptation mechanism enables generalizations and deductions to be made. For example, for a question such as that given above, experiences related to interpersonal problems not necessarily associated with a work structure could be retrieved, provided that they were relevant or enlightening for our particular case.

This type of treatment may enable the creation of an experience database that would be readily accessible to all of the firm's staff. The technology for the implementation of a complete process like that described is not fully available and perhaps may not be in the near future either. The basic difficulty in implementing a system like this is not so much achieving the required results as achieving an easy scale-up that would enable large quantities of information to be processed. The technology currently existing is based to a great extent on the allocation of 'attributes' (generalized keywords) to each case (Kolodner, 1993) or on the use of Internet-type search engines to access the information. These technologies provide a starting point for a search engine to tap a flow of experiences that otherwise could only be stored individually in each individual's perceptional memory.

Competitive knowledge analysis (CKA)

The competitive knowledge analysis (CKA) methodology seeks to identify those knowledge items that are held that can provide a competitive advantage for the firm. A detailed analysis of this issue would mean identifying the uses of knowledge, because knowledge in isolation is rarely part of the service rendered to the customer, and therefore is unable, by itself, to provide competitive advantage. However, to support decision making, it is interesting to design an approximate procedure that gives an idea of the competitiveness associated with each knowledge item.

The central hypothesis behind what follows is that the firm that possesses a higher level of a certain knowledge item is able to make better use of it, either being quicker to use it or providing a better contribution to the service.

Given the above hypothesis, the CKA methodology compares the firm's internal knowledge level with the knowledge level in the business environment, which is given a suitable definition for each use. We can know a lot about a certain subject, but this may not provide us with any advantage because there are many people or organizations in the environment that have a similar level of knowledge.

The stages of a CKA applied to a certain knowledge item are:

- Determination of the internal knowledge level.
- Determination of the environment in which this knowledge is used, depending upon the services-markets being considered.
- Determination of the external knowledge level within each field of use.
- Determination of the competitive advantage existing in each case.

Measuring internal levels

Measuring the internal levels is the first step in comparing the situation of knowledge inside and outside of the firm. An enormous variety of scales can be proposed for this measuring process but, given the difficulty in obtaining precise quantitative observations, we prefer a simple five-category scale. We will not expound on its theoretical rationale here; suffice to say that it is based on cognitive science. The scales' categories are:

1. Know data or *know about* (KA). This means possession of perceptional – and, therefore, unstructured – knowledge. This does not mean that subsequent internalization and comprehension processes do not organize this data into experiential knowledge. But this is another level of knowledge that will be attained at a later stage. To learn by heart the list of Roman Emperors or the rivers in Europe is one way of *knowing about*, as is reading an article in a magazine about laser-induced fusion.
2. *Know how* (KH). This is the knowledge of the operating procedures that make up the performance of a certain task and contains, in the form of routines, the procedure to be followed until the task is completed. For example, a worker may learn to correctly insert a microchip in an electronic card. The procedure is fully specified, but the worker must acquire skill in the application. Learning how to perform household repairs uses this type of knowledge. Hanging a picture is an elementary procedure that is easy to transmit but it requires acquisition of a skill.
3. *Know why* (KW). The firm possesses knowledge at a logical level on a specific phenomenon and is able to create abstract knowledge that predicts the behaviour of the system when the circumstances of its functioning have not been observed previously. It represents the knowledge of the principles by which certain procedures operate. It enables a rational explanation to be given of this functioning and a much deeper understanding of the relationships and interactions underlying it. For example, by knowing the basic model of an internal combustion engine – it is possible to repair failures in the engine that perhaps have not been observed previously by the repairer.
4. *Know how to improve* (KI). This is the possession of knowledge at the level required to solve problems related with change and improvement. Thus, in the

electronic context, an engineer may realize that an error in the insertion of components may cause the entire circuit to fail. This knowledge level must enable him to work on the problem until he finds a solution for it. The solution may be to create a fail-safe insertion procedure: it is only possible to insert the right component in the right position, or design a testing system that tests the components inserted without having any harmful effects on it, or any other system. The knowledge is used in the problem-solving process, not in creating the object that will materialize its solution.

5. *Know how to learn* (KL). The existence of mental models so that future learning takes place effectively and spontaneously. At this level, the firm is able to change the way in which individuals learn. It is not 'learning to learn'. The subtle difference lies in replacing 'learning' with 'knowing how to'. To make it clearer, we ask the reader to let us indulge in a non-academic metaphor. If the human processor had hooks to hang new ideas on, the knowledge level would allow the creation of expandable (prefabricated, polyvalent?) configurations of hooks (drawers, pegs, cupboards, and so on) on which new experiences could be hung easily and in an ordered fashion.

Measuring external levels

The result of the assessment of a knowledge item's external level depends upon how the environment is defined. There is no single way of defining the environment and a good part of strategy creation consists of redefining the environment in which each knowledge item is used.

Among the various alternatives for defining the environment, we would highlight the following:

- The main competitor.
- An industry.
- The market in which the firm operates.
- A geographical area.

To assess the external level, we use the same five-category scale as used in the previous case.[7]

Competitive knowledge analysis

After assigning internal and external levels, we can compare the position of the knowledge within the company with its position in the environment and diagnose the competitive advantage. To do this, we propose using a table, such as that

---

[7] Many students ask us how to obtain knowledge about the external level, especially about competitors. They themselves give the answer when they are asked: 'And what do you think?' The answers are usually: from suppliers, from customers, from our sales department and, above all, from consultants! We would also add specialized research centres that provide this type of information.

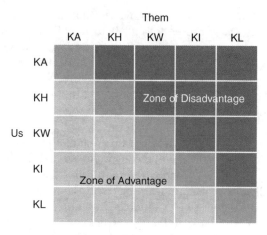

Figure 8.1   Competitive knowledge analysis

of Figure 8.1, whose dimensions represent the internal and external position of each knowledge item.

The area with the light-coloured shading, at the bottom right of the chart, is the zone of competitive advantage. In this zone, the position of the knowledge in the firm is higher than that of the knowledge in the environment. This represents a situation in which the firm is ahead of the environment and offers the possibility of using knowledge that is not within the reach of the other firms in the environment. The area with the dark-coloured shading is the part where there is disadvantage, in the sense that the company's knowledge is in a lower level than in the firms in its environment. Finally, the area with the medium-coloured shading is where knowledge is equally well positioned both in the firm and in the environment.

These positionings give an initial advantage that is neither stable nor even real. A firm may have a highly developed position in a certain type of knowledge but not know what to do with it because it lacks complementary knowledge. Obviously, the analysis does not take into account the relationships and synergies between different types of knowledge. These relationships could be taken into account by placing *competencies instead of knowledge* in the chart. It is slightly more complicated to assess competences than to assess knowledge, because their effect cannot be judged only in a particular knowledge item. Their effect must be judged in a whole body of knowledge and this entails additional complexities. However, the same procedure can be used in this case – and has been used – provided that the assessments are taken with a grain of salt.

Example 8.5 summarizes the knowledge diagnosis of Software Castilla.

Finally, we present a case in Example 8.6 in which a complete knowledge diagnosis was performed.

Example 8.5   Software Castilla, SL (II)

The knowledge diagnosis carried out in Software Castilla yielded the following knowledge list:

- Applications development.
- Local networks.
- Coding.
- Logistics support.
- Configuration control.
- Microcomputing.

Following the methodology described in this chapter, we looked for each knowledge item's external and internal levels. When we had found them, we charted the knowledge in the CKA matrix, taking as our field of work the competitors which the company usually had to compete against. The positioning showed that the competitive knowledge was: logistics support, coding and applications development. Knowledge about configuration control was at the same level both inside and outside of the company, while local networks and microcomputing were more competitive among the competitors.

Example 8.6   A case of using the knowledge portfolio: TECNOEXPO'93

We have already outlined the history of Expo'92 in Chapter 3. Here, we will briefly describe the way in which the TecnoExpo project was carried out. TECNOEXPO'93 was an inventory of the general knowledge held about Expo'92, the Universal Exhibition at Seville, its assessment, and the generation of proposals to use it that would increase the competitiveness of the economies of Seville, Andalusia and Spain.

The publicly-owned company Expo'92 (SEE92) was responsible for organizing the Universal Exhibition. With the purpose of creating something 'unique', SEE92 brought together a large number of professionals from different disciplines. Its activity was essentially concentrated on two aspects: the institutional aspect and that of the participating countries. The goal was to bring together the very best people worldwide in the fields of exhibitions and entertainment. At its height, several thousand people from more than 100 countries were working at the same time in Expo'92.

Conceptualized as an unique, highly innovating entertainment product, Expo'92 agglutinated and materialized a broad spectrum of knowledge. In order to determine the scope of the service developed and, with it, the existing knowledge portfolio, the work began with an analysis of products and services. The company did not exist before 1981. Everything was created during the period 1981–92. This enabled us to make a short cut with respect to the general methodology. Our first activity was to determine what had entered the company during this period. We devised a database which contained all the contractual agreements signed for Expo'92. This analysis gave a preliminary idea of the type of knowledge that had entered the Expo.

The next step was to start a validation process using a series of in-depth interviews carried out during a one-year period with the knowledge custodians. The knowledge base obtained was organized in accordance with its internal structure, and was represented as a semantic network. In our case, most visions of the network had a tree structure. The most important vision was generated from the 'subknowledge of' relationship, where each knowledge item or skill was described in terms of the subknowledges that formed it.

After that, the knowledge underwent a competitive assessment, developing and applying TCA (technology competitive analysis), CKA's predecessor.

As a result of comparing the internal and external level of each knowledge item, the inventoried knowledge was classified by level of competitiveness: competitive worldwide, competitive in Spain (knowledge having similar features could be found elsewhere in the world), and non-competitive (knowledge having similar features could be found in Spain).

Having reached this point, and since the goal was economic development, the Expo's competitive knowledge worldwide and in Spain was assessed with respect to the development requirements of Andalusia's industrial sectors. The idea was to find potential uses for the knowledge existing in the Expo that could have greater effectiveness within the foreseen environment. To do this, a knowledge tree decomposition and recomposition technique was used, seeking to combine knowledge items that could give rise to new products and processes.

The development of a software system that helped us to manipulate the knowledge and simulate its possible future course enabled us to obtain the knowledge items with a potential industrial application. As a result of all the work performed, proposals were made with respect to:

1. Creation of products that could be offered on markets similar to that of Expo'92.
2. Knowledge combinations capable of operating as economic units in present or future markets.
3. Support for the development of knowledge combinations whose market is difficult to foresee.

Finally, with the purpose of maximizing this impact, it was proposed to create a theme park on the Expo'92 site that would integrate education and entertainment. The Expo'92 was a brilliant display of image and sound techniques, accumulating an enormous knowledge potential that could be used for educational applications. The purpose of the theme park would have been to help the visitor gain a better understanding of the world surrounding him, its past and present, highlighting the logical process followed in its evolution. The most advanced technology would have been used to maximize the spectator's interaction with the message.

Source: B. Muñoz-Seca and J. Riverola, 'Proyecto de investigación para la Sociedad Estatal Expo'92', 1992.

Addendum I: Diagnosis of knowledge in services: a simplified method

I. Part one: Knowledge inventory: services and processes

- Start the process by listing the services (hereinafter items) that the business unit actually offers or can offer.
- Do the following for each item at a time.

A. *Inventorying a service*

- In the column with the heading 'Function', briefly state the item's functionality(ies).
- We will now decompose the item into processes. List the processes related to the item we are analysing in the column 'Processes'.
- We can now carry out the first knowledge decomposition. We will use the Operation – Object – Conditions – Goodness system.

We will create entries in the knowledge table with this structure. First list the knowledge items that enable the joint (or integrated) operation of the processes listed.

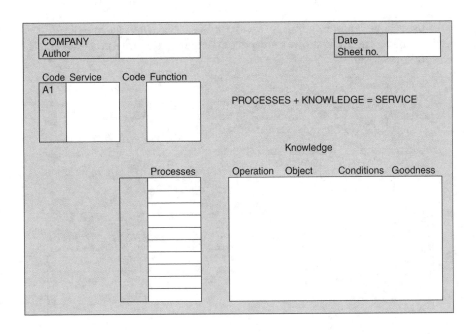

B. *Inventorying a process*

- We will now go to the level of each of the subprocesses. Take each process in Form 1 and decompose it in Form 2, following the same procedure.

Processes

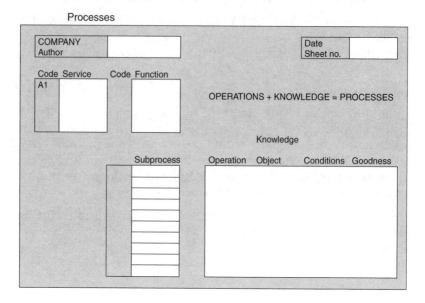

Let us see an example, the inventorying of the service '*home delivery by a super-market*'. The figure below shows the service's decomposition into processes and the relevant knowledge.

Services

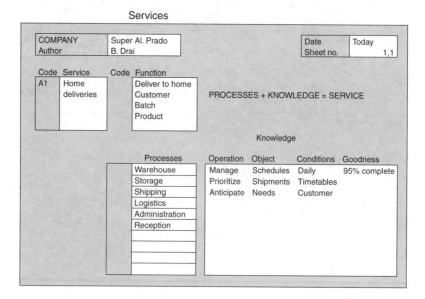

We now decompose the process 'Warehouse' into its subprocesses and list them.

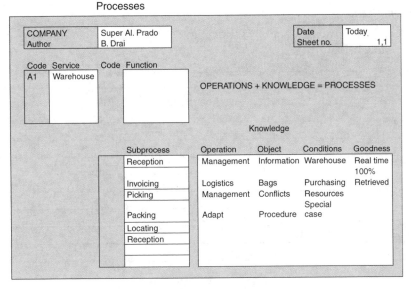

Processes

| COMPANY | Super Al. Prado | | | Date | Today |
| Author | B. Drai | | | Sheet no. | 1,1 |

Code Service   Code Function

| A1 | Warehouse |

OPERATIONS + KNOWLEDGE = PROCESSES

Knowledge

Subprocess	Operation	Object	Conditions	Goodness
Reception	Management	Information	Warehouse	Real time 100%
Invoicing	Logistics	Bags	Purchasing	Retrieved
Picking	Management	Conflicts	Resources	
Packing	Adapt	Procedure	Special case	
Locating				
Reception				

II. Part two: Competitive knowledge assessment (CKA)

Now select a number of knowledge items from the lists you have drawn up. Typically you should select related knowledges with common environments. Then perform the CKA analysis.

- Define the environment in which you will consider the competitors' operation.
- For each knowledge item, assign internal and external knowledge levels.
- Position them on the CKA table.

CKA Table

	I	II	III	IV	V
I					
II					
III					
IV					
V					

III. Part three: Identification of competences

A. *Identification*

To identify competences, start by listing the 15 most competitive knowledge items in the table below.

1	
2	
3	
4	
5	
6	
7	
8	
9	
10	
11	
12	
13	
14	
15	

B. *Grouping*

Now group the above knowledge items, completing them with other knowledge items that have been identified as complementary. The grouping can be carried out using the following criteria:

- Relationship between the knowledge items' purpose.
- Complementarity of the knowledge items.
- Existence of common generalizations with a global purpose.

The grouping can be carried out intuitively or systematically.[8] List the results in the following table:

1	
2	
3	
4	

The knowledge groups obtained are the business unit's 'competences'.

The competences that have been obtained from competitive knowledge are core competences.

Now repeat the process to your heart content!

---

[8] Using for example the KJ methodology, which we explain in the Appendix at the end of this book.

9
Applying Knowledge to Improve the Moments of Truth

Introduction

Before moving on to address the problem of permanent improvement in all its complexity, we will use this chapter to present a simplified version. This should be seen as an intermediate step, more complicated than the project analysis of Chapter 3 but still easy to handle as a complete entity. In this instance, the MOTs are seen as problem generators, problems that must be solved by making maximum use of the knowledge available in the firm.

The application we describe here is not of permanent improvement. In terms of improvement, it would be more like a sporadic improvement process which, at a certain moment in time, creates an action plan which is then implemented to achieve results. If it is wished to improve again on what has been improved, the process can be repeated *ab initio*. The firm's management invariably has the ultimate responsibility for improvement actions, even if it acts jointly with the firm's other agents. Together, they draw up a diagnosis which is then used to generate actions that solve the problems that arise during the MOTs.

Essentially, the method presented here seeks systematically to apply knowledge identification to the goal of improving customer service. The method is applied to each business unit and not simply to the firm as a whole, because the conclusions may vary depending upon the type of customers, suppliers, technology and other components that define a business unit. Typically, a working group, or a team of people from the business unit, work together to improve their work environment. In all cases, it is recommended that all of the unit's agents take part in the activity.

We present a ten-step approach:

1. Analyse the unit's best practices and rules of conduct.
2. Identify and chart the critical processes.
3. Identify the information and decision system.
4. Identify problems occurring in the processes and in the information system.
5. Create the knowledge database.
6. Identify the customers' MOTs.
7. Diagnose the origin of the MOTs' problems.

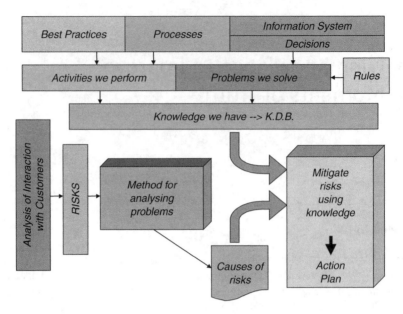

Figure 9.1   Using knowledge to improve the MOTs

8. Propose improvement actions for the MOTs using the knowledge identified.
9. Prioritize the list of actions.
10. Implement the actions.

Figure 9.1 shows the relationship between the various steps. At the beginning of each step, a reproduction of Figure 9.1, with one or more boxes shaded, will indicate the aspects being considered in the section.[1] To illustrate the process with a real-life example, we will use examples taken from a company that has recently implemented this approach and which we will call CORMA. This company is a pharmaceutical laboratory which develops and markets specialized products for hospitals.

*Step 1. Analyse the unit's best practices and rules of conduct

As a starting point for an implementation, the unit concerned must briefly reflect upon the rules of conduct by which it is governed and its best practices. These are the unit's non-typified ways of acting which are critically important for its functioning.

Rules of conduct (Conflict Resolution System, CRS)

As a first step, the team analyses the CRS's 'rules of conduct' that are applied in the firm. The rules are listed, indicating in each case the decisions to which they

---

[1] The tools used in this chapter are described in more detail in other chapters of the book. We refer the reader to the appropriate chapter (which will be indicated in the text when it is relevant) for a deeper analysis.

Table 9.1   Types of rules

Forecasting	Decisions and hypotheses about the future
Planning	Management of high-level or long-term resources
Scheduling	Detailed allocation of resources
Intervention	Manner in which decisions are made

Table 9.2   Rules in CORMA

Marketing and sales	Technical department
• In the decision on 'activities to be carried out in marketing'. —Transmit credibility —Have a scientific/technical approach • In the decision on 'choose publications': Choose only those that are in line with the strategy	• In the decision on 'technician who will carry out a study': —Allocate load to achieve an occupancy of 80 per cent —Maximum 20 cases per person —Apply more resources at the beginning or end of a study than in the middle • In the decision about 'approving centres': —Apply the mandatory criteria as regards facilities, research team, committee, availability of the investigator, existence (or not) of competing studies

are applied. This enables the identification of the business practices and the rules that govern them, including all of the currently valid policies (corporate and local) that affect the unit. One way of helping to identify rules is to divide them into the different types presented in Chapter 6, and in Table 9.1. Some of the 'rules' which were identified[2] in CORMA are shown in Table 9.2.

Best practices

A best practice is a (typically informal) way of doing things adopted by the unit (or part of it) which makes it stand out in the organization, identifying it as the best in a operational specific aspect. In order to isolate these practices, the unit must reflect on its way of acting and list those conducts that make it outperform the rest of the organization.

At CORMA, the best practices were described from the business viewpoint, documenting the main features of the method used in these practices: who is involved, what goal is pursued, and the frequency, form and degree of materialization of decisions. A partial list of the best practices identified:

1. Weekly meetings between the marketing and technical departments.
2. Monthly meetings of mixed areas.
3. Telephone calls between sales representatives and technicians.

---

[2] This list is usually completed when the information system (described further on) is analysed, which is when the decisions made are studied in more detail.

4. Periodic review of best practices between the marketing and technical departments.
5. Weekly technical meetings.

The results of this step are filed for subsequent use in step 5, Knowledge diagnosis.

*Step 2. The critical processes

> See Chapter 5, Section: Processes

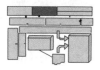
Processes are essential elements in diagnosing the unit's situation. To simplify the work, this can be concentrated on the critical processes. Thus, part of the team is asked to identify those processes that contribute most value to the company's operations. Once these have been identified, they must be charted and each process's operations must be defined. In the case of each process, a custodian or person who holds a critical responsibility in the process's operating result must be identified. Some of the critical processes identified at CORMA are set out in Table 9.3.

When it comes to charting the processes, it is advisable to create small groups who are then assigned selected processes. In this manner, the effort is distributed and the procedure's efficiency is increased. At CORMA, the total task was shared among the unit's members so that each one described the processes he knew and performed. When it was not possible to do this as a team, the process's custodian(s) were identified and a member of the team was made responsible for its experimental validation by observation of the custodian agent.

When the charts have been completed, they must be shared with the rest of the unit for validating, discussing those aspects that pose procedural or interpretation difficulties until they are fully clarified. One of the charts obtained at CORMA is shown as Figure 9.2.

When this stage has been completed, the charts are put away until Step 4, when they will be used to identify the first improvements.

Table 9.3   Some critical processes in CORMA

Marketing	Sales	Technical
• Training • Creating promotional material (publications) and knowledge • Printing technical publications/ communications	• Training • Sales • Recruiting	• Training • Information service • Planning

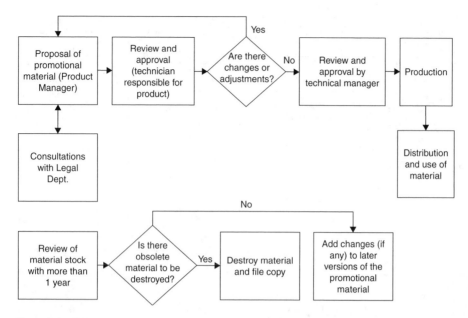

Figure 9.2 Charting a process

*Step 3. Information and decision-making system

> See Chapter 6, Section: Information and conflict-resolution systems

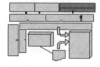 Describing the information system consists of defining what information flows through the processes, identifying who handles this information, describing the resources used to handle the information (documents, records in a computerized system and so on), and identifying the decision intervals.

We remind the reader that the decision intervals are those points at which the information flow stops because a decision must be made. Once the decision has been made, the information continues its flow through the system. The decision intervals implement the decision-making system. For each decision interval, the following must be identified:

- Who decides.
- The information used to make the decision.
- The rules applied to make the decision.
- The results of the decision and the information generated by the decision.

At CORMA, an iterative process was used. The unit's members generally met once for each critical process and documented, with the help of the process's custodian, the process's baseline information. This enabled the path followed by the information to be obtained, from the start to the finish of the process. In order to validate it, this information, summarized in a first draft, was discussed with the

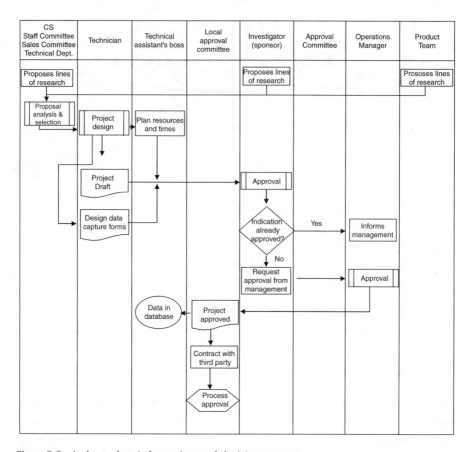

Figure 9.3   A chart of an information and decisions system

entire team. Each process's custodian then used the remarks obtained to develop
the final documentation which he sent for a final validation.

To chart the information system, the techniques described in Chapter 6 were
used. This type of chart enables the inputs and results to be obtained for a given
decision and also identifies the people who are responsible for it and the type of
problem being solved when the decision is made. An example of a complete chart
for CORMA is shown in Figure 9.3.

After charting the information system, the decisions identified must be listed so
that they can be used in a later step.

*Step 4. Problems in processes and information system: initial identification of areas of improvement

To date in our analysis, the work has concentrated on an *'Analysis of the present
situation'*. This has two uses:

- A direct application, which is the result of documenting in chart form a number
  of components that have not been materialized previously. This use is trivial but

having a complete documentation of the processes and information system, that is accepted by all the parties involved, is an important asset for any unit.
• Use of the charts to identify the points at which some type of problem occurs. This identification is the goal of the present step.

To do this, we must consider what things are preventing us from achieving the desired results, with regard to both the process and the information system. One useful technique, which makes use of the work already performed, is to draw 'clouds' connected to the problem areas on both types of chart (processes and information system). Figure 9.4 shows an example of how to insert 'clouds' in a chart of the information system.

Each of the clouds in Figure 9.4 identifies a problem area that requires an improvement action to be taken.

When the first four stages have been completed, the results obtained can be used to construct a *first improvement action plan*, identifying the people responsible for implementation, setting milestones, and determining the timetable and resources required. This action plan includes all those actions that can be implemented immediately to solve the problem areas.

The preliminary improvements could be submitted to management for their approval and implementation. This is a delicate step. Because if management disapproves the plan, the group may become disheartened and withdraw from the whole approach. The result can be a very negative feeling as a considerable amount of time will have been devoted to the process and, now that they are more aware of the problems that exist, the agents need to see solutions to the operating problems that have been detected. The careless approach to this activity is at the root of many failures experimented in improvement efforts.

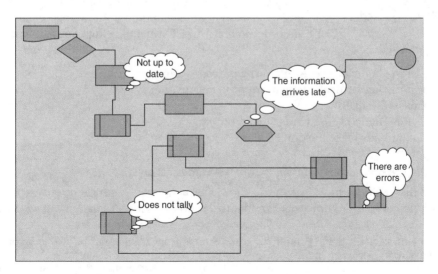

Figure 9.4 Finding the problems in the information and decisions system

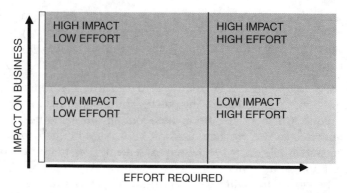

Figure 9.5 Impact matrix

In CORMA, the problem areas were called 'black spots'. A series of actions capable of solving the system's 'black spots' were classified. These actions were then plotted on a matrix (see Figure 9.5) which describes the action's impact on the business and the effort required to perform the action. The preliminary or 'unblocking' actions were submitted to management for approval and execution.

*Step 5. Create the knowledge database

> See Chapter 8: Knowledge diagnosis

 At this point, the unit is in a position to start its knowledge inventory because it now has the necessary elements to do this: the best practices, the processes and the decisions.

We now enter the phase of building a knowledge database (KDB).[3] In order to build a KDB, the following five stages must be followed:

1. List the knowledge existing in the processes and best practices.
2. List the knowledge obtained from the information system.
3. Create the KDB.
4. Define the terms used or create an ontology.
5. Group knowledge in competences.

1. List the knowledge existing in the processes and best practices

As a first stage, we must extract the knowledge contained in critical processes[4] and best practices. This knowledge is contained in the activities. To organize it, we can

---

[3] To be systematic, the KDB must be organized as a database and must be able to accommodate knowledge from other business units and other areas in the company.

[4] This step should be performed with all the processes. However, as this is a simplified version, here we will concentrate solely on the critical processes.

Table 9.4 Knowledge held in CORMA

Process/best practice	Activity	Existing knowledge	Source	Recommended knowledge
Reference to the process or best practice to which the activities belong	Activities within the process or best practice	Things that we know how to do and which enable us to perform these activities	Where does the knowledge reside?	What do we need in order to perform this activity better?
Best practices – weekly meeting	Investigator selection	• Interpret sales data from the potential and actual sales viewpoints	• Marketing and sales • Prior experience • Screening visits	• Know whether there is already information available about a hospital

create a table such as that shown in Table 9.4, which contains fields such as:

- *Process/best practice*: identification of the process or best practice to which the activities belong.
- *Activity*: activities within the process or best practice.
- *Existing knowledge*: things that we know how to do and which enable us to carry out these activities[5].
- *Source*: where the knowledge resides.
- *Recommended additional knowledge*: knowledge which would achieve a greater degree of effectiveness in the activity.

This task is best carried out in a team, systematically analysing each process and drawing up a list of the activities carried out within that process. The next step will be to identify what each person knows how to do and which enables him to perform these activities. This is known as the *knowledge existing in the unit*.

We must also identify the source of this knowledge, – that is, who holds it. At the same time, we must identify what knowledge should be held[6] and is currently not held. This is the *recommended knowledge*. A fragment of a summary table of the knowledge held in CORMA is shown in Table 9.4.

2. Knowledge in the information system

Having found the process and best practices knowledge, the same task must now be performed with regard to the knowledge in the information system.

In order to find the knowledge existing in the IS's decisions, we must identify the problems that this decision is solving. Remember that each time a decision is made, a problem is solved. Therefore, we must find:

- *Problem*: problem solved by making the decision.
- *Methodology*: method or procedure for solving the problem.

---

[5] Here we can use the detailed method described in Chapter 8, although at this stage, a simplified form of the method may be just as useful and less cumbersome.

[6] It should exist to enable more efficient functioning of the unit.

- *Existing knowledge*: what is known that enables this problem to be solved.
- *Source*: where the knowledge resides.
- *Recommended knowledge*: knowledge which would give greater effectiveness to the activity.

An example from CORMA is shown in Table 9.5.

3. Creating the KDB

When all of the previous stages have been completed, we have a prototype KDB. Now we must homogenize all of the components, formulating the knowledge as verb (action), object and qualification, as explained in Chapter 8.

This task may be performed by a small group of representatives drawn from across the areas analysed. It is advisable to add comments that help us to understand the knowledge, the knowledge's source and the materialization of the source, if such materialization exists. In most of the cases we have analysed, the knowledge is usually not materialized – that is, it does not exist as a company asset that can be shared.

Table 9.6 shows a fragment of CORMA's KDB.

As the homogenization process progresses, it is wise to create a dictionary (ontology) of the terms used. For instance it is very common for similar verbs to be used with very different meanings. It is therefore wise to specify definitions, which will be our next step.

4. Defining the terms used

Whenever possible, terms must be used unequivocally. For example, at CORMA, knowledge that used similar verbs such as 'send' and 'dispatch' was listed. By

Table 9.5   Knowledge obtainment at CORMA

Info-decision system	Problem	Methodology	Existing knowledge	Source	Recommended knowledge
Reference to decision and IS	Problem or question solved by making the decision	How do we do it?	Things that we know how to do and which enable us to solve the problems	Where does the knowledge reside?	What do we need in order to enable us to solve this problem or question more easily?
IS: Project planning Decision: Choose studies in which Spain may take part	What projects can it take part in	Discussion at the weekly meeting of the staff committee	Match projects with the local strategy that has been developed	Marketing, Technical Dept., Sales	• Own strategy • Other companies' strategies
IS: Planning systems Decision: Operating plan	Local sales plan	Negotiation and, if conflicts arise, decision by senior management	Management imposes its decision when there is conflict	Marketing and management	Develop sales goal as a more informative medium

Table 9.6 CORMA's KDB: a fragment

Action	Object	Qualification	Remarks	Source	Materialization
Assess	Projects	From technical interest viewpoint	Local projects, best practices	Technical staff	Mental, no materialization
Reuse	Sales experience	By veteran sales representatives to train new ones	Marketing training	Sales force	Mental, no materialization

Table 9.7 Example of verb definition

Verb	Definition
Adapt:	Format, change something's form so that it meets certain requirements.
Allocate:	Devote available resources (people, time, money) to a task.
Assess:	Analyse the impact, interpret, evaluate, draw conclusions from data.
Identify:	Ascertain, investigate and choose among several options.
Obtain:	Attain, gain, have something that one did not have previously.

general agreement, all of these were standardized to 'send' in the thesaurus. A few examples are given in Table 9.7.

This step facilitates the subsequent grouping task, as we will see in the following point.

5. Grouping knowledge in competences

At this point, we have a lengthy list of knowledge items, which we will term *individual knowledge items*. At CORMA, each person contributed on average about five knowledge items. As it is, this knowledge list is awkward to handle and the best option is to group the knowledge items by competences. These competences are identified following the procedure given in Chapter 2. In order to do this, it is recommended that the KJ method[7] or any of its variants is used.

A name must be given to each competence. This name must be representative of the different knowledge items that are grouped. This name is usually a short phrase to which a more precise definition of the competence must be affixed. Two examples of competences found in CORMA are shown in Table 9.8.

Once this stage is completed, we have a KDB, which can be computerized in a simple database.[8] We now have sufficient material to:

- Perform a competitive analysis of existing knowledge.
- Identify what knowledge is materialized and non-materialized.

---

[7] See Addendum at the end of this chapter.
[8] Without any intention to give free publicity (God forbid!), we use Access because it is widely available and is relatively simple. Of course, it is not the best option in the world but it has the advantage of being very well integrated with Excel. And we are great fans of Excel!

Table 9.8   Example of a competence definition

Competence	Definition
Adapt documentation to internal and external requirements	Obtain information about formal documentation requirements and modify its format so that it meets the requirements.
Assess market potential	Draw conclusions about potential sales using the information available about customers and the market.

- Analyse the knowledge we do not have.
- Identify the key holders of the knowledge.
- Apply knowledge to improving the service.

This last point is extremely important. In order to be able to do this, we must first identify the interactions with the customers (the moments of truth) and the problems that arise in the course of these interactions. This procedure is explained in the following step.

*Step 6. Interaction with customers – moments of truth

See Chapter 4: The beginning of good doing: the world of operations

 It is preferable that this step should be performed by homogenous teams or teams of people who deal with the same customers. The goal is to identify the critical points of the interaction with the customers, or MOTs,[9] and to assess their present functioning. Normally, all subgroups have some type of interaction with end or internal customers.

In order to enumerate the MOTs, the following must be identified:

- *The points of interaction*: the times when there is an interaction with the customer.
- *The risks*: analysis of what can go well and what can go wrong in each interaction.
- *The interaction process*: analysis of the company-customer interaction process.

Because the work is carried out in homogenous teams, we must group *a posteriori* all the homogenous interactions that have been identified in the various subgroups. This enables all of the customer interactions to be summarized in a complete list of the MOTs.

Table 9.9 gives a sample of the MOTs found at CORMA.

When this step is completed, we have a list of MOTs.

We also have a list of risks that may prevent a MOT from being positive. In order to understand the causes of this risk, or problems in the MOT, we need to identify

---

[9] One of the members of the team of the company we use as an example defined the MOTs as those situations when 'it's make it or break it' with the customer, those times when something can go well or wrong and, therefore, may have a totally different outcome.

Table 9.9 MOTs at CORMA

Interaction points	Risks: What can go well/wrong?	Interaction process
Times when there is an interaction with the customer	*Analysis of what can go well and what can go wrong, or of what the risks are*	*Brief description of the interaction process*
Working meeting —Sales —Marketing	*General* — Risk: close a commitment (take part in a study, take part in something you want the customer to do, obtain support). — Good: increases information, the longer time gives the opportunity for issues not on the agenda to be aired. *Sales* — Bad: there is a misunderstanding between your idea and what the customer interprets. — Bad: information that you do not have on hand to answer something that the customer knows. *Marketing* — Risk: create/not create a favourable environment for addressing the business issue it is wished to talk about. — Risk: spoil a relationship with a customer.	*Sales* Very similar to an arranged call but with the intention of increasing personal contact, the customer is isolated from the environment and the call time is increased. *Marketing* An appointment is made and the customer is invited. As a general rule, all the issues are broached but without getting immediately to the point.

its origin. In order to find the causes of each potential problem, we will use a classic quality technique – the fishbone or Ishikawa chart[10]. The next step explains this procedure.

*Step 7. Methodology for analysing problems (Ishikawa)

In contrast to the previous step, this exercise must be carried out in heterogeneous groups. These groups will contribute different viewpoints on the same problem and thereby enrich the diagnosis. The best size for such a group is 2–3 people, so that every member can take an active part in analysing a group of problems.

The number of cause and effect analyses (Ishikawas) generated must equal the MOTs listed. In the case of CORMA, five teams were created in which marketing, sales and technical skills were combined and the moments of truth were distributed among them. An example of one of these charts is shown in Figure 9.6.

When this stage is completed, we will have the following:

- The KDB (Knowledge Data Base).
- The competences.

---

[10] See Addendum.

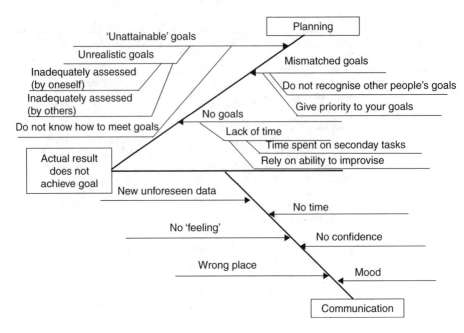

Figure 9.6 Ishikawa chart of a MOT at CORMA

- The moments of truth.
- The Ishikawa charts (root causes of the risks).

We are now reaching the last phase, when we will combine our competences with the causes of problems in order to improve the MOTs and, by this means, the company's competitiveness.

*Step 8. Apply competences to the causes

The purpose of this step is to combine the existing competences, found in Step 5, with the root causes of the risks in the MOTs, obtained in Step 7. It therefore focuses on how to use the competences that the firm possesses in order to destroy the risks or ascertain whether any of the existing competences are useful for permanently solving all of the problems.

In order to achieve this purpose, problems are crossed with competences, in each case asking whether or not the competence can be used to address the cause. In this stage, we need only to be concerned with the possibility of action, not with the action itself, which will be determined next. Table 9.10 shows a useful form for this exercise.

Having identified the possibility of using a competence, it is necessary to investigate the possible use of the individual knowledge items that make up this competence. The ultimate goal is to generate a specific improvement action. Table 9.11 shows a standard form that can be used to carry this out. This form has the information given in Table 9.10 but has been expanded with the individual knowledge items and finally reaching an action.

Table 9.10 Form for crossing problems with knowledge

		Competences				
		KG1	KG2	KG3	KG4	KG5
MOT with	MOT					
transcribed	cause 1					
Ishikawa	cause 2					

Table 9.11 Form for generating knowledge-based actions

Difficult MOT		Knowledge group	
Move MOTs here	Mark applicable MOT	Move knowledge here	Mark applicable knowledge
Action		MOT	Individual knowledge item
Give name to action which will use the knowledge to solve the conflict		Origin of problem	Identify the knowledge item which will be used
Description of action			

Since this is a creative exercise, it is a good idea to use small heterogeneous groups that complement each other, supplementing this with techniques designed to support creativity.

The list of actions must be given some sort of organization as it is usually fairly long, as was the case with CORMA, where a list of 64 actions was obtained. After detailing the actions, it is advisable that a working party group them by similarity, paying particular attention to their complementariness. The 64 actions mentioned were grouped into the following categories:

- Information actions.
- Event preparation actions.
- Plan creation actions.
- Personal ability actions.
- Knowledge-sharing actions.
- Organizational actions.
- Forecasting actions.
- Operation actions.

Step 9. Prioritized action list

Once the actions are grouped together into categories, they can be ordered according to their priority. Priorities should be based on objectives derived from the company's mission. One way is to use a numeric scale where, for example, 5 points means that the action is important and 1 point means that the action is irrelevant. Table 9.12 shows a form for carrying out this task. One way to obtain the group's assessment is by weighted voting. Each individual makes their own assessment and the individual assessments are added together. This gives the overall priority that the group has assigned to the actions. It is a quick and rather crude procedure, but it is often sufficient. The curious reader can consult the available literature on multicriteria analysis.

Step 10. Implementation of actions

Although this final step may seem to be obvious, this is in practice far from being the case. After an exercise such as the preceding one, which takes up a considerable amount of time and effort in analysing their own work, the agents reveal two types of improvement opportunity: (i) opportunities whose implementation depends solely upon the agents involved in the process; and (ii) opportunities that require the involvement of other levels in the firm.

The former are the easiest to deal with but this requires management acceptance that the initiative for action is not in their hands, but at lower operating levels.

Table 9.12   Form for prioritizing actions

MOT	Action category	Action	Classification					Order of priority
			1	2	3	4	5	

1	Highly irrelevant
2	Irrelevant
3	Relevant
4	Important
5	Highly important

The latter require a management commitment which must be made *a priori* and maintained at all times. Nothing is more demoralizing for a group of people interested in improving than to see that any effort to identify actions fails to reach a practical conclusion because of problems at the higher levels of the firm. If in the end there is not going to be any implementation, it is best not to start the process.

Conclusion

In this chapter, we have described how to use knowledge to improve the MOTs. The Addendum to this chapter contains all of the forms that the reader will need in order to perform a similar action in his own company.

Addendum: forms and summary of the stages

I. Starting point

- Best practices
- Rules of conduct

II. Processes

- Critical processes
- Process charts

III. Information systems

- Information system
- Decisions

IV. Blockages and improvements

V. Database (KDB)

- Knowledge assessment based on processes and best practices
- Knowledge assessment based on the information system
- Construction of the KDB
- Definition of the terms used
- Knowledge grouping
- Definition of knowledge groups
- List of knowledge groups with their individual knowledge items

VI. Customer

- Moments of Truth (MOT)
- Identification of the source of the problems

VII. Improvement actions for the MOTs using knowledge

- Application of knowledge to the MOTs
- Prioritized improvement actions

I. Starting point

1. List of best practices

2. *The firm's rules of conduct*

Functional area

Rules

II. Processes

1. *Identification of critical processes*

Functional areas

Critical
processes

2. *Charting each critical process by operations*

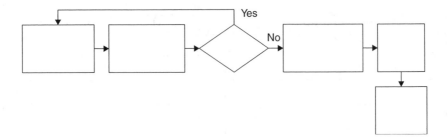

III. Information system

1. Graphic representation of the information system

☐ Written document   ☐ Operation on the information   ◯ File
(normally computerized)

☐ Decision   ◇ Alternatives   △ Information obtained
by (telephone) query

⬡ Complex process that will not be detailed in this chart

2. Diagram

People through which the information passes and/or who make decisions

Representation

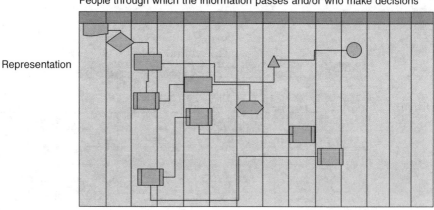

III. Information system: summary of decisions

1. Identification of decisions

Who makes the decision	What is the decision

IV. Blockages in processes and information system

Using the charts for the critical processes and information systems (IS), those points where there has been some type of problem are identified, painting a 'cloud' on that part of the process or IS.

1. Processes

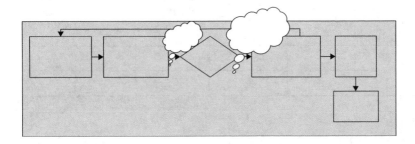

2. Information system

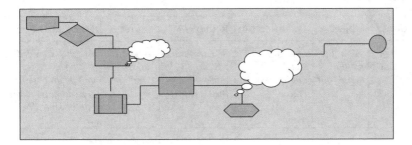

V. Building the KDB (Knowledge Data Base)

1. Knowledge assessment based on processes and best practices

Process/best practice	Activity	Existing knowledge	Source	Recommended knowledge
Reference to the process or best practice to which the activities belong	*Activities within the process or best practice*	*Things that we know how to do and which enable us to perform these activities*	*Where does the knowledge reside?*	*What do we need in order to perform this activity better?*

2. Knowledge assessment based on the information system

Info-decision system	Problem	Methodology	Existing knowledge	Source	Recommended knowledge
Reference to decision and IS	*Problem or question solved by making the decision*	*How do we do it?*	*Things that we know how to do and which enable us to solve the problems*	*Where does the knowledge reside?*	*What do we need in order to enable us to solve this problem or question more easily?*

3. Build the KDB

Action	Object	Qualification	Remarks	Source	Materialization
Verb that expresses the knowledge	*What the action carries out*	*Elements that qualify the object*	*Remarks that will help understand the knowledge*	*Who has the knowledge?*	*Are they recorded in some way so that they can be an asset for the company and can be shared?*

4. Define the terms used

Verb	Definition	Occurrences
Insert the verbs used	*Give a definition of each verb*	*Number of times*

5. *Group the knowledge*

Action	Object	Qualification	Knowledge	Knowledge group
Transfer the list generated in Table 3 and organize by similarity of action				*Define a new knowledge that groups the previous knowledge items*

6. *Define the knowledge groups*

Knowledge group	Definition
Transfer the knowledge grouped in Table 5	**Look for the most suitable definition**

7. *List the knowledge groups with their individual knowledge items*

Knowledge group	
	Individual knowledge items

VI. Interaction with the customers

1. The moments of truth

Interaction points with the customer	Risks: What can go well/wrong?	Interaction process
Identify the times when there is an interaction with the customer	*Analysis of what can go well and what can go wrong, or of what the risks are*	*Brief description of the interaction process*

2. List of MOTs

MOT	MOT	MOT

3. Identify the origin of the risks: the root of the problems, cause and effect or Ishikawa chart

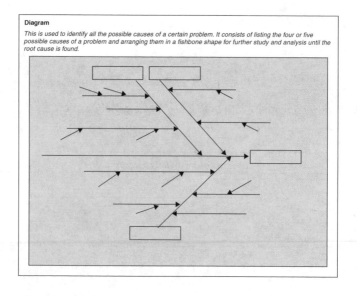

Diagram

This is used to identify all the possible causes of a certain problem. It consists of listing the four or five possible causes of a problem and arranging them in a fishbone shape for further study and analysis until the root cause is found.

VII. Application of knowledge to MOTs

1. Compile

A. The KDB (Knowledge Data Base)

Knowledge group	
	Individual knowledge items

B. Definition of the KDB's knowledge groups

Knowledge group	Definition

C. Definition of verbs

Verb	Definition

D. The moments of truth

MOT	MOT	MOT	MOT

E. The Ishikawa charts (root causes of the risks)

MOT

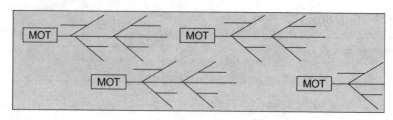

2. Execute

A. Matrix with the moments of truth and knowledge

Knowledge groups

		KG1	KG2	KG3	KG4	KG5
MOT with transcribed Ishikawa	MOT					
	cause 1					
	cause 2					

B. Action form

Difficult MOT		Knowledge group	
Move MOTs here	Mark applicable MOT	Move knowledge here	Mark applicable knowledge
Action		**MOT**	**Individual knowledge item**
Give name to action which will use the knowledge to solve the conflict		Origin of problem	Identify the knowledge item which will be used
Description of action			

C. List of actions

Action	MOT originating the problem	Number

10
Knowledge Generation

Introduction

In the previous chapter, we presented a systematic way of using the firm's knowledge to improve the service rendered to the customer. In this particular case, it was a procedure in the form of an improvement project – that is, a one-off event within the firm's life. But how can this approach be transformed into a permanent improvement system? At first sight, the answer might be: 'Well, let's carry out the method once a day.' However, when put into practice in this manner, the process suffers from two basic drawbacks:

1. *The preparation is costly.* Any knowledge identification process, discovery of moments of truth, and the like, that is needed to arrive at a list of actions, is time-consuming. To perform it every day is costly. But, on top of that, it is redundant. Because, unless drastic changes are made within the firm, we will discover the same knowledge that we had the previous day. And in the process, we will perform that wondrous act of carrying out a costly process that contributes nothing new. This is logical, because knowledge is only changed by our actions and subsequent learning. However, in one day, not enough time will have passed to perform actions that change the knowledge base. One possible modification is to lengthen the time between analyses. However, now the opposite effect happens. If we lengthen it too much, we will miss opportunities because the knowledge is not detected when it is generated.

2. *It is a system of plans.* The outcome of the process is an action plan consisting of a sequence of actions that encompass a not insignificant time period. The plan represents a commitment to future action by the individuals involved, sanctioned by the firm's management. This has three effects. First, it gives the plan an internal application logic, with precedents and synergies between activities. Generally speaking, it is difficult to separate the plan into individual actions that can be performed concurrently by the agents and which can be generated by each agent in the course of interacting with his daily work environment. Second, the plan must be reviewed by consensus and iteration. With this method, it is unlikely that each agent will have the initiative to change actions as problems are detected. The result of the analysis is both too

detailed – with too many coordinated actions – and too broad to enable rapid review of the plans. And lastly, in order to assess actions, they must all be available and have been described in sufficient detail.

Because of these two drawbacks, the technique described in Chapter 9 is not practical for creating a complete permanent improvement system. If we wish to obtain a permanent improvement system, we must study in greater depth the context in which the improvement takes place and adapt the ideas of the previous chapter – and not the procedures – which must be substantially modified.

Permanent improvement and PDM

A permanent improvement system is very different from an improvement plan: an improvement plan seeks to find better actions, an optimal plan for solving current problems. Optimizing means having alternatives, centralizing them, subjecting them to a comparative assessment, and choosing the best actions to pursue in solving the problem. It is a monolithic approach, in which the entire organization moves towards a suitable plan (Figure 10.1).

By contrast, an improvement system must take a completely different approach. In this instance, the emphasis is on *flexibility*. When a problem is found, action is taken. This has the disadvantage that the action applied may not be the optimal action and that, later on, we will end up again faced with a problem that has not been satisfactorily resolved.

The solution to this dilemma is a radical one. An improvement system must perform *actions to destroy problems*, not solve them. This way, we make sure that we will never see the problem again. We can say that the approach moves from optimization – the best solution for solving a problem – to feasibility – a feasible action (not necessarily the best action) that destroys the problem. And when actions are repetitive, it does not matter much that each one is optimal so long as, collectively, they take the system to its competitive purpose. (See Figure 10.2.)

Therefore, a PDM system must possess the following qualities:

1. There is a state of continual watchfulness regarding the diagnosis of problems. These must be identified 'on the spot' by any agent that encounters them. This

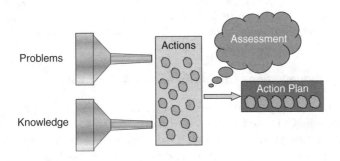

Figure 10.1   The approach described in the previous chapter

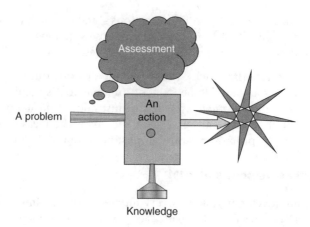

Figure 10.2 The permanent improvement approach

implies decentralization. Whoever finds a problem acts to resolve the situation, without waiting for more to be found.

2. People do not wait until all of the problems are catalogued and all of the actions are listed before performing an action. Prompt action would be impossible in such conditions. Initiative must be delegated to the agents.
3. The agents can work in parallel if necessary, each one undertaking their own improvement process. However, their actions will be coordinated if this enables joint problems to be solved. This requires understanding the process and creating an environment of mutual help.
4. Steps are taken to ensure that learning is obtained from the actions performed. Just as in the previous point, an environment that supports mutual help must be created.
5. The assessment made of the actions is the outcome of a continuous evaluation process. This can be achieved, and this is a key idea, by evaluating the *problems*, not the actions.

Therefore, the next two chapters will focus on understanding the process for designing a support system, rather than an action plan.

This is the framework for action that we outlined in Chapter 7. Sometimes, management has difficulties in adopting this new approach. Remember, *the goal is not that management make action plans but that it create a context in which others can make action plans.*

Knowledge management and permanent improvement

The permanent improvement system must make sure that learning takes place and that the knowledge is used in the best manner possible in order to achieve the firm's goals. Other authors (Nonaka, 1991, 1994) seem to associate knowledge management with the firm as a whole and propose concepts such as that of 'learning organization'. Indeed, the term has been used in a multitude of meanings,

Example 10.1   Some answers to what knowledge management is

What is Knowledge Management? Some Answers to an Informal Survey

The following answers were obtained by one of the authors during a number of seminars held on the subject. Of course, these answers were given at the start of each seminar. The respondent's position or profession is given in brackets beside each answer.

- An approach to Human Resources management (Human Resources manager).
- The valuation of intellectual capital (accountant).
- The technology for storing and distributing knowledge (Information Systems manager).
- A branch of artificial intelligence (engineer).
- What philosophers do (lawyer).
- An empty box with a label (professor).
- What we are going to talk about in this seminar (business).

---

many of them contradictory. In most instances, it is already synonymous with document management, people are even starting to talk about knowledge management as document management. None of these conceptions is very operational and they place little emphasis on the achievement of results for the firm. We are only interested in knowledge management insofar as it makes the firm more productive and more competitive.

We think that the true nature of the knowledge management system *is being the operating implementation of the permanent improvement system*, one of the many systems that must function within any company. It does not replace any of the classic systems, except the quality system, which it transcends and clarifies. Therefore, knowledge management is not a new approach to the firm's organization, nor is it a new management philosophy. It is simply the body of elements that ensures the best use of an asset that has always been present in the firm, but whose right to be one of its basic resources is only just being recognized. And which tries to guarantee that this use is focused deliberately in the same direction – *the constant improvement of the firm's productivity and competitiveness*.

Learning as a knowledge acquisition process

The word 'learning' encompasses a broad spectrum of situations and it has been used with very different meanings. Argyris (1990, 1993) defines it as 'a process in which people discover a problem, devise a solution for the problem, produce the solution and evaluate the result, which leads to the discovery of new problems'. More recently, Pérez López has said that learning is 'any change that takes place as a consequence of an interaction process (between two agents), provided that the modification is significantly important for the explanation of future interactions'.

The learning process is a personal improvement mechanism, the complex result of all the experiences that the individual encounters in his progression. All of the specialists agree that learning only occurs if it is ultimately reflected in action. An individual only learns if there is a change in his behaviour, in his 'decision rules'.

In his definition, Argyris (1990, 1993) explicitly mentions the mechanism that generates learning: problem solving. Pérez López is not as explicit, but in his study of the relationship between two agents, he defines the interactions as 'the result of problem solving by the active agent'. With such illustrious forerunners and with the specialists in virtually unanimous agreement, we feel authorized to formulate our basic hypothesis: *problem solving produces learning and, reciprocally in adults and in a context of action, learning takes place basically by problem solving.*[1] This means that the reader is not learning anything by reading this book. In fact, he will not learn until he immerses himself in the real-life solution of permanent improvement problems.

The problem-solving process modifies the agent who executes the action. By doing so, the agent acquires a methodology that helps him to solve more problems and improve the solutions. However, that is not all. In industrial practice, we have observed – and Jaikumar (Jaikumar and Bohn, 1986) also hints at this – a much more important second-order effect. The agent, the person who solves the problem, reconfigures himself in a structure that enables him to perform new problem-solving procedures.

We must differentiate between memory and learning. Memory is increased, by definition, when the agent's *perceptional* knowledge increases. Learning refers to the other types of knowledge – *abstract and experiential.* Popularly, learning is linked more directly with knowledge acquisition while memory is more associated with retaining the knowledge that has already been acquired.

One aspect that is inherent to learning is forgetting past conducts that were not successful or decision rules that proved to be wrong. Implicit in the development of knowledge is its obsolescence when reality changes. Understanding new events implies learning new knowledge and discarding obsolete knowledge. This discarding activity – unlearning – is almost as important as the creation of new knowledge. A slow unlearning process is a weakness of many organizations.

Problems lead to solving problems – and this, in turn, leads to learning. But what generates problems? If a problem is characterized as the existence of a situation that is not 'pleasant' for the individual, as we suggested in Chapter 1, defining what causes 'unpleasant' situations may help us to identify what causes problems.

In a stable environment, given sufficient time for the mist to clear, everything is pleasant. Unpleasant situations appear as a consequence of *change.* Change

---

[1] Those of us who teach in business schools, such as ours (IESE), have absolute faith in this. And our belief is so deep that our teaching process is based almost entirely on confronting the student with cases that raise management problems.

creates its share of unpleasant situations, things that turn out in a manner that is not pleasing to us. Anything that is 'new' is the outcome of a change. In any action situation, problems are generated if the agent's environment changes to include new situations. *Problems are generated by 'change'.*

In the business world, change has been analysed for many years under the heading of *innovation*. But the reader should not just think of major innovations. Most of the innovations that take place in a company are changes in the way in which certain operations are performed. They are often small changes, without any dramatic effect on the lives of the people affected by them. Innovation is only doing *new, or old, things in new ways.*[2]

Innovation is, therefore, a sufficient condition for the existence of problems. An organization that does not innovate does not have problems. Not to innovate is simply not to do anything new. And what is known or stable never causes problems. Absolute stability is death. Therefore, innovation generates problems that must subsequently be solved by means of a problem-solving process. This problem-solving process produces *learning*. And learning increases the *knowledge base*.

The causal chain therefore stretches over all four basic components: innovation, problems, problem solving and learning.

To close the cycle which will establish the learning context, we must recognize the existence of a feedback mechanism which makes the causal chain turn back on itself. Indeed, it is known (Boden, 1994) that improvement ideas appear in proportion to the volume of knowledge existing in the agent. A very broad knowledge base is normally a more productive source of ideas for change. As a consequence of the high level of knowledge and the greater understanding of the function and state of the environment, traditional ways of working are questioned and ideas for improvement are proposed. These improvement ideas – even when they exist only in an intellectual state – become a source of innovation, proposals for implementing new ways of doing things.

This observation closes the loop by making learning depend upon the knowledge base. Since growth of the latter depends upon learning, the result is a dynamic loop which describes a context that causes the knowledge base to evolve in the right direction. We call this causal sequence the *knowledge generation cycle or internal cycle* and it is one of the core ideas in the construction of an improvement system (Figure 10.3).

Idea generation is the result of the *creativity* of the people in the organization. Therefore, everything that is known about creativity can be used to encourage and further the creation of ideas.

Of these variables, *problem solving* was discussed in the first chapter of this book and we refer the reader to what was said there. Suffice to say here that this problem-solving process's internal structure must help the manager to identify how and when the process's elements can be supported. Further on, we will enter

---

[2] This outlook is shared by many experts in innovation. As an example, Juran (1988) says that innovation is 'to create and introduce original solutions for new or already identified needs'.

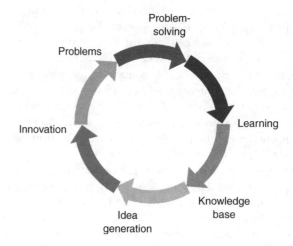

Figure 10.3   Knowledge generation cycle or internal cycle

into greater detail about how the problem-solving process's structure gives clues as to how to support it within the firm.

Innovation

Innovation is the manner in which new ideas are put into practice. Perhaps this is one of the variables – within the manager's reach – that is most important in controlling the internal cycle. Implementing innovations lies at the very heart of the manager's profession. A manager can control his company's innovation portfolio by deciding what innovations will be introduced and how.

In order for innovations to be implemented, they must first be introduced to the organization's members. In any innovation, three types of agent are involved: the innovator, the innomanager and the innoreceiver. The *innovator* is the person who introduces the innovation into the firm. He is responsible for securing the implementation of the new way of doing things. It may be the managing director if the innovation consists of introducing an ERP, for example, or the maintenance manager if it is a new safety door. The *innomanager* is responsible for ensuring the innovation's success. His job is to guide the implementation and to provide support to the people who must live with the innovation. These people are the *innoreceivers*.[3]

The problem-solving activity, essentially, performed by the innoreceiver, may be subject to significant input from the innomanager. Specifically, the innomanager can provide tools, create an environment and provide training to make the receivers more efficient in problem solving.

---

[3] Sometimes also called innosufferers, because they are the ones who end up suffering the effects of the innovation.

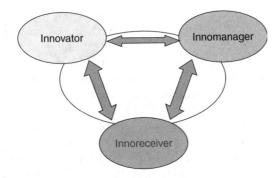

Figure 10.4   The agents involved in innovation

The success of innovations, in the sense of increasing the knowledge base, depends to a great extent upon the way in which absorption of the innovations is assigned to the organization's components, and, more specifically, to its associated agents. The innovator must consider the type of effect that will be caused before introducing the innovation. The innoreceiver will have to adjust to the innovation, solve its problems, and be the active subject of the learning. And the innomanager, normally a line manager, has the responsibility – probably the most important responsibility of all – of ensuring that the problems generated by the innovation can be absorbed by the innoreceivers in such a manner as to obtain maximal learning. The relationship between these three agents is shown in Figure 10.4.

Innovation action

For innovation to be successfully implemented, a genuine change must take place within the firm. In this sense, innovation is merely the *implementation* of a change. If new ideas are to be turned into innovation, they must be transformed into action. And this action comes about after a mental creativity process that is based on the knowledge currently held. Therefore, innovation is ultimately the result of a knowledge application process aimed at *changing* (some part of) the firm.

Many schools of thought have been developed around innovation and there is insufficient room in this book to consider all of them. We present here the line of work that is most akin and from which we have borrowed some of the ideas to establish the manner in which innovation affects the learning process.

This school of thought is represented by the work of Abernathy (Abernathy and Clark, 1985). This author proposes that, at any given moment in time, all firms have a series of relationships or *links*, which are both internal (with the firm's other processes and agents) and external (with the environment in which it operates). The internal links form the business system's invariants. They are those things that 'do not change', even when everything else changes. To put it in plain language, 'those things that we have always done that way'. The external links play the same role to anchor the company's relationship with the environment. They are the invariants of that relationship. Furthermore, they are related, in a more or less stable manner, to the processes that take place within the company. Employees can either understand the nature of all these stable links or can simply accept them as the 'way things are done'. For example, the firm's relationship with its suppliers, customers and even competitors may be the outcome of a ritual or accepted way of operating, typically part of the CRS.

The internal and external links form a basic unchanging fabric – a surface on which the firm's action is developed. According to Abernathy, when innovation comes onto the scene, it disrupts these links and then modifies the behavioural patterns of the people who work in the firm. The surface undergoes changes in its curvature that distort the existing force field. According to this proposal, the mechanism that accounts for the appearance of problems – is the disruption of the (internal and external) links that exist in the environment in which the innovation is introduced. The causal chain:

Links → innovation → disruption → change → problem

summarizes the problem-generating mechanism caused by innovation. Innovation and change are, therefore, two related but different concepts. One is related to doing things and the other to experiencing results. To explore in greater depth the structure of the effect caused by the phenomenon, we must classify the types of innovation and the nature of their influences.

All of the classifications of the types of innovation that have been proposed have sought to show the size of the internal or external disruption brought about by the innovation. As our purpose is to relate innovation with learning, we propose to relate first with the type of problem it generates. Therefore, our innovation typology is based upon the internal conditions for learning that are created within the firm.

*Types of innovation

In order to classify the problems generated by innovation, we consider two dimensions. Two dimensions are sufficient because they provide a good separation of the types of innovation and intuitively reflect the nature of the phenomenon.

When choosing the two dimensions, the idea is that the total quantity of change in the existing links and, consequently, the quality of problems generated by innovation is, in some way, the product of its intensity and extension. As a measure of the *intensity* of the problems generated, we can take their degree of structure: structured problems versus non-structured problems, in the sense explained in Chapter 1.

The second dimension must be related with *extension*, the number of links existing within the firm, or between it and the environment, which are disrupted by the innovation. Among the various choices available, we will take as second dimension the variety of problems generated by innovation. If the problems generated are of very different types, it is logical to assume that the innovation has disrupted a large number of links when it was introduced. A large part of the

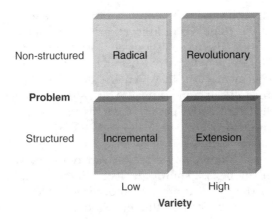

Figure 10.5 Innovation typology

organization will be affected by it and many people will be exposed to potentially unpleasant circumstances. If, on the other hand, the variety is limited, only a few links will be disrupted, the problems generated will be confined to one area of the firm and, probably, the number of people affected will be much less.

Therefore, we select the two variables:

- The problem structure.
- Variety of problems generated.

To simplify the presentation even more, let us only consider two extreme values in each dimension: high and low. Crossing these two dimensions gives the following innovation typology (Figure 10.5).

In accordance with this figure, we classify innovations into four categories, depending upon the nature and variety of the problems generated,[4] and the four varieties will be given the names stated in the corresponding quadrants of Figure 10.5.

1. *Incremental innovation* is produced by the implementation of changes that have a local scope and modify only a small number of the firm's links. For example, most of the innovations that are implemented as a result of the firm's suggestions system are of this type. These are minor changes aimed at improving the functionality and performance of certain work units. They affect a limited area and create operating problems which, as we know, are mostly structured. These innovations do not require a great variety of knowledge in order to deal with them. The problem solving is confined to a limited amount of domain or task knowledge. Changes in how the performance of a certain activity is reported; changes in the method for carrying out customer service operations; design

---

[4] We said previously that our classification of innovations is based on the ideas of Abernathy. We have therefore taken the liberty of using names similar to his to define our typology.

changes that make the assembly process easier, etc., are some examples of this type of innovation. Hundreds of innovations of this type occur in the firm's day-to-day activities. The repercussions are basically financial – that is, their impact is on the firm's productivity. Their net result is to keep the firm within a certain improvement path, in which the difference between the present situation and the following one is small. This type of improvement has sometimes been called continuous improvement, as its time course has a certain continuity, with small changes in small intervals of time.

2. *Extensive innovation* entails an increase in the variety of problems caused by innovation. It therefore requires a greater variety of knowledge in the firm, much of which will be task knowledge. Its main drawback lies in the coordination between the different areas of knowledge, which must cooperate to solve the problems generated by the innovation. If an extensive innovation could be reduced to a slow sequence of incremental innovations, it would not give rise to any stress in the firm's daily life. In practical reality, the firm often tries to reduce extensive, radical and revolutionary innovations to a succession of incremental innovations. 'Do it step by step', 'introduce the novelty using a pilot implementation' is classic advice that *a priori* seems to offer a good approach to implementing change.

   The problem arises with the speed of change. A sequence of incremental innovations that take place at great speed ceases to be an incremental innovation and becomes an extensive innovation. Many small but very quick changes cause 'confusion' and 'stress'. Extensive innovation also has the added requirement of involving many people, giving rise to coordination problems that are not encountered with incremental innovation.

The next two types of innovation generate non-structured problems. Solving these problems typically requires solving two different types of subproblems to be pursued. On one hand, structuring problems that can eliminate part of the confusion. By structuring a part of the problem one simplifies its solution. However there is always an unstructured leftover problem that cannot be structured easily. This part requires management talent to attack the problems generated and the knowledge required for this is biased towards experiential knowledge. The non-structured part thereby tests the risk-taking and entrepreneurial capacities of the organization's managers.

3. The problems generated by *radical innovation* are difficult, but they all have a similar nature so that solving one type (perhaps in an eminently exploratory phase) may eventually give rise to approaches that solve other problems. One example of radical innovation (for customers) was the introduction of automatic cash dispensers by the banks. The way in which exchange operations are carried out between the bank and the customer changed significantly. Human contact was replaced by a machine, with all of the associated relational problems. For the customer, the innoreceiver, the innovation was radical. However, for the banks productivity side the introduction of cash dispensers was not a radical innovation. For many banks this innovation simply generated a variety of well-structured problems, so it could be said to have been an extensive innovation.

4. *Revolutionary innovations* generate a greater variety of unstructured problems and require a higher level of coordination. The coordination now takes place between decision makers solving problems that are unstructured and, therefore, difficult to specify. The very nature of the solution itself is in question and the interrelation problems that arise between individuals will be acute. The great variety of knowledge required to solve the extensive range of problems is combined here with the difficulty in applying this knowledge. When people try to enumerate examples of this type of innovation, they often lapse into a technology fantasy. Nothing could be further from the truth. For example, the authors experienced a revolutionary innovation when the walls were removed in an R&D department and the engineers started to work in a large open-plan office. A wide variety of problems were generated – friction between people, physical problems caused by noise, lack of privacy, etc. – all of them largely unstructured problems. In fact, the problems were so unstructured that even the people affected by them were unable to diagnose them. They complained of environmental factors when, in fact, the underlying cause was one of territoriality.

In contrast, the introduction of digital television, which some believe to be a revolutionary innovation, is almost an incremental innovation for the user. His relationship with the television set will only be affected as regards the number of channels available. If this number is high, perhaps one could call it a radical innovation, since this generates non-structured problems (the stress of not being able to see everything may force the user to resort to frantic zapping, causing clearly non-structured purpose or relation problems ...).

For most companies, a typical revolutionary innovation is the introduction of an ERP-type information system. The problems generated are companywide and affect how all of the company's staff work, their habits and the ways they have always done things. The large number of failures occurring in this field is due to the inadequate approach taken to implementing this type of innovation.

Example 10.2 shows the differential effect of innovations and also their impact even when firms have the necessary knowledge.

At any given point in time, a company might have a certain number of innovations in progress, belonging to all four types. In a similar manner to the knowledge portfolio we presented in the first chapter, now the *innovations portfolio* is the combination of innovations confronting a firm at any given moment. Through the innovative agent, the firm can control the rate and type of innovation so that learning could be controlled within the firm. A carefully managed innovations portfolio must produce increases in the firm's knowledge base. Managing the innovations portfolio means selecting – for subsequent implementation – the proposals that are best matched to the abilities and knowledge of the people in the firm. This critical element will be the subject of the next section.

We alert the reader once again about the possible confusion that the words revolutionary, radical, etc., may create when they are used to describe innovation. Remember that these are only names for types of innovation that are defined by

Example 10.2   Innovation at EFA

Effects of Innovations: EFA's Radar

In 1986 Inisel, a Spanish company specializing in professional electronics, was involved in an international defence programme. The firm, which was the largest in this industry in Spain and was very interested in developing its technology base, viewed the project as an unique opportunity to achieve its goal. Under instructions from the Spanish government, it formed an international consortium with another three European companies to tender for the development of the European Fighter Aircraft's (EFA) onboard radar. The EFA is a plane produced by a consortium of four aviation companies in each of the four participating companies: Germany, Italy, the United Kingdom and Spain. The four companies formed a company, Eurofighter, which was responsible for coordinating and subcontracting all of the project's activities. The four member companies of the radar consortium were Inisel, AEG (Germany), Marconi (United Kingdom) and FIAR (Italy).

When Eurofighter published the radar's preliminary specifications, the four companies realized that it was a very advanced device and only two of the consortium's companies had experience in similar developments. By contract, each of the four participating companies was responsible for developing 25 per cent of the project. It was estimated that the duration of the project would be of two years. The complete project was divided into four clearly differentiated parts: emitter, receiver, signal processor and antenna. As the engineers considered that each part had the same quantity of work, it seemed logical to allocate one part to each company.

Eurofighter asked the consortia to submit preliminary tenders to judge the project's feasibility and to determine its final configuration. The consortium developed a series of rules for drawing up the preliminary tender, which were circulated among the four companies. In order to have the best information on the project's costs and prevent possible imbalances, it was decided that each of the consortium's companies would tender for all of the radar's components, without taking into account the possible preliminary allocation of the components.

As part of preparing the tender, an estimate was made of the workloads that the project would entail for each company. The outlay that would be required in development, production and testing was quite sizable and seemed to be project-specific, so it all had to be recouped during the project's life. Another major cost component was materials, because it had to be electronics in a militarized version.

Each company drew up its tender and sent it to the coordinator, AEG, in Ulm (Germany). The tenders were kept sealed until all the companies met at Ulm. At the meeting, the different parts of the system were listed one by one on a board and each company gave its quote, which was written on the board. Even the first quote caused considerable surprise. The quantities varied over a broad range, with differences of up to 60 per cent. Even the two companies with most experience showed differences of 30 per cent. However, when they got to the signal processing module, muffled laughs started to be heard. This module showed differences ... of several orders of magnitude!, and all the companies had given wildly different estimates.

A subsequent analysis revealed that the cause of the cost deviations was to be found in the workload estimates. The signal processor specified was something completely new for all of the companies. It required implementing revolutionary innovations whose effect was difficult to foresee, although all of the companies agreed that the two-year time period given was long enough to solve the problems generated by the innovation.

the type of problems they generate ... Revolutionary innovation does not mean that it must organize a revolution (although in some cases it may do this). Likewise, an incremental innovation may have a dramatic effect on the firm's competitiveness and, perhaps, on its relationship with the environment. For example, buying telephones for all of the firm's employees may not be a revolutionary innovation, but for a sales company it is likely to have a dramatic effect on its relationship with the market.

The type of problems generated by an innovation depends upon the baseline situation of the firms concerned. The same innovation may be revolutionary in the case of one firm and incremental in the case of another. But the reader should not forget that the semantic charge associated with adjectives such as 'revolutionary' or 'radical' often distorts the reasoning.

Innovation and learning

All four types of innovation generate problems that produce learning. But this learning is not always immediate. A more detailed analysis leads to a series of qualifications that are of great importance for innovation management. The most significant point to consider is that, in any type of innovation, there is a serious danger of the innoreceiver not experiencing any learning. Indeed, an innovation may generate frustration, without this being accompanied by any type of learning. The degree of learning created by an innovation depends upon the degree of *challenge* created for the firm's agents by the problems generated. Therefore, management of innovation with the goal of achieving learning also requires managing the right type of *challenge*.

De Treville (1987) has documented by experiment that the problem-solving activity produces learning provided that the challenge posed by the problem to the person who has to solve it, remains within certain limits. If the challenge is too small, the problem is trivial, no effort is required to solve it, and very little learning takes place. If the challenge is too large, the person trying to solve the problem is unable to have any impact on it, he feels frustrated, and he withdraws

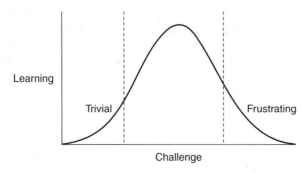

Challenge

Figure 10.6   De Treville's curve

from it. In this case, frustration, rather than learning, takes place. Maximum learning occurs when the problem's intrinsic challenge is matched to the capacity of the person solving it. Figure 10.6 illustrates these effects of challenge on learning.

The phenomenon is very familiar to teachers and it is unsurprising that it appears in business contexts. However, it has important implications. For example, it raises a series of questions about the traditional ways of allocating tasks. Traditionally, it is recommended that a task should be allocated to a person who is qualified to perform it. De Treville says that, from the learning viewpoint, it should be allocated to a person whose qualifications place the challenge in the best position for learning. In other words, the match should not be between task and skills but between skills and challenge. Some may think that this approach goes against the quality of the task performed. According to traditional wisdom, the worker will perform his task best if it does not pose him any challenge. This is true to some degree, but it relies upon a static view of the world, in which the worker will never learn enough to perform tasks that are more complex or require a greater level of knowledge. The challenge is related with the type of innovation. Ceteris paribus revolutionary innovations have a higher level of challenge than incremental innovations. A revolutionary innovation necessarily represents a significant change for the organization. If the organization has an adequate knowledge base, the resulting challenge may be located in the learning zone of De Treville's curve. However, if this is not the case and the challenge is too great, the firm's people will be unable to cope with the innovation.

The idea generation process or creativity

Creativity is a complex phenomenon and has been the subject of considerable study for many years in the psychological literature. However, until recently, these studies have appeared to have little relevance for improvement. What is creativity and what are its mechanisms? The experts generally agree that there is something – which we may call the creative process – that is performed by individuals and which consists of five basic stages (Guilford, 1979).

1. *Preparation*. The acquisition of skills, general information about the subject, resources, experiences and definitions of the problem.
2. *Concentration*. The individual concentrates deeply on the problem, to the exclusion of virtually everything else. This is a trial and error stage, which includes failed attempts and, probably, frustrations.
3. *Incubation*. Separation of the problem and ordering, integration and clarification, all of this at an unconscious level. If often includes contemplation, relaxation and solitude actions.
4. *Illumination*. The 'Aha!' phenomenon, which often happens suddenly and which brings to the surface an idea, an image or a perspective that suggests a solution or a direction for exploration.
5. *Verification and elaboration*. Testing of ideas, evaluation, development, implementation and convincing others about the idea's worth.

These stages need not occur separately from each other and there may even be complex interconnections and feedbacks between them. Torrance (1969) defined creativity, in a broad sense, as 'the process of perceiving a problem, looking for possible solutions, proposing hypotheses, testing and evaluating them, and communicating the results to others'. He also adds in this definition that the creative process must have original ideas, a different viewpoint, break moulds, and recombine or discover new relationships between different ideas.

There is a significant body of literature that addresses the problem of creativity through the impact that its environment has on it. Thus, Hamel (1999) mentions how a certain number of firms try to generate this environment in a much more radical manner by developing entrepreneurship within the company. Thus, the so-called 'innovation laboratories' create a favourable environment for idea generation, trying to reproduce the so-called Silicon Valley spirit within their company. These laboratories generate risk-taking and new idea- and service-generating environments similar to those created in their day by firms such as Motorola and 3M. In our approach, the environment becomes important for the *entire permanent improvement creation process*.

T. Amabile (1998) conceives creativity as the ability to order ideas that already exist in new combinations, in which three components intersect (see Figure 10.7): experience, motivation and mechanisms or skills for generating creativity. In her opinion, managers must influence these three components in order to generate new ideas.

Amabile defines experience[5] as 'the intellectual space that each person uses to explore and solve problems'. The larger this space is, the more idea-generating capacity the person has. The second component, motivation, focuses on the cause–effect relationship, arguing that the greater the internal motivation to rise to the challenge is, the more idea-generating capacity the person has. This could be combined with the four elements suggested by Torrance (1969) for generating

---

[5] 'Knowledge is experience. The rest is just information.' Albert Einstein.

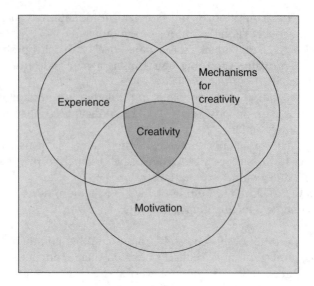

Figure 10.7   The three components of creativity according to Amabile

individual creativity:

1. *Fluidity of ideas*: skill for producing a large number of ideas.
2. *Flexibility*: skill for producing a great variety of ideas.
3. *Elaboration*: skill for developing, embellishing or filling an idea.
4. *Originality*: skill for producing ideas that are unusual or statistically infrequent, in addition to not being banal or obvious.

Our goal is to understand how creativity functions so that we can develop it in people. To do this, we start by defining creativity as 'the generation of ideas to enhance a normal intelligence'.[6] For us, creativity is the development of ideas that are new for the individual. According to Boden (1994), there are two levels of new ideas: surprising and impossible. A surprising idea is an unexpected idea, but as soon as it arises, it is assimilated and the agent's thinking is reorganized. The impossible ideas are those that are paradoxical breaking structures and turning what was impossible into something that is now possible. (See Example 10.3.)

The creativity we are interested in is the so-called *structured imagination*.[7] *Structured imagination occurs when people perform a task in which a new reality (a new object or operation, a modification of existing objects or designs, etc.) is generated*. In most cases, structured imagination in the business world has been studied using *ad hoc* techniques, with no substantive knowledge of the underlying mechanisms.[8]

---

[6] We take the Aristotelian definition of intelligence – the ability to use knowledge – specifically 'teleological intelligence', that is, the ability to use knowledge for a purpose.

[7] A concept taken from Boden's P creativity.

[8] This does not mean that the results are bad. Quite the contrary, the intuition of some people who achieve results without any mechanism to account for them is admirable.

Example 10.3 A case of structured imagination

Aries Balanzas, S.L.

At the end of the 1970s, Aries was a Barcelona-based company specializing in the manufacture of precision scales. The scales they made were renowned throughout Europe for their quality and reliability. In addition, their business was successful and very profitable. The scales were classic mechanical precision scales that were extensively used in scientific laboratories. They were very light, mounted on wedges that used semi-precious materials, with extra-rigid arms, etc. The company had accumulated an appreciable quantity of knowledge in mechanics and was constantly introducing modifications in its scales that enabled it to continue offering the highest precision for its price band. However, in 1981, Aries encountered the first electronic scales imported from Japan. A Japanese company was offering scales with slightly less precision but 50 per cent cheaper. Aries' managers immediately realized the potential offered by electronic technology in precision measurements and decided that they had to design and manufacture a new line of electronic scales.

The initial design for the new scale was subcontracted to a university department, who did an excellent job and designed a prototype that performed better than the Japanese model and still offered many possibilities for further improvements. However, the most serious problem arose when the prototype was passed on to Aries so that it could be integrated in its operations. Although all of the company's engineers were highly proficient in mechanics, their knowledge of electronics was virtually non-existent. Their great intuition in mechanics was of no use to them in electronics, as they hardly ever knew what bit was doing what. Learning was progressing at a very slow pace and problems of a very elementary nature were starting to delay industrial-scale implementation of the prototype. As on other occasions, the company's management tried to apply more pressure but this only led to more frustration. With the help of experts, the company was able to diagnose this situation and draw up an action plan. The company decided to recruit someone part-time who could help them.

A middle-aged engineer, with a solid background in electronic and mechanical design, was hired as a consultant to provide first-hand assistance in solving the implementation problems that were arising in the company. This consultant was asked to identify and eliminate possible obstacles but to leave sufficient difficulty so that the others could learn. For example, the consultant would meet once a week with the design group and together they would review the problems that had arisen during the previous week. The consultant solved some of them but allocated tasks to the group members that they themselves had to solve, asking them to report back with the results in the following meeting. The presence of this consultant engineer led to a drastic increase in the

> rate of progress of the new product line and, in less than a year, the company
> had a very decent version of an electronic precision scale on the market.
>
> *Source*: Based on an original case study by F. Serra, 'Instrumentos de precisión, S.A.
> IPRESA', IESE, case no. P-420, Barcelona, 1982.

We start from the idea that creativity can be developed in adults: that is, one can become creative by learning to be creative. This is an important point to stress: just as one can be taught to solve problems, one can be taught to generate ideas. Of course, there will be adults who have an innate ability to generate ideas. But this does not mean that less fortunate people cannot do the same.

A second critical point to stress is that creativity is developed by education: education in tools, to be able to think in a more systematic manner, education in new ways of thinking (Boden). The case study method is a typical example. Through constant effort and systematic preparation, students acquire a mental framework that enables them to diagnose and analyse situations in a different light. The specification of facts, the systematic search for alternatives, and the weighing of the different elements of the decision, make the mind think in a different way.[9]

What is the mechanism of creativity? M. Boden (1994) identifies three idea-generating mechanisms that are very useful for our purpose:

- *Combining*: Grouping known and used ideas in an unusual manner. This is the most widely used mechanism in most activities. Many psychological exercises are based on this mechanism to obtain new ideas.
- *Exploring*: This is a progressive change in the conceptual structure through systematic application of known transformations, but used in an unusual manner. Exploring is closely linked to the exploration process for solving problems analysed in Chapter 1.
- *Transforming*: This is the creation of a new framework, a different way of thinking. This is the most complex mechanism and that which provides the greatest capacity for viewing situations under a totally different light.

Everyone has these three mechanisms (Figure 10.8).

1. Combining

This is the most usual way of generating ideas. When we join together two concepts that do not have a usual or even logical relationship, the mind analyses the problem in a different light. Combining does not require any significant investment in training. Commonly used creativity techniques are sufficient to rapidly achieve an adequate level of training and provide the necessary background for using this form. It is a style of creativity that is often used by graphic designers to produce new presentations. For example, a small number of concepts are used to

---

[9] One of the authors takes pride in being able to identify those people who have been MBA students at IESE simply by discussing a problem.

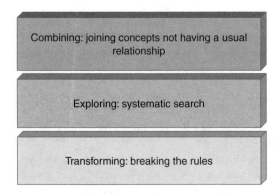

Figure 10.8 The three mechanisms of creativity

create websites. The aim is to combine them so that they produce a new perception on the part of the user.[10] An example of this type of creativity was presented to one of the authors when he was asked to draw 'an original arrow' in a drawing program. The problem is simply to combine the basic forms available in the program to obtain a 'different' result. Let the reader test his skill by trying to perform the exercise himself.

A certain type of literary creativity is combinatory. For example, one successful Anglo-Saxon author composed novels by combining the same ingredients in different ways.[11] When the possible combinations are few, one could hardly call the result creative. However, if the number of possible combinations is high, one obtains an interesting level of creativity.

2. Exploring

Curiously enough, creativity can often be thought of as a problem-solving process. One just poses the problem of finding an 'unusual' or 'novel' object. The problem proposed has one important property: The specification of the goal is diffuse and, therefore, it is difficult to define the evaluation functions. In the extreme case, one could say that the problem that it is wished to solve is 'incorrectly formulated' because we only know that the result must be 'unusual' without it being possible to define a clear criterion for this objective. This is why this type of problem does not lend itself very readily to the use of knowledge. The knowledge phase is very small, perhaps non-existent, and the exploratory phase takes up most of the process because of the ambiguity in defining a satisfactory solution. The features of an exploratory process have already been described in detail in Chapter 1. The ability

---

[10] Although, curiously enough, all of the websites are very similar. Most of the pages designed professionally have a heading, a menu on the left and along the top, a central text column and occasional inserts on the right. Did all professional designers study the same book?

[11] Someone remarked to the authors that the James Bond films always have the same ingredients in the plot, combined in different ways.

to obtain a satisfactory solution obviously has a random component; we may apply by chance the right transformations at the first try and set what we need.

Some people seem to always have luck on their side – they seem to have special skills, probably heuristics, to choose the right transformations that lead to an unusual solution without resorting to an exhaustive exploration. What is more, they seem to know how to do it systematically. Architects, designers, painters, musicians, and many others, seem to have this sixth sense that enables them to choose a path towards the solution scarcely having to backtrack. An extreme case was that of Mozart who, apparently, wrote the scores of his compositions without making a single correction (backtracking), although some of his biographers assure us that the backtracking took place in his mind before he physically wrote the score. In any case, the power of his heuristics enabled him to compose at a speed that made the use of extensive exploratory phases largely unnecessary. This property, often called 'creativity' and shrouded in mystery, has led many to think that it is an innate quality whose identity is unknown and people are called creative or uncreative depending on whether or not they have this quality.

Our analysis of the problem-solving process shows that this ability is just a property of an individual's personal problem-solving process. Whether they are heuristics or transformations, they are more powerful in these people than in most of us. It is this capability to find the best path 'at the first go' that constitutes the differential source of creativity.

3. Transforming

This is the most complex mechanism of all and the most difficult to explain. It consists of a fundamental modification in the individual's mental structure that comes about by introducing conditions (premises) that were not explicit in the problem and which drastically alter its solution process. These conditions do not change the way in which the solution process is performed but the formulation itself of this process. It is therefore a kind of metacreativity. However, although it can be explained and presented in these terms, this would not contribute anything meaningful and would probably confuse the reader. The best way to understand this creativity is to give an example of how it can be obtained. We invite the reader to examine Example 10.4 and, when he gives up, the footnote[12] will give him a 'transformational' approach.

*An integrative model

The complete creativity mechanism is probably a combination of the three mechanisms listed in the previous section. One integrative model which has been

---

[12] In actual fact, four triangles can be formed. But the trick is to do it … in space, not on the plane! In space, a tetrahedron has four equal faces and six sides, so it can be built with the six matchsticks. The problem-solving process itself – exploring with pencil and paper – automatically limits us to the plane. And on the plane, it is not possible to form more than two triangles. The dramatic change in one of the problem's non-explicit conditions has provided the means to solve the problem.

Example 10.4   Triangles

Transformational Creativity

The task is to form the largest possible number of equal triangles using six matchsticks, each one having the same length. The triangles must have one matchstick for each of their sides. A little experimenting with pencil and paper shows that two triangles can be obtained with some matchsticks left over. How many can the reader obtain?

---

proposed for combining all three mechanisms in a coherent structure is that offered by Finke, Ward and Smith (1992), who have developed the Geneplore (Generate and Explore) model. The model introduces the idea of pre-inventive structures, the metablocks which are combined in the problem-solving process. Figure 10.9 is a scheme of the Geneplore model adapted to our needs.

Using Boden's concepts we could say that the Geneplore model postulates the existence of two parallel processes:

- *P process.* This is a *problem-solving* process (exploration component) in the general sense outlined in Chapter 1. This is shown with medium shading in Figure 10.9.
- *C process.* This is also called the pre-inventive structure-generating process. It is a process of loading the inputs required to solve the problem – that is, for the P process to function. The C process is placed between the individual's knowledge base and the problem-solving process. The C process extracts elements from a knowledge database and combines them, obtaining structures that can be used by the P process and that are not in the database. These new structures can be obtained either by combining or by breaking the rules to generate transformations. This is shaded in a light colour in Figure 10.9.

The complete system functions as follows: The knowledge base contains knowledge which can be used to solve problems. Some of this can be transferred directly as inputs to the P process to help in solving the problem. They can be obtained from the knowledge base by the simple procedure of accessing it. However, these ready-to-use elements may not be ideas that can be used immediately to solve the current problem. They probably come from the solution of previous problems, where they proved to be useful. In Newell's (1982, 1990) jargon, they are 'chunks' obtained from previous problem-solving activity.

Thus, the elements that can be used for the P process should be obtained from the knowledge base. This raises the question of how to generate elements that do not exist in the individual knowledge base. There are two answers to this. First, it is possible to use the other knowledge bases. Therefore, if there is an efficient way of sharing knowledge, this considerably enriches the individual knowledge base, contributing both perceptional (memory) and abstract knowledge. The former can

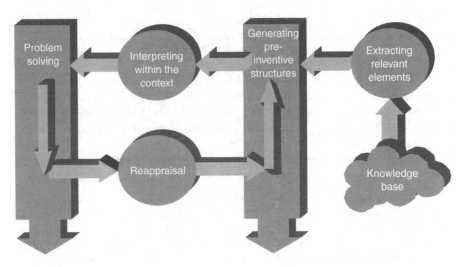

Figure 10.9   The Geneplore model

be used to induce, creating experiential knowledge that represents a new element that does not exist in the knowledge base.

Second, the agent's system is a TMS (Chapter 2). Consequently, he possesses inference mechanisms that are capable of obtaining new results if the baseline premises are modified. For example, an idea retrieved from the knowledge base may be modified by applying known transformations to produce a new idea that does not exist in the database.

This problem-solving mechanism is fed by the C process. *The C process initially obtains primitive ideas from the knowledge base that seem to be interesting. Afterwards, in an exploratory phase, it considers the possible variations and alternatives to the original idea.* Finally feeds the results to the P Process.

The authors of the Geneplore model use the term pre-inventive structures to refer to the structures obtained by the C process.

There is no room here to describe and discuss in detail the transformation categories that can be used to massage the primitive ideas and we refer the reader to the original work. We will simply say that the simplest is the rule that De Bono calls the lateral thinking (De Bono, 1977). It consists of systematically changing some of the properties of an idea from one context to another, to move 'laterally' (De Bono, 1992) (in our language, a combination mechanism).

The C process has an exploratory component, which is fairly unstructured because the transformations are difficult to specify systematically.

By giving meaning the results of the C process to, the individual can recompose the idea in his mind and process it using tools that are more akin to logic and intended to provide a full understanding of the situation. The association of meaning to ideas is usually done through their representation in a language and many people are capable of choosing languages from among a wide range of possibilities.

The C process eventually constructs a mental object to deliver to the P process. *The P process now uses the input received from the C process in its problem-solving task.* In the P process, the structures received are assessed and this assessment is transmitted back to the C process, enabling the latter to refine its elaboration mechanisms. Here too there is a feedback mechanism which accounts, to a certain extent, for the relationship between knowledge and creativity. As the active agent solves problems and learns, he helps to generate better transformations for the C process which, in turn, produces better inputs for solving the creative problem.

Two conclusions are important here:

1. By improving the problem-solving methodology, creativity is improved by improving the P process – the process for solving the creative problem.
2. The process that is most specific to creativity is the C process and its interaction with the P process. Therefore, the actions that seek to develop creativity independently from the actions associated with problem solving, should concentrate on *enhancing the C process in our agents*.

11
Taking Knowledge to Service Excellence

Introduction

In the previous chapter, we saw how knowledge is generated. As was suggested there, a firm whose internal cycle functioned perfectly would be something like a perfect university. Everyone would learn a load of totally useless things.

The problem is that agent involvement in problem solving is not enough to bring about improvement in the firm. The solution of any type of problem increases knowledge, but it may be irrelevant unless the problem is directly relevant to improving the firm's service.

Therefore, we must provide a *means of linking the internal cycle with the service so that the problem-solving activity can have an impact upon the firm's competitiveness.* We want to transfer knowledge generation to the service, to the customer's perception of goodness and consistency with what has been promised. We look for synergies among all of the organization's endeavours in order to increase long-term competitiveness.

In order to do this, the firm must focus its efforts in idea generation and problem solving focused towards excellence in service, as stated in the firm's mission. This is achieved when the priority in problem solving in all of the organization's members is synchronized with the priorities stated in the mission. We will call the mechanism that assures this *the relevance mechanism.* We will often simplify and just call it *relevance.* Understood in this sense, *relevance* is the property that ensures that any *agent in the firm is capable of applying the mission's basic criteria to assess a priori whether the solution of a problem increases the firm's competitiveness.* In more precise terms, one could say that relevance must ensure that everyone knows, shares and uses the mission. However this formulation would make it necessary to talk about the theory and mechanisms of motivation, which we prefer to leave to those specialists in human psychology. (See Example 11.1.)

Likewise, in our desire not to waste a single drop of the energy produced within the organization, it is necessary to implement mechanisms that ensure that every agent perceives *the effect that their own problem-solving activity* has on the firm's level of competitiveness. This mechanism will enable the firm's agents to observe and reflect on both the successes and the errors that have taken place as a result of the problem-solving process and, consequently, to validate them and learn from them. The mechanism that makes sure that his feedback takes place will be called *the importance mechanism* or simply *importance*.

This chapter presents the basic concepts that take us from knowledge generation to the production of tangible benefits for the firm, through relevance and importance.

General approach

How is the link to be made between the firm's internal cycle and its competitiveness? In principle, this should be straightforward. The firm's competitiveness is the outcome of a differential service. This service is attained through the firm's operations which, by definition, are the service's providers. Any improvement in operations will lead to an improvement in service and, eventually, an improvement in competitiveness.

Thus, competitiveness only improves when the problems solved lead to improvements in the operations' structure or performance. There is a causal chain that takes us from knowledge to competitiveness, which appears in the form of what we call the *external, or competitiveness, cycle*.

Figure 11.1 shows the external cycle and its connection with the internal cycle. We can see in this figure that the 'jump' between the internal cycle and the external cycle requires an *a priori* evaluation of the problem to be solved. This in turn requires relating competitiveness with the type of problems which are solved on a day-to-day basis.

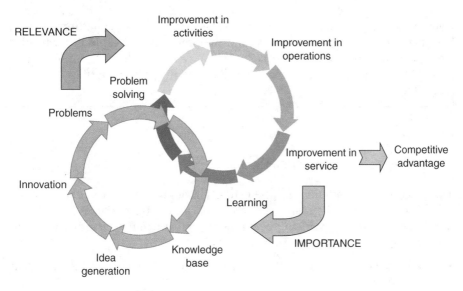

Figure 11.1   The external cycle

Example 11.1   An example of the lack of relevance mechanisms

One of the present authors worked for several years for a company that specialized in the manufacture of aeronautical products. This company had a machining section which manufactured titanium parts for fighter aircrafts. For unknown reasons, the designers of titanium parts never tired of specifying extremely low tolerances. The parts machined in the company had such tight specifications that the contraction and dilation of the machine tools caused the production of defects. The machines started the day at a certain temperature but, as the day progressed, the temperature in the building, and that of the machine itself, changed. The machine's bedplate expanded and the result was a higher number of defects. To prevent this, the company installed glass cubicles with air conditioning, similar to offices with glass enclosures, around the process's critical machines. Because of this, the machine could be maintained at a constant temperature without having to air condition the entire building which, like any industrial building worth its salt, had thousands of places where air could come freely in and out. One day, when the author was walking through the machining building with the company's managing director, he noticed that the cubicle door of one of machines was wide open, rendering the (costly) air conditioning completely totally ineffective. When this was mentioned to the foreman, he also expressed his surprise. Finally, the machine's operator said that he had opened it because he suffered from claustrophobia and could not work in such a small place without any openings. The worker was not aware that this was a problem and he thought that instead of bothering the foreman with work reassignments, it would be better to take immediate action to solve the problem. So he opened the door. This situation shows that the perception of the relevance of individual decisions is far from automatic. The company should have explained why the air conditioning was installed to the workers concerned and the problems that could occur if the temperature was changed. If he had been given this information, our man would have known that opening the door solved the problem in the worst way possible.

Conditions for the cycles' functioning

The function of a firm's internal and external cycles is to achieve sustained, long-term competitiveness. This has important implications. For example, according to our model, a firm that starts off being more competitive than another will continue to enjoy this advantage, provided that:

- Its knowledge base is composed of relevant knowledge and it is larger than that of the other firm.
- It knows how to keep both cycles working with equal effectiveness.

The working of the cycles is not automatic and, in the absence of any controls, it is very likely that they will stop and fail.

For the internal cycle to function adequately, it is not enough to act on its three variables. There are additional conditions that could block it.

1. *Problems as a learning opportunity*. In order for the cycle to function and for there to be problem-solving activity, the organization must find problems. This may seem obvious, but this is not always so. There are organizations that do not find problems, as their organizational style prevents this activity. We will give two examples of this:

   (a) *Organizations who look for people to blame (kill the messenger)*. When an organization has this culture, it immediately proceeds to point to someone who is to blame for its existence[1] whenever it encounters a problem. This imposes considerable limits on the discovery of problems. Anyone who notices a problem passes carefully beside it, trying not to raise any dust, so that it can be found by someone else who will shoulder the blame.

   (b) *Bureaucracies*. Bureaucracies do not solve problems – they simply carry out procedures. A bureaucracy is normally obsessed with the opposite situation, with preventing any problem from appearing that could overwhelm existing procedures and make it necessary to perform a genuine problem-solving activity. Some government departments are good examples of this type of organization.

2. *Obstacles to creativity*. In order for creativity to develop, the organization must encourage independent thinking by its agents. Any structure that concentrates decision-making capacity in one level of management and relegates lower levels to the mere implementation of decisions, usually has problems in promoting creativity. In many cases, it is simply a problem of trust on the part of the employees. Although the organization issues formal messages that it expects creativity from everyone, the informal message is usually understood as 'I give the ideas and you do the work'. Another way of stifling creativity is to praise the ideas but then not to apply the solutions proposed. Many organizations have suggestions boxes and offer prizes for the best suggestions. Some implement the suggestions immediately and keep its promises regarding prizes. Others simply process the results and there is never any evidence that the suggestions have been implemented. In the end, such organizations cease to receive suggestions. (See Example 11.2.)

3. *Innovation-related problems*. These are normally obstacles to the implementation of accepted ideas. They often arise from the non-acceptance of the solutions by the person responsible for implementing them. On other occasions, they arise

---

[1] In many organizations, the buck is passed from one person to another, or it is kept in a cupboard for it to be found by someone else. This is typical of an organization that 'kills the messenger', in which the problem's discoverer is typically landed with the blame. The reader should carefully check whether this is happening in the organizations he works with or knows. The problem is much more common than would seem; it seems to be part of human nature, including that of the authors.

because the organization is incapable of supporting individuals risk-taking by abandoning people to their own limitations.

Just as was the case with the internal cycle, spontaneous functioning is not guaranteed in the external cycle either. In practice, intervention is required to ensure that the functioning takes place and that it functions in the right direction.

The external cycle may break down for the following reasons:

(a) *Definition of the mission.* People may not have enough information about the relevance of their actions, either because of a lack of access to the firm's

Example 11.2   A suggestions system

Toyota's Kobe Plant

In 1984, a group of IESE alumni, including one of the authors, went to Japan to visit a number of companies. At that time, trips to Japan were a common occurrence, with the aim of getting a close-up view of the miracles that the new approaches were working on operations productivity. Some of the trips were almost pilgrimages to the sancta sanctorum of Just in Time, quality and involvement. During the visit that our group made to Toyota's plant, one of the firm's managers talked about the suggestions system. Always with the inevitable consecutive translation, at some time during the presentation he said that the number of improvement proposals (suggestions) received by the company amounted to about 40 per person per year. As about 7,000 people were working in the plant, a quick calculation gave a figure of 280,000 suggestions per year. A ripple of surprise ran along the group. There was some background murmuring, in which one sceptic said that 'they must do it to give a good image but probably none of the suggestions are actually implemented ...'. Unable to repress his curiosity, one of our entrepreneurs finally dared to ask. He raised his hand and asked, 'How many suggestions are implemented in the company?' The Japanese managers conferred for a few moments and then the spokesman answered, '80 per cent'. Everyone was amazed. 'How can you do that?' another participant exclaimed. The reply was conclusive. 'One out of every three employees in the plant works in operations engineering.' The company assigned more than 2,000 people to implementing about 200,000 suggestions a year, or 1,000 changes a day! Of course, some refused to believe it, but the questions that followed only confirmed what had already been said. The incredulity turned into admiration as soon as we entered the plant. It was obvious that the workers had a big say in how their jobs were structured. Not one unnecessary movement, intelligent use of compressed air, very simple and cheap but highly efficient conveying systems, clear signs that the people who experienced the problems had taken part in solving them ...

mission or a lack of definition of the mission in categories that can be used in their daily work.

(b) *Effect on operations*. There may be a lack of knowledge that enables actions to be related to its effects on operations. Chapters 4 and 5 contain the appropriate baggage for most situations. However, many people are not aware of the basic logic, unless the firm takes specific action in this respect.

(c) *Lack of feedback*. If there is no feedback, it is impossible to know the outcome – positive or negative – of actions. Therefore, there is a risk of repeating errors, with the resulting attrition of the agent.

Breakdowns in the functioning of the external cycle lead to a loss of competitiveness or a loss of organizational focus on competitiveness (which amounts to almost the same thing). The internal cycle's efficiency, the speed at which the cycle operates, determines the rate of knowledge accumulation – that is, the learning obtained in the company. The external cycle's speed determines the rate at which the improvements influence the firm's competitive position. Both efficiencies play a key role in the firm's ability to exploit its advantages before its competitors. A firm that starts at a low level of knowledge may become an industry leader if it transforms its knowledge into improvements of its operations' structure at a faster rate than its competitors. Other firms may have a better knowledge position but, because of inefficiencies in the external cycle, may be unable to convert its potential into a competitive advantage.

These aspects illustrate once again the role of management in the cycles' functioning. The cycles must evolve so that the net result is a movement towards the desired competitive improvement. If the cycles function properly, there will be improvements both in the short-term achievement of the firm's mission and in the construction of knowledge assets that will bring competitiveness in the medium and long term.

Relevance

The term *relevance* is taken from the classic context (Wilson and Sperberg, 1992). In this context, it is proposed that the information is relevant if it interacts in a specific manner with the hypotheses that the agent makes about the world – that is, with the world model that each agent possesses. For this to be possible, it is required that: 'other things being equal, the greater the contextual effect, the greater the relevance, and other things being equal, the smaller the processing effort the greater the relevance'.

The basic hypothesis for the study of relevance is the *rational selfishness* hypothesis,[2] which assumes that a human being will always take the action that he believes is best for him, assessing it in accordance with his own perception of the action and its present and future results, both for him and for others, within a timeframe determined freely by the individual himself.

---

[2] We have referred to this hypothesis several times in the course of the book, in different contexts but dealing with the same phenomenon in all cases.

So what should be done to ensure that the agent includes the appropriate criteria in his decision process to unify his action with the firm's mission and, consequently, to increase the customer's satisfaction?

From the innovation viewpoint, relevance must put into motion a satisfaction transmission mechanism. That is, the agent must include in his decision criteria the satisfaction that another agent – in our case, the end customer – obtains from the outcome of the agent's problem-solving process. Formulated in this manner, relevance is too grandiose for our modest purpose. To attenuate it, we will restrict our relevance (now rather less grand) to the situation's *rational* components.

When the individual has previously experienced the effect of his actions and has direct experiences that are identical to the action problem at hand, he can foresee the satisfaction that a certain action will give him and, therefore, take it into account in his decision process. However, people's actions that have an effect on the firm's competitiveness are rarely repetitive. Indeed, if they are going to produce learning, by definition, their effect cannot have been experienced beforehand. Therefore, one way in which the individual can take into account his actions' effect is *by rational reasoning*, applying (see Chapter 2) abstract knowledge to give predictive mechanisms to the agents.

The management of relevance must therefore *give individuals the rational ability to predict the outcome of their actions*, before they are executed. After that, whether or not he will take the action will depend upon motivation. If, for example, the individual does not predict how his individual action decreases everyone's benefit – including his own – the individual arguments could be reduced to a poor issue of personal credibility: 'because I think that you must do this'. At such a level, mutual understanding between individual and firm is unlikely to occur. To note, even once he has understood the situation's rationality, the agent can still choose to not do what the logical process recommends. But this is a problem of human behaviour and motivation, which is beyond the scope of this book.

*Designing the relevance system

The only way in which the firm can instil in individual decisions a rational component that is consistent with (contributing to the achievement of) the overall mission is to create an environment in which the actions that are necessary for achieving collective satisfaction are also the most rational actions (with bounded rationality) for the individual. For this to be possible, the individual must:

- *Have the possibility* of addressing problems from the viewpoint of the firm's overall competitiveness, introducing the appropriate premises in his TMS.
- Exploit the *opportunities that arise for his own learning*, in particular learning on his impact on the other agents, with a possible contribution to the general knowledge base.

One simple way of working towards the first point is to assign explicit goals to each agent. These goals are inferred by adapting the firm's mission to the agents' environment. If the firm uses management by objectives, it may only have to take the objectives down to the operating levels. However, to go beyond this initial action, more sophisticated approaches are needed.

To probe deeper into the phenomenon it is useful to consider a concrete situation. As part of a worker's job in a sheetmetal shop, he must understand issues such as the shop's context, how it operates, what is expected from his work, what tools he can use and what their effect is. The knowledge that the worker brings with him – his previous experience, training, and so on – are sufficient to understand part of the structure he encounters in the workshop. Part of his knowledge has a logical structure; another part is pure experience or skill.

In order that the worker can foresee by rational reasoning what the consequences of his acts will be, he must have a deeper understanding of the structure of the workshop in which he works. That is, he must establish a *model* of the environment, a model of how his world functions. Any experienced welder has an idea of the temperature of his welding torch's flame by looking at its colour, and he can take this knowledge with him to any workshop. However, in a certain workshop, there are other important issues that must be defined: what the materials used there are like, what features the product to which they belong has, what the customer is like and what he wants, what his fellow workers are like and how they behave, what things are valued in the company, and so on.

In his action within the workshop, the agent will accumulate observations that he will eventually interpret. Everyone accumulates observations, but not everyone is an intelligent observer. Perception may often make false judgements because of emotional, perceptive or other states. Therefore, our agent must have *observational* elements that enable him to compare and interact with the workshop's functioning, instruments for measuring (objectifying and rationalizing) reality. For example, he may find that a pyrometer is useful for measuring whether the welding torch's flame is at the right temperature or not. Of course, here we are referring only to observation of the simpler phenomena, interactions with stable objects, not with agents who learn or with people.

In the latter case, observation is a much more delicate process, because the observing agent's very presence influences the phenomenon's result and, therefore, the observation depends upon the observer's internal state. Instruments and knowledge are needed both to perform the observation correctly and to interpret the results.

The agent must act on his world, he must be able to consider different types of actions that interact with him. What actions are possible, desirable or recommendable, again depends upon his relationship with the rest of the environment. In order to be able to take actions, the agent must understand what is the *scope of actions* he can choose from, what actions are expected from him. Can he change the way he welds? Between what limits is he authorized by the product's specifications to make such changes? What about the sheet's thickness?

Thus, we have identified three basic elements for achieving (a better) harmony between the individual and the environment and, by this means, ensure the relevance of his actions. First, the individual must *form an idea of the environment's functioning* which will enable him to predict and/or anticipate his behaviour if a certain event occurs. Second, the individual must have *measuring and diagnostic tools* that help him in his interaction with the world. Finally, since the agent does not act in isolation the agent's actions must be coordinated through an understanding of the *logic of his actions*, which includes both feasibility conditions, criteria and relationships with other agents' actions.

As a result of what we have said so far, we can say that the following conditions are necessary for relevance:

- *Anticipate*. The agent must possess a model (a theory of expectations) that is consistent with the environment.
- *Detect*. He must have tools for observing and diagnosing reality.
- *Act*. He must share and understand an action logic.

In order for the system to operate, the firm must provide all of its participants with mechanisms that help them to achieve this purpose. Consequently, systematic and concrete actions must be developed to *anticipate, detect and act (ADA)*. These three aspects make up the core on which the relevance system rests. A general outline of their relationship is shown in Figure 11.2. As can be seen, there is a feedback relationship which links the three ADA functions. The expectations theory determines the manner in which the agent understands the world, the test enables him to validate his perceptions with facts and the action logic determines the action context.

Of course, these three ADA functions are related to the problem-solving mechanism introduced in Chapter 1. The expectations theory assumes control of the logical causality context, in which the individual's deductive processes can operate in order to make the best possible use of existing knowledge in determining transformations and criteria. The action logic identifies the way in which the different transformations can be handled, including, significantly, the action heuristics, the rules that determine the use of certain operators.

In order to obtain a *model of the world*, we must appeal to rational knowledge and, in particular, to scientific knowledge. However, other types of knowledge, whose structure is not as logical as scientific knowledge, are possible and important. In the latter case (see Example 11.3), the role of the facilitator, of the manager, is to make the necessary tools available to the individual to enable him to realise the existing model's full potential, ensuring at least the results' consistency with the intra- and interpersonal hypotheses.

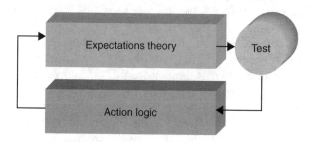

Figure 11.2   Diagram of the relevance system

Example 11.3   A non-scientific model

Folk Psychology

Most people have partial models of the world which contain important relationships for predicting conducts. Although the power of these models is less than that of their scientific counterparts, they offer the advantages of availability and generality. In Western culture, most people have an intuitive, or natural, framework that has no solid scientific basis but which we often call upon to explain other people's behaviour. This conceptual model, which some call *folk psychology*, rests upon a series of categories and relationships that anticipate the outcome of our interactions with other individuals. A simple example is given by a reasoning such as the following:

'John is a decent chap. He very rarely takes offence at anything. However, he has really put his foot in it in his management of the warehouse and he'll have to be told this. The thing is, John doesn't like being corrected in those things which he thinks he is an expert in. And one of them is management of the warehouse. So, if we tell him directly, he'll get upset and feel less motivated about his job. Let's do it indirectly. Let him see for himself where he has gone wrong.'

As the reader will readily see, many of the categories used here cannot be considered scientific knowledge. What is a 'decent chap'? What are its properties? What is meant by 'put his foot in it'? Why will he get upset? And so on. This ambiguity, irrationality or bounded rationality is what triggers heated debate on how to act in personal issues. However, the model is useful, widely used and relatively consistent. The problem is not so much its elimination as its rational basis and logical use. This can be enhanced by providing suitable tools for supporting it.

In order to achieve this goal – that is, to add logical and consistency aspects to a model – firms have used (probably unconsciously) a wide variety of tools. Most of them have been found on a shelf within the quality movement. For instance, we can use tools to facilitate coherence and logic, such as priority matrixes and tree charts (Brassard, 1990). None of them adds much of significance to the basic model. They are simply aids for ensuring that the results obtained match the hypotheses.

As regards the *test* function, we must have suitable observation tools that enable us to distinguish facts from opinions. This principle of measurement is crucial in any scientific knowledge and has also been adopted by the quality movement. 'Measure everything that can be measured and, if that isn't possible, make it measurable', as Galileo said. Of course, there is a long-standing tradition in the development and use of measuring tools. But there is also knowledge that deals with the use of measurement to induce hidden properties, mainly statistics. Statistical tools are very important for diagnosing and testing the results of agents actions.

Example 11.4   Attitudes towards measurement

Two Attitudes Towards Measurement

Do NOT trust words because words are blown away by the wind. Do NOT trust books because they are written words. Do NOT trust women because they are word-speaking machines... Facts, only facts! (Santiago Rusinyol, *L'Auca del Senyor Esteve*.)

Grownups love figures. When you talk about a new friend with them, they never ask you what really matters ... They always ask: How old is he? How many brothers and sisters does he have? How much does he weigh? How much does his father earn? Only when they have found out all this do they think that they know him ... But, in all sureness, we who understand life, we don't care a bit about numbers! (Antoine de Saint-Exupéry, *Le Petit Prince*.)

Where most difficulties are encountered in finding tools is in *action logic*. Perhaps the best approach is to turn back to the ideas on the conflict-resolution system discussed in Chapter 6. Typically, the logic of action is expressed by means of a system of rules or premises which must be added to each decision maker's TMS, integrating them in his own reasoning.

It is significant that the three mechanisms specified can be matched with the three types of functional knowledge. Expectations theory requires the existence of domain knowledge, especially ontologies, knowledge on objects that populate the agent's immediate world and the relationships between them. The observation function requires task knowledge, that is, knowledge about how to proceed and how to interpret the results. Action logic requires that the agent have inference knowledge. This correspondence provides hints on the type of tools that be added to the relevance system.

Figure 11.3 shows some of the classic quality tools associated with the various components of the relevance system. We will not go into detailed descriptions of these techniques, which the reader can find in any treatise on quality.[3]

Importance

In previous sections, we have defined importance as the mechanism which shows the decision maker the effect that his problem solution has had on the firm's competitive advantage so that he can complete his learning process. This requires us to address a fundamental issue: how can the information obtained from observations be turned into learning? In a way, this is the reverse process of creativity. Now, our task is not to obtain a new result from old knowledge, but new knowledge from observed results.

---

[3] See Brassard, 1990. The knowledge profile is explained in the addendum to this chapter.

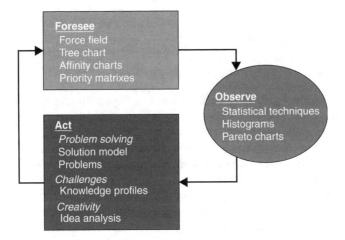

Figure 11.3 Tools for relevance

Importance is very much related to induction and the creation of experiential knowledge (Chapter 2). Among the theories of induction, we borrow from Holland (Holland *et al.*, 1989) and other authors the following phases for importance:

- *Forecasting the result or establishing uncertain expectations based upon existing knowledge.* Using his TMS and applying the rules obtained in it, the decision maker is able to obtain a forecast of the result. This forecast is associated with an assessment of the potential surprise caused by the possible results.
- *Obtaining new information.* This must be done in a way that makes it easy to compare the observations with the forecast. A quantitative forecast, for example, requires measuring the observations. In this phase, the individual must know how to observe, since an incomplete observation reduces subsequent learning capacity.
- *Comparing between what is observed and what is expected.* This process requires the simultaneous presence of both components, what is observed and what is expected. This requires the existence of recall mechanisms on the part of the agent that remind him of the forecast while he is carrying out the observation. This presence has many forms, due to the possibility of partially contradictory avenues of explanation. In order to solve the paradox, it is necessary to identify the rules and mechanisms that lead to the prediction and allocate them a responsibility in the result. Here, a cause and effect analysis may be the appropriate tool, although it is not always easy to find causes.
- *Restructuring rules or the framework.* Of course, the rules that have produced results that are consistent with the observation will come out strengthened from this process, and those that have failed to do so must be penalized. By observing the role played by each rule, the agent reviews the weight and, therefore, the priority in the use of a rule. This will influence how the rules will be used in subsequent deductions by the agent.

- *Creating new rules or induction.* The results produce new rules, perhaps by a process of collapsing rules with similar results and *reinterpreting* them in a more general context, giving rise to new frameworks which have been 'induced' from the observation process. This rule generation is guided by the relationship between forecasts and results.

Importance must transmit not only the actions' operational results but also their complete result, including the emotional, learning and interpersonal aspects.

In service operations, it is often simple to transmit importance to the people providing the service. The agent can observe at first hand, if he knows how to and wants to, all of the results obtained with his action. If an air hostess spills a glass of lemonade over a customer, the customer reacts immediately to the action. In industrial companies, the transmission of importance may be much more complicated because the factory may be 'buffered' and the information has to overcome barriers in its path towards the agent.

For importance to work effectively, it must contribute to learning. Completion of the learning process requires a reaction of the agent to the results reaching him. We can distinguish the following types of reaction to the stimulus represented by the results.

- *Resolution of paradoxes.* The resolution of an apparent contradiction between what is observed and what is forecast. It requires the presence of abstract knowledge and of research procedures that enable exploration of the apparent contradiction and its eventual resolution. The TMS mechanism offers an explanation of what is involved here. For this type of reaction, it is often useful to be able to access real or virtual replications of the phenomenon observed.
- *Lack of alternatives.* In this reaction, the agent observes that there have been no actions that have solved the problem. This must lead the agent to consider new alternatives, obtaining further understanding of the model that relates causes with results. In this type of learning, it is important to have access to previous experiences and/or the advice of experienced agents.
- *Induction.* The detection of several similar situations must lead to the appearance of mental objects that did not exist previously. Induction requires the simultaneous presence of the objects that must take part in the process. Therefore, the individual must be able to access similar situations which he can use to carry out the synthesis.
- *Generalization.* Extraction of elements that are applied to classes of objects of which the observed phenomenon is a specific case. For this process, it is important to have object hierarchies on which the generalizations can be performed.

*Designing the importance system

An agent's learning must lead to learning for all of the organization's agents – that is, to collective learning. Importance is not a mechanism for the individual, but rather its purpose is to look for synergy among all the learning performed each day. To do this, the firm must establish systems that are able to smoothly channel

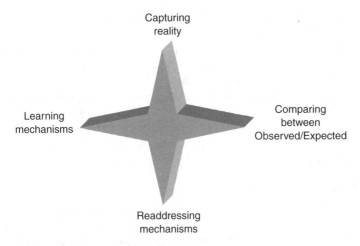

Figure 11.4   The four functions of the importance system

individual experience and learning to convert it into collective experience and learning.

The design of the importance system, is composed of the following functions:

1. *Capturing* reality.
2. *Readdressing* to the origin, sending it to the decision makers concerned.
3. *Diagnosing* or comparing between what is observed and what is expected.
4. *Learning* obtainment mechanisms.

Figure 11.4 shows the four functions of the design of the importance system.

1. Capturing reality

The first step is to capture information on the reality that is taking place. The attempt to capture data on all of the aspects of reality that may interest a firm's agents is an arduous and futile task. Indeed, people capture reality in the form of sensations that are more or less difficult to communicate and which, when formalized, take on the appearance of written or verbal communiqués or reports.[4] In short, sentences expressed in a certain language.

The recent emphasis on content management systems arises from the abundance of relevant information lacking the necessary features to enable easy access. A written report can only be accessed as such and it is often difficult to find, among the mountains of written communications, those documents that are significant for a particular situation.

---

[4] Working with this type of information presents considerable difficulties. However, it is usually very rich in nuances and, when suitably analysed, provides very important information about the system. However, its automated processing will require the development of reliable techniques for analysing content and extracting meaning. Judging from the lack of success of the projects undertaken, it does not seem that such techniques will be available in the short term.

It is important to organize the flow of importance. For instance, one of the ways of is by the moments of truth. An interaction at a moment of truth takes place between two agents: the customer and the agent responsible for providing part of the service. Each interaction has two components: the customer's perception and the agent's perception. A diagnosis will require both versions of the moment of truth, as each one provides the particular view of one of the two participants in the interaction. In this case to diagnose the customer's and the agent's perception, we can use tools such as questionnaires, after-service assessments, customer panels, statistical tests. The literature provides a large number of procedures for carrying out this task.

2. Readdressing to the origin

Once the information has been obtained, it must be readdressed to the originating agent. In many companies, complaints are only treated as problem events and once the problem in solved, the incident is forgotten. This hampers learning. Complaints must be captured and readdressed within the firm by mechanisms that refer them to the person who can implement corrective actions on their root causes.

Example 11.5   A case of the implementation of importance

A Case of Importance

A pharmaceutical laboratory was organized by operating units corresponding to groups of diseases for which the company had medicines. Each unit had certain common services, represented by a small group of technical staff (physicians, pharmacists, biologists, ...) who dealt with the common issues and distributed the necessary knowledge to the front-line staff. The front-line staff visited the customers and observed their needs. These employees were responsible for all sales-related operations with customers. They held a large quantity of first-hand experience on the customer that was not readily systematized. Typically, each front-line employee reported on the outcome of his calls to his unit manager, in accordance with his own perception of the importance of the situation and the observations. This meant that the level of standardization of the information was very low. Each representative reported his visits in accordance with his own theory of the situation, his own criteria and other components of his vision of reality. The most commonly used reporting system was by e-mail. When a member of the technical staff wished to know the outcome of a given action program, he had to retrieve all the e-mails on the subject and get a general idea by reading them. The company attacked the problem of rationalizing importance on two fronts. First, a clear typology was established for the moments of truth. The representatives had to give priority to reporting the outcome of the different moments of truth. Second, an e-mail filing system was created in which these were classified in accordance with a series of criteria. In fact, the representatives themselves underlined the key sentences in

---

their e-mails in different colours, which were associated with different subjects by a colour code. The result was used to develop a software system that obtained the relevant documentation indexed by subject and moment of truth.

According to the company, the system enabled the teams to monitor the sales actions performed to a degree that would not have been attainable using other more traditional methods, including the commercial CRM systems available at that time.

Some typical forms of readdressing that can be considered are:

- *Reporting by exception*. Each event has an associated seriousness indicator and the events are sent to a unit when they exceed a critical value. This system is specially suitable when the relationships between operating units are hierarchical.
- *Reporting by request*. Each unit provides information only when another unit asks for it. This technique must be supplemented with some other mechanism that ensures that all the relevant information is sent.
- *Reporting by origin*. Each origin receives all the information on certain events, selected by their origin.
- *Summary reporting by profiles*. Here, the information obtained is aggregated in accordance with certain want profiles specified by each unit.
- *Statistical synthesis*. Numerical summary indicators are allocated to all of the information and regularly distributed.

3. Diagnosing reality

The agent must understand and internalize the phenomenon observed. The goal is to modify the model in order to understand why what has been observed has happened and what has been the mechanism linking the decision with the result. One procedure is for the person responsible for the interaction to perform a cause and effect analysis on the interaction, perhaps using an Ishikawa chart or other similar technique.

4. Learning mechanisms

In this final phase, the agent must use his knowledge of the interaction's causal model to propose actions that prevent the result from recurring (if it is negative) or ensure that it is obtained (if it is positive). In order to obtain learning, we can use:

- *Model banks*: Theories of the world related to the target environment to be tested. They can be formalized as libraries, documentation services, and so on.
- *Experience banks*: Case-based reasoning (CBR). This technique will be discussed in greater detail in Chapter 13, but it consists of the use of case or experience databases which can be accessed by analogy with the situation it is wished to analyse. This enables analogous situations to be retrieved which show possible action alternatives and offer explanations for the results observed.

- *Experimentation elements*: Simulation. When it is necessary to perform tests, it is possible to use the interaction with simulated worlds. These techniques, limited at one time to the analysis of abstract models, have achieved a considerable degree of sophistication, providing the possibility of interacting with virtual worlds offering a high degree of realism and detail.
- *Feedback providers*: Groups or people who interact with the agents to give them the opportunity to observe the effects of their behaviour. In the 1970s, these ideas were popularized by behaviour observation techniques (e.g. the T-groups). However, in many cases, they proved to be too aggressive and the consequences of their use were ill-defined. As a result, new, less aggressive formats were developed such as the advisory and consulting boards, coaching groups, and so on.
- *Benchmarking*: Information about the behaviour of other competing agents.

*The use of e-mail as a source of importance

Some companies have observed that the firm's main source of feedback is e-mail. Indeed, the mail documents many of the interactions between different agents of the firm – often with supplementary documentation defining problems and providing results.

The implementation of importance can be simplified and enhanced if a read-dressing and indexing system is superimposed on the mail system, structured in accordance with people's roles. The readdressing system is implemented in some systems by working or discussion groups. Other systems use special programmes which are superimposed on the e-mail system to produce full-blown discussion and exchange forums.[5] A good feedback system may be obtained by implementing any of these systems and adequately designing the forums and groups.

An e-mail can be traced from its originator to the resulting effect and the material related to the result can be returned to the agent that sent the message. As the problem-solving process normally concludes with internal action orders that are the subject of written communication, this system can provide effective feedback to the participants on most occasions.

A simple way of classifying e-mail and associating it with specific subjects is to use the body of the message itself to highlight words that play a key role in it. This technique – word highlighting – is very powerful and some applications, such as PCPack (a knowledge engineering system), use it to obtain knowledge structures from raw text. Other applications associate a path with each e-mail, together with the names of the agents who are interested in the subject and the reason for this interest. These indexes are then used to construct a return route for the information that provides the desired feedback.

In short, a good e-mail system, or a few simple applications on top of the existing e-mail system, can provide a relatively easy and incremental implementation of the importance mechanism. (See Example 11.5.)

---

[5] See, for example, the Groove application (http:www.groove.net), which has the added advantage of being low-cost.

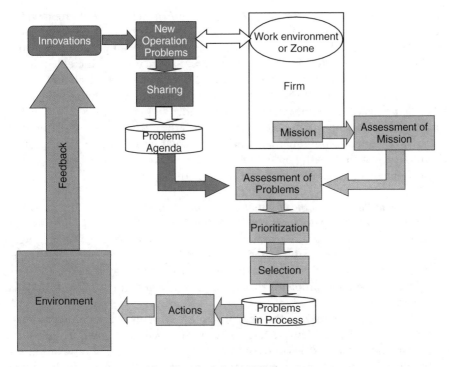

Figure 11.5 Competitive problems methodology (CPM)

The competitive problems methodology (CPM)

In this section, we present a cycle-based improvement system implementation plan. This is a development from the methodology explained in Chapter 9, which meets the conditions for being considered 'the permanent improvement system' defined at the beginning of Chapter 10. The crucial difference with respect to the methodology of Chapter 9 is a change of perspective. We now consider *problems* – and not *actions* – as the core element. This methodology, which we will call the 'competitive problems methodology (CPM)', is an implementation of a major part of both cycles and uses some tools that have been used in the implementation of quality processes.[6] This methodology is intended for individual work, complemented with group participation, and, in our experience, is relatively easy to integrate in daily work. The CPM is the skeleton of the knowledge-based permanent improvement system and, therefore, one of the central issues of this book.

The CPM is a zonal approach which takes an agent's work environment as the basic span of activity. The agent should keep two basic agendas. In one of them, he keeps a list of problems detected, problems that have yet to be analysed and solved. In this list, the problems are ordered on the basis of their relevance. In the other

---

[6] Thus, the reader will recognize obvious analogies with the QFD (Quality Function Deployment) technique.

list, he keeps his action plan, that is, the list of actions that are pending performance, in process, and completed and pending feedback. These actions have been carried out to solve certain problems chosen from among those included in the first list. As the system evolves, the two agendas are updated incrementally.

The process has the steps shown in Figure 11.5. There are three chains, shaded dark, light and medium, respectively. The first is the analysis chain, which contains elements from the internal cycle. The reader will recognize in it a structure for a problem-solving methodology and this is effectively its purpose. The other two chains contain components from the external cycle. The lightest-coloured chain is the relevance path and the medium-shaded chain is the importance path.

The following paragraphs describe the different components:

1. *Continuous diagnosis of the operation's problems.* A model (expectations theory) is kept continually up to date about the environment and the processes surrounding the agent, that is, his 'area of influence' or 'Zone.' A complete review of the entire area can be based on the WWWWH questioning technique described in Chapter 5. However, this 'major overhaul' is rarely necessary. If the agent has a series of problems that have been detected, the list can be updated *incrementally.*

   This requires identifying the new things that happen in the immediate environment and the problems that have been generated as a consequence of their introduction. The reader will recognize here the monitoring of innovation and the diagnosis of the problems that this generates in the agent. Each time an innovation[7] takes place, the problems must be recorded, associating them with the innovation and taking note of their innovator and innomanager. The ultimate goal is to understand the operating environment and to detect the unpleasant situations that are found in it. The problems exist as such because that is how the agent sees them; therefore, this list of problems is basically a subjective list, a vision of the world seen from the agent's perspective. When this analysis is completed, the new problems diagnosed in the agent's environment are added to the list of problems pending solution.

2. *Sharing.* This phase consists of a simple but continuous review of the information accumulated in day-to-day operations to construct a general model that can be applied to the interaction between the agent's zone and the firm's other zones. In practice, the aim is to bring together the knowledge held by the related agents to progressively construct 'the best' joint theory, given existing time and space limitations. Conceptually, the agent is already immersed in a problem-solving process, which begins as soon as he has the updated problems list. As a first part of the learning process, the agent compares his individual position with that of the other agents. Since each agent maintains a local problem list, probably he does not take into account the common causes that may be influencing problem generation. The agent must interact with other agents in related zones to broaden his horizons. This may be done either in a task force or

---

[7] Or novelty.

by another technology-enabled means. A simple way of systematizing scattered observations way is to construct a hierarchically organized master problems agenda from the individual problems agendas. Considering that the goal of this sharing is to create a synthesis model, it often becomes necessary to aggregate using similarity criteria. To do this, we can use the KJ technique.

3. *Problems agenda.* This phase consists of updating the problems pending solution, now reformulated after the agents' interaction. A typical, although not very systematic way used by many people is to write all the issues pending solution on post-its and stick them in some visible place. The problem is that the process's lack of confidentiality means that agents do not list some of the problems that worry them and which are often the most important ones. Relational, insecurity or other problems are never written down on the post-its arrayed around many computer screens. Computer technology may be a good medium but, and the most significant tool is the virtual post-it that can be easily managed (and hidden).

4. *Assessing the firm's or business unit's mission.* This is where the relevance path begins. The firm's mission must be decomposed and specialized. To perform this task, we recommend using the ideas put forward in Chapter 4 about the mission and its dimensions. When creating the goals systems used for employee compensation, many firms perform a mission cascading process, although these systems' format is not necessarily the most appropriate for relevance. Many systems contain generic goals, beyond the individual's control and associated with things such as 'corporate earnings' and other similar parameters. This type of goal is superfluous – and can even be harmful – for relevance because it can lead the agent to try to solve problems that he believes are 'strategic' for the firm, neglecting the operating improvement problems that surround him and which only he can attack. It is therefore essential that the agent's goals are focused on his task's results for the customer. If the agent does not see the external customer, the technique of creating internal customers – people who act as such with respect to the agent's work – can be used.

5. *Assessing the problems with respect to the mission.* The methodology now requires that each agent prioritize the problems included in his problems list in accordance with the mission specified in step 4. One simple way of performing this assessment is to carry out an analysis of the problem's impact on the criteria. There are two possibilities for this:

   • Determine the effect that solving the problem would have directly on each of the mission's assessment dimensions. In this case, the result is assessed positively if the solution adds positive value to the dimension, that is, increases its value, and negatively if it decreases its value. The problems are then weighted using the weights assigned to them (Muñoz-Seca and Riverola, 1997).

   • A better way of addressing the evaluation problem is to do it in two steps, following the logic of the external cycle. The first step establishes the relationship between the problem's solution and the operations' functioning. This is done by determining what activities in the BAS are going to be affected and what happens to the values of the six variables studied in Chapters 5 and 6. The second step uses the relationship between the variables and the firm's goals to complete the assessment. A detailed description of the procedure is beyond the scope of this book. However, this system has advantages that should be taken into account. First, it is possible to prepare the second step beforehand, so that the agent only has to concentrate on the first step. The BAS–goals relationship can be filed as a spreadsheet, for example, in which it is only necessary to fill in the parameters' values. This enables a more complete and sophisticated expectations theory to be constructed than with other procedures. Also, with this procedure, it is easier to include criteria that determine the action's logic for the agent.

6. *Choosing a problem to attack and solving it.* We will now go back to the medium-shaded sequence in Figure 11.5. We already have a problems list, with the problems sorted by their impact. The first decision is to choose a problem to work on. This problem is added to the in-process problems list, indicating that it is in the initial phase. Now we must attack it. We start by asking ourselves whether the problem can be destroyed. One way of answering is to carry out a causal analysis of the problem (which may perhaps be already available if the results of the previous task have been filed). For each problem, a series of root causes on which to act is identified. This step concludes with the creation of a list of specific actions to destroy the problem, to eliminate its root causes, if this is possible. If it is not possible to destroy the problem, the agent must proceed to solve it (Chapter 1). In this process, useful knowledge for solving the problem must be identified, together with their availability within the firm. This can be done by using the firm's general knowledge database, always assuming that this is updated to reflect the agent's learning. Finally, it is necessary to explain how the residual exploratory phase should be performed if the knowledge is not sufficient to solve the problem completely. All of these activities must be supported, either within the information system or by specific management action from the firm's organization structure.

7. *Actions.* Each agent has a personal action plan – a calendar of actions currently in process, with specific milestones and commitments. For each new problem, the agent decides the specific actions to be performed and adds them to his personal action plan. At the same time, a note is made that actions have been begun to solve the problem and the problem enters the 'pending feedback' status. The agent carries out the actions indicated, either within his own sphere of action or within other agents' spheres, in accordance with the action logic valid for the zone.

8. *Feedback from the environment.* This is the sequence with medium shading, the importance. Here, the environment can react to the agent's actions. The reaction must be readdressed so that it returns to the originating agent, identifying the reaction in some manner with the action that caused it. The goal is to enable the agent to associate results with actions and, through the observation mechanism, induce results. This requires implementation of the importance mechanism. The information system may help in this, provided that the effects are singularized within the general process.

Addendum: the knowledge profiles*

The idea behind profiles is very simple. In order to prevent frustration when faced with an excessively challenging task, it is necessary to diagnose the knowledge gaps that may cause this frustration.[8] As was seen in the previous chapter, when there is a high degree of frustration, the agent becomes blocked and no learning takes place. It is therefore necessary to determine each agent's gaps by determining his level of knowledge in the areas that are relevant for the problem. To measure the level, we will use the five levels of knowledge listed in Chapter 8. As the reader will remember, these levels are: know about (KA), know how (KH), know why (KW), know how to improve (KI), and know how to learn (KL).

The profiles' technique is as follows: The first step is to assess the profile of knowledge *already held* by the agent. To this end we suggest using a description of the processes and knowledge that make up the job. This analysis enables existing knowledge to be assessed using the five levels. If the firm has already performed a knowledge diagnosis, as proposed in Chapter 8, it will also have each agent's knowledge profile.

The next step is to diagnose the knowledge *required* to solve the situations that the agent must face. The five levels are used for this too.

Finally, a knowledge acquisition path is drawn between what the agent has and what he should have. These steps are summarized in Figure 11.6.

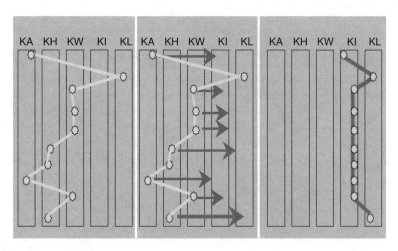

Figure 11.6   Current profile, path of the target profile, final profile

---

[8] We remind the reader what was said previously about this subject in the section on Innovation in the previous chapter.

In term of competences, sometimes an even better approach, we can:

1. *Describe each agent's job.* Using the analysis of the firm's processes and knowledge, we must describe each agent's job, specifying the tasks that he performs or can perform. Many companies keep staff files with the relevant information for this analysis.

2. *Identify the competences on the agent's profile.* In this phase, we must list the competences that will make up the agent's profile. This list of competences will be used to compare present and desired profiles. Each competence must be decomposed into knowledge items which are assigned to a particular level. It is a good idea to involve the agent's immediate superior, who has the ineluctable responsibility of knowing him thoroughly.

3. *Define the profile required for competitiveness.* This profile must be generated from the knowledge requirements that the agent must acquire to perform his new tasks, or for the natural evolution of these tasks. Figure 11.6 shows the current knowledge profile with a light-coloured line and the agent's required profile with a dark-coloured line.

4. *Analyse the competences that must change.* In this step, the effort is focused on diagnosing the competences that need to change. The arrows on the right of Figure 11.6 show these desirable changes.

5. *Actions.* The final step is to list specific actions that can change the profile, assuming that the one ultimately responsible for the change is the agent himself. The main tool used for change is training, which will be the subject of the next chapter.

12
Training, Information and Participation

Introduction

Having completed our analysis of the components of the cycles, in this chapter we propose to explore the horizontal measures required to implement PDM and the permanent improvement system. It is possible to identify a series of levels or strata in the implementation, which we represent graphically in pyramid form. We have chosen to call this pyramid, whose three strata indicate the different layers into which any implementation of a PDM system can be decomposed, the knowledge management implementation actions (KIA[1]) pyramid (Figure 12.1).

The pyramid's three levels are:

- A base level which concentrates on the generation of *learning*. This is focused on the ability to solve problems, generate ideas and implement them.
- A second level which concentrates on the *competitive use* of that learning. This focuses on the relevance and importance mechanisms.
- A top level which designs *organizational* policies and tools to facilitate the previous levels. The organization is configured by comprehensive or higher-order decisions which define an environment which affects all of the other variables. This environment consists basically of information, training and participation (ITP) actions.

The specific actions taken by management at the bottom level of the pyramid are indirect; improving abilities is a strictly personal matter. The firm can execute actions that change the environment with relative ease, but it is not easy to directly influence the way in which each individual responds to these changes to improve his personal abilities. It must be the people themselves within the firm who take the specific actions aimed at developing their abilities.

This is typical. As we have already said, one of the basic difficulties encountered in the implementation of improvement is precisely the indirect role played by management. In other aspects, the firm's management draws up action plans to

---

[1] Admittedly a rather lame acronym. But it has a justification. In this field dominated by three-letter acronyms, an acronym with more than three letters seems to be beyond the reach of most professionals in the discipline. For their sake, we have reduced it to three letters.

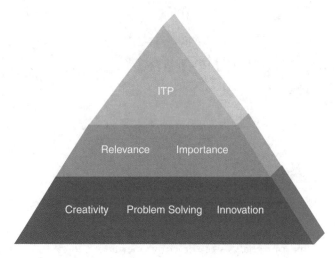

Figure 12.1   The KIA pyramid

achieve goals. Here, the management prepares actions so that others, in turn, may prepare actions that achieve the desired goals. In addition, it is a task that must be undertaken by all of the line managers, not just the senior management. Responsibility for success is shared by all of the organization and, much more directly than in other areas, depends upon both the acceptance of a number of general principles and the unity of action by all of the participants. It is something that requires a change of management mentality.

Management creates the necessary conditions for each person in the firm to develop his initiative and carry out detailed actions that enable him to improve his abilities. These necessary conditions are created at the higher levels of the pyramid. At progressively higher levels in the pyramid, the initiative for action depends upon an increasingly smaller number of managers. For example, training actions can, and should, be undertaken by the senior management.[2] In the case of training, decentralizing decisions does not generate increments in the overall competitiveness as much as it does in other aspects. The higher levels of the KIA pyramid therefore pertain to senior management, which concentrates its actions on importance, relevance and the ITP level.

As a general rule, in order to obtain results at the lower level of the pyramid, it is critical to simultaneously address its higher levels. ITP, relevance and importance form the substrate on which creativity, problem-solving and challenge-assigning actions are developed.

---

[2] Many companies entrust training management to specialized departments. We think that these departments should disappear or be radically changed, turning them into internal consultants. Education is one of the great levers of action that management has and to delegate it to a specialized department is to relinquish a duty and privilege that cannot, nor should not, be shirked by managers.

In this chapter and the next, we will focus on the tip of the pyramid – on the ITP actions. We will see how these three terms, Information, Training and Participation, take on a new meaning. Training concentrates on providing the core competences that each individual needs to realize his individual competitiveness and participate in that of the firm. Participation is a key element for the use of knowledge. Finally, information takes on a new dimension when it is viewed as a knowledge exploitation system in operations (presented in the following chapter).

*Training which is not 'training': the new role

In the context of knowledge management, at a first level, training must ensure the acquisition of skills in problem-solving, innovation and creativity. On the other hand, training is a tool for generating relevance and educating agents in its management. Finally, through virtual situations, training must train the organization to focus on importance.

However, the type of training that can achieve these results is not the traditional type, focused on more or less active 'courses'. The type of training we are talking about is based on the performance of formative actions. A *formative action* consists of a series of previously defined – and sometimes artificial – action situations, designed so that the individual, once he is immersed in them, gradually, naturally and spontaneously achieves the desired learning goal.

This change of approach to training presupposes the use of new teaching techniques and models. The rules of the game change and, with them, the way people learn. (See Example 12.1.)

The power of *formative actions* has been validated experimentally in research projects conducted both by us and by other groups. Throughout Europe, companies are clearly moving away from the traditional training models towards new ways of generating the skills that their workers need to gain maximum benefit from knowledge. (See Example 12.2.)

The approach is nothing more than a return to the Socratic approach to learning. It is a master–disciple learning process in which the master teaches the disciple how to solve problems, understand the world and act on it (Shank, 1997).

It is an almost one-to-one training process which, to date, has been enormously expensive and unthinkable in a world of economies of scale. In this world, a good education – a learning process in which a few students are taught by one master – is expensive, because the cost of the master must be divided among a small number of students. The possibility of change arises when direct labour – the master – can be replaced by capital goods capable of performing part of his work. This can be achieved in the world of 'mass customization', which is gradually becoming possible thanks to technology. In this world, it is possible to individualize teaching at a reasonable cost, developing approaches that individualize knowledge acquisition and generate a customized design using technology as facilitator.

Knowledge management provides an explicit methodology for achieving this new approach without getting bogged down by fixed costs. The crucial observation *is that the cycles model can also be used as a model of the training process itself.*

Example 12.1   A new approach to training

KUST, a British building products manufacturer, needed to change the profile of its workers, who were accustomed to repetitive work. Now, they had to perform a range of new tasks with proactive approaches. The workers' average age was 45 years. The company's staff had been under no need to innovate for many years. Futhermore, they had been performing mostly simple, low-content and basically manual tasks. The company realized that the workers were set in their ways and, before undertaking an ambitious change programme, they needed to exercise their minds. In addition, this had to be done in a non-aggressive manner so that the slower ones would not become frustrated. It was proposed that they follow classes during working hours in whatever subject appealed to them. Some took music classes; others learned how to paint, etc. After a little while, the company proposed that they start to learn new ways of working, based on an interactive, non-passive approach. The programme was a success and the workers found it much easier to adapt to their new tasks.

Example 12.2   The master–disciple learning process

Germany used to be one of the leading exponents of this teaching method, with one of the best apprentice training systems in Europe. For economic reasons, many German companies ceased using this system, losing in the process a significant competitive advantage. Germany is currently reassessing its entire training policy and is recovering old master–disciple methods. Something similar is happening in the United Kingdom where the apprenticeship system has taken a new direction with the goal of finding new jobs for the unemployed. As part of a movement promoted by the Labour government, training plays a vital role in the fight against unemployment and forward-looking measures are being implemented to bring down the unemployment rate. Many of these measures are taken with the corporate viewpoint in mind so that workers' profiles are matched to future needs. The logic is that the present worker must be made ready for an uncertain future and must acquire the necessary knowledge to enable him to seek his own competitiveness, without having to depend totally on the company he currently works for.

In accordance with this observation, the design of a training plan should seek to implement both cycles virtually – minimizing the negative impact of the failures and adapting the challenges to the ability of each individual involved. The master then supports the disciple in the functioning of both the internal and external cycles while both do profitable work for the firm.

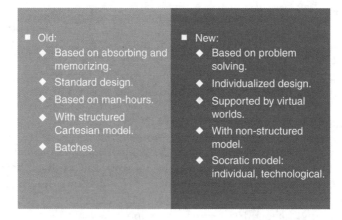

■ Old:
  ◆ Based on absorbing and memorizing.
  ◆ Standard design.
  ◆ Based on man-hours.
  ◆ With structured Cartesian model.
  ◆ Batches.

■ New:
  ◆ Based on problem solving.
  ◆ Individualized design.
  ◆ Supported by virtual worlds.
  ◆ With non-structured model.
  ◆ Socratic model: individual, technological.

Figure 12.2   The new approach to training

Example 12.3   An example of training and use of technology

Training in the Art of Cutting Ham

As an example of this new model, we could mention formative actions that are being carried out in several companies with the help of specific software. One example, which is a favourite of one of the authors, is the case of a supermarket chain which has trained its butchers with the support of a virtual world. This example clearly illustrates the difference between the traditional approach and the new approach to training.

The traditional approach to training butchers is that used by the El Corte Inglés department stores in its training centre. In its magnificent facilities, young apprentices learn from a master the art of cutting Parma ham. El Corte Inglés can afford to make the investment of buying hams, albeit of second-class quality, so that they can be 'hacked to pieces' by the apprentices in the course of their training process. The result, as consumers well know, is excellent and both the butchers and the fishmongers who are employed by El Corte Inglés are one of the differential competitive competences of the company's hypermarkets. The new approach is represented by a small chain of supermarkets who wished to address the problem with the help of technology. It developed a virtual program in which the young apprentices learned at their own speed. The technology enabled the process to be performed in accordance with each one's needs. The apprentices learnt to use the software very quickly and the result was excellent, at a very reasonable cost.

This approach drastically changes the conception of the training model. The conventional model is based upon absorbing, memorizing and teaching by horizontal groups, without individualizing. The training process's design is standard. It is taught in batches and based on man-hours – hours spent by the teacher in transmitting ideas. Rarely does the student undertake the solution of real problems, the emphasis is often more on examples than on problems.

*The manager as an educator

The new design for training implies a qualitative change in management. On the one hand, the idea that one learns in day-to-day work and, on the other hand, the possibility of imitating good habits of superiors or colleagues, lead ineluctably to the conclusion that the people who interact with the trainee in the firm during the daily routines have a decisive influence upon his education – particularly if the trainee assigns them the (subconscious) role of instructors, tutors or masters.

This gives rise to a new role for the manager: that of trainer and educator. The manager must accept his responsibility, his role as a reference point for those who are around him, who can use his help for their professional and personal development. The ability to educate becomes a necessary management skill in the development of organizations. This management role can be found in many companies, although generally in an embryonic state. For example, Xerox designed the LUTI (learn, use, teach, inspect) approach as one of the main-stays of its quality plan. This approach has also been used at Hughes as a step towards the implementation of a quality programme. However, the few empirical studies performed on this subject (for example, Ellinger *et al.*, 1999) have focused on the manager's role as instructor, rather than educator.

What is the difference between the two? An instructor teaches domain and/or task skills; an educator also teaches inference skills. An instructor focuses on the transmission of knowledge; an educator supports and transfers to his subordinates the skills that help them to learn. It is only logical that the subordinates, who are the people who face the every day operating realities, should know more about specific subjects than the manager, limiting his possibilities as an *instructor*. There are very good instructors on the market specialized in great varieties of domain and task knowledge. However, this is not the case of inference knowledge. And here is where the manager could be the best trainer.

Different people prefer different learning styles and, in order for learning to be effective, the teaching style must be adapted to their learning style. This requires identifying the way in which people learn so that it can be developed, applied and improved. In other words, the manager must try to understand the singularities of his people in order to facilitate knowledge generation most effectively. Honey's well-known learning typology (Honey and Mumford, 1992) lists four different ways of learning approaches: activist, reflector, theorist, and pragmatist.

- *Activist*: they enjoy the here and now, they like their life to be full of immediate experiences. 'I'll try anything once'. They tend to act first and consider the consequences later.

- *Reflector*: for them, the key is to compile and analyse information on experiences and events. 'You've got to be careful'. They prefer to remain in the background in any meeting or discussion.
- *Theorist*: they view problems from a logical stance. They like to analyse and synthesize. They prefer rational goals to subjective or ambiguous positions. 'If it is logical, it's got to be good'.
- *Pragmatist*: they are experts in testing ideas, theories and techniques to see if they really work. 'If it works, it's got to be good'. They are eminently practical in making decisions and solving problems.

For the manager, these four types owe their importance to the statistically observed fact that the *learning style is equal to the teaching style*. If, for example, the manager learns theoretically, he will tend to train and educate in the same way. This has one immediate consequence. If the manager does not understand the relationship between teaching and learning styles, he teaches (unconsciously) in accordance with his own learning style. This leads to a *dysfunctionality* with those subordinates who do not share the same way of learning. It is therefore vital, on one hand, that the manager identifies his way of learning and, on the other hand, that he be aware of his subordinates' styles so that he can adapt his teaching style to their learning style.

This book has actually developed a general structure to help the manager focus his role as educator. In synthesis he must teach by giving people problems to solve, offering support and knowledge in the process. He manages through an understanding of each individual's knowledge needs for action. With this approach to knowledge management, the ability to educate is placed within the reach of any manager.

*Designing the training system

Designing the training system becomes a systematic review of each of the steps involved in implementing PDM, creating virtual environments that allow it to develop. There are very simple virtual implementation of the cycles and the reader should not allow himself to frightened by the word 'virtual'.[3]

We should distinguish between *system design* and *training plan design*. In the former, a framework is defined within which it is possible to construct training programmes that are consistent with the firm's strategy. A *training plan* proposes a series of actions in response to certain needs that are stated *a priori*. The system

---

[3] The world of the classic classes is also virtual, where the teacher assigns mathematical problems, for example, to his students, establishing virtual relevance by assigning points to the different answers and generating virtual importance by correcting and discussing the exercises. In this case, the teacher has introduced the abstract knowledge so that the students can attain the solution (challenge), provided the methodology for solving the problems (for example, by teaching integration by transposing variables) and developed creativity (perhaps by establishing a series of reference cases to illustrate how variables are transposed).

design avoids having to intervene in the plan. If the system is well designed, it will favour the creation of consistent plans at all levels of the organization and at any given moment in time. The steps listed below are a proposal for designing the training system:

1. *Develop competitiveness criteria: in which areas does the company wish to excel?* The plan's design must always be referenced to the mission's priority dimensions. It is therefore essential to use these priorities as a reference and involve all of the organization in them. Therefore, as a first step, management must specify the priority criteria by which the service's excellence will be measured. The procedure for doing this was explained in Chapter 4.
2. *Generate problems to be solved.* This is the core part of the design, as the task now is to combine the problem diagnosing and solving capacities that are relevant for the firm. Although we are dealing with virtual situations, there must exist a solid relationship between the problems generated and the situations that the firm is experiencing at any given time. This accelerates the learning, since the problem's relevance is accepted with greater ease.
3. *Add aids to creativity that is to generate ideas about specific problems.* The goal here is to help the participants to generate ideas. To do this, remember that creativity, is not innate to the individual. Creativity is something that is taught and any adult can be creative. We refer the reader to Chapter 10 for a more detailed discussion of this matter.
4. *Determine innovations.* We now reach another crucial idea. Innovations should generate the problems whose solution is desired, as stated in 2 above. Here is where abstract knowledge can be incorporated in the individual to match his capacity to face challenges. As a first step in identifying the challenge, and the resulting danger of frustration, it is necessary to diagnose the level of knowledge held by each individual and map the path towards the profile required to solve the problems that have been identified. This gives a gap between what exists and what is required which must be filled by the acquisition of knowledge, integrated within the formative action. For this stage, the profiles technique briefly described in the addendum of Chapter 11 can be useful.
5. *Eliminate the frustration associated with too high a level of challenge.* In a previous study (Muñoz-Seca, 2003), we identified four educational dimensions that help to assimilate the challenge. Each individual has a certain intensity, a specific profile in these dimensions which produces what we may call his *challenge profile.*
   The dimensions making up the challenge profile are: analyse alternatives, deliver experiences, guide through the process and provide knowledge. An individual may be more inclined to solve problems when they are proposed to him with an analysis of the *alternatives* for solving them. In the same manner, there are individuals who accept innovations and their associated problems more easily if they are given *experiences* of similar situations. Others need *support* during the problem-solving process, indicating milestones and stages which must be met. Finally, there are people who need a *conceptual*, theoretical framework to guide them in understanding the problem. Figure 12.3 shows the challenge

	Activist	Pragmatic	Theoretic	Reflexive
Guiding through the process	+	++	+	−
Delivering experiences	++	+	−	+
Analyse alternatives	+	−	+	++
Providing knowledge	−	+	++	+

Figure 12.3 The challenge profile and learning styles

profile associated with each of the four Honey's – learning styles. The reader should reflect on what his learning style is and analyse his challenge profile.[4]

In order that the individual can assimilate the challenge, the problems generated by innovation must be biased on his favourite dimension. The manager must know his own profile[5] and that of his subordinates. This will enable him to adjust the challenge along the appropriate dimensions so that learning can better take place.

6. *Design relevance mechanisms: implementation focused on the firm's priorities.* This stage concentrates on teaching participants to assess the different problems' relevance for the firm's operations. This involves training in the three components of relevance: anticipate, observe and act. This learning can take place quite naturally by means of exercises in the workplace, using guided learning. In this type of learning, the tutor – someone in whom the trainee trusts – assigns relevance to each of a series of pre-established situations, which for comparison purposes he shares with the trainee after the latter has performed his own assessment.

7. *Design importance mechanisms: feedback to complete learning.* The last stage in the design consists of establishing mechanisms to generate feedback on the effect of the improvements made. This stage requires again guided learning mechanisms. The use of indicators, control panels and other similar tools[6] should provide the feeling that the trainee controls the situation.

With these rules for the training system, we can establish a methodology for designing *training plans*.

This methodology is summarized in Table 12.1, which gives an 11-step guide for devising training plans in PDM.

---

[4] If the reader would like to explore this subject in greater depth, he can read Muñoz-Seca. If he wishes to know his challenge profile, he can go to the website iese.edu/bms where he will find a test in the learning and technology section.

[5] As one participant in a session told us: 'So it's not that I have problems with people but that I don't understand how I am and how the others learn ...'.

[6] What the current experts call the 'balanced score card' and which is simply a system for monitoring the main vectors that govern the situation. And yes, we realize that we have written a sentence that is almost as complicated to understand as the original one.

Table 12.1   Guide for a training plan

Guide for Designing a Training Plan
1. Make a list of knowledge and skill requirements. The knowledge diagnosis will have helped in this task.
2. Group them, assess them and choose those that have most priority.
3. Identify the type of (virtual) problems that must be solved in order to attain the desired learning.
4. Design a virtual world where these problems have meaning. Establish this world's rules of conduct and cause and effect mechanisms.
5. Think what type of innovations will be made to generate the desired problems. Identify the challenge profile and your knowledge gaps.
6. Think what you will do so that the innovations' challenge is within the participant's reach.
7. Say how you will support the participants' creativity.
8. Say how you will support the problem-solving process.
9. Identify how you can introduce relevance into this virtual world.
10. The same for virtual importance.
11. Analyse which technologies will help you perform the above steps.

Participation which is not 'participation'

We now turn to the second component of the vertex of the KIA pyramid: participation. People often talk about this subject. Even measures have been taken to ensure the participation of all of the firm's agents in management, creating laws that regulate it. Mostly, the result has not gone beyond the presence of workers' representatives at board meetings.[7] Mere formalities or, in the best of cases, well-intentioned acts based on a vague idea that 'everyone is entitled to take part'.

In PDM, participation is a logical consequence of the approach. We are not talking about more or less charitable events in which everyone is invited to participate. If the firm wishes to tap into all of its brains, this can only be done if each individual can develop his problem-solving activity in his own sphere of responsibility.

Likewise, in all service activities, the server's profile requires his involvement in operating decisions. It is the server who is in contact with the customer and who must solve the problems that the latter experiences. The server takes on the risk and, therefore, must feel that his decisions are accepted by all of the organization.

*Knowledge and organization structure: LMO (learning management organization)

The development of PDM system in the firm raises new problems within the organization. We now discover that, in addition to any firm's primary goals,

---

[7] A friend of ours describes this situation as 'give a worker a place at your table' by analogy with a ridiculous campaign ran in Spain some years ago which invited people to share the Christmas spirit with the slogan 'Give a poor person a place at your table'...

people's development must now be included as an indispensable requirement for attaining its primary aims. Until recently, this task corresponded to the firm's environment; it was a task that was, to be carried on by society and the role of the corporate world was much less important. Now, as a cell of society, the firm must perform part of a process that was previously outside its formal sphere of action.

PDM processes are consubstantial to organizations of people and no explicit start-up process is required for them to be active. The structures that support these processes have always been part of the firm's informal organization, developed by evolution because they are a function that must be performed if the firm is to continue living.

The purposeful implementation of PDM acknowledges the reality of this situation, identifies its roots and considers how the whole should be managed in order to achieve maximum accumulation of knowledge and its competitive use. We are not creating anything that did not exist previously – we are trying to channel and exploit a natural resource that the firm was already generating spontaneously.

In order to create the appropriate context, some firms have implemented parallel organization structures whose specific purpose is the development of the knowledge resource.[8]

When proposing new organization structures, there are certain pitfalls that must be avoided. First, there is nothing worse than implementing *unnatural* organization structures. A formal organization structure must naturally facilitate the development of a function. Otherwise, people flee from the formal structure to seek refuge in the informal structure and the former becomes dysfunctional, an object in a glass case. There is nothing more likely to ensure that an organization loses its natural structure than to make it excessively complicated or rigid. Anyone who designs a complicated organization is guaranteed to produce a monster of reason.

Second, highly formalized organizations are rigid, perhaps very efficient, but slow in adapting either to the environment or to the needs of its own members.

Any organization that wishes to make its knowledge available to everyone needs to possess a very high degree of adaptability. The "chaotic" organization, which is continually reconfiguring itself, is probably the ideal that everyone dreams of in such circumstances.

This idea has been explored in some depth in environments characterized by a high degree of innovation. Why should the firm want stable managers? To perpetuate power relationships? Who can guarantee that the present managers will be the best managers for the firm tomorrow, when the circumstances have changed?[9] Why is there a class who does not contribute all its knowledge to achieving the firm's mission?

---

[8] One of these firms is IBM, which has implemented a group and leaders structure that is very much in line with what is described below.

[9] A friend of ours says that this may be another reason why many companies have to change their managers after they are 50. The only way to flexibilize the organization chart, eliminating positions, is to eliminate the people who hold them, because the organization assumes that person = job. Of course, the elimination should be virtual, not real ...

Leadership must be variable and changing, adapting to the capabilities that are required for each situation. Examples in HP, Wal-Mart and others prove that it can be done.[10] In some companies, the managers are chosen for each situation by their 'subordinates' (Quinn, 1997). Again, the need for flexibility is a logical consequence of our approach, to the point that if the firm's senior management is not convinced that this is a natural structure for the firm, the ideas of PDM will contribute very little to improving the firm.

In the following, we will examine a kind of parallel structure designed to support the complete process of the internal cycle, providing a model that seeks to enrich the formal-virtual relationships between the firm's people.

The idea is very simple, consisting of imitating the social structure of the clubs. A society's citizens belong to clubs or associations in which they find an atmosphere that is conducive to their physical, intellectual or professional development. The clubs offer activities to their members, led by a management committee who is responsible for these activities. A citizen may belong to as many clubs as he wishes and this structure is superimposed on his own chrematistic activity. At these clubs, he can leave messages and hold meetings. The implementation makes all of the firm's employees to belong to whatever clubs they may need to obtain adequate support for their development.

This organizational proposal, which we can call *learning management organization*, or simply LMO, has the following formal characteristics:

1. *It is a polymorphous, multidimensional matrix structure.* Each person in the organization can belong to different organizational groups in interlaced structures, whose only limit is set by the organization's intrinsic operating capacity.
2. *One of the dimensions is the business unit.* The organization of business units subsumes all of the traditional results-oriented organization. Therefore, the traditional organization can be immersed in an LMO. Highly hierarchized organizations with very strict authority relationships will find it very difficult to be compatible with a polymorphous LMO. On the other hand, organizations that already have a diffuse structure based on delegation and trust provide a suitable environment for this evolution.
3. *The relationships between the organization's members are based on support and development*, not on action and command. In this sense, it is inappropriate to talk about superiors and subordinates; correct terms would be facilitators and supporters.
4. *It can be conceived as a virtual structure.* Although it is based on the group, it does not need the group's physical existence nor the exchange of experiences by physical contact between its participants. The exchange may be virtual insofar as physical contact is not indispensable for PDM. This sentence should be

---

[10] We ourselves have helped many companies to remodel their organization to increase their flexibility. We have done this by creating project-specific organizations in which the project manager has powers so long as the project is in progress but, upon completion, can join another project as simply another member. The firms we have helped have survived and improved, which is a wonder in itself ...

understood in its exact sense. We are not implying that group work is not necessary. The meeting of the group puts into motion personal and social processes that are extremely important for achieving structural goals such as cohesion, understanding, acceptance, and so on. PDM can use techniques that capitalize on this type of process. For example, creativity sometimes attains its best expression in group work techniques. However, when the processes described are not crucial for the result, the interaction can be structured in other ways that avoid the combinatory problem of coordinating several separate agendas. Virtual dialogues, through e-mail, telephone or videoconferencing, can be excellent tools for these purposes.

*Implementation of a LMO

In this section, we will describe the stages into which the preparation of a LMO project can be decomposed. We will confine our discussion to its design, without entering into the actions required to implement it. We will apply the idea of converting the firm's *competence structure* into the base of the LMO structure. To illustrate the ideas contained in this section, we will use the PETESA case presented in Example 12.4.

Example 12.4   PETESA

PETESA: Productos Electrónicos de Telefonía, SA

PETESA is a firm specializing in the development and manufacture of innovative telecommunication products. In 1993, the firm (which was in a perilous finalcial position) banked all its hopes for future survival on being able to quickly start production of a new wireless local telephony product. Any entity, company or family group who wished to have a group of mobile extensions connected to the same switchboard could buy PETESA's new product, which would provide this service. The goal of the design was to enable a switchboard connected to the telephone network to handle up to 16 mobile extensions operating simultaneously, without interfering or overhearing each other, provided that they were no more than 300 metres from the switchboard. Likewise, the system had to be secure between subscribers, so that two subscribers with overlapping coverage would not suffer mutual interference problems.

PETESA had high hopes of this system, which it considered could give it a competitive product for the world market. However, the research and development engineers who were taking part in the project had little experience in dealing with a product of this type. Likewise, the factory was not used to working together with engineering. In addition to obtaining the product, the project had to be a source of valuable knowledge for the company's future and possession of this knowledge had to be assured. The company recruited two experienced foreign engineers to direct the project. The contract was for the specific project and, as soon as the development was completed, the engineers would return to their country. The complete team was composed of 23 people, of which 10 were design engineers and 5 were production employees. The other 8 people were auxiliary staff (designers, sales engineers, clerical staff). One doctoral student of ours worked with the project team for a number of months.

The project was organized in five task forces or working groups which designed each of the product's basic systems. One group designed the switch-board, a second group designed the system's radio frequency system, and another was responsible for the software. Of the two remaining groups, one was assigned to the system's ergonomic design and the last group was concerned with the manufacturability of the result. It soon became apparent that the way the project was going, it would be very difficult to secure the desired learning. The foreign engineers often designed a critical component themselves, without it being very clear what process they had followed.

By common agreement with the company's management, a PDM formalization process was begun. To simplify, the study's scope was limited to the project unit (equivalent to a business unit).

The steps for implementation an LMO structure are as follows:

1. *Identify the knowledge units.* The knowledge units are the virtual groups of an LMO. *A knowledge unit is an organization unit which contains the knowledge related to a competence.*

    Therefore, by diagnosing the firm's competences we can obtain the knowledge units. As can be seen, with this structure, a person can belong to a very varied group of knowledge units, depending upon his knowledge profile. Due to the virtual, polymorphous nature of the knowledge unit, this multiple affiliation is feasible without producing any serious complications.

2. *Identify the knowledge unit's components.* The next step is concentrated on identifying the people who must belong to each knowledge unit. This requires identifying the competence's carriers. This task is simple and normally overlaps with the previous step. Everyone in the firm should be assigned to at least one knowledge unit. If we can not assign it easily, we have identified a person who does not contribute knowledge to the firm. This situation is a sign that the knowledge inventory process has been superficial or incomplete, and the analysis should be re-examined in order to identify the cause of the anomaly.

3. *Document the relationships between the knowledge unit's components.* Now the knowledge unit must be given an internal structure. In a knowledge unit, instead of bosses there are masters. And since it is not a structure based on 'potestas', it is easier to form it around the existing (and probably accepted) natural relationships between the knowledge unit's members.

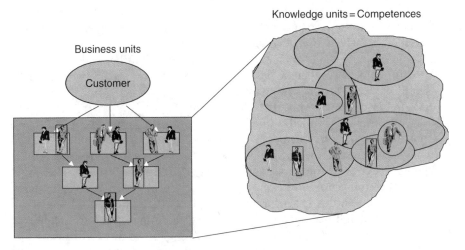

Figure 12.4 The knowledge units (KU)

Example 12.5 Competences in PETESA

Our associate performed a preliminary analysis of the competences that already existed in the project group. To do this, he interviewed all of the group's members, identified knowledge items and established the necessary groupings to identify the competences. The result was presented to the group for review. Eight main areas of competence were identified: wave propagation, coding, transmission with frequency jumps, control software, electronic packaging, materials processing, electronic components, and reliability.

The roles played by each carrier must be identified along three dimensions, derived from the three control variables of the internal cycle: creativity, problem solving and innovation. This requires identifying the people who:

- Facilitate the solution of other people's problems.
- Are seen by the others as being more creative.
- Other people turn to them to implement ideas.

The next task is to understand each virtual group's internal structure in terms of this three dimensions outlined above. For example, for creativity (and the same thing goes for the other), we must understand which people within the group are accepted as being references for all the others, and will be asked for support and so on.

Here, we can use group structure and operations analysis techniques.[11] In a classic work, Allen (1984) used a simple method for documenting the

---

[11] And the reader will say: 'There they go again! These people solve everything by creating groups'. Perhaps the only answer we can give to this objection is that the important point

relationships existing in a R&D structure, which can be readily applied to any competence in the firm and which we recommend to the reader. It is an intuitive method which can be applied in diagram form. However, if necessary, there are a multitude of different techniques which can be used in this field, with the help of competent professionals[12] who can separate what is really useful from what is purely accidental.

Allen's procedure is simple but illuminating.

Let us assume a knowledge unit composed of three carriers: A, B and C. We represent each person by a node, a circle on a diagram. An arrow connecting two nodes will represent a relationship between the two, which is described in the text associated with the arrow. For example, the arrow and the text leaving B represent a connection of the 'problem-solving' relationship. A accepts advice, or help, from B in this specific aspect. We will say that B helps A. This relationship is potential, it need not actually have existed in practice, but it represents a predisposition on the part of A to accept B's superior ability in this particular aspect. On the same diagram, we can see influences belonging to other relationships. Specifically, A can help C in implementing actions and C can help B in generating ideas. A diagram constructed in this way is a good summary of the complete set of relationships among the knowledge unit components.

4. *Identify the critical people within the knowledge unit.* The diagram shows the critical people in each knowledge unit. By definition, the critical people are those who carry the highest number of relationships. (See Figure 12.5.)

At least one of them must play the role of custodian of the knowledge unit. However, this role may be played by several people, one for each type of relationship, if there are no agents who combine several influences. The main role of the knowledge unit's custodian is to manage and operate the unit so that the knowledge contained in the competence defining the unit is improved. The

Example 12.6   Knowledge units at PETESA

People were assigned to knowledge units at PETESA on the basis of the profile obtained in the interviews. The eight competences gave rise to eight units with the following number of members: 3, 2, 5, 10, 5, 4, 14, and 8. Three people did not fit in any of the competences listed. As the total assignments are 41, each person was assigned to approximately 2 units.[13]

---

of our approach is not creating groups but the reason why groups are created. Having understood this reason, we have probably felt compelled to use them as a standard procedure. But as one of the authors says in an authoritarian voice, '...but it is forbidden to waste time in meetings!'

[12] Which, of course, we authors are not as at least one of them is a total unbeliever in the usefulness of these tools.

[13] The result of the advanced mathematical expression: $41/20 = (2 + \text{an insignificant quantity})$.

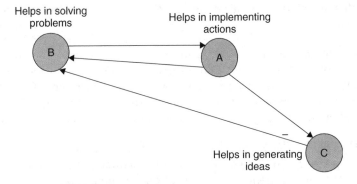

Figure 12.5 Relationship between the carriers of a KU

Table 12.2 Questions to be considered when developing the capacity of a KU's components

---

- How are problems solved within each KU affected by the problems?
- How can we improve the way ideas are generated?
- How can we discover alternatives for using the knowledge unit's knowledge in the business units?
- What blocking factors prevent implementation of new ideas?
- What problems will arise when different knowledge is applied to current activities?
- What prevents us from thinking in another way? What internal barriers do we have?
- What tools would we need to develop our way of thinking?
- What supports are needed to improve creativity? The capacity to take on challenges? The capacity to diagnose and solve problems?

---

knowledge unit's custodian catalyses the improvement of the internal cycle and must have a very proactive role.

5. *The knowledge unit's tasks.* The goal of each of the participants in a knowledge unit is to identify ways of applying knowledge to improve the BU they belong to. To do this, the knowledge unit's leader must consider the questions listed in Table 12.2.

In each case, after having detected an improvement need, it is important to bear in mind the creativity model introduced in Chapter 10. The decomposition of the creative process into components, and the nature of these components should help generate actions to support improvement.

Note that, through the custodians, common support actions are proposed for all of the people in the knowledge unit. This is because we implicitly assume that belonging to a certain knowledge unit implies a certain type of personal typology, for instance, a cognitive style. If it is necessary to adapt the process to the person, the profiles of Chapter 11 are helpful, which individualize the need for specific knowledge.

*The influence of the organization structure: the project-oriented organization

Permanent improvement through PDM flourishes in certain types of organizations and withers in others. If the whole pyramid is to be implemented, certain important conditions must be met, which we will review in this section. To conclude, we will propose a type of organization structure which is proving to be suitable for our purpose.

Organizational conditions for the personal stratum

We have already seen in Chapter 11 that there are conditions that restrict the functioning of the internal cycle. The organizational complications defined there are fairly obvious. Less obvious is the fact that as the level of mental sophistication of the firm's staff increases, the classic motivation techniques become increasingly less effective. Without going into the essence of the phenomenon, which corresponds to organization theory, we will briefly describe here some of the effects that we have observed in practice (deMarco and Listes, 1999).

1. *Lack of confidence in management ability.* In high technology or knowledge-intensive companies, many of the people at lower levels in the organization are highly educated and have developed their analysis and synthesis abilities to a very high degree *throughout their lives.* It is not uncommon for the organization to include among its inhabitants PhDs who are universally acknowledged within their fields. Often, these people feel (legitimately) proud of their own knowledge, which is often the only asset that can make them competitive and provide them with opportunities for advancement. Such people tend to analyse the outcome of the decisions made within the firm in the light of their own knowledge and they can readily detect irrationalities, inconsistencies and errors. Management must be aware that their decisions will be judged and criticized because they affect everyone's lives. Some types of manager feel insecure and tend to retreat into arbitrariness, power (*potestas*, not *autoritas*) and aloofness from those who criticize them. The gap between management and subordinates widens until it becomes unbridgeable.
2. *Knowledge of each other's abilities.* In this type of organization, people usually have a clear diagnosis of the various agents' knowledge profiles. Each one is weighed according to what he knows and contributes. Thus, inconsistencies for example, in status or compensation, are rated depending upon each person's level. This leads to the perception of unfair treatment by all those who think that their ability is superior to that of others who hold positions of higher rank or earn a higher salary.
3. *Responsibility towards the customer.* Qualified staff usually bear a high level of responsibility towards the firm's customers and this responsibility manifests itself in day-to-day activities. An ERP installer may have highly qualified implementation staff, who are the people who are answerable to the customer. If any mistake is made in planning, resource estimation or duration, customers will

look to these people for an explanation and may rightly complain to them, even though these staff might not have any control over what is happening. In such cases, the agents may dissociate themselves from the organization, making a clear separation between 'the company' and 'us'.

4. *Lack of suitable challenges.* This type of person usually gives a high value to personal development opportunities, which are often more highly valued than their salary. Their high level of qualification means that the tasks undertaken have a low level of challenge for the participants. This demoralizes and minimizes learning. The resulting sensation of lack of progress will lead the individual to look for more attractive openings. These people often look for opportunities for initiative, decisions and, in short, to feel that they have a significant influence on the collective future.

As can be seen, most of these issues are in fact ways of inhibiting learning and the use of knowledge for improvement. If the organization does not overcome these conditions, knowledge will have almost no chance of influencing the firm's improvement. However, if the organization is able to overcome them, the cycles' functioning is facilitated and the organization learns and solves problems, developing its competitiveness.

Thus, there are organization forms that are better matched to PDM, while others are counterproductive or may even prevent it altogether.

The organization forms that effectively facilitate the cycles' functioning have yet to be studied, which is a task that should be left to the experts. For us, such forms are few in number[14] and they have common features.

In the following paragraphs, we will concentrate on an organization structure known as 'management by projects'. This type of organization has the following properties:

1. *It is polymorphous and changing.* The organization does not have a rigid, stable reporting structure. It is structured in task forces, which are often given the name of 'projects'. A task force or working group undertakes a certain task, a project, which has a well-defined beginning and end. The nomenclature of 'projects' is suggestive, because the groups are normally surrounded by the paraphernalia that forms part of a project group and everything that has been said in Chapter 4 is also applicable to them. Generally speaking, the group has certain generic goals obtained by specialization of the firm's general goals. Relevance is assured by this definition process and by the subsequent formal motivation structure created *ad hoc* for each group. They have both fungible and recoverable resources assigned to them, especially people who enter and leave the project as it progresses and in accordance with its needs. The organization maintains pools of resources which it assigns to the groups and which it recovers as soon as these groups release them. No group should have resources

---

[14] In the technical literature, they are known as heterarchies, a nice little word that is obtained from hierarchy and changing the prefix. However, the meaning is dramatically different.

that it does not need. The groups have a control structure based on tasks and milestones based on projects management but which is applied even to potentially repetitive situations.

2. *It is flat.* There are usually very few organizational layers. If possible, there are only two. One of them is senior management, whose job is to create and change the groups, design the organization system, guarantee and safeguard the common resources, and, in general, perform all the support tasks for the project leaders. Typically, this support is focused on representation tasks, because the group leader needs an external image that he cannot project himself and then delegates upwards, relying on the firm's management to obtain the necessary impact.

   The second level is composed of the project managers. A potential project manager is a job category that assures that the individual is able to manage a project but does not necessarily mean that the individual has a project assigned to him. A project manager may be assigned to a group that has another leader.

   These two levels may be assisted by staff groups who own the resources. The staff groups propose initiatives for assuring functioning of the pyramid and, in particular, that of the two cycles. On a general level, there are often three leaders – a technology leader, a general resources leader (including finance) and a human resources leader. For example, the financial leader's sole mission is to supply the money resources required by the groups at the lowest cost and invest surplus resources in the best possible manner.

3. *There is no command by position, by potestas.* Command is by *autoritas*. A group may be assigned resources consisting of people with different levels of experience and position within the organization. At a certain point in time, the group has a leader, normally appointed by the senior management, whose mandate expires after a certain time (which coincides with the project's life time). The leader is responsible for his group's efficiency and goals. The group's members accept his leadership because of his match with the group's purposes. In some firms and in specific cases, the managing director himself is a member of a working group and performs functions in it (typically sales-related) under the orders of the project manager.

4. *It has a high degree of initiative.* If they are to fulfil their mission of intensively exploiting knowledge, the working groups must be designed so that they can use the knowledge they hold in the immediate solution of the problems, particularly in those that arise in dealings with customers. The treatment of the moments of truth, for example, requires a high degree of initiative to be given to the customer–group interface, which is where the problems affecting service occur. Many companies that are implementing this type of organization recognize the working group as a mini-company led by the group leader, who acts as its general manager. Once the resources have been allocated, the responsibility for future competitiveness, based upon the group's learning, is placed within the group itself.

5. *It delegates by trust.* The type of delegation required in this type of organization is delegation by trust (Riverola & Muñoz-Seca, 1989). This is a form of delegation

that has been studied relatively little, but which is found with some frequency in environments such as those described here. In a modern organization, with thousands of knowledge items continually being processed, any manager must trust in the decision-making capacity of those who work under him in the hierarchical sense but, as we have said earlier, often know more about a certain area of competences. Delegation by trust provides the manager with a means to succeed in situations in which, otherwise, the lack of knowledge would leave him not knowing what to do. The power held by this form of delegation is based on the following idea: 'I trust in you, because both you and I are committed to this idea, because you know the importance that this matter (and you yourself) have for the company; and as I know that you are fully motivated to succeed, you have full authority in this project.' This idea seems to have provided the basis for a number of studies in human resources management but it has not, in our opinion, been fully developed and applied. Delegation by trust is the culmination of the implementation process represented by the KIA pyramid. For this delegation to take place, at least the following conditions must be met:

- Implementation of the other actions of the KIA pyramid.
- Existence of an atmosphere in which information and communication is open.
- Acceptance of the loss of power on the part of the manager.
- Management must maintain an open attitude in which changes are welcome.
- The individuals must share both success and failure at the same levels and with mutual understanding.
- The individual has full responsibility for achieving his goal, but is free to ask his superiors for advice and support.
- The manager must create an atmosphere of acceptance that facilitates the provision of assistance.
- The agent must understand that asking for help is not a sign of weakness but a normal part of daily life.

Another prerequisite of delegation by trust is that the higher levels of the firm trust in the level formed by the group leaders and, by extension, in its members. The compensation system applied to such people must also be in accordance with this approach. Typically, these professionals are well paid, because of their high level of qualifications and their integration with the firm. Normally, the compensation contains a part that is indexed to the goals and results achieved, and which are attainable by the group, being subsumed within relevance. At these levels, compensation is not a primary issue and the recognition of others, satisfaction with one's own work, and other similar factors hold great importance for the agent.

When this type of organization is implemented, it is common for agents to ask themselves how they can show the world the true value that the firm gives to them. The world is usually full of people exhibiting titles of 'managers' of this and that and, in certain situations, the title of 'project manager' is not of a high social status. The Y career system, in which each person has a professional category and a managerial category that are parallel and superimposable, is one way of addressing this problem. In this type of career, two different ladders are created in which the 'technical' rungs are the recognition of each individual's merits, rather than of the hierarchical position he holds within the organization.

6. *It requires significant changes in the information and control systems.* As a consequence of its micro-company structure with the features described in Chapter 4, a project-driven organization requires the implementation of information and monitoring mechanisms specifically designed for the group's goals. These systems' design is referenced to relevance. Generally speaking, it is based upon the identification of each group's drivers or critical efficiency (effectiveness) factors. Once they have been identified, ways to measure and present the drivers' evolution are created. The result is something akin to the balanced score cards technique. The information system, based upon the concepts described in Chapter 6, identifies the invariant process sequences but maintains a high level of flexibility as regards the DSS, accepting the potential differences between the different working groups.

To summarize, an organization such as that described above changes the organizational invariants. Traditionally, the invariants that appear as a consequence of power relationships are summarized in the organization chart. In organizations by projects, the invariant is the body of rules that are used to create and destroy groups, allocate resources, delegate and provide the necessary information and control mechanisms for their functioning. Any firm that is able to create this type of organization will find fertile ground for learning and the application of PDM.

13

Information Systems for Knowledge Management

In this chapter, we will establish the starting points for the construction of a KMS (knowledge management system). This is a technological subject and therefore has a specifically contemporary component which we shall try to avoid by not entering into any description of the various products available on the market and concentrating instead on their immanent functional features.

Introduction

Information systems are the fundamental vehicle for processing symbols in any firm. Insofar as knowledge can be materialized, the information systems have the potential of storing, transmitting and making available the firm's knowledge to all of its personnel.

The traditional information systems have generally confined themselves to processing data – particularly quantitative data. From a well-designed information system it is easy to obtain answers to questions such as: 'What is the output for the last 12 months from the Valladolid plant?' But these information systems encounter serious problems in answering questions such as: 'What happened in February at the Valladolid plant that made its output fall so low?', even though everyone who works in the company knows that there was a strike in February.

The new role of the information system is to handle knowledge, and not just data. To highlight this new role, we propose using the term knowledge management system (KMS), instead of Information System.

Key aspects of the KMS

This KMS approach is becoming possible thanks to the slow but fruitful development of the techniques used in (albeit incorrectly termed) artificial intelligence. Although this discipline has a long history, its appearance on company managers' desks has been relatively recent. People have started to use the term 'knowledge engineering' to refer to the techniques that are used to take people's knowledge, store it and process it on computers. For many years, and in spite of its age, artificial intelligence has retained the seductive power of a person in the flower of youth.

Although its successes to date are much less than had been promised and desired, the truth is that it is starting to give results that are only possible in the context of the KMSs.

1. *The treatment of perceptional knowledge.* This issue can be treated as case storage and retrieval. There are many situations in which the mere retrieval of stored cases may hold considerable interest. We will mention, for example, the retrieval of pre-inventive structures in creativity, the retrieval of transformations in problem solving, the isolation of challenges similar to an assigned challenge in innovation, etc. If the reader takes another look at the different aspects of the KIA pyramid, he will note that there are many places where the activity of a case retrieval system can provide relevant information. Even in teaching, the identification of forms of behaviour by the agent and the retrieval of stored experiences relevant to the situation are being successfully used in some advanced experiments.

2. *The treatment of abstract knowledge.* The storage and retrieval of this type of knowledge has been based on the use of rules having the structure IF <conditions> THEN <results or actions>. In operational situations, it is often possible to summarize the knowledge embedded in procedures by using this type of rule. In order to process the rules, one implements a TMS system capable of drawing conclusions from premises perhaps using a search process similar to that presented in Chapter 1.

   The (limited) applications of this type of technique have been called 'expert systems' and they have been used in highly operational aspects, where the entire environment can be summarized in a few dozen rules. Although the idea is attractive, the basic problem is scaling up the deductive techniques. When the problem refers to an extensive environment, the possibility of performing deductions within a reasonable time limit becomes unacceptably low. We have already seen the causes in Chapter 1. However, we would emphasize here that this happens because the inference mechanism has little knowledge, little capacity for solving problems directly, and must resort to exploration by searching, which leads to interminably long processing times.

3. *Induction; data mining.* This is a range of computer technologies whose purpose is to discover structure in a heap of data. Often, the information available in the firm is too extensive and unstructured for it to be summarized in a reasonable form using statistical techniques.

   In order to discover causes, we need an adequate 'representation' of the data. For example, if we look for: 'What percentage of the products account for 80 per cent of the sales?', a raw listing of sales by products is not very useful (particularly if there are several thousand products). An ABC chart may be the adequate representation for answering this question.

   The Data Mining techniques can help in cause recognition processes in complex situations. Basically, they offer the possibility of using a different (and extensive) number of representations using graphics, colours, statistics, etc. They should be considered whenever, at some point in a process, massive quantities of data can (should) be interpreted that cannot be processed by any other procedure.

4. *Anticipation and relevance.* An intuitively obvious way of predicting the outcome of an agent's actions is to carry out these actions experimentally. Obviously, this experimenting cannot be carried out on the real system, since the system often cannot be regenerated to undo the consequences of a wrong decision. In such cases, simulation techniques are a valuable aid. They build a symbolic model of the world in the computer which can be used under a variety of circumstances, even if the decision maker has incomplete knowledge.

The drawback of the simulation techniques is the considerable time it takes to construct and validate a model that adequately represents reality. Even using modern simulation tools, it is quite a complicated task to develop a model, even in very simple cases. Furthermore, it is not easy to find the experience required to do this and even less common to have it available routinely in the firm. Therefore, this type of technique is not used generally, although progress continues to be made in studying simple forms of representing real worlds for processing on computer systems.

When designing a KMS, particular attention should be paid to the simulation techniques. If it proved to be possible to isolate a few situations where one can construct adaptable models, the result may be spectacular. As a specific example, we could mention the use of these techniques in product development. It has become routine to simulate the mechanical, hydraulic, electrical or thermal behaviour of a design before building it, as this enables the design cycle to be completed much more quickly than using the normal method. In fact, simulation has become integrated in CAD (computer assisted design) systems and is a mandatory step in most cases. It could be said that it no longer contributes any significant competitive *advantage* since it already is standard knowledge to be used by any company wishing to compete today.

5. *Importance and its perception.* Finally, the perception of an action's results is becoming increasingly possible through the use of virtual reality techniques. Although for the time being confined to strictly operating problems, their scope of application is becoming wider every day. Popularized by the science fiction films and computer games, they have become part of everyday vocabulary. Apart from a few applications, they are still in their infancy for knowledge management applications in companies, because everything has proved to be much more complicated to scale up than was thought a few years ago.

*Information systems and KMS

Although the KMSs contain the ERPs (enterprise resource planners), they go far beyond them. An ERP is the part of the KMS that provides the administrative and operational support. Many systems currently used by companies are ERPs. Contained in a more or less distributed database, they store, distribute and exploit the quantitative information related with the firm's operations.

Table 13.1   MySAP modules

• MySAP Enterprise Portals	• MySAP Exchanges
• MySAP Supply Chain Mgmt.	• MySAP Business Intelligence
• MySAP Customer Relationship Mgmt.	• MySAP Financials
• MySAP Supplier Relationship Mgmt.	• MySAP Human Resources
• MySAP Product Lifecycle Mgmt.	• MySAP Mobile Business
	• MySAP Hosted Solutions
	• MySAP Technology

Some ERP systems claim that they can become virtual KMSs. In order to ascertain what is true in these claims, it is necessary to analyse the capacities of most of the present ERPs.

In recent years, ERP systems have undergone considerable growth and as an alternative to inherited systems. In many firms, the complexity of keeping up to date the historic system, consisting of disjointed applications developed at different times and by different people, has led senior management to consider a drastic new approach. Many companies have chosen to buy standard systems that can be adapted to a greater or lesser extent to the firm's reality, but do not require the enormous amount of software talent of the early applications.

As an innovation, ERPs can not be considered revolutionary. We could classify them as extensive innovation. They are designs evolved from the old MRPs logic (material resources planning) and refined using the current information technologies (distributed processing, client-server architecture, databases, and so on).

Most of the inherited systems had been customized exactly to the way the firm operated. This was both their strength and their weakness. It was a strength, because if they were well implemented and supported the firm's distinctive features, by definition the system helped the firm to be more competitive. But it was also a weakness, because they were difficult to change and, therefore, hampered the firm's natural development.

The ERPs are an attempt to standardize the traditional systems. Taking the best ideas from a sample of companies, the ERPs standardize the process. Theoretically, they can be adapted to any company by changes of their parameters.[1] The classic systems were bespoke suits made by mediocre tailors. The ERPs are off-the-peg suits made by an excellent tailor. They have the same advantages and disadvantages as their textile counterparts.

The ERPs are decomposed into modules (see Table 13.1 for the modules offered in the MySAP system). For example, the accounting module implements financial accounting in an adaptable format, the customers module does the same with the customer accounts and the production module seeks to perform an identical function with production.

One key point is that the different modules can be implemented separately. However, the implementation and adaptation is normally so complex that the

---

[1] One of the best-known systems offers the possibility of adjusting more than 8,000 parameters…

involvement of top-notch consulting firms is required. The outcome of all this is that the implementation of a more or less complete ERP can cost several million euros.

Some ERPs offer 'knowledge management modules'. None of these modules offers support for an approach as the one in this book. Most are mainly systems for maintaining and distributing documentation. In fact, they are starting to be known as 'content management modules' and not as 'knowledge management modules'.

Dedicated systems

Other software manufacturers have put special systems on the market that are advertised as knowledge management systems. Few of them really get this far. The larger systems are basically information distribution systems that are capable of addressing information to people who have stated at some time that they are interested in it. However, these systems can be quite complex. They usually include complicated search engines – that build queries by asking the user the types of information required, and that are capable of sorting out the most relevant stored items answering the query.

A dedicated system of this type normally does not integrate with the ERP and basically forms a parallel world.

Specialized and local systems

These constitute the most interesting alternatives – at least from the viewpoint of this book. The few existing systems that can provide support to the cycles have been developed as local applications within this category. Some include fairly sophisticated tools, such as the Kads system (Schreiber *et al.*, 1999).

Of course, their main drawback lies precisely in their locality. They support individual processes, but cannot cope with the collective process, particularly when it comes to companywide knowledge sharing.

*The structure of a KMS

Of course, a KMS is not knowledge management, just as an ERP is not the firm's operations. However, they are a very important tool for supporting knowledge management, just as the ERPs are very important for supporting operations.

Ideally, there are three main areas which a KMS should cover. These are shown in Figure 13.1:

- Maintain the firm's relevant databases, particularly the knowledge database.
- Provide selective communication between the agents. The communication should cover not only the interaction – the most traditional form of communication – but also selective knowledge exchange. This can take the form of a request – direct request of knowledge requirements – by default – an instruction to inform the interested person when a certain type of knowledge is in the system.
- Support the entire KIA pyramid, at both the individual and the organizational levels. This function should try to supplement individual capacities with

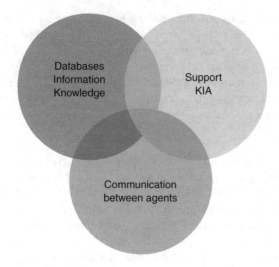

Figure 13.1   The action areas of a KMS

appropriate support for each basic variable. These components have been described in previous chapters and their descriptions should point the reader to the type of support that can (should) be given.

With the technology available in 2002, some of these functions are available immediately, perhaps for the price of buying a software package and installing it.[2] However, for the moment, there is no system (integrated or otherwise) which fully covers these specifications. In more detail:

- *Maintaining databases.* Database technology has advanced significantly in recent years. The present systems can do a good job in handling classic data, so it can be said that this technology is already in general use (particularly in the ERPs). However, this is not the case with regard to the part of the database which must deal with knowledge. There is no accepted, effective way of storing and retrieving information in a free format. The typical solution is to combine classic databases with free-format documents. The former maintain different types of indexes on the documents and these indexes are used to extract information by means of traditional techniques. Even with these limitations the technology is ready to perform well.

- *Communication between agents.* Message exchange technology is moving forward at a dizzy pace. Communication systems have exploded in the last ten years and it can be said that, at present, the problem is basically one of content, not of infrastructure. The technology is ready to transmit information but the

---

[2] Sometimes tremendously expensive. People talk of installations that have cost tens of millions of dollars. You can pay a lot of salaries with that money. The authors would be willing to assist actively in implementing such a system for just 5 per cent of this figure. Anyone interested?

problem is what information and for what purpose. The requests must still be processed by a painfully inadequate indexing system. The same difficulty arises with defaults. Deep down, we are up against the same obstacle as in the previous case: obtaining meaning from a document in free text. There are search engines that try to do that. But most of them are rudimentary, often requiring intensive training by the user, a very boring and difficult task. Typically they only work well in stable environments.

- *Support for the KIA pyramid.* Here, the situation is very primitive. As a general rule, there is technology available at least to attempt it. Further on in this chapter, we will comment on the most promising. However, to make progress, a much deeper understanding is required about the nature of the processes to be supported. Again most applications deal with local environments, without trying to combine them into an overall system. However, even simple applications can be very helpful if they are carefully designed. In the last section of this chapter, we will briefly describe a very simple system which we have used in practice to implement some of the improvement ideas explained in the book.

*The components of a KMS

Figure 13.2 shows a possible architecture for a KMS that would cover the entire spectrum of potential applications implied by this book. Of course, many other configurations are possible, so this architecture should only be understood as an example of a design covering the functions that should be contained in a KMS.

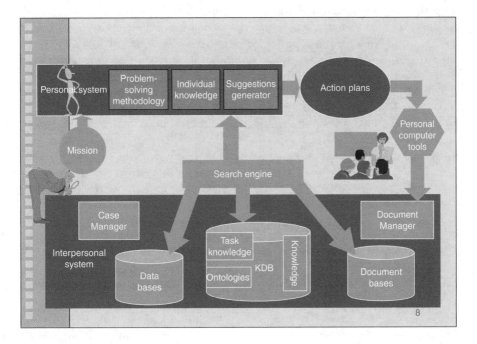

Figure 13.2 A comprehensive KMS

There are three different subsystems within this design.

- *Personal system.* The support system for all processes whose centre is a single agent. The personal system supports the bottom layer of the KIA pyramid and provides the necessary interfaces to obtain inputs from the second layer.
- *Interpersonal system.* This is responsible for coordinating and obtaining synergies through the use of interpersonal data and knowledge.
- *Action system.* This is composed of the normal applications that the firm uses for control and decision making in operations. This subsystem must provide the interfaces so that the agent's problem-solving activity, which takes place mainly within the personal system, can reach the BAS in a form that can improve customer service.

Personal system

The personal system includes three functions: support for problem solving, individual knowledge handling, and suggestions generation.

The support for problem solving should cover the basic aspects explained in Chapter 1. Specifically, Figure 13.3 shows a number of issues in which technology could contribute to expanding the individual agent's capacities, indicating the issues' present status (by means of faces[3]). We have confined ourselves to identifying the most feasible aspects. All of the areas indicated have been studied (particularly in the literature on artificial intelligence) and offer the promise of simple applications with real usefulness, even though they are currently in the prototype stage and lack any actual practical application.[4]

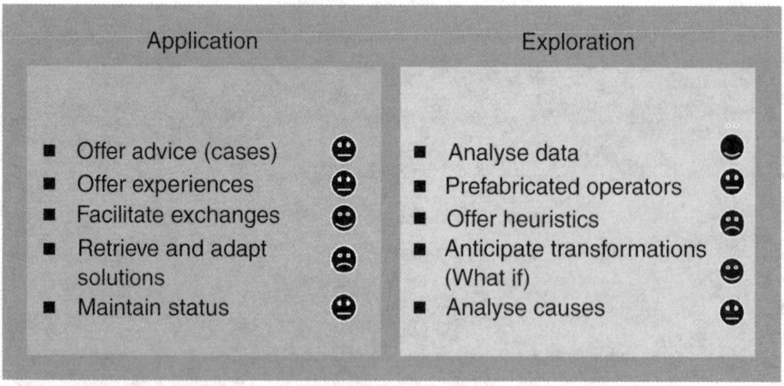

Figure 13.3 Support needs in problem solving and state of the art in 2002

---

[3] We use unsmiling smileys because we do not dare to design a reasonable scale for judging applicability. If the reader does not like our method, he can replace our smileys by others he can design himself.

[4] Possibly because there has not yet been a market that demands them. We are sure that when this book is published, an enormous market will be created which will be screaming for this type of application, which will be pioneered by our country. And, in gratitude, they'll build a monument to us in a street of some town … right?

Individual knowledge handling requires tools that assist in the formulation of hypotheses, performing deductions, doing preliminary analyses, or creating association of facts – All of these aspects are typically related with creativity or innovation. Decision making, particularly in intellectual services, requires a great number of different types of knowledges. When a wage scale is modified, for example, it is necessary to view the situation from different angles, relate it to previous experiences and other types of activities contemplated within this subsystem.

Finally, the suggestions generator is a type of functionality which must recognize the basic features of the problem being addressed and help to find, within the knowledge to which the system has access, the stored knowledge that can provide anchors, references or examples to the agent. We will talk about this subsystem in greater detail later. For the moment, suffice to say that this aspect has been studied in some depth by the ILS group (Shank, 1997).

Interpersonal system

The interpersonal system is more complex. On one hand, it includes the three main databases: the firm's database, the knowledge database (KDB), and the document database. The firm's database can be managed with the ERP or by using conventional applications. However, the other two databases require specialized managers that retrieve stored items according to their structure. The greatest difficulty with these managers is the interfaces, how to recognize the object's structure and how to recognize the agent's desires. To address this, advanced search engines need to be developed, somewhat along the lines of web search engines but with improved capacities.

Action system

The action system must contain the agent's desktop. The personal computing tools are probably the best tools to use in implementing an action system, and we have found this to be so in several companies. For example, a simple spreadsheet, combined with some simple Basic programmes, can provide a large part of the necessary functionality. The addition of a sophisticated electronic mail programme,[5] such as Lotus Notes, completes a context in which the agent's work can be performed with ease. Some companies have used these tools to implement complex support systems, which include some forms of knowledge management. The chief design criterion is to keep it simple. The agent will carry out most of the interactions in this subsystem and complications will add an additional challenge that is irrelevant[6] for competitiveness.

*KMS for the people: a 'simple system'

A KMS that sought to encompass the entire spectrum of knowledge management would be a very complicated system. It would probably require a major overhaul

---

[5] We remind the reader that we have already discussed the use of e-mail in Chapter 11.

[6] In the explicit sense of relevance used in this book.

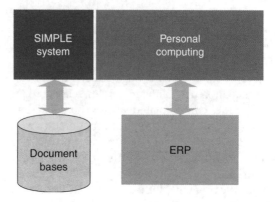

Figure 13.4 A simple system

of the firm's information system from a completely different viewpoint. The datum is no longer the information unit but the elementary knowledge item, and processing this information would require the presence of sophisticated reasoning tools which are not even fully available at prototype stage.

But there is hope! The hope consists of implementing only the personal subsystem, supplementing the action system's personal computer tools. In Figure 13.4, this object is called a simple system. This system concentrates solely on the permanent improvement system's basic processes. But it has the great advantage in that it can be developed on top of the existing IS and technologies can be used in its development that can be found on the shelves of computer stores. In most cases, it is necessary to supplement the existing databases with a document database to capture the relevant documental information. In personal applications, it is not difficult for the agent to index the documentation that he/she handles.

It is essential to integrate the single system in the agent's desktop. The tools must be readily available and organized so that no mental leaps are needed to use them. Remember that, under knowledge management, an agent does not follow just procedures, as in many traditional companies. Therefore, the work environment cannot be organized by procedures, as most ERPs do, but following the internal cycle model and the elementary processes described in Chapter 1.

The next few years will probably witness a change of paradigm in personal computer applications related to the aspects we are discussing. The work environment must change dramatically. The present computer environments, based on the desktop paradigm (Macintosh type), are insufficient for easily including the required permanent improvement tools. An example of what this new environment could be like, albeit still in a very primitive form, can be found in Epistemics' PCPACK system [www.epistemics.co.uk].

*An example of a simple system

In this section, we present a summary of a simple system used in a pharmaceutical company in order to improve its activities.

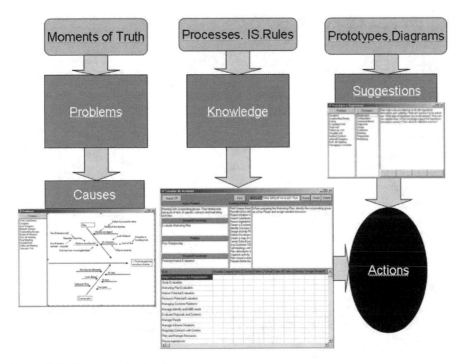

Figure 13.5   Structure of a simple system

This case concerns a business unit specialized in cardiology which sells pharmaceutical products to hospitals. The firm's ultimate customer is the hospital's physician and the unit's efforts are focused on giving him a good service.

The purpose of the simple system in question is to help in using the knowledge existing in the company to improve customer service. The system's methodological substrate originates in the approach of Chapters 9 and 11. The system revolves around a database which forms the system's backbone. See Figure 13.6 for a partial listing of tables in the database.

Of the tables contained in the database, we would like to highlight the following:

- *Moments of truth.* A detailed analysis of the moments of truth, including all firm's interactions with the customer throughout the product's lifecycle.
- *Knowledge database.* A list of the knowledge existing in the business unit using a format similar to that in Chapter 8.
- *Problems.* A problems table obtained by analysing each interaction within the moments of truth.
- *Ishikawa.* Cause and effect charts for each problem, made by the team members (in this case, in two-person groups).
- *Suggestions.* Lists of possible actions and the scope of their application, obtained from other business units that had performed a similar process.
- *Actions.* Actions to solve the problems specified and thus improve the service.
- *Process analysis.* A table with the results of the analysis of the unit's processes, obtained using the WWWWH technique.

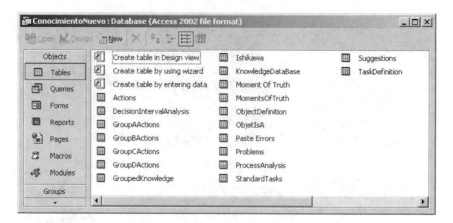

Figure 13.6   Databases of a simple system

- *Standard tasks.* A table in which cognitive operations are decomposed into subtasks in accordance with the KADS methodology (Schreiber *et al.*, 1999). This table is useful for suggesting possible actions.

The system tries to guide the user in creating actions that use existing knowledge to destroy the detected problems. The basic tool is the table of Figure 13.7, the core structure for the process. The table contains a matrix with problems in columns and knowledge groups (the different types of knowledge are grouped to make them more manageable) in rows. Each intersection is an action possibility. The top right window is an editor where the user can enter the description of his suggested action(s).

Figure 13.8 shows a suggestions window that the user can pop up at any time. This window lists the problems and the KADS prototypes that help in formulating suggestions. A suggestion appears in the window on the right.

The knowledge database is handled from another window (Figure 13.9), providing a layered access to the KDB's entire structure. In the middle window, the user can disaggregate knowledge, ask for explanations and select knowledge items for the object and action given in the description.

Lastly, the system provides access to the Ishikawa charts and other chart-type information. Figure 13.10 shows the window corresponding to an Ishikawa chart.

Figure 13.11 gives a complete view of the application with several windows open simultaneously around the actions window.

In the figure, the actions window is in the centre, the suggestions window at the bottom right, the knowledge handler at the top right, the Ishikawa chart window at the top in the middle, with a fragment of a KADS chart appearing behind it. An outliner is shown in the middle left and finally at the bottom, appears the knowledge group query window, which changes the several level of aggregation.

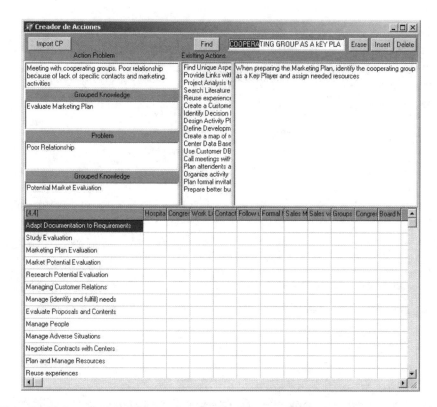

Figure 13.7 Crossing knowledge with problems to generate action

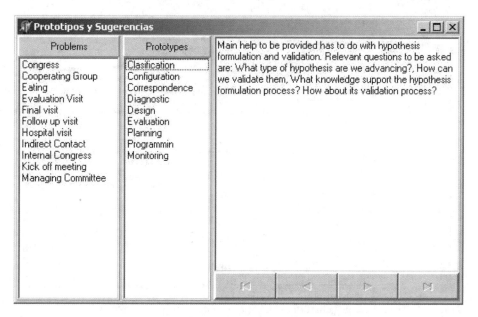

Figure 13.8 Suggestions window

308

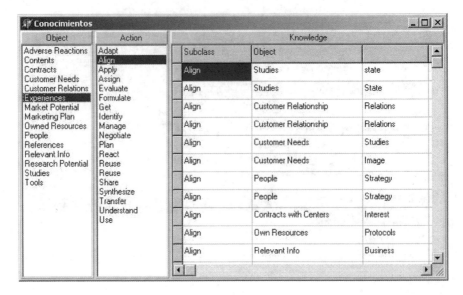

Figure 13.9   Knowledge base

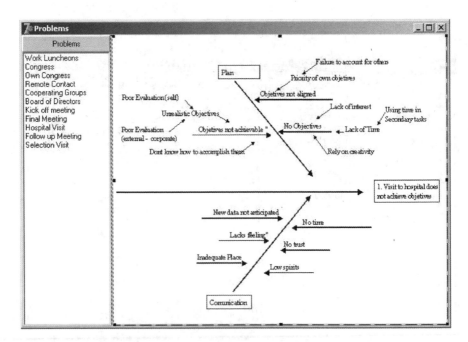

Figure 13.10   An Ishikawa chart of a critical moment of truth

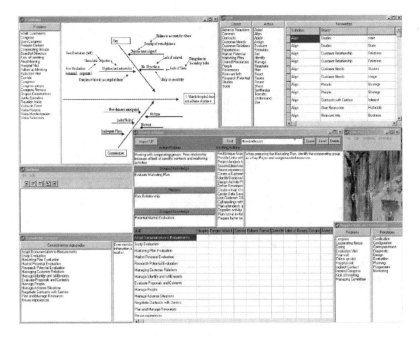

Figure 13.11   Complete view of the application

In practice, all of these windows will never be active simultaneously. The figure is simply intended to show the system's complete functionality.

*The implementation technology

Many approaches are possible to support the basic processes. The technology that is currently most promising is the case-based reasoning (CBR) technology.[7]

What is a case in this sense? A case is a textual description of a situation that includes the following items

1. A description of the context in which a decision had to be made.
2. The alternatives available.
3. The decision made.
4. The reasons for the decision.
5. The result obtained.
6. The learning resulting from the entire situation.

A case is therefore a brief description of a complete experience, including its moral[8]. A case is simply an element of the firm's perceptional memory, a memory of a certain action and the results obtained when it was performed.

---

[7] Mentioned in Chapter 8.
[8] Something like a modern version of an Aesop's fable. A proverb is a case too, but a very short one!

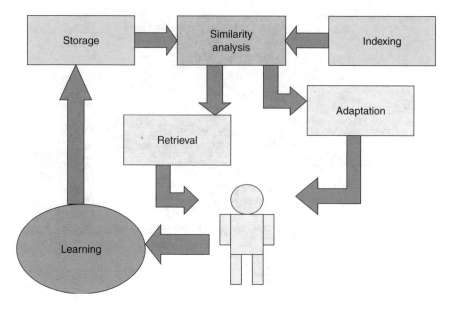

Figure 13.12   The services of a CBR

If we could file all of the firm's cases, we would have a repository of everything that has happened in it for the betterment of future generations. A good idea, but rather unwieldy ...

Things start to look up when we find out that the technology for handling case databases is already (fairly) available if we are dealing with a few hundreds of cases. And that acceptable procedures are available for finding cases that are 'similar' to a certain case. Technology enables cases to be retrieved from a description of a situation from which we wish to obtain 'similar situations'. Therefore, a case database enables access to the firm's historic memory with relative ease, retrieving and comparing previous situations that have a specifiable similarity with the situation facing us.[9] Figure 13.12 shows the services of a CBR.

A case database renders services that go beyond the mere retrieval of cases. Specifically, typical CBRs can provide the following services:

- *Storage*. Storage of cases in textual form.
- *Indexing*. Creation of indexes for the rapid retrieval of similar cases.
- *Retrieval*. Mechanisms for specifying the desired search, the degree of similarity desired in the result, etc.
- *Analysis of similarity*. Determination of the significant differences between the situation specified in the search and the cases retrieved.
- *Adaptation*. Forms of adapting the retrieved cases to the situation on hand.

---

[9] Let's say that it is the firm's old-timer who, at its employees' request, recounts the company's past feats ...

- *Learning or broadening.* Automatic filing of the experiences obtained by the system itself or from the interaction with the user.

An important point to make at this point is that a CBR is not just a textual search engine like, say, Yahoo! or Lycos. In many search engines, the system simply checks whether the words specified are present in the text being analysed. With a CBR, the search is much more intelligent, since its purpose is to identify situations that are *similar* to a described situation. Perhaps an example will help understand the subject better.

Let us suppose that a bank has a CBR for handling customer complaints. Here, a case is a complaint (Example 13.1).

Assume that a clerk at a branch receives a complaint of the type 'I've been debited a bill that isn't mine.' What should he do? Many times the normal procedure would be to ask his boss. This enormously underuses people's talent. What would be done if there was a CBR? The complaint would be entered in text form. The computer could obtain the case given in Example 13.1 by a reasoning such as the following:

1. The sentence doesn't say who is making the complaint. However, as it is a complaint, I assume that it is being made by a customer.
2. An 'invalid commission' is a 'collection error'. As an 'invalid bill' debited is also a 'collection error', the present case is relevant.
3. Failing further information, the story explained in Example 13.1 is relevant for the present complaint and is retrieved from the case database.

Note the key points 1 and 2, that include the need to make a hypothesis and the deduction of similarity between two concepts. This is not a heroic exploit by the computer. It needs the right technique, but it is within the reach of technology. In our desktop computer, we have a file with more than 65,000 terms interrelated by similarity. For example, the computer 'knows' that a chair is a piece of furniture. It knows, in the sense that it is capable of calculating that a chair and a settee are both specific cases of items of furniture and, therefore, similar. Semantic networks (see Appendix) are one way of implementing these wonderful operations.

Example 13.1 Case of a complaint

'The customer complained because we had charged commissions for conversion from pesetas to euros, arguing that, according to the European Union, no commissions should be charged for this operation. After consulting with the head office, it was seen that the customer was right and the commission charged was returned to him. The customer came back, quite annoyed, saying "How many commissions have you charged me illegally without me realising it?" To settle the matter, we offered to compensate him, paying default interest, and this was done shortly after. We have learned that returning the money does not settle the problem; compensation must be offered for the harm caused.'

The CBR databases are a suitable information substrate for supporting the KIA processes. In their most elementary form, any of the KIA processes can be supported simply by providing cases similar to a current situation, with the concept of 'similarity' depending on the process in question. More specifically, the role of the CBRs in the basic processes is as follows:

1. *Creativity*. Here the type of retrieval to be performed depends upon the type of creativity. For example, in the case of exploratory creativity, the system must provide user-guided navigation capacities. In this way, it can go from one case to another 'similar' case, suggesting possible paths for exploration and enabling the exploration of situations that are increasingly distant but 'relevant' for the initial situation.
2. *Innovation*. The system must retrieve experiences on how to solve the blocking factors. The plausible presence of particular blocking factors must be deduced from the description of the situation. Then, the system must offer help in the form of related cases with their solution. The interaction with the IS may help understand the blocking factors.
3. *Problem solving*. This is the most natural domain of the CBRs. In this aspect, they are very similar to the use of cases in teaching. The description of a problem must be compared with cases that contain specific methodologies. The methodologies are then the plausible action guidelines.
4. *Relevance*. Here, non-interactive extraction must be used. The CBR's engine must analyse the similarity of existing cases on the basis of the company's service policies. It must then determine the discrepancies or adaptation defects and list the potential service problems. This list of problems helps the user in setting priorities.

Example 13.2 NEC's system

All of these actions have been put into practice by pioneering companies in this field. For example, NEC has implemented a case-based system for software quality control. The system uses a specific approach, the Experience Sharing Architecture, to share knowledge between the organization's members. From the software viewpoint, the system has been mounted on top of an ERP's database so that the extractions are performed using SQL (the query system of the ERP's database). A front end interacting with the user converts the text of the case queries into SQL commands, which interrogate the database. This minimizes the number of elements to be developed and makes use of the existing traditional infrastructure.

Developing the complete system took more than 20 man-years. The most complicated task is preparing the cases. Ten people are assigned full-time to this operation. To date, 20,000 cases have been filed but the number of new cases included each month has decreased considerably in recent years due to saturation of subjects. NEC estimates the benefits of the application in several million dollars.

5. *Importance*. This is a case diffusion activity adapted to individual profiles. When the cases enter the CBR, the CBR's engine (or manager?!) decides which people may be interested in them and offers them information about the case.

*Implementation of a CBR system

To implement a CBR, certain organizational measures are required. Let's consider some of these:

1. *Implement a case collection organization*. It is necessary to identify who is authorized to enter cases in the system, the type of approval required, how to assess the cases' quality, etc. One typical way is to use e-mail to receive the cases from the users. Next, a working group is made responsible for evaluating all the cases and deciding which one to include into the CBR. Often, large case databases are not required and this function should keep the case database to a reasonable size. In many situations, a few hundred cases are more than enough to characterize the typical situations that arise in the firm.
2. *Index cases* and maintain the index structure between concepts. It is necessary to develop and maintain a thesaurus of relationships[10] between the concepts handled routinely in the firm. A standard dictionary or a body of general rules does not enable similar cases to be retrieved with the necessary precision. The similarity depends upon the context and each firm is different in this aspect. Normally, a number of people are responsible for maintaining the thesaurus, assisted by general ontologies.
3. *Design the processes* that interact with the user, on top of the CBR. The form that this process must be adapted to the firm's policies.
4. *Supervise the operation*. The firm's managers still have primary responsibility for ensuring that the learning takes place. The Simple system is a simple way of facilitating the storage and distribution of experiences, but it does not guarantee learning and, much less so, the learning's quality. This is a task that corresponds to managers in their role as educators.

The magic formula is usually to keep the case database simple and well-structured. Current technology cannot deal with thousands of cases. In contrast to the traditional databases, here the search is complicated because it requires deduction and search. Thus, the system's power rapidly decreases as the size growths large. The road is long, the pay is poor and the hardships are many.[11] As always, being competitive is being unique, different, and implementing a simple system is just one way of progressing along this road.

---

[10] Does the reader remember the 'ontologies'? Well, here they are again!

[11] As the long-suffering Roman soldiers in the Asterix series would say, as well as that oft-quoted 'Join the Legion and see the world...'.

14
Final Synthesis: Designing a PDM System

In this chapter, we conclude our work by presenting a list of actions which, if they are fully performed, will produce a rather complete implementation of PDM. Of course, considerable effort is required to implement the system in all its glory. However, the possible results are equally impressive. They represent a complete change in the way the firm works and point to goals that, until now, many companies have not even considered.

Implementation: general considerations

Implementing a complete system requires innovating to the very highest level and, probably, is beyond the reach of most companies. An innovation like this cannot be conjured up overnight and must be carried out step by step to adjust the challenge to the agents' capacity. However, we have decided to present a global design so that the reader can choose the path he wants to follow and how much he wants to implement from what has been presented here.

Of course, it is not necessary to implement most of the recommendations in order to start working. Implementation of the system must be decomposed into fragments, each one of which has a particular beginning and end, so that each fragment leads to specific advantages that everyone in the firm can see. As always, the KISS principle[1] operates here.

Likewise, it is not necessary to implement the system across the entire company. It is much more advisable to start the implementation in those parts of the company that can set an inspiring example to others. It should be remembered that implementing the entire system ends upon the company in question, its baseline situation, and management commitment and style. Creating expectations only to disappoint them should be avoided and the best option is to progressively deliver results that increase the system's appeal to the other people in the firm.

Each implementation project is a world in itself, as each company is too. Here, there are no standard solutions. For this reason, the largest hurdle in the implementation process is understanding how the ideas presented in this book can be

---

[1] KISS: Keep it simple, stupid – a basic principle in the world of operations.

adapted to the way the company works and how they modify the basic premises of its functioning. This adaptation process is individual for each company and must be monitored by senior management.

Implementing PDM is implementing an *organization system*, not a computer system. Therefore, the computer experts should stay out of it until they are needed to provide information system support to the system designed. The KMS – should be the culmination of the process, never the initiator. This has been one of the errors behind the failures of some companies that have mistaken knowledge management for the implementation of a certain ERP module having the same name, or even worse, for the implementation of a specialized information processing system. Likewise, the human resources and training departments should play the role of technical advisors, without any controlling role in the implementation process.

The methodologies

In this book, we have highlighted certain methodologies. As always happens in practice, a methodology is a procedure that is known but rarely followed. All of the known methodologies share this property to some extent. From the Cartesian methodology, *divide et impera*, to those presented in different chapters of this book, all of them share one important property: few use them explicitly. And yet they are so useful.

The secret behind this apparent contradiction was explained back in Chapter 1. A methodology is a set of rules for solving a problem. The more general it is, the wider the spectrum of problems in which it can be used, the less specific it is. Therefore, the less powerful it is in finding the solution. In other words, the general methodologies have significant exploratory phases. As they can solve any problem, it takes an effort to adapt them to the specific structure of a particular problem. When there is knowledge, this provides a straight path. Therefore, as our knowledge grows in a range of problems, we need less general methodologies, to the point of dispensing with them entirely. Only when we suddenly find ourselves immersed in a new problem does the need for the method appear.

This is well known in the research and consulting worlds. When there is a precedent, everything is simple. The reader should know that he has achieved his greatest success in applying the ideas given in this book when he is able to forget about their methodological content. Know, to forget. This will mean that he has knowledge, that he now 'knows' in its truest sense.

A general implementation scheme

The operating implementation of a permanent improvement project consists of identification, improvement and action in the seven action blocks shown in Figure 14.1.

Each block is identified by a different shading.

I. *The mission*: identification of the company's mission and its relevant dimensions.

II. *The operations*: the six action variables of operations that make up the basic elements to increase the company's efficiency and productivity.

III. *The customer*: identification of the interactions (MOT) and improvement in operations for customer satisfaction.

IV. *Knowledge generation system*: the three variables of knowledge generation: problem solving, innovation and creativity.

V. *The organization's knowledge bases*: the structure of the KDB, the configuration of how the knowledge is filed, making it available to the rest of the organization.

VI. *The mechanisms for taking knowledge to operations and service excellence*: relevance and importance.

VII. *Supporting elements*: the organization structure, ITP and use of technology.

These seven blocks break down into 14 tasks which are outlined in the following tables. These tasks are based upon a general vision of the firm's position (preliminary phase), a second vision that is more concentrated on a specific area, a business unit or a specific part of the firm's BAS (local phase), and a third where the general mechanisms are considered (general phase).

The 14 tasks are described below. We have highlighted in grey those tasks which are not directly discussed in this book.

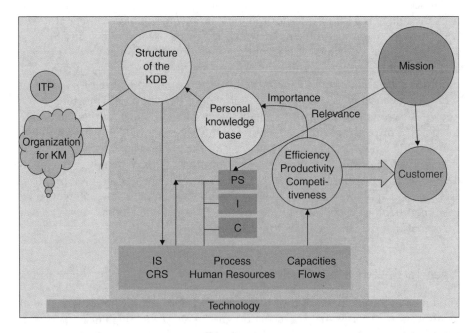

Figure 14.1 Action blocks for implementation (PS = problem-solving; C = creativity; I = innovation)

I. Preliminary phase

Task	Subtask	Comments
1. Diagnose operations. (References: Chapters 4, 5 and 6)	Analyse mission, way of competing, customer, most critical MOTs.	As a first step, it is necessary to ascertain the state of the operations' structure. This requires identifying the firm's mission and the priority dimensions.
	Analyse the BAS and the six variables.	The BAS's critical activities and adequate configuration of the six variables in accordance with the way of competing must be analysed, identifying the priority dimensions.
2. Identify the sources of problems, areas where problems are generated in the firm and which will be included in the scope of the improvement system. (References: Chapters 5 and 6)		The task is to make a map of the main problem sources in the firm, without going into details, because the problems are defined in the course of day-to-day activities.
	In processes.	Highlighting the parts of the process which can be improved.
	In the information system.	Highlighting the decision intervals.

II: Local phase

Task	Subtask	Comments
3a. Problem areas and competences for each area. (References: Chapters 1, 2 and 8)		List the general competences involved in the operation.
	List the main problem areas that may appear.	List the types of problem that may appear in the area, by order of probability and using a top-down method.
	Establish the competences that ideally should be held. Establish the competences that are currently held.	Develop a list of the necessary areas of competence, using the lists of problem areas. List the competences that are held now, performing a knowledge diagnosis.

II: Local phase (continued)

Task	Subtask	Comments
3b. Ontology. Creation of a basic ontology for the entire company. Participation and discussion. (Reference: Chapter 2)		Definitions of all of the objects that appear in the system, with their attributes and mutual relationships. Probable construction of a semantic network of relationships.
4. Problem-solving methodologies. (Reference: Chapter 1) For each problem area do:	Define an acceptable exploring strategy.	What is the exploration percentage that we are prepared to accept?
	Objects involved in solving a problem.	For each type of problem, list the objects that will be used in analysing the problem.
	Way of describing the problem at any given time.	Alternative ways of describing the problem's status at any given time, degree of detail and way of reporting progress.
	Basic transformations and how they are used.	Main types of operations that are used in the area to transform problems.
	Goals.	Way of measuring the solution's quality at any given time.
	Exploration management: Heuristics and possible methods.	Rules that must guide the exploration when it takes place. Possible aids and stop criteria.
	Establish quality criteria in problem solving.	Description of the way to measure the solution's quality and when it is possible to stop the exploration on the basis of its quality.
	Tools.	Supports required for the problem-solving process and supports available.
	Group work.	Role of the task forces, membership rules and functioning.

II: Local phase (continued)

Task	Subtask	Comments
5. Types of innovation to be introduced. (Reference: Chapter 10)		Innovation strategy in the area, in accordance with the firm's needs. Horizon and type of change.
	Innovators, innomanagers, innoreceivers	Relationships between the different agents involved in innovations, focusing on the agents who operate in the area.
	Type of problems generated: classification.	Types of innovation and determination of the knowledge profiles required for innovations. (Reference: Chapter 11)
6. Competence profiles. (Reference: Chapter 8)		Detailed knowledge profiles of the people operating in the area.
7. Challenges produced by the innovations. (Reference: Chapter 10)		Estimation of the size of the challenge that each type of innovation will pose to the agents, considering the knowledge required and actually held.
8. Type of creativity required to find actions. (Reference: Chapter 10)		Analysis of the type of creativity able to propose solutions for the area's problems.
	Procedures for developing it.	Ways of developing creativity that are applicable to the area.
	Tools.	Possible supports for creativity, including software support.
	Ways of creating groups.	Role of groups in the development of creativity.
	Resource allocation.	Resources that can be allocated to the development of creativity, particularly the agents' time availability.
	Suggestion mechanisms.	Suggestion systems and their internal functioning. Rewards and incentives.
	Implementation resources.	Resources allocated to the development of creativity.

III. General phase

Task	Subtask	Comments
9. Relevance. (Reference: Chapter 11)	Decomposition of general goals into subgoals.	Top-down decomposition of the firm's mission and creation of a quantification of the mission.
	Critical drivers.	Determination of the activity's critical drivers in each area.
	Reporting format: Balanced Scorecard.	Creation of an interrelated system of indicators, construction of reports and ways of evaluating actions.
	Expectations theory.	Ways of seeing the world that are needed in each area. Ways of addressing the cause and effect relationship.
	Observation tools.	Ways of measuring the impact of the problem to be solved on the internal or external customer.
	Local action logic.	Logical limits on the action depending on resource requirements and agent's initiative. Rules applied to the area.
10. Feedback. (References: Importance Chapters 9 and 11)		How the information about the results of our decisions is received, ways of obtaining short and long-term (internal and external) customer satisfaction.
	Identification of the critical MOTs.	What are the MOTs that have most effect on service and what are the root causes of the problems.
	Types of information to be supplied.	Relevant information according to the indicators system obtained.
	Accessibility of the information in each area.	Availability of data through the information system. Who is entitled to know what.
	Application of knowledge to MOT.	Generate improvement in service by applying knowledge and developing learning from this.
11. Scope of responsibility (Reference: Chapter 12)		How service responsibilities are distributed throughout the firm.
	Possibilities for initiative.	What is the initiative domain in which the agent can operate.

III. General phase (continued)

Task	Subtask	Comments
	Group versus individual.	Role of the group in decision-making.
	Organization by projects.	Ways of structuring the teams, duration, position and functioning.
12. Development plan for functional management. (Reference: Chapter 12)		Establishment of the features and responsibilities of the participants' different management levels.
	Working style.	Leadership style and ways of supplementing and supporting other people's work.
	Learning and teaching styles.	Identification of styles and establishment of the basic features of the educator manager.
	Responsibilities.	Basic roles of each management function throughout the system's structure.
	Indicators.	Basic for measuring management's performance from the improvement viewpoint: teaching and support.
	Motivation system.	The intrinsic, extrinsic and transcendent motivation systems used by management.
13. Technological support. (Reference: Chapter 13)		The knowledge exploitation system: management analysis for subsequent computerisation.
	Competence databases and their handling.	Creation of the knowledge databases. Initializing structure and uploading knowledge depending on the diagnosis.
	Search engines.	Identification of search and knowledge-sharing requirements. Determination of the properties required from the search engine.
	Document handling system.	Organization for handling all of the documents generated within the firm. Employee responsibilities and criteria.
	Indexing and retrieval.	Types of indexes to be maintained, responsibility for indexes.

III.   General phase (continued)

Task	Subtask	Comments
	Other sources of information: way of using e-mail. Application to areas.	The events register. Way of using e-mail and ways of retrieving the information. Detailed designed of the operation in each area.
	Integration.	Specifications of the complete system, particularly on the way of sharing knowledge. Limits and requirements.
	Definition of knowledge custodian groups.	Organization structure for formal progress of knowledge, form of knowledge units and people responsible for units.
14. Organization and role of management. (References: Chapters 12 and 13)		General organization system not considered previously.
	System monitoring, indicators.	Database updating system, monitoring of system's progress.
	General training plans.	External provision of knowledge for each area depending on needs and possibilities. The same for development of management support. Types of training and how to obtain it.

Remarks

We insist on starting the implementation with a pilot project in one of the company's units. This gives the opportunity for a compact group within the company to adapt the ideas to its environment. This group will become the internal 'crusader' of the approach's worth and disseminate it through the organization. Anybody who prefers to be cautious[2] is advised to implement first the approach presented in Chapter 9, which encompasses the following subset of the previous tasks:

- Task 2. Identify the areas where problems are generated in the company and which will be the target of the improvement system, concentrating on the processes and the information system.
- Task 3a. Identify knowledge and competences. Establish the knowledge currently held.

---

[2] Although we say that one wild duck is worth more than a 100 chickens ...

- Task 6. Identify the competence profiles.
- Task 10. Feedback. Identify the critical MOTs and apply knowledge to the MOTs.

Future developments

Problem Driven Management (PDM) is starting. There is no reason to think that a fully operational tool for its implementation will be available in the near future.[3] From this book's viewpoint, we end up with more questions than answers and, in this section, we would like briefly to list the main issues that remain to be solved.

1. The implementation of knowledge management (KM) is not well developed. There are very few actions that are specifically for KM. The originality of the general approach is not complemented with the possible detailed action.
2. There is no complete implementation methodology. The rough summary given in this chapter is only a list of things to be remembered, but is far from being a detailed methodology, such as that given in Chapter 9. The reason is obvious. There are virtually no precedents of the need to design and implement a meta-system – a system where, instead of performing actions, the environment is prepared so that others can perform the actions. A lot remains to be done here.
3. It is not clear what kind of support to give to problem solving and how to do it. Describing the process helps understand it, but it does not help much to support it. Classes of general transformations, criteria and heuristics should be typified so that they are readily available for use. The same thing happens with creativity.
4. Relevance and importance need a more extensive conceptual foundation than is given here. Experiences must be documented, establishing certain general guidelines to facilitate implementation.
5. There is no experience in organizational measures. It seems that the results reported are good, but there is no solid evidence of this. There may be other possibilities that are not even suspected today. Some serious empirical research is required that relates learning to organization structure.
6. The technological development is very elementary. All aspects of knowledge management should be supported by technology but, as yet, these objects are not receiving the required treatment. Both the rules and the cases systems are very primitive and have not given the results that were hoped.
7. A new paradigm is needed to enable the information system to put the improvement system on the agent's desktop. The system should be accessible

---

[3] The authors are helping a large software company in implementing a system along the lines in this book. Curiously enough, as usually happens, knowledge management seems to have gone slightly out of fashion without ever having been used to its full potential. This is one more example of how quickly concepts wear out in a market that needs new concepts with increasing frequency to 'sell new things' to companies. *O tempora, o mores!*

as simply another element from among those handled during daily work – something like an extension of the electronic mail program. If this is not so, the attempts to develop technological support systems will encounter application problems. The paradigm must also be very simple to use – within the reach of anyone who can operate a computer. The present systems are excessively time- and effort-consuming.

8. Being dependent upon many technologies and methodologies, knowledge management inherits the primitive state of many of them. Not even psychology has answers for many of the questions that are raised. As we have seen, sometimes the answer is hinted in the field of Artificial Intelligence, which is one of the few sciences that has concerned itself with implementation problems. A review of the true value of what is available and the ease with which it can be implemented has yet to be performed. We have no idea what part of the research performed in Artificial Intelligence during the last forty years may be really useful for PDM. For example: 'Does Soar provide a suitable foundation for an improvement support system? What can it contribute from the practical day to day viewpoint? Can it act as a complement to reasoning? How does one implement an effective TMS, assuming that it can be done?' If these understanding-facilitating concepts were ready for use in applications of some significance, knowledge management would be able to draw on a highly developed, unique technology based on decades of high-quality work.

We insist that there is no reason to think that these issues will be solved immediately. In fact, many of them continue to be in the same state as when we decided to explore this field more than 15 years ago. A lot has been done but what we have found out is more related with understanding than with action and often borrowing concepts from other disciplines. In their prologue to *Theory of Games*, John Von Neumann and Oskar Morgenstern say: 'It took physics more than 2,000 years of careful observation, culminating with observers of unparalleled calibre such as Tycho Brahe, Copernicus and Galileo, to create the substrate for the brilliant synthesis of Isaac Newton. There is no reason to think that progress will be quicker in the field of social science.' Well, dear reader, we must part here until 2,000 years from now, when we will meet again to witness the wonderful synthesis. Until then, may the gods smile on you!

Appendix: Some Basic Techniques

In this appendix, we summarize some of the basic tools used in most of the procedures presented in this book. Our purpose is to show the reader that a lot has been written in this field and that, therefore, there is more than one way of doing things. Almost any reasonable procedure can be justified. So the reader is advised to decide which is his favourite procedure and use it in applications. The most important thing is to maintain consistency over time. Once a procedure is chosen, it should not be changed unless the defects should prove to be overwhelming.

This appendix only contains a brief description of the possibilities. We refer the interested reader to the specialized literature for more details.

Influence diagrams and semantic networks

An influence diagram is the graphic representation of the relationships between a series of objects. The objects are portrayed as nodes (circles) on a chart, which is constructed using the relationships between objects as arrows. For example, the chart in Figure A1 shows a diagram associated with accounting. Specifically, it is the influence diagram of a group of ledger accounts concentrating in a single relationship which shows how the accounts are closed. Each node on the chart represents an account and each arrow represents 'the account is closed on' relationship.

As the reader can see, in this chart all of the arrows point in a certain direction, because the direction in which the accounts are closed is significant. If we have an arrow pointing from node i to node j. Node i, the arrow's origin, is usually called the 'father' (or ascendant) of j. Reciprocally, j is usually known as a 'son' (or descendant) of i. There are relationships that must be represented by an arrow pointing in both directions. This is the case of the symmetrical relationships, such as 'i is a brother of j'.

Sometimes in a chart of this type information is added about the attributes of the nodes and possibly of the arrows. In Chapter 3, we saw a classic case: the PERT chart, in which the nodes represent operations or activities, and the arrows relationships of precedence between activities.

Various relationships can be represented on the same chart if different types of arrows are inserted. This is usually done by associating with each arrow a label indicating its type. The result is a semantic network. In these networks, a node can represent either an object or a class of objects. In semantic networks, the different nodes are joined by varied relationships. Two of the most frequently used relationships are IS_A and IS_PART. The IS_A relationship specifies that the destination of an arrow is a subtype (or a specific case) of the object associated with the arrow's starting point. The IS_PART relationship indicates that the target node is a part of the object associated with the starting node. However, there are many other possibilities, such as 'speak-with', 'is-influenced-by', etc. Allen uses this type of diagram in his classic study on innovation to represent the communication relationships between the members of research units, which led him to discover the most influential agents. The diagram of Figure A2 shows a communication network between people. There are four types of relationship, differentiated by the different types of arrow. For example, the dark-coloured arrows mean 'trusts technical competence', the light-coloured arrows mean 'personally distrusts', and so on.

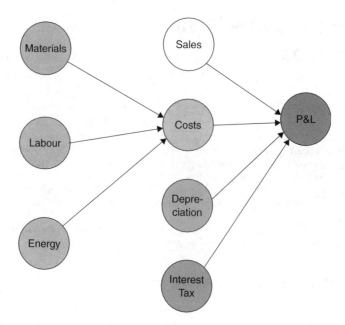

Figure A1 Diagram associated with accounting

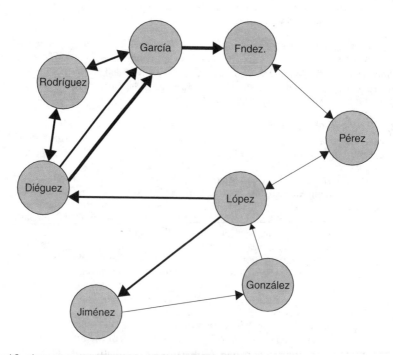

Figure A2 A communication network between people

In its general state, this type of diagram is a graph, or rather a multigraph, a mathematical object with a long history behind it since Euler strolled around Koenisberg.[1]

A particular case, perhaps the most interesting one, is the class of tree-shaped graphs, without cycles between nodes (closed paths). Many tree-shaped graphs have appeared in this book. The most commonly used have been: the hierarchical or top-down decomposition tree and the grouping tree.

A note about implementation

The graphic representation of a series of relationships is interesting because its overall structure can be seen at a glance. Globalness is a known property of these representations. Why is it that way is not clear, but it is probably associated with the perception of shapes by humans. However, a graphic structure can be time-consuming to create and maintain. Drawing directly a two-dimensional graphic representation, gives rise to topological problems of locating the nodes and arrows on the medium. This rapidly gives rise to the need to move things from one place to another, to make room or to enable the representation to be seen more clearly. On paper, this means continually erasing, with all of the problems this causes. On the computer, the visible work area is normally small. Screens have a very limited space and on them, globalness is soon lost – with only the immediate drawing area being visible, and with that, one of the most prized features of graphic representations is lost too.

For this reason, other methods of representation have been developed that provide a simpler way of handling objects. In the case of tree-shaped graphs, a two-dimensional representation can be reduced to a one-dimensional or sequential representation, which simplifies its construction enormously. The simplest way to do this is using an indenter or outliner. Figure A3 shows a simple but effective indenter. These tools are extremely useful for the applications described in the next section. Sometimes, the indenter helps to construct a tree, and then the tree is represented in chart form to improve communication. Good indenters can do this automatically.[2]

Hierarchical or top-down decomposition

This consists of representing the relationship 'is a subclass of' so that the decomposition into subclasses of a node is a partition, that is, is exhaustive and exclusive. This means that the group of sons of the same 'father' is composed of classes that have an empty intersection (they have no common individuals) and, together, account for all of the possibilities (each individual in the father class is a member of one or other of the 'son' classes). This type of

---

[1] One of the first appearances of the graph concept is related with Euler's strolls around the centre of the city of Koenisberg, in Germany, where he lived. The city was parted in the middle by a river, with a central island. The banks and the island were joined by an elaborate system of bridges. Euler wondered on one of his walks whether there was a way to do the complete route and come back home crossing all the bridges, but only once. From this trivial exercise was graph theory born!

[2] But not the primitive indenters included in Microsoft Office. Some day, Microsoft should package a decent indenter with this product, as Symantec did with More. Although for some reason More fell by the wayside, its implementation of the indenter-presenter-document organizer combination was so much better than the tools available in Office.

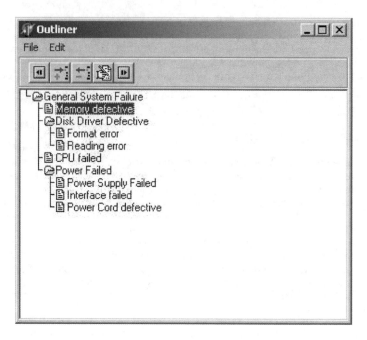

Figure A3   A simple outliner

chart has a tree shape and is usually built by starting with the highest-level 'father', progressively decomposing each of the 'sons' until the person performing the operation decides he has had enough. Of course, the sooner he tires, the 'grosser' the decomposition obtained is. The longer he continues, the 'finer' the decomposition is.

The procedure for carrying out this decomposition is the following:

1. The starting point is a single general node.
2. A split is generated for each of the tree nodes that are already represented. One way of generating a split is to concentrate on one of the object's attributes and write a partition of its values. For example, if we are decomposing the object 'man', we can concentrate on his attribute 'height' and split its values into two categories, 'tall' and 'short'.
3. This procedure is repeated in an arbitrary order until a sufficiently fine decomposition has been generated for the purpose of the analysis.

Generating a grouping tree

Here the process is the reverse of the previous paragraph. The starting point is a list of all the objects that must be grouped. In addition, the agent has an explicit or implicit set of similarity criteria. These criteria form the basis of the grouping process. Often, objects have attributes whose values are used to compute the similarity criteria.

There is an enormous variety of grouping methods, devised for different types of similarity criteria and object attributes. We will mention a few here, referring the reader to the specialized literature for further information.

With attributes

This case is applied when the objects can be described fully by a series of attributes. This offers the possibility of using powerful calculation methods, depending upon the grouping criteria.

1. *When a distance between two objects given by a function can be defined.* For example, in many applications, the distance between two objects is measured by the sum of the squares of the differences between individual attributes. This criterion is called the Euclidean distance, or sum of squares. In this case, the use of statistical methods can be considered, and the most commonly used of these are the clustering methods. The idea behind these methods is to perform successive groupings, putting together first those that have the smallest distance between them. As there are many ways of carrying out this procedure, this process can produce a large number of different groupings.
2. *When a distance cannot be defined,* more general methods can be used, such as the Classweb, or Coweb (Russell and Norvig 198/95). This method is based upon the creation of a classification tree which uses the attributes to obtain the right group for each object. For example, in a grouping of people, the method can conclude that the most discriminatory attribute is height, obtaining a group of tall people and a group of short people. It can then decide that the next attribute is the weight, obtaining two additional groups, and so on.
3. *Constraint satisfaction methods.* In these cases, a series of conditions that must be met by the grouping's objects are defined and a search process is begun which tries to meet these conditions. The process must be performed mechanically and, being based on exploration, it may be very time-consuming.

No attributes are defined

1. *A general method when qualitative relationships can be defined* between objects, for instance, when a semantic map of similarities can be constructed, is the application of graph concepts. For example, one of these methods considers similarities called *subsumptions*. One graph is subsumed in another when the former is part of the latter, in the sense that a correspondence can be found between the two which includes one in the other. This criterion is used as a comparison criterion, for example, in [Arcos and Plaza 1993]. A major drawback of the criterion is the intrinsic difficulty in calculating it, with increasingly lengthening times as the graph's size increases.
2. *Logical methods.* In this approach, each object is associated with a set of logical propositions. Propositions characterizing the grouping are also defined. The calculation process tries to deduce a result which meets the desired conditions, starting from the axioms established for the objects. The difficulty with this method lies in the process's explosiveness due to exploration. One advantage is that the method renders it necessary to give a detailed description of the process's starting point and result, which may enable shortcuts (knowledge) to be used. This method is closely related to the constraint satisfaction methods.
3. *Intuitive methods.* Here, one or more agents cooperate in defining groups without having an explicit grouping procedure. One of these methods, our favourite, is the KJ method. It often happens that either not all of the power of the KJ is needed or it is not wished to spend the necessary time to do it or simply the agent must perform the grouping himself, without any help from others. In these cases, a simplified KJ works reasonably well. An outliner is used to create brief descriptions of the objects and they are progressively

grouped in folders, using personal semantic similarities. However, there are many other methods that the reader can consult in the specialized literature. These methods suffer from two problems. On one hand, they cannot be computerized, which means that they are difficult to implement for large grouping problems. Second, being intuitive methods, they depend on the agents performing the grouping.

As can be seen, the agent has a wide variety of techniques available to him. This often causes perplexity. Therefore, we have taken the liberty to give our favourite techniques, which may guide the reader in creating his groupings. We use the following process:

1. Try to give attributes to the objects.
2. If the Euclidean distance (or a similar distance) is meaningful, use a clustering technique. Here, 'similar' means that our statistical programme includes that distance among the usable distances.
3. If the Euclidean distance does not work, use the classweb method.
4. If there is no possibility of defining numeric attributes and you do not wish to use the complete KJ, use a simplified version.
5. In all other cases, use the complete KJ.

Cause and effect chart

This consists of listing the four or five main causes of a problem and arranging them in a fishbone style to analyse and explore them until a sufficient level of description is reached that identifies the ultimate causes. This implies the involvement of the people directly related with the problem. (See Figure A4.)

To construct a cause and effect chart, the following procedure must be used.

(a) Place the problem in a square on one side of the work surface.
   Suggestion: Make sure that everyone agrees on how the problem is approached. Include all the information you can on the problem's 'what', 'where', 'when' and 'how much'. Use data to specify the problem.
(b) Write the main cause categories, connecting them to the fishbone or Ishikawa chart's backbone.
   • Be flexible regarding the main cause 'fishbones'. In a service process, the most traditional categories are: policies (decision rules), procedures (steps of a task), plant (equipment and space), and people. Also the medium (buildings, logistics and space) and measurement (calibration and data collection). There is no perfect set or number of categories. Fit the categories to the problem.
(c) Place the causes in the appropriate category.
   • During the search and analysis process, the possible causes can be placed in a category as it is generated, or after the entire list has been created. Both work well, but creating the entire list first maintains the creative flow of ideas without suffering any constraints from the categories of main causes, or the place in which the ideas fit in each 'bone'.
   • Some causes seem to fit in more than one category. Ideally, each cause must go to only one category but some of the causes related with 'people' may legitimately belong to two places. Place them in both categories and see what it looks like. Since this type of chart is a tree graph one can use an outliner to advantage.

The KJ grouping technique

The KJ method originated in anthropological science. Drawing from the idea that hieroglyphs transmitted messages, KJ proposes judging the similarity of concepts through the images evoked by each one. This method is particularly suitable when there are many

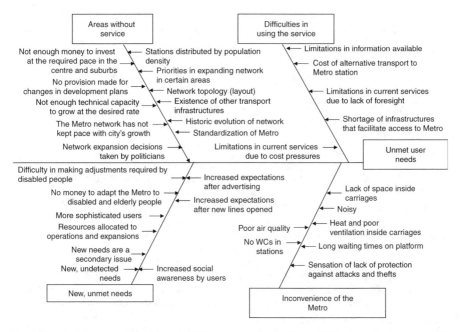

Figure A4   An Ishikawa chart for part of the metropolitan railway (Metro) service in a large city

non-numerical data, as the lack of options for statistical analysis makes it difficult to process them.

The KJ method is a bottom-up approach that starts with a list of concepts that are associated by affinity of images. The similarity between concepts is not syntactic (by words that are similar) but semantic (by images that suggest similar concepts). The emphasis on semantics rather than syntax arises from the recognition that there are certain features of language that inhibit human beings' creativity. A deliberate effort is required to break the dependence upon syntax and liberate the true meaning of qualitative data. The method postulates that the best way of summarizing the meaning of a sentence is through the images it evokes in the person reading it. Therefore, in order to judge the similarity between two concepts described by propositions, it is sufficient to compare the images evoked by each one in the recipient. The images evoked are based upon individual perceptions and may be different for each person. The perception of the same event by two people may give rise to totally different images.[3]

The KJ method is designed to exploit the group's creative potential. The level of creativity increases with the number of participants until it peaks when there are about 10–12 individuals in the group. From then one, including more people in the group is dysfunctional.

---

[3] This phenomenon is exploited in some psychological tests, such as Roxach's test, where the person expresses his vision of the world by verbalizing the perception conjured up by a certain drawing. In contrast to the test, which takes the figure as the datum and produces the verbal description, the KJ method takes the verbal descriptions and associates them with the images.

A detailed description of the KJ method[4] is beyond the scope of this book and the reader should refer to the specialized literature.[5] However, in the following pages, we briefly summarize each step's goals (Figure A5) and the tasks performed in each step.

Step 1: Prepare the material
The material is distributed to each participant in the group. The subject to be analysed is chosen.

Step 2: Hand out blank sheets
In this step, each participant is given some blank sheets.[6] A brief discussion is held on the subject in question.

Step 3: Write down problems
Nobody speaks during this step. Each group member writes down facts about the subject under discussion. The sentence should explain the problem's objective facts. Implied statements or sentences with only a few words are not accepted.

Step 4: First grouping level
The first objective of this step is to clarify the contents of each sheet. Once they are clarified, the sheets are pasted (in any order) on the wall. The second goal is to group the sheets by similarity of images. There should not be more than three sheets in each group. Each participant must think about the image suggested by each sheet and place those above images that are similar beside each other. Nobody speaks during this step. If there is repeated disagreement between two members of the group, each one draws the image evoked by the sentence and the images are compared, and the contradiction resolved.

Step 5: First-level titles
Each grouping must be given a title. The title must be a concise phrase which expresses the grouping's common feature. Each participant suggests a title and the group selects the most appropriate.

Step 6: Second grouping level
Step 4 is repeated by grouping the titles.

Step 7: Second-level titles
Step 5 is repeated again with the new titles of the second level groups.

Step 8: Compose the panel
Now the relationship between the top-level groupings is fully displayed and analysed. The participants use arrows to indicate the causal dependence or antagonism relationships.

Step 9: Assessment
In the last step of the methodology, the importance of the top-level titles is assessed.

---

[4] The methodology, as applied by us, has undergone some alterations and adaptations. This is due to its application and the authors accept full responsibility for this. According to the method's creator, there are 19 steps. Likewise, certain changes have been made in the methodology's application to make it culturally more acceptable and efficient. If the reader wishes to explore the methodology as it has been described by the original author, he can see (Shiba, 1993).

[5] The reader can find a more detailed description of the adaptation made by the authors of the KJ tool in B. Muñoz-Seca and J. Riverola, *Riqueza y conservación. La planificación de espacios naturales protegidos* (Publicaciones de la Conserjería de Medio Ambiente de la Junta de Andalucía, Seville, 1997). We have observed that the modifications make the method easier to use in a non-Japanese cultural environment. Of course, we have not tested it in a Japanese environment.

[6] Normally post-its or substitutes are used. A total of 20 are given to the entire group.

333

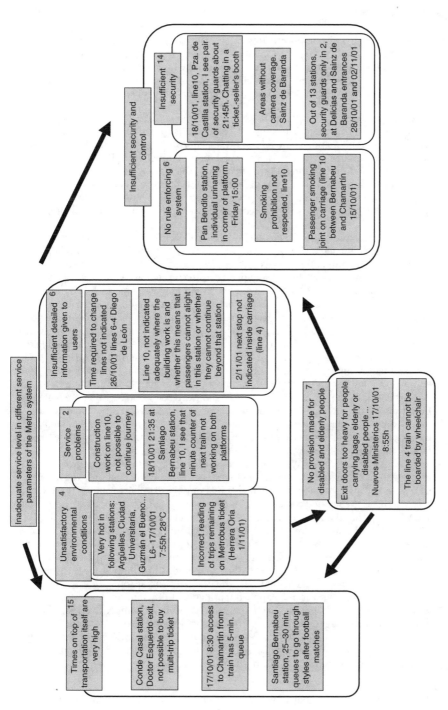

Figure A5 Example of a KJ

Assessing actions

When it comes to assessing and prioritizing actions, the variety of procedures that have been proposed is almost infinite. Therefore, there is no room in this appendix to review this field in depth. We will confine ourselves to a few approaches which we use and have given good results, particularly when working in a group. We assume the existence of a collection of objects that must be ordered under a series of criteria that are also stated explicitly.

1. *Individual assessment*
   - *Simple assignment* method. The simplest procedure is to define a scale, typically with five or seven grades, and assign values to the actions using this scale. If there are several criteria, the same procedure is performed for each one. The critical problem here is combining the different criteria into just one. If the scale is numerical and a mathematical operation can be used to combine the results of the individual assessments, one quick solution is to add each criterion's values. Better still, define weights and use them to weight the values. This is the procedure that we normally use to relate actions with the company's mission through the five criteria given in Chapter 4.
   - When the individual *scales are not numeric*, things become more complicated. One can use multi-valued preference assignment procedures (Raiffa and Keeney), but this is time-consuming and complicated and is only justified in important cases. Often, a simple process drastically reduces the number of objects to consider, if the number of criteria is small. This is the possibility of identifying the non-dominated objects. In a multicriteria classification, it is said that one object dominates another when the values of all the criteria in the former are equal to or greater than those of the latter. By eliminating the dominated objects, the alternatives are reduced to those that are not dominated, which often simplifies the process of evaluation. There are more sophisticated ways of exploiting the group of non-dominated solutions. One of the most interesting is the DEA (Data Envelopment Analysis) method (Cooper *et al.*, 1999). This method tries to identify non-dominated solutions under different conditions that add additional structure to the set of objects. For example, one could consider the existence of objects that are scaled-up from those of the sample (a company, for example, that is several times larger than one of the companies that are explicitly available). In this case, an object may be dominated by any of the 'virtual' objects introduced by the scaling and cannot not be chosen as the best. For further information, we refer the reader to the above reference.
   - *Assignment with restrictions.* When there is a risk that the agents will always give the highest score to all alternatives, it is common to restrict the possible valuations. The most typical way is to assign a total number of points that must be distributed among the different objects. This is the method we use to assess the mission's criteria. A good way is to assign 100 points so that the result can be easily interpreted in terms of percentage.
   - The literature abounds in methods for combining different criteria in a total order or at least for choosing the best from a number of objects. We will just mention Saaty's (Saaty and Vargas, 1994) AHP (Analytic Hierarchy Process), which compares all the pairs of criteria and the result is processed by logical methods to obtain weights that enable them to be combined while maintaining the original comparison.
   - All of the above methods can be applied repeatedly at different levels to combine and group criteria from a top-down decomposition of a general competitiveness criterion. The weights (or averages) method in particular is very simple to use and is our favourite, in spite of all the conceptual difficulties associated with it. In our experience, it is understood well and the result is explained easily in terms of the baseline components, which is usually a necessary condition for practical application.

2. *Group assessment*
   - The simplest method is that of weighted assignment. In this procedure, each participant performs an individual assessment of the objects. The participant states out loud

his individual assessments, which are summarised on a presentation medium (blackboard, projector) in view of everyone. The individual assessments are averaged and the result is used to set priorities. An important and highly recommended variant of this method is to criticise the assessments as they are presented. This way, the agent can see whether his assessment agrees with that of the rest and, if it does not, explain why. Thus, a kind of simplified Delphi method is performed, which helps enormously to decrease the scatter of the results.

- The group assessment is a special case of a multicriteria assessment. Consequently, all of the remarks made in the previous section are also applicable to this situation.

References (by Chapters)

Not all of the references included here are quoted in the text. There, we only included those that were directly relevant to the subject under discussion. In these references, we include most of the books that we consider to be useful for a comprehensive study of the subject and in which the reader can find ideas for applications or to improve his understanding.

Prologue

The literature on knowledge management is extensive, although not very concrete. There is an abundance of general books that highlight the concept's importance but offer few alternatives for implementation. As the reader will see, our preferences revolve around five books. Any reader wishing to progress in this area should acquire them and read them, although he should be warned that he won't find them easy going. These books present the five basic ideas that we use in the book. They are Pérez-López on organizations, Russell and Narvig on artificial intelligence, Schreiber et al. on intellectual processes, Newell on problem solving, and Simon on all the rest. Those five will be enough ... But for certain details[1] that have given us ideas on certain subjects throughout the book, we would like to quote a more detailed literature.

For a general approach, we recommend Morris, Quinn, 1992 and Quinn, 1997. Some classics are Polyani, Senge. Nonaka (Nonaka, 1991; Nonaka, 1994) was one of the first to draw attention to tacit and explicit knowledge, which is an interesting classification, but which we use little in this book because it does not seem very operational to us. As knowledge management is a basically interdisciplinary subject, we recommend reading certain classics on business management. We have already said that Simon is indispensable and we thoroughly recommend Pérez-López, although he is not easy to read. We include one of the few published attempts to apply these ideas to a specific field (Vidorreta). If the reader wishes to explore the nature of the problem in greater depth, he must read some of the basic texts such as Bunnin and Tsui-James, a compendium of philosophical issues, and Fetzer for a view of cognitive science. The book (Russell and Norvig) on artificial intelligence has had a decisive influence on the way we approach the transition between ideas and practice and the reader may find it interesting, even if the formal contents do not appeal to him. Of course, as all authors do, we must say that the best introduction to this book is our other book, perhaps a little outdated but still interesting (Muñoz-Seca). Of course IDE is not a book for the mind but rather for the stomach, but as they say, *primum vivere*.

Barancatto, R. *The Knowledge Connection*. Harvard Business School Press, 1991.

Bohn, D. and Peat, P.D. *Science, Order and Creativity* (2nd ed.). Routledge, 2000.

Bunnin, N. and Tsui-James, E.P. (eds), *Blackwell Companion to Philosophy*. Blackwell Publishers Ltd., 1996.

Clark, K. 'Knowledge, Problem Solving and Innovation in the Evolutionary Firm'. Harvard Business School Report, 1989.

Fetzer, J.H. *Philosophy and Cognitive Science*. Paragon, 1996.

Guilford, J.P. *Cognitive Psychology with a Frame of Reference*. Edits. Publishers, 1979.

Handy, C. *The Age of Paradox*. Harvard Business School Press, 1995.

IDE. 'La cocina del IDE'. Instituto de Desarrollo Empresarial, 1998.

---

[1] In a learned book, we must give the impression that we have read a lot. In this case, it is true, we have.

Morris, T. *If Aristotle ran General Motors: the New Soul of Business*. Henry Holt and Company, Inc., 1997.

Muñoz-Seca, B. and Riverola, J. *Gestión del Conocimiento*. Folio, 1997.

Nonaka, I. 'The Knowledge Creating Company'. *Harvard Business Review*, November–December (6), 1991, 96–194.

Nonaka, I.A. 'Dynamic Theory of Organizational Knowledge Creation'. *Organization Science* (February), 1994, 14–37.

Pérez-López, J.A. *Teoría de la Acción Humana en las Organizaciones: la acción personal*. Rialp, 1991.

Polyani, M. *The Tacit Dimension*. Doubleday, 1966.

Quinn, J.B. *Intelligent Enterprises*. The Free Press, 1992.

Quinn, J.B. *Innovation Explosion: Using Intellect and Software to Revolutionize Growth Strategies*. The Free Press, 1997.

Ruggles, R. 'The State of the Notion: Knowledge Management in Practice'. *California Management Review*, 40(3), 1998, 80–9.

Russell, S. and Norvig, P. *Artificial Intelligence: a Modern Approach*. Prentice Hall, 1995.

Senge, P.M. *The Fifth Discipline*. Doubleday/Currency, 1990.

Simon, H.A. *Science of the Artificial*. MIT Press, 1981.

Vidorreta, Joseba. *La gestión del conocimiento en el sector sanitario*. Asociación de Economía de la Salud, 1998.

Von Krogh, G. and Roos, J. (eds), *Managing Knowledge: Perspectives on Cooperation and Competition*. Sage Publications, 1996.

1 Knowledge and Problem Solving

This chapter draws its sources from an enormous quantity of literature that has analysed this subject during the last 40 years. In the references, we have included literature from three sources: artificial intelligence, methodology and cognitive science. In artificial intelligence, the book that should be read by anyone who wishes to gain more knowledge is Newell, 1990. This is a very readable synthesis of all the work on Soar, on which we have based a large part of our discussion. Other interesting works for this viewpoint are Newell and Bobrow. Russell and Norvig is, for us, the best general reference on AI. For methodology, an indispensable book is Polya, a classic that still has a great deal to say. The attempted sequel by Michalewicz and Fogel does not have the quality of Polya's book, but it is interesting for the good coverage of certain recent techniques, such as heuristics, genetic methods and others. For cognitive science, we have included different types of reference. Some (Jackendoff, Mayer) are more philosophical, while others are much more general (Anderson, Osherson and Smith) or applied (Cherniak). Fagin *et al.* is an excellent reference on formalization of reasoning about 'knowing', although it is very advanced and difficult to assimilate. Finally, we would stress the role that decisions analysis has played in structuring problem solving. From this viewpoint, Raiffa is still very valid and exciting to read.

Anderson, J.R. *Cognitive Psychology and its Implications*. W.H. Freeman, 1990.

Bobrow, D.G. and Collins, A. *Representation and Understanding: Studies in Cognitive Science*. Academic Press, 1975.

Cherniak, C. *Minimal Rationality*. MIT Press, 1990.

Dreidstadt, R. 'The Use, of Analogies and Incubation in Obtaining Insights in Creative Problem Solving'. *Journal of Psychology*, (7), 1969, 159–75.

Fagin, R. *et al. Reasoning about Knowledge*. MIT Press, 1995.

Flood, R.L. and Jackson, M.C. *Creative Problems Solving: Total Systems Intervention*. John Wiley & Sons, 1991.

Jackendoff, R. *Consciousness and the Computational Mind*. MIT Press, 1990.

Luce, R.D. and Raiffa, H. *Games and Decisions*. John Wiley & Sons, 1957.

Mayer, R. *Thinking, Problem Solving, Cognition*, 2nd ed. W. H. Freeman and Co., 1992.

Michalewicz, Z. and Fogel, D.B. *How to Solve It: Modern Heuristics*. Springer Verlag, 1999.
Newell, A. 'The Knowledge Level'. *Artificial Intelligence*, 18, 1982, 87–127.
Newell, A. *Unified Theories of Cognition*. Harvard University Press, 1990.
Osherson, D. and Smith, E. (eds), *Thinking: An Invitation to Cognitive Science. Visual Cognition and Action*. The MIT Press, 1990.
Polya, G. *How to Solve It: a New Aspect of the Mathematical Method*. Princeton University Press, 1945.
Raiffa, H. *Decision Analysis: Introductory Lectures on Choices Under Uncertainty*. Addison-Wesley, 1973.
Russell, S. and Norvig, P. *Artificial Intelligence: a Modern Approach*. Prentice Hall, 1995.
Simon, H. *Science of the Artificial*. MIT Press, 1981.
Springer, S.P. and Deutsch, G. *Left Brain, Right Brain: Perspectives from Cognitive Neuroscience*. W. H. Freeman and Company, 1997.

2   The Properties of Knowledge Within the Firm

For a general focus of knowledge in the firm and some applications, see Badaracco. As the subject is linked with the scientific method, anyone wishing to know more about it should see Popper. From the philosophical viewpoint, the subject has been discussed since (before) Aristotle. We recommend reading the classics and Bunnin gives an excellent historical synthesis, although the first part of the book dwells too much on Anglo-Saxon philosophy. To learn more about the classifications of knowledge Pérez-López is essential reading. Lamberts deals with other knowledge categories and types. For a view of the Kads methodology and its implications, see Wielinga. This same group has written a complete book on the subject (Schreiber). The book gives a detailed and very interesting presentation of a methodology for analysing intellectual processes. Some implications of this approach, particularly highlighting the excellent work of the Bellaterra group, can be obtained from Arcos, 1995, 1997. The definitive work on TMS is Forbus, which includes a detailed implementation of several types of TMS. Prahalad is the standard reference on the subject of competences, seen from the firm's viewpoint. Finally, an excellent book on bounded rationality, and which we have found very useful because it provides a very good summary of the different approaches to the subject that are possible, is Rubenstein.

Arcos, J.L. 'The Noos Representation Language'. Thesis, Polytechnic University of Catalonia, 1998.
Arcos, J.L. and Plaza, E. 'Learning and Reflection with Noos'. IIIA Report, Autonomous University of Barcelona, 1993.
Badaracco, J.L. *The Knowledge Link: How Firms Compete Through Strategic Alliances*. Harvard Business School, 1991.
Bunnin, N. and Tsui-James, E.P. (eds), *The Blackwell Companion to Philosophy*. Blackwell Publishers Ltd., 1996.
Clark, K.B. and Fujimoto, T. *Product Development Performance: Strategy, Organization and Change in the World Auto Industry*. Harvard Business School Press, 1991.
Forbus, K.D. and De Kleer, J. *Building Problem Solvers*. MIT Press, 1994.
Lamberts, K. and Shanks, D. (eds), *Knowledge, Concepts and Categories*. MIT Press, 1997.
Muñoz-Seca, B. 'Training for Continuous Improvement in the Firms and its Operations'. PhD thesis, University of Navarre, 1992.
Newell, A. 'The Knowledge Level'. *Artificial Intelligence*, 18, 1982, 87–127.
Pérez López, J.A. *Teoría de la Acción Humana en las Organizaciones: la acción personal*. Rialp, 1991.
Popper, Karl. *The Logic of Scientific Discovery*. Routledges, 1992.
Prahalad, G. and Hamel, C.K. *The Core Competence of the Corporation*. Harvard Business Review, 1990.
Rubinstein, A. *Modelling Bounded Rationality*. MIT Press, 1997.

Schreiber, G., Akkermans, H. and Angewierden, A. *et al. Knowledge Engineering and Management: the Common KADS Methodology.* MIT Press, 1999.

Wielinga, B., Van De Velde, W., Schreiber, G. and Akkermans, H. 'Towards a Unification of Knowledge Modelling Approaches'. In *Second Generation Expert Systems*. Eds David, J.M., Krivine, J.P. and Simmons, R. Springer Verlag, 1993.

3 First Practical Implications: Project Management

Mountains of paper have been written about project management. Most of this literature is fairly useless because once you have read one book, you have read them all. Representatives of this school, with more content than many others, are Graham and Karzner. Knowledge in project management has been addressed basically with respect to the development of 'intelligent' project management systems. For example, see Russell and Sathi, 1985 and 1986, which are old references, but not much progress seems to have been made in this field. For organizational issues, the reader can see Ancona and Cross. Finally, for intellectual processes, the authors' favourite is (once again) Common Kads Schreiber.

Ancona, D., Bresman, H., Kaeufer, K. *et al.* 'The Comparative Advantage of X-Teams'. *MIT Sloan Management Review*, Spring 2002.

Cross, Rob, Nohria, N. and Parker, A. 'Six Myths About Informal Networks'. *MIT Sloan Management Review*, Spring 2002.

During, W.E. 'Project Management and Management of Innovation in Small Industrial firms'. *Technovation*, 4, 1986.

Fox, J.R. 'Estimating the Cost of Large, Complex Projects'. Working Paper. Harvard Business School, 1986.

Graham, R.J. *Project Management: Combining Technical and Behavioral Approaches for Effective Implementation.* Van Nostrand, 1985.

Karzner, H. and Tramhein, U.J. *Project Management Operating Guidelines.* Van Nostrand, 1986.

Lynn, G.S., Morone, J.G, Paulson, A.S. Marketing and Discontinous Innovation: the Probe and Learn Process. *California Management Review*, 38, 1996.

Russell, S. and Norvig, P. *Artificial Intelligence: a Modern Approach.* Prentice Hall, 1995.

Sathi, A., Fox, M.S. and Greenberg, M. 'Representation of Activity Knowledge for Project Management'. *IEEE Transactions on AI*, 5 September, 1985.

Sathi, A., Morton, T.E. and Roth, S.F. 'Callisto: An Intelligent Project Management System'. *The AI Magazine*, Winter 1986.

Schreiber, G. *et al. Knowledge Engineering and Management: the Common KADS Methodology.* MIT Press, 2000.

4 The Beginning of Good Doing: The World of Operations

The world of operations arises from the production environment. Hodson is an encyclopaedia on the traditional approach to operations, based on industrial engineering, in the Anglo-Saxon meaning of the term. It should be in the reference library of anyone interested in the subject.[2] A text that is representative of the old school is Buffa's book. Without forgetting its origins, which date back to Taylor, its content today has undergone a complete transformation. It is expanded and enhanced with research on the other activities that make up the development and implementation of a service and with the consideration of its

---

[2] Although we do not know of anyone who has read it from beginning to end and lived to tell the tale.

strategic role in the firm. Although somewhat antiquated now, Skinner is the pioneering work on operations strategy and Uncle Wick is the putative uncle of an entire generation of specialists in these subjects, including the authors and all those mentioned here. Some of the classics on the subject are the works of the Harvard group, Hayes, Wheelwright and Clark. Followers of Skinner and fore-runners of a new school, they have been the inspiration for many of the subjects discussed in this chapter. Wheelwright and Clark have focused on the study of product development and we recommend them to anyone interested in the subject. There are several books on operations by Spanish authors, although most of them have a marked academic content and relatively little business content. However, see Díaz and Fernández. Although both are highly geared towards production, the latter contains ideas on the productivity–competitiveness relationship. Biasca is probably the closest to our approach, possibly because the second author is a former IESE student.

For a study of the firm's mission, Porter's book is a classic and almost compulsory reading. The BAS owes much to Porter's value chain. If the reader wishes to find a guide on how to operationalize the firm's mission, we recommend the book of our friend Arnoldo Hax. One of the authors carried out a comprehensive implementation of his methodology in his company and found it very useful. A more modern vision that is closer to the spirit of this book is Grant, especially because knowledge can be seen as the firm's chief resource. Rafael Andreu has an article on this subject in the process of being published.

We always say that all companies are service companies, but there are unique features that should be stressed. Here, Carlzon's book about his MOT approach is interesting, particularly because he was the first to draw attention to the subject, but see also Berry. A standard reference work that we recommend for the subject of services is Heskett.

Other references that discuss the subject of competitiveness from the operations viewpoint, although not so comprehensive, are Carlsson, Foster, Johne. Even if it only be for the quote in the chapter, we cannot exclude one of the books that has marked the twentieth century. Few people have read it but it is still fully relevant today and is very thought-provoking. The book is Von Neumann.

Berry, L. *On Great Service*. The Free Press, 1995.

Biasca, R. and Paladino, M. *Competitividad*. Editorial Atlántida, 1991.

Buffa, E. *Dirección de las Operaciones*. Limusa-Wiley, 1983.

Carlsson, M. 'Aspects of Integration of Technical Functions for Efficient Product Development'. *R&D Management*, 21(1), 1991, 55–66.

Carlzon, I. *El momento de la verdad*. Asociación para el Progreso de la Dirección, 1988.

Clark, K.B. and Fujimoto, T. *Product Development Performance: Strategy, Organization and Change in the World Auto Industry*. Harvard Business School Press, 1991.

Clark, K.B. and Wheelwright, S.L. 'El desarrollo de productos como ventaja competitiva'. *Harvard Deusto Business Review* (564), 1993, 72–84.

Cyert, R. and March, J. *Teoría de las Decisiones Económicas en la Empresa*. Herrero Hermanos, 1965.

Diaz, A. *Producción, Gestión y Control*. Ariel Economía, 1993.

Dumbleton, J.H. *Management of High Technology Research and Development*. Elsevier, 1986.

Fernández-Sánchez, E. *Dirección de la Producción*. Civitas, 1993.

Foster, R. *Innovation: the Attacker's Advantage*. McKinsey, 1986.

Grant, R. 'The Resource Based Theory of Competitive Advantage. Implications for Strategy Formulation'. *California Management Review* (Spring), 1991, 114–35.

Hamel, G. 'Bringing Silicon Valley Inside'. *Harvard Business Review*, September–October, 1999.

Hax, A. and Majluff, N. *The Strategy Concept and Process: a Pragmatic Approach*. Prentice Hall, 1991.

Hayes, R.H., Wheelwright, S.C. and Clark, K.B. *Dynamic Manufacturing: Creating the Learning Organization*. The Free Press, 1988.

Heskett, J.L., Sasser, W.E. and Hart, C.W. *Service Breakthroughs*. The Free Press, 1990.

Hodson, W. (ed.), *Maynard's Industrial Engineering Handbook*, 4th edn. McGraw-Hill, 1992.

Johne, F. and Snelson, P. 'Success Factors in Product Innovation: a Selective Review of the Literature'. *Journal of Product Innovation Management*, 5, 1988, 114–28.

Nelson, R. and Winter, S. *An Evolutionary Theory of Economic Change*. Harvard University Press, 1982.

Porter, M. *Competitive Advantage: Creating and Sustaining Superior Performance*. The Free Press, 1995.

Quinn, J.B. 'Technological Innovation. Entrepreneurship and Strategy'. *Sloan Management Review* (Spring), 1979, 1–30.

Riverola, J. 'Perspectivas de la dirección de operaciones'. *Revista de Economía*, 7, 1990.

Rosenthal, S. *Effective Product Design and Development: How to Cut Lead-Time and Increase Customer Satisfaction*. Irwin Professional Publications, 1992.

Rubinstein, A. *Modeling Bounded Rationality*. MIT Press, 1997.

Simon, H. *The Sciences of the Artificial*. MIT Press, 1969.

Skinner, W. *Manufacturing: the Formidable Competitive Weapon*. John Wiley & Sons, 1985.

Taylor, F.W. *The Principles of Scientific Management*. Dover Publications, 1998. Originally published New York: Harper and Bros, 1999.

Von Neumann, J.V. and Morgenstern, O. *The Theory of Games and Economic Behavior*. Princeton University Press, 1944.

Wheelwright, S.C. and Clark, K.B. *Revolutionizing Product Development*. The Free Press, 1993.

5   The Basic Variables of Action in Operations (I)

Most of the material included in this chapter is standard in operations but organized in a different way, more geared towards its use by firms' senior management. Therefore, we have only included the classic references or others that are on specific subjects that the reader may find relevant. The classics are Clark, Dodgson, Forrester, Gilbreth and Hammer. Forrester continues to be the precursor of Supply Chain Management, since he discovered the famous bullwhip effect. However, in the work quoted, he also classified the main flows in the firm. Hammer is the standard reference on process analysis. Although incomplete and out of vogue in parts, it should still be read with care. A text providing a broad coverage of the most useful techniques for operations analysis, although approached from a more general viewpoint, is Wagner, which has been reprinted in many new editions since 1971. It is very long, but very readable. Many techniques have been designed to systematize the entire operations structure in the firm. For a summary, see Larios. The SEM method – another approach is discussed in Wallace. Riverola is a detailed discussion of the procedures required to implement the ideas given in this chapter and is compulsory reading for those who wish to undertake this task.

Chew, W., Clark, K. and Breshanan, T. 'Measurement, Coordination and Learning in a Multiplant network'. *Working Paper*. Harvard Business School, 1989.

Clark, K. 'Knowledge, Problem Solving and Innovation in the Evolutionary Firm'. *Harvard Business School Report*, 1989.

Couger, J.D. *Creative Problem Solving and Opportunity Finding: Decision Making and Operations Management*. Boyd and Fraser Pub. Co., 1995.

Davenport, T., Javernpaa, S. and Beers, M. 'Improving Knowledge Work Processes'. *Sloan Management Review*, 37 (Summer), 1996, 53–66.

Dodgson, M. *The Management of Technological Learning*. De Gruyter, 1991.

Edosomwan, J. *Integrating Innovations and Technology Management*. Wiley Inter-science, 1989.

Forrester, J.W. *Industrial Dynamics*. Pegasus Communications, 1961.

Gilbreth, J. *Motion Study*. Hive Pub Co., 1972.

Hammer, P. *Business Process Reengineering*. Addison-Wesley, 1992.

Larios, F. 'Métodos tipo GRAI: para el análisis de procesos'. *Research Document*. University of Valencia, 1995.

Riverola, J. and Muñoz-Seca, B. *El análisis de procesos y la reducción del tiempo de servicio*. Biblioteca IESE de Gestión de Empresas, Folio, 1997.

Taylor, F.W. *The Principles of Scientific Management*. Dover Pubns, 1998. Originally published New York: Harper and Bros, 1911.

Van Gundy, A.B. 'How to Get the Idea that Leads to the Product'. The National New-Products Conference, Chicago, 8–9 May, 1984.

Wallace, R.H., Stockenberg, J.E. and Charette, R.N. *A Unified Methodology for Developing Systems*. McGraw-Hill, 1987.

6 The Basic Variables of Action in Operations (II)

The first part of this chapter is based on standard tools, particularly for the analysis of waiting phenomena (Wagner). However, see Beer for qualitative aspects of human resources. The information systems' approach owes much to Anthony, Dretske, Kerr and was put down in print, we believe for the first time, in Riverola, 1975. The techniques required to design information systems, from the technical viewpoint, can be consulted in Sommerville, a very complete manual on software engineering. From the management viewpoint, Andreu, 1991, is the best that has been written on the subject. The conflict-resolution systems are a development of our own which took shape from Andreu, Fox. Subsequent works such as Jaikumar, Kerr further contributed to their development. In any case, it is not an absolute novelty but simply the reformulation of well-known concepts that are difficult to trace. Not even we can clearly trace the origin of the term and its associated ideas.

Andreu, R. 'Designing from Specifications'. PhD Thesis. Sloan School of Management, MIT, 1980.

Andreu, R., Ricart, J. and Valor, J. *Estrategia y sistemas de información*. McGraw-Hill, 1991.

Anthony, R. and Govindarajan, V. *Management Control Systems*. McGraw-Hill/Irwin, 2001.

Beer, M. *et al. Human Resource Management*. Free Press, 1985.

Dretske, F.I. *Knowledge and the Flow of Information*. MIT Press, 1981.

Dyer, J.H. *Collaborative Advantage: Winning Through Extended Enterprise Supplier Networks*. Oxford University Press, 2000.

Fox, M.S. *Constraint-Directed Search: a Case Study of Job Shop Scheduling*. Morgan Kaufmann, 1985.

Jaikumar, R. and Bohn, R. 'The Development of Intelligent Systems for Industrial Use'. *Research on Technological Innovation, Management and Policy*, 3, 1986, 169–211.

Kerr, R. *Knowledge Based Manufacturing Management*. Addison-Wesley, 1990.

Larios, F. 'Métodos tipo GRAI para el análisis de procesos'. *Research Document*, University of Valencia, 1995.

Riverola, J. and Andreu, R. 'Porque no funcionan los sistemas integrados'. *Proceso de Datos*, 1982.

Riverola, J. and Andreu, R. 'Spags, un nuevo concepto'. *Proceso de Datos*, 1982.

Russell, S. and Norvig, P. *Artificial Intelligence: a Modern Approach*. Prentice Hall, 1995.

Simon, H. *The Sciences of the Artificial*. MIT Press, 1969.

Sommerville, I. *Software Engineering*. Addison-Wesley, 2001.

Wagner, H. *Principles of Operations Research*. Prentice Hall, 1975.

7 Quality and Service

The literature on quality is again enormous, much of it merely repeating a few basic sermons. We have confined ourselves to pointing out those references which we think contribute the field's original ideas and on which all the rest has been built. Of course, the basic books are Deming, Juran, written by the gurus on the subject. An attempt to revitalize the field, introducing new ideas and techniques, is Shiba. This should be compulsory reading for all those who wish to know more about how to apply quality ideas in practice. It has a different, refreshing and very useful approach. Curiously, in spite of the time that has passed since it was published, it has not become very popular among the Spanish-speaking entrepreneurial class. Garvin is a readable and sensible textbook on quality. After having read this book, the reader should avoid reading any other general text on the subject. For specific techniques related to the firm's general management, see Hauser. Continued improvement was popularized by the book Imai, which, curiously, was a book that addressed the subject in a rather superficial and sermonish manner. Cole is a lucid synthesis of quality problems. The quality approach in services has its origin in Maslow and is applied to hotels in Muñoz-Seca.

Asbhy, Ross W. *An Introduction to Cybernetics*. Chapman & Hall, 1956.

Cole, R.E. *The Death and Life of the American Quality Movement*. Oxford University Press, 1995.

Cole, R.E. 'Learning from the Quality Movement: What Did and Didn't Happen and Why?' *California Management Review*, 41(1), 1998.

Deming, W. 'Improvement of Quality and Productivity through Action by Management'. In Tushman and Moore (eds), *Readings in the Management of Innovation*. Harper Business, 1988.

Garvin, D.A. *Managing Quality*. The Free Press, 1988.

Hauser, J. and Clausing, D. 'The House of Quality'. *Harvard Business Review*, 6 (May–June), 1988, 63–73.

Imai, M. *Kaizen: the Key to Japan's Competitive Success*. Irwin-McGraw-Hill, 1986.

Juran, J. *Juran on Planning for Quality*. The Free Press, 1988.

Juran, J.M. and Grina, F.M. *Quality Planning and Analysis: From Product Development through Use*. McGraw-Hill, 1993.

Maslow, A.H. 'Theory of Motivation'. *Psychology Review*, 50, 1943, 370–96.

Muñoz-Seca, B., Riverola, J. and Sprague, L. 'A New Way to Define Operations in the Hotel Industry'. *IESE Research Paper*, 34, May 1997.

Shiba, S., Graham, A. and Walden, D. *A New American TQM: Four Practical Revolutions in Management*. Productivity Press, 1993.

Walton, Mary and Deming, W.E. *Deming Management Method*. Perigee, 1986.

8 The Knowledge Inventory

The knowledge inventory has received little coverage in the literature. If is often said that it must be done but little is said about how it should be done. One of the articles which discusses the subject is Bohn. Heibeler addresses knowledge comparison and Glazer considers the subject from an accounting viewpoint. Kolodner, in his treatise on case-based reasoning, remarks on the subject, although without giving any details regarding implementation. Another reference is Zack. Some applications carried out by one of the authors are found in Andreu, Riverola.

Alder, P. 'When the Knowledge is the Critical Resource, Knowledge Management is the Critical Task'. In *IEEE Transactions on Engineering Management*, 3, 1989, 87–94.

Andreu, R., Riverola, J. and Valor, J. *Proyecto Tecnolímpica 9*. IESE internal report, 1991.

Arcos, J.L. and Plaza, E. 'Learning and Reflection with Noos'. IIIA Report. Autonomous University of Barcelona, 1993.

Bohn, R.G. 'Measuring and Managing Technological Knowledge'. *Sloan Management Review*, 3(1), 1994, 61–73.

Glazer, R. 'Measuring the Knower: Towards a Theory of Knowledge Equity'. *California Management Review*, 40(3), 1998, 175–94.

Heibeler, R.J. 'Benchmarking Knowledge Management'. *Strategy & Leadership*, 30(24) (March–April), 1996, 22–9.

Kolodner, J.L. *Case Based Reasoning*. Morgan Kaufmann Publishers, 1993.

Matchlup, F. *Knowledge: Its Creation, Distribution and Economic Significance. Volume 1: Knowledge and Knowledge Production*. Princeton University Press, 1980.

Riverola, J. 'Análisis competititvo de la tecnología (ACT)'. Technical Note PN-310 IESE, Barcelona, 1992.

Schneider, B. and Bowen, D. *Winning the Service Game*. Harvard Business School Press, 1995.

Zack, M.H. 'Managing Codified Knowledge'. *Sloan Management Review*, 40(4) (Summer), 1999, 45–58.

9   Applying Knowledge to Improve the Moments of Truth

There are few references that can be given for this chapter, which is basically a 'how to implement' of the previous chapters. In certain details, however, there are some interesting subjects. Action assessment is a case of multiple-objective comparison. This subject has been discussed extensively in the literature. There are many sophisticated procedures and one of the most popular is AHP (Saaty). Rosenhead is a general reference on how to rationally structure non-structured situations, as also is Van Gundy. The other references are supplementary.

Ashby, William Ross. *An Introduction to Cybernetics*. Chapman & Hall, 1956.

Cohen, W.M. and Autry, D.A. 'Absorptive Capacity: a New Perspective on Learning and Innovation'. *Administrative Science Quarterly*, 3, 1990, 128–52.

Howard, W. and Guile, B. *Profiting from Innovation*. The Free Press, 1992.

Kogut, B. and Zander, U. 'Knowledge of the Firm, Combinative Capabilities, and the Replication of Technology'. *Organization Science* (August), 1992, 383–97.

Rosenhead, J. (ed.), *Rational Analysis for a Problematic World*. John Wiley & Sons, 1989.

Saaty, T.L. and Vargas, L. *Decision Making in Economic, Political and Technological Environments with the Analytical Hierarchy Process*. RWS Publications, 1994.

Van Gundy, A.B. *Techniques of Structured Problem Solving*. John Wiley & Sons, 1988.

10   Knowledge Generation

This chapter takes its sources for ideas from a wide range of disciplines. We can identify several currents of thought in the references. On one hand, the current on creativity. Here, the work that has interested us most is probably that of Boden, although we have considerably appreciated others (De Bono). There seems to be limitless choice in techniques, which is a good indication that none of them is perfect – see Crawford, De Bono, Goldner, Kim, Michalko, Ray, Scott. Analyses of the creative process can be found in Holyoak and, particularly, in Finke, where the Geneplore model is discussed in depth. Dartnall, a collection of somewhat mixed papers, seeks to show how creativity can be associated with artificial intelligence. The book shows some technological approaches that can be used for enhancing creativity, particularly in product development. An interesting, and curious experiment is Turner, which describes a computer programme which makes up stories about knights errant and damsels in distress. The second current is innovation. Here, the classic is

Abernathy and, from the management viewpoint, Burgelman. De Treville is the discoverer of the challenge–learning relationship, a keystone of our presentation. The third current is learning. Here, the real driving force is Argyris, 1978, 1990, 1991, 1993. The references do not show sufficiently the author's influence on this chapter. Attendance of his lectures by one of the authors has had a decisive influence on the design of the internal cycle. Although mentioned in other chapters, we must also acknowledge the influence of Pérez- López throughout the chapter.

Abernathy, W.C. and Clark, K.B. 'Innovation: Mapping the Winds of Creative Destruction'. *Research Policy*, 114, 1985, 3–22.

Alder, H. *The Right-Brain Manager*. Piatkus, 1993.

Amabile, T. 'How to Kill Creativity'. *Harvard Business Review*, September–October 1998.

Argyris, C. *Organizational Learning: a Theory of Action Perspective*. Addison-Wesley, 1978.

Argyris, C. *Overcoming Organizational Defenses: Facilitating Organizational Learning*. Allyn and Bacon, 1990.

Argyris, C. 'Teaching Smart People How to Learn'. *Harvard Business Review*, 6(3), 1991, 99–109.

Argyris, C. *Knowledge for Action*. Jossey-Bass, 1993.

Boden, M.A. *La Mente Creativa, Mitos y Mecanismos*. Gedisa, 1994.

Burgelman, R. and Maidique, M. *Strategic Management of Technology and Innovation*. CRC Press, 1988.

Crawford, R.P. *The Techniques of Creative Thinking*. Prentice Hall, 1954.

Dartnall, T. (ed.), *Artificial Intelligence and Creativity*. Kluwer Academic Publishers, 1994.

De Bono, E. *Lateral Thinking*. Penguin Books, 1977.

De Bono, E. *Serious Creativity: Using the Power of Lateral Thinking to Create New Ideas*. Advanced Practical Thinking, 1993.

De Treville, S. 'Disruption, Learning and System Improvement in JIT Manufacturing'. Thesis GSB, Harvard University, 1987.

Doheny-Farina, S. *Rhetoric, Innovation, Technology*. MIT Press, 1992.

Finke, R.A., Ward, T.B. and Smith, S.M. *Creative Cognition: Theory, Research and Application*. MIT Press, 1992.

Goldner, B.B. *The Strategy of Creative Thinking*. Prentice Hall, 1962.

Guilford, J.P. *Cognitive Psychology with a Frame of Reference*. Edits. Publishers, 1979.

Hamel, G. 'Bringing Silicon Valley Inside'. *Harvard Business Review*, September–October 1999.

Holyoak, K. and Thagard, P. *Mental Leaps*. MIT Press, 1996.

Kao, J. *Jamming*. Harper Business, 1996.

Kim, S.H. *Essence of Creativity: a Guide to Tackling Difficult Problems*. Oxford University Press, 1990.

Lumsdaine, E. and Lumsdaine, M. *Creative Problem Solving*. McGraw-Hill, 1995.

Mackay, D.M. *Information, Mechanism and Meaning*. MIT Press, 1969.

Mcfadzean, E. 'The Creativity Continuum: Towards a Classification of Creative Problem Solving Techniques'. *Creativity and Innovation Management*, September 1998.

Michalko, M. *Thinkertoys*. Ten Speed Press, 1991.

Muñoz-Seca, B. 'Training for Continuous Improvement in the Firms and its Operations'. PhD thesis. University of Navarre, 1992.

Nadler, G. and Hibino, S. *Breakthrough Thinking*. Prima Publishing, 1992.

Nonaka, I.A. 'Dynamic Theory of Organizational Knowledge Creation'. *Organization Science*, 5 (February), 1994, 14–37.

Pérez López, J.A. *Teoría de la Acción Humana en las Organizaciones: la acción personal*. Rialp, 1991.

Ray, M. and Myers, R. *Creativity in Business*. Doubleday, 1989.

Rickards, T. *Problem Solving Through Creative Analysis*. Gower Press, 1974.

Scott, G. *The Empowered Mind: How to Harness the Creative Force Within You*. Prentice Hall Trade, 1994.

Turner, C.C. *The Creative Process*. Lawrence Erlbaum Assoc., 1994.

11   Taking Knowledge to Service Excellence

In this chapter, we have borrowed ideas and techniques from many sources. The focus is how to take knowledge to service excellence. Thus, Fahey and Prusak study the problems in a sample of companies in the United States and Pfeffer and Sutton give examples of actions that some companies are undertaking. In Bukowitz, we find a detailed description of how to attack the problem. The term relevance has its origin in Wilson and Sperberg. The design of the relevance system is influenced by techniques of Shiba, Juran and Brassard. To design the importance system, we have used the work of Holland as our starting point. The CPM (Competitive Problems Methodology) described in this chapter is based on previous publications by the authors (Muñoz-Seca and Riverola) and is influenced by the work of Leonard-Barton and Vail.

Brassard, M. and Ritter, D. *El impulsor de la memoria II*. Goal/QPC, 1990.
Bukowitz, W.R. and Williams, R.L. *The Knowledge Management Fieldbook*. Prentice Hall, 1999.
Fahey, L. and Prusak, L. 'The Eleven Deadliest Sins of Knowledge Management'. *California Management Review*, 40(3), 1998, 265.
Holland, J., Holyoak, K., Nisbett, R. and Thagard, P. *Induction: Processes of Inference, Learning and Discovery*. MIT Press, 1986.
Ingram, P. and Baum, J.A.C. 'Opportunity and Constraint: Organizations Learning from the Operating and Competitive Experience of Industries'. *Strategic Management Journal*, 18, 1997, 75–98.
Juran, J. *Juran on Planning for Quality*. The Free Press, 1988.
Leonard-Barton, D. 'Implementation as Mutual Adaptation of Technology and Organization'. *Research Policy*, 1, 1998, 251–67.
Leonard-Barton, D. 'La fábrica como laboratorio de aprendizaje'. *Harvard-Deusto Business Review*, 58(6), 1988, 46–61.
Leonard-Barton, D. *Wellsprings of Knowledge*. Harvard Business School Publishing, 1995.
Muñoz-Seca, B. and Riverola, J. *Riqueza y Conservación. La planificación de espacios naturales y protegidos*. Publicaciones de la Consejería de Medio Ambiente de la Junta de Andalucía, 1997.
Pfeffer, J. and Sutton, R. *The Knowing–Doing Gap: How Smart Companies Turn Knowledge into Action*. Harvard Business School Press, 2000.
Quinn, R.E. and Cameron, K.S. (eds). *Paradox and Information*. Ballinger, 1988.
Shiba, S., Graham, A. and Walden, D. *A New American TQM: Four Practical Revolutions in Management*. Productivity Press, 1993.
Vail, P. *Learning as a Way of Being*. Jossey-Bass, 1996.
Wilson, D. and Sperberg, D. *Pragmatics and Modularity. Pragmatics: a Reader*. Ed. Steven Davis. New York: Oxford University Press, 1991.

12   Training, Information and Participation

The chapter is divided into two main sections. The first presents an approach to training that is different from the traditional approach (for the traditional approach, see Bentley and Goldstein). The new approach presented requires a new role for the manager: the educator manager. To broaden this idea, see Honey, Ellinger, Knowles, Muñoz-Seca, Shank and Torrance. The second section is devoted to the organization structure based on a study performed by the authors and published in Escorsa. We present the knowledge units, with a certain similarity to the concept presented in Nonaka and influenced by Argyris and Schein. The project-based organization is presented, which can be related to Ancona and Cross and is influenced by the work of Garvin and Kanter.

Allen, T. *Managing the Flow of Technology*. MIT Press, 1984.
Ancona, D., Bresman, H. and Kaeufer, K. 'The Comparative Advantage of X-Teams'. *MIT Sloan Management Review* (Spring), 2002, 33–9.

Andrew, B.H. 'Firms as Knowledge Brokers: Lessons in pursuing Continuous Innovation'. *California Management Review*, 40(3), 1998, 209–27.

Argyris, C. *Integrating the Individual and the Organization*. Transaction Publishers, 1990.

Bentley, T. *The Business of Training*. McGraw-Hill, 1990.

Birell, N.D. and Gould, M.A. *A Practical Guide for Software Development*. Cambridge University Press, 1985.

Brown, J.S. and Duguid, P. 'Organizational Learning and Communities-of-practice: Toward a Unified View of Working, Learning and Innovation'. *Organization Science*, 2 (February), 1991, 40–57.

Buckley, R. and Caple, J. *Theory and Practice of Training*. Kogan Page, 2000.

Butler, A.S. *Team Think: 72 Ways to Make Good, Smart, Quick Decisions in Any Meeting*. McGraw-Hill, 1996.

Cross, R., Nohria, N. and Parker, A. 'Six Myths about Informal Networks'. *MIT Sloan Management Review*, 43(3) (Spring), 2003, 67–76.

Damanpour, F. 'Organizational Innovation: a Meta-Analysis of Effects, Determinants and Moderators'. *Academy of Management Journal*, 34(3), 1991, 555–90.

Davenport, Thomas H. and Prusak, Lawrence. *Working Knowledge*. Harvard Business School Press, 1997.

Demarco, T. and Lister, T. *Peopleware: Productive Projects and Teams*, (2nd edn). Dorset House, 1987.

Ellinger, A., Watkins, K. and Barnas, C. *Responding to New Roles: a Qualitative Study of Managers as Instructors*. Management Learning. Thousand Oaks, 1999.

Escorsa, P. (ed.), *La gestión de la empresa de alta tecnología*. Ariel Economía, 1990.

Garvin, D.A. 'Building a Learning Organization'. *Harvard Business Review*, 71(4), (July–August), 1993, 78–91.

Goldstein, I.L. *Training and Development*. Jossey Bass, 1989.

Hodgestts, R., Luthans, F. and Sang, M. 'New Paradigm Organizations. From Total Quality to Learning to World-Class'. *Organizational Dynamics*, 22(3), 1994, 5–19.

Honey, P. and Mumford, A. *The Learning Styles Helpers Guide*. Peter Honey Publications Limited, 1992.

Huber, G.P. 'Organizational Learning: the Contributing Processes and the Literatures'. *Organization Science*, 2(1), 1991, 88–115.

Kanter, R.M. *The Change Master*. Touchstone Books, 1985.

Knowles, M. and Associates. *Andragogy in Action: Applying Modern Principles of Adult Learning*. Jossey-Bass, 1984.

Langer, E.J. *The Power of Mindful Learning*. Addison-Wesley, 1997.

Lynn, Gary S. 'New Product Team Learning: Developing and Profiting From Your Knowledge Capital'. *California Management Review*, 40(4), 1998, 74–93.

Muñoz-Seca, B. and Silvia Santiago, C. 'Four Dimensions to Induce Learning: The Challenge Profile'. *IESE working paper*, no. 520, September 2003.

Nonaka, I. and Konno, N. 'The Concept of "Ba": Building a Foundation for Knowledge Creation'. *California Management Review*, 40(3), 1998.

Payne, L.W. 'Unlocking an Organization's Ultimate Potential Through Knowledge Management'. *Knowledge Management in Practice*, 31(1), April–May, 1996.

Pérez López, J.A. and San Román, R. *Enseñanza de economía a profesionales no economistas*. Fondo para la Investigación Económica y Social de la Confederación Española de Cajas de Ahorros, 1973.

Purser, R. 'Redesigning the Knowledge Based Product Development Organization'. *Technovation*, 11(7), 1991, 403–15.

Quinn, J.B., Anderson, P. and Finkelstein, S. 'Managing Professional Intellect: Making the Most of the Best'. *Harvard Business Review*, 74(2), 1996, 71–82.

Schein, E.H. *Organizational Culture and Leadership*, 2nd edn. Jossey Bass, 1997.

Schein, E.H. 'How Can Organizations Learn Faster?, The Challenge of Entering the Green Room'. *Sloan Management Review*, 34(2), 1993, 85–92.

Shank, R. *Virtual Learning: a Revolutionary Approach to Building a High Skill Workforce*. McGraw-Hill, 1997.

Sherwood, J.J. 'Creating Work Cultures with Competitive Advantage'. *Organizational Dynamics*, 16(3), 1988.

Torrance, P. *Creative Ways of Teaching*. Casete 283, Edition, Jeffrey Norton Publishers, 1969.

13   Information Systems for Knowledge Management

This chapter is heavily influenced by the case-based reasoning school, whose chief exponent has been Roger Shank (Shank, Riesbeck). Curiously, Shank has published relatively little and most of the contributions have been made by disciples of his, such as Kolodner, an encyclopaedic work but too verbose and detailed. The organization of a KMS is drawn from Bradshaw. Sage, written many years ago, is a precursor work that summarizes some useful techniques for implementing these systems. Rasmussen gives a detailed design of a multi-level information system which has properties similar to our KESO. Something similar is done by Wallace in the context of the SEM. Kuipers is a key work for qualitative simulation. The other references present some experiences in the implementation of systems which can be vaguely considered KMSs.

Bradshaw, J. (ed.), *Software Agents*. MIT Press, 1997.

Davenport, T.H. and Klarh, P. 'Managing Customer Support Knowledge'. *California Management Review*, 40(3), 1998, 195–208.

Kolodner, J.L. *Case-Based Reasoning*. Morgan Kaufmann Publishers, 1993.

Kuipers, B. *Qualitative Reasoning*. MIT Press, 1994.

Leake, D.B. *Case Based Reasoning: Experiences, Lessons and Future Directions*. MIT Press, 1996.

Morik, K. (ed.), *Knowledge Representation and Organization in Machine Learning*. Springer-Verlag, 1989.

Olife, M. (ed.), *Intelligent Manufacturing*. Benjamín/Cummings, 1988.

Rasmussen, J., Pejtersen, A.M. and Goodstein, L.P. *Cognitive Systems Engineering*. Wiley-Interscience, 1994.

Riesbeck, C. and Shank, R. *Inside Case Based Reasoning*. Lawrence Erlbaum, 1989.

Sage, P. *Large Scale Systems: Analysis and Design (Sistemas a Gran Escala: Análisis y Diseño)* Prentice Hall, 1982.

Schreiber, G., Akermans, H., Anjewierden, A. *et al. Knowledge Engineering and Management: the Common KADS Methodology*. MIT, 2000.

Shank, R. *Virtual Learning: a Revolutionary Approach to Building a High Skill Workforce*. McGraw-Hill, 1997.

Wallace, R.H., Stockenberg, J.E. and Charette, R.N. *A Unified Methodology for Developing Systems*. McGraw-Hill, 1987.

Wright, P.K. and Bourne, D.A. *Manufacturing Intelligence*. Addison Wesley, 1988.

14   Final Synthesis: Designing a Continuous Improvement System

The material of this chapter is a synthesis of what has been presented throughout the book. Perhaps the only new reference that can be mentioned is a preliminary application of knowledge management to new product design by one of the author's doctorate students (Revilla).

Revilla, E. *Factores determinantes del aprendizaje organizativo: un modelo de desarrollo de productos*. Club Gestión de la Calidad, 1995.

Appendix: Some Basic Techniques

Many of these techniques can be found in the literature mentioned above. Muñoz-Seca provides a good compilation of the techniques commonly used by the authors.

Muñoz-Seca, B. and Riverola, J. *Riqueza y conservación. La planificación de espacios naturales protegidos*. Publicaciones de la Consejería de Medio Ambiente de la Junta de Andalucía, 1997.

Bibliography

Abernathy, W.C. and Clark, K.B. 'Innovation: Mapping the Winds of Creative Destruction'. *Research Policy*, 114, 1985, 3–22.

Alder, H. *The Right-Brain Manager*. Piatkus, 1993.

Alder, P. 'When the Knowledge is the Critical Resource, Knowledge Management is the Critical Task'. In *IEEE Transactions on Engineering Management*, 3, 1989, 87–94.

Allen, T. *Managing the Flow of Technology*. MIT Press, 1984.

Amabile, T. 'How to Kill Creativity'. *Harvard Business Review*, Sep.–Oct. 1998.

Ancona, D. *et al.* 'The Comparative Advantage of X-Teams'. *MIT Sloan Management Review*, (Spring) 2002, 33–9.

Anderson, J.R. *Cognitive Psychology and its Implications*. W.H. Freeman, 1990.

Andreu, R. 'Designing from Specifications'. PhD Thesis. Sloan School of Management. MIT, 1980.

Andreu, R., Ricart, J. and Valor, J. *Estrategia y sistemas de información*. McGraw-Hill, 1991.

Andreu, R., Riverola, J. and Valor, J. *Proyecto Tecnolímpica 92*. IESE internal report, 1991.

Andrew, B.H. 'Firms as Knowledge Brokers: Lessons in Pursuing Continuous Innovation'. *California Management Review*, 40(3), 1998, 209–27.

Anthony, R. and Govindarajan, V. *Management Control Systems*. McGraw-Hill/Irwin, 2001.

Arcos, J.L. and Plaza, E. 'Learning and Reflection with Noos'. IIIA Report, Autonomous University of Barcelona, 1993.

Arcos, J.L. 'The Noos Representation Language'. Thesis, Polytechnic University of Catalonia, 1997.

Argyris, C. *Integrating the Individual and the Organization*. Transaction Publishers, 1990.

Argyris, C. *Knowledge for Action*. Jossey-Bass, 1993.

Argyris, C. *Overcoming Organizational Defenses: Facilitating Organizational Learning*. Allyn and Bacon, 1990.

Argyris, C. 'Teaching Smart People How to Learn'. *Harvard Business Review*, 6(3), 1991, 99–109.

Asbhy, Ross. W. *An Introduction to Cybernetics*. Chapman & Hall, 1956.

Badaracco, J.L. *The Knowledge Link: How Firms Compete Through Strategic Alliances*. Harvard Business School, 1991.

Barancatto, R. *The Knowledge Connection*. Harvard Business School Press, 1991.

Beer, M. *et al. Human Resource Management*. Free Press, 1985.

Bentley, T. *The Business of Training*. McGraw-Hill, 1990.

Berry, L. *On Great Service*. The Free Press, 1995.

Biasca, R. and Paladino, M. *Competitividad*. Editorial Atlántida, 1991.

Birell, N.D. and Gould, M.A. *A Practical Guide for Software Development*. Cambridge University Press, 1985.

Bobrow, D.G. and Collins, A. *Representation and Understanding: Studies in Cognitive Science*. Academia Press, 1975.

Boden, M.A. *La Mente Creativa, Mitos y Mecanismos*. Gedisa, 1994.

Bohn, D. and Peat, F.D. *Science, Order and Creativity* 2nd edn. Routledge, 2000.

Bohn, R.G. 'Measuring and Managing Technological Knowledge'. *Sloan Management Review*, 3(1), 1994, 61–73.

Bradshaw, J. (ed.). *Software Agents*. MIT Press, 1997.

Brassard, M. and Ritter, D. *El impulsor de la memoria II*. Goal/QPC, 1990.

Brown, J.S. and Duguid, P. 'Organizational Learning and Communities-of-Practice: Toward a Unified View of Working, Learning and Innovation'. *Organization Science*, 2(Feb.), 1991, 40–57.

Buckley, R. and Caple, J. *Theory and Practice of Training*. Kogan Page, 2000.

Buffa, E. *Dirección de las Operaciones*. Limusa-Wiley, 1983.

Bukowitz, W.R. and Williams, R.L. *The Knowledge Management Fieldbook*. Prentice Hall, 1999.

Bunnin, N. and Tsui-James, E.P. (eds). *The Blackwell Companion to Philosophy*. Blackwell Publishers Ltd., 1996.

Burgelman, R. and Maidique, M. *Strategic Management of Technology and Innovation*. CRC Press, 1988.

Butler, A.S. *Team Think: 72 Ways to Make Good, Smart, Quick Decisions in any Meeting*. McGraw-Hill, 1996.

Carlsson, M. 'Aspects of Integration of Technical Functions for Efficient Product Development'. *R&D Management*, 21(1), 1991, 55–66.

Carlzon, I. *El Momento de la Verdad*. Asociación para el Progreso de la Dirección, 1988.

Cherniak, C. *Minimal rationality*. MIT Press, 1990.

Chew, W., Clark, K. and Breshanan, T. 'Measurement, Coordination and Learning in a Multiplant Network'. *Working Paper*. Harvard Business School, 1989.

Clark, K. 'Knowledge, Problem Solving and Innovation in the Evolutionary Firm'. *Harvard Business School Report*, 1989.

Clark, K.B. and Fujimoto, T. *Product Development Performance: Strategy, Organization and Change in the World Auto Industry*. Harvard Business School Press, 1991.

Clark, K.B. and Wheelwright, S.L. 'El Desarrollo de Productos como Ventaja Competitiva'. *Harvard Deusto Business Review*, 56(4), 1993, 72–84.

Cohen, W.M. and Autry, D.A. 'Absorptive Capacity: a New Perspective on Learning and Innovation'. *Administrative Science Quarterly*, 3, 1990, 128–52.

Cole, R.E. 'Learning from the Quality Movement: What Did and Didn't Happen and Why?'. *California Management Review*, 41(1), 1998, 43–73.

Cole, R.E. *The Death and Life of the American Quality Movement*. Oxford University Press, 1995.

Cooper, W.W., Seiford, L.M. amd Kauro, T. *Data Envelopment analysis: a Comprehensive Text with Models, Applications, References*. Kluwer Academic Publishers, 1999.

Couger, J.D. *Creative Problem Solving and Opportunity Finding: Decision Making and Operations Management*. Boyd and Fraser Pub. Co., 1995.

Crawford, R.P. *The Techniques of Creative Thinking*. Prentice Hall, 1954.

Cross, R., Nohria, N. and Parker, A. 'Six Myths about informal networks'. *MIT Sloan Management Review*, 43(3) (Spring), 2002, 67–76.

Cyert, R. and March, J. *Teoría de las Decisiones Económicas en la Empresa*. Herrero Hermanos, 1965.

Damanpour, F. 'Organizational Innovation: a Meta-Analysis of Effects, Determinants and Moderators'. *Academy of Management Journal*, 34(3), 1991, 555–90.

Dartnall, T. (ed.). *Artificial Intelligence and Creativity*. Kluwer Academic Publishers, 1994.

Davenport, T.H. and Klarh, P. 'Managing Customer Support Knowledge'. *California Management Review*, 40(3), 1998, 195–208.

Davenport, T., Javernpaa, S. and Beers, M. 'Improving Knowledge Work Processes'. *Sloan Management Review*, 37 (summer), 1996, 53–66.

Davenport, T.H. and Prusak, L. *Working Knowledge*. Harvard Business School Press, 1997.

De Bono, E. *Lateral Thinking*. Penguin Books, 1977.

De Bono, E. *Serious Creativity: Using the Power of Lateral Thinking to Create New Ideas*. Advanced Practical Thinking, 1993.

De Treville, S. 'Disruption, Learning and System Improvement in JIT Manufacturing'. Thesis GSB, Harvard University, 1987.

Demarco, T. and Lister, T. *People Ware: Productive Projects and Teams*, 2nd edn. Dorset House, 1999.

Deming, W. 'Improvement of Quality and Productivity through Action by Management'. In Tushman and Moore (eds), *Readings in the Management of Innovation*. Harper Business, 1988.

Diaz, A. *Producción, Gestión y Control*. Ariel Economía, 1993.

Dodgson, M. *The Management of Technological Learning*. De Gruyter, 1991.

Doheny-Farina, S. *Rhetoric, Innovation, Technology*. MIT Press, 1992.

Dreidstadt, R. 'The Use of Analogies and Incubation in Obtaining Insights in Creative Problem Solving'. *Journal of Psychology*, (7), 1969, 159–75.

Dretske, F.I. *Knowledge and the Flow of Information*. MIT Press, 1981.

Dumbleton, J.H. *Management of High Technology Research and Development*. Elsevier, 1986.

During, W.E. 'Project Management and Management of Innovation in Small Industrial Firms'. *Technovation*, (4), 1986.

Dyer, J.H. *Collaborative Advantage: Winning Through Extended Enterprise Supplier Networks*. Oxford University Press, 2000.

Edosomwan, J. *Integrating Innovations and Technology Management*. Wiley Inter-science, 1989.

Ellinger, A., Watkins, K. and Barnas, C. *Responding to New Roles: a Qualitative Study of Managers as Instructors*. Management Learning. Thousand Oaks, 1999.

Escorsa, P. (ed.). *La gestión de la empresa de alta tecnología*. Ariel Economía, 1990.

Fagin, R. *et al. Reasoning about Knowledge*. MIT Press, 1995.

Fahey, L. and Prusak, L. 'The Eleven Deadliest Sins of Knowledge Management'. *California Management Review*, 40(3), 1998, 265.

Fernández-Sánchez, E. *Dirección de la Producción*. Civitas, 1993.

Fetzer, J.H. *Philosophy and Cognitive Science*. Paragon, 1996.

Finke, R.A., Ward, T.B. and Smith, S.M. *Creative Cognition: Theory, Research and Application*. MIT Press, 1992.

Flood, R.L. and Jackson, M.C. *Creative Problems Solving: Total Systems Intervention*. John Wiley & Son, 1991.

Forbus, K.D. and De Kleer, J. *Building Problem Solvers*. MIT Press, 1994.

Forrester, J.W. *Industrial Dynamics*. Pegasus Communications, 1961.

Foster, R. *Innovation: The Attacker's Advantage*. McKinsey, 1986.

Fox, J.R. 'Estimating the Cost of Large, Complex Projects'. Working Paper Harvard Business School, 1986.

Fox, M.S. *Constraint-Directed Search: a Case Study of Job Shop Scheduling*. Morgan Kaufmann, 1985.

Garvin, D.A. 'Building a Learning Organization'. *Harvard Business Review*, 71(4) (July–August), 1993, 78–91.

Garvin, D.A. *Managing Quality*. The Free Press, 1988.

Gilbreth, F. *Motion Study*. Hive Pub Co., 1972.

Glazer, R. 'Measuring the Knower: Towards a Theory of Knowledge Equity'. *California Management Review*, 40(3), 1998, 175–94.

Goldner, B.B. *The Strategy of Creative Thinking*. Prentice Hall, 1962.

Goldstein, I.L. *Training and Development*. Jossey Bass, 1989.

Graham, R.J. *Project Management: Combining Technical and Behavioral Approaches for Effective Implementation*. Van Nostrand, 1985.

Grant, R. 'The Resource Based Theory of Competitive Advantage. Implications for Strategy Formulation'. *California Management Review* (Spring), 1991, 114–35.

Guilford, J.P. *Cognitive Psychology with a Frame of Reference*. Edits. Publishers, 1979.

Hamel, G. 'Bringing Silicon Valley Inside'. *Harvard Business Review*, Sep.–Oct. 1999.

Hammer, P. *Business Process Reengineering*. Addison-Wesley, 1992.

Handy, C. *The Age of Paradox*. Harvard Business School Press, 1995.

Hauser, J. and Clausing, D. 'The House of Quality'. *Harvard Business Review*, 6 (May–June), 1988, 63–73.

Hax, A. and Majluff, N. *The Strategy Concept and Process: a Pragmatic Approach*. Prentice Hall, 1991.

Hayes, R.H., Wheelwright, S.C. and Clark, K.B. *Dynamic Manufacturing: Creating the Learning Organization*. The Free Press, 1988.

Heibeler, R.J. 'Benchmarking Knowledge Management'. *Strategy & Leadership*, 30(24) (March–April), 1996, 22–29.

Heskett, J.L., Sasser, W.E. and Hart, C.W. *Service Breakthroughs*. The Free Press, 1990.

Hodgestts, R., Luthans, F. and Sang, M. 'New Paradigm Organizations. From Total Quality to Learning to World-Class'. *Organizational Dynamics*, 22(3), 1994, 5–19.

Hodson, W. (eds). *Maynard's Industrial Engineering Handbook*, 4th edn. McGraw-Hill, 1992.

Holland, J. *et al. Induction: Processes of Inference, Learning and Discovery*. MIT Press, 1989.

Holland, J., Holyoak, K., Nisbett, R. and Thagard, P. *Induction: Processes of Inference, Learning and Discovery*. MIT Press, 1986.

Holyoak, K. and Thagard, P. *Mental Leaps*. MIT Press, 1996.

Honey, P. and Mumford, A. *The Learning Styles Helper's Guide*. Peter Honey Publications Limited, 1992.

Howard, W. and Guile, B. *Profiting from Innovation*. The Free Press, 1992.

Huber, G.P. 'Organizational Learning: the Contributing Processes and the Literatures'. *Organization Science*, 2(1), 1991, 88–115.

IDE. 'La cocina del IDE'. Instituto de Desarrollo Empresarial, 1998.

IMAI, M. *Kaizen: the Key to Japan's Competitive Success*. Irwin-McGraw-Hill, 1986.

Ingram, P. and Baum, J.A.C. 'Opportunity and Constraint: Organizations Learning from the Operating and Competitive Experience of Industries'. *Strategic Management Journal*, 18, 1997, 75–98.

Jackendoff, R. *Consciousness and the Computational Mind*. MIT Press, 1990.

Jaikumar, R. and Bohn, R. 'The Development of Intelligent Systems for Industrial Use'. *Research on Technological Innovation, Management and Policy*, 3, 1986, 169–211.

Johne, F. and Snelson, P. 'Success Factors in Product Innovation: a Selective Review of the Literature'. *Journal of the Product Innovation Management*, 5, 1988, 114–28.

Juran, J. *Juran on Planning for Quality*. The Free Press, 1988.

Juran, J.M. and Grina, F.M. *Quality Planning and Analysis: From Product Development through Use*. McGraw-Hill, 1993.

Kanter, R.M. *The Change Master*. Touchstone Books, 1985.

Kao, J. *Jamming*. Harper Business, 1996.

Karzner, H. and Tramhein, U.J. *Project Management Operating Guidelines*. Van Nostrand, 1986.

Kerr, R. *Knowledge Based Manufacturing Management*. Addison-Wesley, 1990.

Kim, S.H. *Essence of Creativity: a Guide to Tackling Difficult Problems*. Oxford University Press, 1990.

Knowles, M. and Associates. *Andragogy in Action: Applying Modern Principles of Adult Learning*. Jossey-Bass, 1984.

Kogut, B. and Zander, U. 'Knowledge of the Firm, Combinative Capabilities, and the Replication of Technology'. *Organization Science* (August), 1992, 383–97.

Kolodner, J.L. *Case Based Reasoning*. Morgan Kaufmann Publishers, 1993.

Kuipers, B. *Qualitative Reasoning*. MIT Press, 1994.

Lamberts, K. and Shanks, D. (eds). *Knowledge, Concepts and Categories*. MIT Press, 1997.

Langer, E.J. *The Power of Mindful Learning*. Addison-Wesley, 1997.

Larios, F. 'Métodos tipo GRAI para el análisis de procesos'. *Research Document*, University of Valencia, 1995.

Leake, D.B. *Case Based Reasoning: Experiences, Lessons and Future Directions*. MIT Press, 1996.

Leonard-Barton, D. 'Implementation as Mutual Adaptation of Technology and Organization'. *Research Policy*, 1, 1998, 251–67.

Leonard-Barton, D. 'La fábrica como laboratorio de aprendizaje'. *Harvard-Deusto Business Review*, 58(6), 1988, 46–61.

Leonard-Barton, D. *Wellsprings of Knowledge*. Harvard Business School Publishing, 1995.

Luce, R.D. and Raiffa, H. *Games and Decisions*. John Wiley & Sons, 1957.

Lumsdaine, E. and Lumsdaine, M. *Creative Problem Solving*. McGraw-Hill, 1995.

Lynn, G.S., Morone, J.G., Paulson, A.S. 'Marketing and Discontinous Innovation: the Probe and Learn Process'. *California Management Review*, 38, 1996.

Lynn, Gary S. 'New Product Team Learning: Developing and Profiting from your Knowledge Capital'. *California Management Review*, 40(4), 1998, 74–93.

Mackay, D.M. *Information, Mechanism and Meaning*. MIT Press, 1969.

Maslow, A.H. 'Theory Of Motivation'. *Psychology Review*, 50, 1943, 370–96.

Matchlup, F. *Knowledge: Its Creation, Distribution and Economic Significance. Volume 1: Knowledge and Knowledge Production.* Princeton University Press, 1980.

Mayer, R. *Thinking, Problem Solving, Cognition*, 2nd edn. W.H. Freeman and Co., 1992.

Mcfadzean, E. 'The Creativity Continuum: Towards a Classification of Creative Problem Solving Techniques'. *Creativity and Innovation Management*, Sept., 1998.

Michalewicz, Z. and Fogel, D.B. *How to Solve It: Modern Heuristics*. Springer-Verlag, 1999.

Michalko, M. *Thinkertoys*. Ten Speed Press, 1991.

Morik, K. (ed.). *Knowledge Representation and Organization in Machine Learning*. Springer-Verlag, 1989.

Morris, T. *If Aristotle Ran General Motors: the New Soul of Business*. Henry Holt and Company, Inc. 1997.

Muñoz-Seca, B. 'Training for Continuous Improvement in the Firms and its Operations'. PhD thesis. University of Navarre, 1992.

Muñoz-Seca, B. and Riverola, J. *Gestión del Conocimiento*. Folio, 1997.

Muñoz-Seca, B. and Riverola, J. *Riqueza y Conservación. La planificación de espacios naturales y protegidos*. Publicaciones de la Consejería de Medio Ambiente de la Junta de Andalucía, 1997.

Muñoz-Seca, B., Riverola, J. and Sprague, L. 'A New Way to Define Operations in the Hotel Industry'. *IESE Research Paper*, 34. May, 1997.

Muñoz-Seca, B. and Silvia Santiago, C. 'Four Dimensions to Induce Learning: the Challenge Profile'. *IESE Working Paper*, no. 520, September 2003.

Nadler, G. and Hibino, S. *Breakthrough Thinking*. Prima Publishing, 1992.

Nelson, R. and Winter, S. *An Evolutionary Theory of Economic Change*. Harvard University Press, 1982.

Newell, A. 'The Knowledge Level'. *Artificial Intelligence*, 18, 1982, 87–127.

Newell, A. *Unified Theories of Cognition*. Harvard University Press, 1990.

Nonaka, I. 'The Knowledge Creating Company'. *Harvard Business Review*, November–December (6), 1991, 96–194.

Nonaka, I.A. 'Dynamic Theory of Organizational Knowledge Creation'. *Organization Science*, 5 (Feb.), 1994, 14–37.

Nonaka, I. and Konno, N. 'The Concept of "Ba": Building a Foundation for Knowledge Creation'. *California Management Review*, 40(3), 1998, 40–54.

Oliff, M. (ed.). *Intelligent Manufacturing*. Benjamín/Cummings, 1988.

Osherson, D. and Smith, E. (eds). *Thinking: an Invitation to Cognitive Science Visual Cognition and Action*. MIT Press, 1990.

Payne, L.W. 'Unlocking an Organization's Ultimate Potential Through Knowledge Management'. *Knowledge Management in Practice*, 31(1), April–May, 1996.

Pérez López, J.A. *Teoría de la Acción Humana en las Organizaciones: la acción personal*. Rialp, 1991.

Pérez López, J.A. and San Román, R. *Enseñanza de economía a profesionales no economistas*. Fondo para la Investigación Económica y Social de la Confederación Española de Cajas de Ahorros, 1973.

Pfeffer, J. and Sutton, R. *The Knowing–Doing Gap: How Smart Companies Turn Knowledge into Action*. Harvard Business School Press, 2000.

Polya, G. *How to Solve it: a New Aspect of Mathematical Method*. Princeton University Press, 1945.

Polyani, M. *The Tacit Dimension*. Doubleday, 1966.

Popper, Karl. *The Logic of Scientific Discovery*. Routledge, 1992.

Porter, M. *Competitive Advantage: Creating and Sustaining Superior Performance*. The Free Press, 1995.

Prahalad, G. and Hamel, C.K. *The Core Competence of the Corporation*. Harvard Business Review, 1990.

Purser, R. 'Redesigning the Knowledge Based Product Development Organization'. *Technovation*, 11(7), 1991, 403–15.

Quinn, J.B. 'Technological Innovation. Entrepreneurship and Strategy'. *Sloan Management Review*, (Spring), 1979, 1–30.

Quinn, J.B., Anderson, P. and Finkelstein, S. 'Managing Professional Intellect: Making the Most of the Best'. *Harvard Business Review*, 74(2), 1996, 71–82.

Quinn, J.B. *Intelligent Enterprises*. The Free Press, 1992.

Quinn, J.B. *Innovation Explosion: Using Intellect and Software to Revolutionize Growth Strategies.* The Free Press, 1997.

Quinn, R.E. and Cameron, K.S. (eds). *Paradox and Information*. Ballinger, 1988.

Raiffa, H. *Decision Analysis: Introductory Lectures on Choices under Uncertainty.* Addison-Wesley,1968.

Rasmussen, J., Pejtersen, A.M. and Goodstein, L.P. *Cognitive Systems Engineering*. Wiley-Interscience, 1994.

Ray, M. and Myers, R. *Creativity in Business*. Doubleday, 1989.

Revilla, E. *Factores determinantes del aprendizaje organizativo: un modelo de desarrollo de productos.* Club Gestión de la Calidad, 1995.

Rickards, T. *Problem Solving Through Creative Analysis*. Gower Press, 1974.

Riesbeck, C. and Shank, R. *Inside Case Based Reasoning*. Lawrence Erlbaum, 1989.

Riverola, J. 'Análisis competitivo de la tecnología (ACT)'. Technical Note PN-310 IESE, Barcelona, 1992.

Riverola, J. 'Perspectivas de la dirección de operaciones'. *Revista de Economía*, 7, 1990.

Riverola, J. and Andreu, R. 'Spags, un nuevo concepto'. *Proceso de Datos*, 1982.

Riverola, J. and Andreu, R. 'Porque no funcionan los sistemas integrados'. *Proceso de Datos*, 1982.

Riverola, J. and Muñoz-Seca, B. 'Implementing Innovation Projects: a paradigm and its implications'. *IESE Research Paper,* no. 154, Barcelona, 1989.

Riverola, J. and Muñoz-Seca, B. *El análisis de procesos y la reducción del tiempo de servicio.* Biblioteca IESE de Gestión de Empresas, Folio, 1997.

Rosenhead, J. (ed.) *Rational Analysis for a Problematic World*. John Wiley & Sons, 1989.

Rosenthal, S. *Effective Product Design and Development: How to Cut Lead-Time and Increase Customer Satisfaction*. Irwin Professional Pub, 1992.

Rubinstein, A. *Modeling Bounded Rationality*. MIT Press, 1997.

Ruggles, R. 'The State of the Notion: Knowledge Management in Practice'. *California Management Review*, 40(3), 1998, 80–9.

Russell, S. and Norvig, P. *Artificial Intelligence: a Modern Approach*. Prentice Hall, 1995.

Saaty, T.L. and Vargas, L. *Decision Making in Economic, Political and Technological Environments with the Analytical Hierarchy Process*. RWS Publications, 1994.

Sage, P. *Large Scale Systems: Analysis and Design (Sistemas a Gran Escala: Análisis y Diseño).* Prentice Hall, 1982.

Sathi, A., Fox, M.S. and Greenberg, M. 'Representation of Activity Knowledge for Project Management'. *IEEE Transactions on AI*, Sep. (5), 1985.

Sathi, A., Morton, T.E. and Roth, S.F. 'Callisto: an Intelligent Project Management System'. *The AI Magazine* (Winter), 1986.

Schein, E.H. 'How Can Organizations Learn Faster? The Challenge of Entering the Green Room'. *Sloan Management Review*, 34(2), 1993, 85–92.

Schein, E.H. *Organizational Culture and Leadership*, 2nd edn. Jossey Bass, 1997.

Schneider, B. and Bowen, D. *Winning the Service Game*. Harvard Business School Press, 1995.

Schreiber, G., Akkermans, H., Angewierden, A. *et al. Knowledge Engineering and Management: the Common KADS Methodology*. MIT Press, 1999.

Scott, G. *The Empowered Mind: How to Harness the Creative Force Within You*. Prentice Hall Trade, 1994.

Senge, P.M. *The Fifth Discipline*. Doubleday/Currency, 1994.

Shank, R. *Virtual Learning: a Revolutionary Approach to Building a High Skill Workforce*. McGraw-Hill, 1997.

Sherwood, J.J. 'Creating Work Cultures with Competitive Advantage'. *Organizational Dynamics*, 16(3), 1988, 5–27.

Shiba, S., Graham, A. and Walden, D. *A New American TQM: Four Practical Revolutions in Management*. Productivity Press, 1993.

Simon, H. *Science of the Artificial*. MIT Press, 1981.

Skinner, W. *Manufacturing: the Formidable Competitive Weapon*. John Wiley & Sons, 1985.

Sommerville, I. *Software Engineering*. Addison-Wesley, 2001.

Springer, S.P. and Deutsch, G. *Left Brain, Right Brain: Perspectives from Cognitive Neuroscience*. W.H. Freeman and Company, 1997.

Taylor, F.W. *The Principles of Scientific Management*. Dover Publications, 1911. Orginally published. New York: Harper and Bros, 1999.

Torrance, P. *Creative Ways of Teaching*. Casete 283, Edition, Jeffrey Norton Pub, 1969.

Turner, C.C. *The Creative Process*. Lawrence Erlbaum Associates, 1994.

Vail, P. *Learning as a Way of Being*. Jossey-Bass, 1996.

Van Gundy, A.B. *Techniques of Structured Problem Solving*. John Wiley & Sons, 1988.

Van Gundy, A.B. 'How to Get the Idea that Leads to the Product'. The National New-Products Conference, Chicago, 8–9, May 1984.

Vidorreta, J. *La Gestión del Conocimiento en el sector sanitario*. Asociación de Economía de la Salud, 1998.

Von Krogh, G. and Ross, J. (eds). *Managing Knowledge: Perspectives on Cooperation and Competition*. Sage Publications, 1996.

Von Neumann, J.V. and Morgenstern, O. *The Theory of Games and Economic Behavior*. Princeton University Press, 1944.

Wagner, H. *Principles of Operations Research*. Prentice Hall, 1975.

Wallace, R.H., Stockenberg, J.E. and Charette, R.N. *A Unified Methodology for Developing Systems*. McGraw-Hill, 1987.

Walton, Mary and Deming, W.E. *Deming Management Method*. Perigee, 1986.

Wheelwright, S.C. and Clark, K.B. *Revolutionizing Product Development*. The Free Press, 1993.

Wielinga, B., Van De Velde, W., Schreiber G. and Akkermans, H. 'Towards a Unification of Knowledge Modelling Approaches'. In *Second Generation Expert Systems*. Eds. David, J.M., Krivine, J.P. and Simmons, R. Springer Verlag, 1993.

Wilson, D. and Sperberg, D. *Pragmatics and Modularity. Pragmatics: a Reader*. Ed. Steven Davis. Oxford University Press, 1992.

Wright, P.K. and Bourne, D.A. *Manufacturing Intelligence*. Addison Wesley, 1988.

Zack, M.H. 'Managing Codified Knowledge'. *Sloan Management Review*, 40(4) (Summer), 1999, 45–58.

Index

Notes: * = 'material that may be skipped on first reading' (cf. pages xiv–xv); **bold** = extended discussion or heading/word emphasized in main text; *e* = example; *f* = figure; *n* = note; 100n = denotes that there is only one footnote on the particular page; 100(n3) = footnote specifically numbered if there is more than one footnote on any page; *t* = table.